W0254549

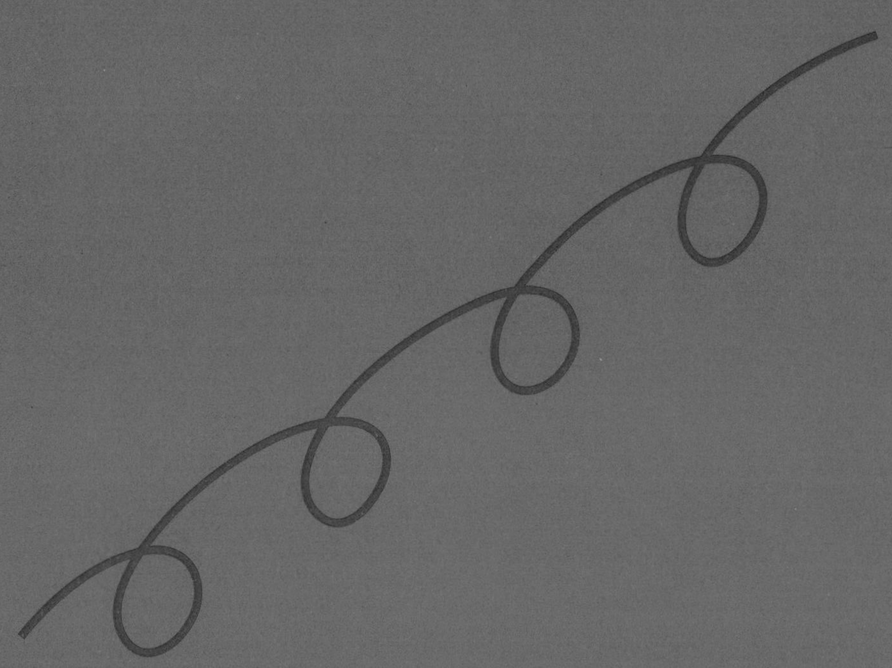

HOW COUNTRIES GO BROKE

ALSO FROM RAY DALIO

Books:

Principles: Life & Work
Principles for Navigating Big Debt Crises
Principles for Success
Principles for Dealing with the Changing World Order
Principles: Your Guided Journal

Additional research publications available at economicprinciples.org

Animations (available on YouTube):

How the Economic Machine Works
Principles for Success
Principles for Dealing with the Changing World Order

Apps and social media:

All of Ray's content, as well as interactive case studies created at the company he founded, Bridgewater Associates, can be found in the Principles In Action app, available in the iOS and Android app stores. Follow Ray on LinkedIn, Facebook, Instagram, X, YouTube, and TikTok.

Digital course:

Ray has partnered with the Wealth Management Institute of Singapore and ADGM Academy of Abu Dhabi to offer a digital course based on his investment and economic principles. Information on the Dalio Market Principles course can be found at principles.com.

HOW COUNTRIES GO BROKE

THE BIG CYCLE

RAY DALIO

SIMON & SCHUSTER

London · New York · Amsterdam/Antwerp · Sydney/Melbourne · Toronto · New Delhi

First published in the United States by Avid Reader Press,
an imprint of Simon & Schuster, LLC, 2025

First published in Great Britain by Simon & Schuster UK Ltd, 2025

3 5 7 9 10 8 6 4 2

Simon & Schuster UK Ltd
1st Floor
222 Gray's Inn Road
London WC1X 8HB

www.simonandschuster.co.uk
www.simonandschuster.com.au
www.simonandschuster.co.in

Simon & Schuster Australia, Sydney
Simon & Schuster India, New Delhi

The authorised representative in the EEA is Simon & Schuster Netherlands BV, Herculesplein 96, 3584 AA Utrecht, Netherlands. info@simonandschuster.nl

A CIP catalogue record for this book
is available from the British Library

Hardback ISBN: 978-1-3985-5146-6
eBook ISBN: 978-1-3985-5147-3

Interior design by Creative Kong

Printed and bound in India by Replika Press Pvt. Ltd.

WHY I'M SHARING THIS BOOK

I wrote this book to pass along what I have found to be invaluable timeless and universal understandings and principles that I have learned over my 50-plus years as a global macro investor. I don't think that anyone has worked harder for more years and with better resources to acquire these understandings and principles. They have rewarded me and others abundantly, and I don't want them to die with me. I believe that the concepts I explain can make the world run better when put in the hands of policy makers and investors. Above all else, I hope you will take away from reading this book:

1. A complete and practical understanding of the Big Debt Cycle. If you want a very brief summary of that, read Part I, and for a more in-depth understanding, read Part II.
2. A much more practical understanding of how supply and demand really work compared to the conventional economic thinking. This is covered in detail in Chapter 2 but you can see it at play throughout the book.
3. A complete and practical understanding of the Overall Big Cycle, which is driven by the Big Debt Cycle and the other major cycles, including the big political cycle within countries that changes political orders and the big geopolitical cycle that changes world orders. One of my main goals for this book is to help you understand how this Overall Big Cycle brings about these big shifts as I believe that we are now on the brink of such a period of major change. If you read only one chapter in this book, Chapter 8 covers it.

The material in this book complements and helps complete my explanations of the understandings and principles conveyed in my other books, most importantly *Principles for Navigating Big Debt Crises* and *Principles for Dealing with the Changing World Order.* Because that's a lot of interrelated stuff, I am putting all that and more into an AI avatar of myself that you can easily communicate directly with. If you want to try that out, you can sign up at principles.com.

WITH APPRECIATION

I am incredibly fortunate to be able to triangulate my thinking with some of the most knowledgeable people in the world. This is particularly important because much of my thinking is unconventional. I am especially grateful to former Treasury Secretaries Larry Summers and Timothy Geithner, former Speaker of the House Paul Ryan, former European Central Bank President Mario Draghi, former Bank of Japan Governor Haruhiko Kuroda, International Monetary Fund Managing Director Kristalina Georgieva, and Committee for a Responsible Federal Budget President Maya MacGuineas.

The deep historical analysis on which I base my ideas requires a great amount of analytical work. It would not have been accomplished without the help of my excellent research team, including Steven Kryger, Bill Longfield, Udai Baisiwala, Hemanth Sanjeev, Kaus Bansal, Jonah Garnick, Nick Brown, and Eric Styrcula.

Converting my big piles of research and writing into book form is also no small feat and would not have been possible without the quick and expert help of Mark Kirby, Chris Edmonds, Julie Farnie, Brian De Los Santos, Martha Merrell, Millissa Henaire, and Zoe Petkanas.

I am also deeply grateful to my literary agent, Jim Levine, and my editor at Simon & Schuster's Avid Reader Press, Jofie Ferrari-Adler. Their help has been indispensable in the publication of all my books.

PART III
LOOKING BACK

PART IV
LOOKING AHEAD

HOW TO READ THIS BOOK

- Because I recognize that there are different readers who have different levels of expertise and want to give different amounts of time to this and because I want to help you get what you want out of this, **I have put the most important points in bold so you can read just the most essential stuff and optionally dive into the details that interest you**. If you are a professional or aspiring professional who is really into economics and markets, I recommend that you read the whole thing because I believe that it will give you a unique perspective that you will enjoy—and it will help you be successful in your job. If you are not, I recommend just reading what is in bold.

- I also want to convey some principles that are timeless and universal truths for dealing with reality well, which I have denoted by ● ***putting a red dot in front of them and italicizing***.

- Because I love having two-way conversations with people rather than just sharing what I think and because I find these conversations give me invaluable feedback that improves my own thinking, I am working on a few new technologies for doing that, including an AI version of myself. If you'd like to learn more about this, I recommend you sign up for updates at principles.com.

- Finally, to keep this book from becoming much too long, there is also a lot of supplemental material available at economicprinciples.org, including reference material, citations, more data on the indices, etc.

INTRODUCTION

Are there limits to a country's debt and debt growth?

What will happen to interest rates and all that they affect if government debt growth isn't slowed?

Can a big, important country that has a major reserve currency like the US go broke—and, if so, what would that look like?

Is there such a thing as a "Big Debt Cycle" that we can track that will tell us when to worry about debt and what to do about it?

These aren't just academic questions for academic economists. They are questions that investors, policy makers, and most everyone must answer because the answers will have huge effects on all our well-beings and what we should do. But definitive answers don't currently exist.

At this time, some people believe that there isn't any limit to government debt and debt growth, especially if a country has a reserve currency. That's because they believe that the central bank of a reserve currency country that has its money widely accepted around the world can always print the money to service its debts. Others believe that the high levels of debt and rapid debt growth are harbingers of a big debt crisis on the horizon, but they do not know exactly how and when the crisis will come—or what its impacts will be.

And what about the big, long-term debt cycle? While the "business cycle" is widely acknowledged and some people recognize that it is driven by a short-term debt cycle, that is not true for the big, long-term debt cycle. Nobody acknowledges it or talks about it. I couldn't find any good studies or descriptions of it in textbooks, and even the world's leading economists—including those who are now running, or in the past ran, central banks and government treasuries—didn't have much to say about this critically important subject when I explored it with them. That is why I did this study and am passing it along.

Before I get into all that, I should begin by explaining where I'm coming from. I don't come to this subject as an economist. I come as a global macro investor who for over 50 years has been through many debt cycles in many countries and has had to navigate and understand them well enough to bet on how they would go. I have carefully studied all the Big Debt Cycles over the last 100 years, and superficially studied many more from the past 500 years, so I believe that I understand how to navigate them. Because I am deeply concerned about what I'm seeing, I feel a responsibility to pass along this study for others to assess for themselves.

To gain my understanding, I look at many cases like a doctor studies many cases, examining the mechanics behind them to understand the cause/effect relationships that drive their progressions. I also learn from being in these experiences, reflecting on what I learn, writing it up, and having smart people read and challenge it. Then I build systems to place my bets on what I learned and have new experiences. I do that over and over and will do it until I die because I love it. Because my game has been to bet on the markets and because the debt markets drive just about everything, I have been obsessed with studying debt dynamics for decades. I believe that if you understand these dynamics, you can do very well as an investor, businessperson, or policy maker, and if you don't, you ultimately will be hurt by them.

Through my research, I discovered that there are big, long-term debt cycles that have unfailingly led to big debt bubbles and busts. I saw that only about 20% of the roughly 750 debt/currency markets that have existed since 1700 remain and that all the remaining ones have been severely devalued through the mechanistic process I am going to describe in this study. I saw how this big, long-term debt cycle was described in the Old Testament, how it repeatedly played out in Chinese dynasties over thousands of years, and how time and again it has foreshadowed the fall of empires, countries, and provinces.

These Big Debt Cycles have always worked in timeless and universally consistent ways that are not well-understood but should be. In this study, I hope to explain how they work with such clarity that my description will serve as a template that can be used to see what is going on with, and what is likely to happen to, money and debt. While I recognize that my Big Debt Cycle template is unconventional, I am confident that it exists because I've made a lot of money using it to bet on how things would go. I am sharing it and other key concepts that have helped me because I am now at a stage of life in which I want to share what I have learned that I have found of value in the hope that it will help others, too. You can do what you like with it.

Why do I think I understand something that others don't? I theorize that this is for a few reasons. First, this dynamic is not widely understood because big, long-term debt cycles typically last about one lifetime—roughly 80 years, give or take 25 years—so we don't get to learn about them through experience. Second, because we focus so much on what is happening to us at the time it is happening, people overlook the big picture. I also think there are biases against being concerned about too much debt because most people like the spending ability that credit gives them, and it is also true that there have been many warnings about pending debt crises that never happened. Memories of big debt crises like the 2008 global financial crisis and the European debt crisis of the PIIGS countries (Portugal, Italy, Ireland, Greece, and Spain) have faded, and since we have gotten past them, many people assume that policy makers learned how to manage them rather than view these cases as early warnings of bigger crises on the horizon. But whatever the reason, it doesn't matter exactly why these dynamics are overlooked. I am going to paint a picture of what happens and why, and if there is enough interest in what I'm saying, my template will be assessed and will live or die on its merits.

That leads me to a principle:

● ***If we don't agree on how things work, we won't be able to agree on what's happening or what is likely to happen.*** **For that reason, I needed to lay out my picture of how the machine works and triangulate it with other knowledgeable people before moving on to look at what's happening and what might happen.**

At a time when government debt is large and increasing rapidly, it seems to me dangerously negligent to assume that this time will be different from other times without first studying how other cases transpired. It would be like assuming that we will never have a civil war or world war again because they haven't happened before in our lifetimes without studying the mechanics that brought them about in the past. (By the way, I believe that both the civil war and world war dynamics are also going on today.) As in my other books,[1] I will create a description of the archetypical dynamic and then look at how and why different cases transpired differently so that one can track current cases relative to the template and put into context what's happening and what's likely to happen. In that way, you will both see many cases of this happening and get a peek into the future. Comparing what is happening with that template leads me to believe that we are head-

[1] While debt and currency cycles are comprehensively covered in my book *Principles for Navigating Big Debt Crises* (which looked at all of the 48 biggest debt crises in the 100 years between 1918 and 2018, the year I published the book) and in Chapters 3 and 4 of my book *Principles for Dealing with the Changing World Order* (which looked at the rises and declines of the world's reserve currency markets over the last 500 years and 750 currencies since 1700), in this study, I am going to get much more granular in explaining the last and most dramatic breakdown part of the cycle that leads to changes in currency orders.

ing into one of those cases in which central governments and central banks will "go broke" in the ways that have happened hundreds of times before and have had big political and geopolitical consequences.

This brings me to an important point. **The Big Debt Cycle is just one of several interrelated forces that together make up what I call the "Overall Big Cycle" (or just "Big Cycle"). For example, 1) Big Debt Cycles influence and are affected by largely coinciding 2) big cycles of political and social harmony and conflict within countries that both are affected by and affect 3) big cycles of geopolitical harmony and conflict between countries. These cycles in turn are affected by both 4) big acts of nature (droughts, floods, pandemics, etc.), and 5) developments of big new technologies. Combined, these forces make up the Overall Big Cycle of peace and prosperity and conflict and depression as things progress from one "order" to the next.**

What do I mean by order? Orders are ways of operating that change when systems break down. There are monetary orders that determine how the monetary system works, political orders that determine how governance works within countries, and geopolitical orders that determine how governance works between countries. Big Cycles go from one order (i.e., one system of operating) to the next one. Big Cycles end when these orders break down, usually in a big crisis.

As I described in my book *Principles for Dealing with the Changing World Order*, these Big Cycle breakdowns and big changes in orders typically occur about once in a lifetime and are traumatic. The changes from one monetary system to the next, from one system of governance within a country to the next, and from one system of governance between countries to the next typically take about the same amount of time because they have big effects on each other.

These changes from one set of orders to another have always happened in basically the same ways for the same reasons, but they aren't well-understood because they come along so infrequently. Yet they happen in highly mechanistic ways that can be measured and monitored. I provide an overview of the forces that drive the Big Cycle in Chapter 8, and I explain what they may mean for the future in

Chapter 19, which is the concluding chapter. I believe that, once you read about them, they will be obvious to you and will help you understand where we are in the Big Cycle and what is likely to come. If you take nothing else from this book, I hope that you get a much better understanding of the Big Cycle template so that you can apply it to understanding the seemingly improbable events happening today. While these events would have seemed unimaginable just a few years ago, they make perfect sense once you understand the Big Cycle and the mechanics of the five forces that drive it.

This study consists of four parts and 19 chapters. Part I describes the Big Debt Cycle, at first very simply, then in a more complete and mechanical way, and then with some equations that show the mechanics and help with making projections of what is likely to happen. Part II lays out a detailed template, derived from 35 Big Debt Cycle cases, that shows the typical sequence of events that signifies how a cycle is transpiring and shows symptoms that can help identify how far the cycle has progressed. It also contains a chapter that walks through how the Overall Big Cycle works. Part III reviews the most recent Big Debt Cycle, which started when the new monetary and world orders began at the end of World War II and brings it up to the present. In that part, in addition to looking at the Big Debt Cycle and the Overall Big Cycle with a focus on the US (because it has been the world's major reserve currency country and the world's leading power, thus making it the world's leading shaper of what one might call the American world order since 1945), I also very briefly describe the Big Cycles of both China and Japan, showing them from the 1800s until now. This will give you a more complete picture of what has happened in the world since 1945 and provide two other Big Debt Cycle cases to look at. Finally, in Part IV, I will peek into the future, looking at what my calculations say about what is required for the US to manage its debt burden and how the five big forces might unfold in the years ahead.

PART I

OVERVIEW OF THE BIG DEBT CYCLE

Part I provides a comprehensive picture of the Big Debt Cycle, which has occurred again and again throughout history but isn't widely recognized because big shifts in it come along so infrequently, only about once in a lifetime. The purpose of this part is to describe how the natural mechanics of money, credit, debt, and economic activity, combined with human nature, add up over time to create the Big Debt Cycle. In it I explain the stages of how the Big Debt Cycle progresses and what happens when it unravels. In the first chapter, I provide an overview of how the cycle unfolds in a nutshell, and in the following two chapters I dive into more detail, explaining the mechanics that drive the debt cycle both in words and concepts and in numbers and equations. These chapters have a lot for both the general reader and the investor, and I'd encourage you to either read just the bold or explore the details as it suits you.

CHAPTER 1

THE BIG DEBT CYCLE IN A TINY NUTSHELL

My goal for this chapter is to convey a very brief but complete description of the mechanics of a typical Big Debt Cycle. If you read only one chapter to understand how debt works, this is the one to read.

HOW THE MACHINE WORKS

Credit is the primary vehicle for funding spending and it can easily be created. Because one person's spending is another's earnings, when there is a lot of credit creation, people spend and earn more, most asset prices go up, and most everyone loves it. As a result, central governments and central banks have a bias toward creating a lot of credit. Credit also creates debt that has to be paid back, which has the opposite effect—i.e., when debts have to be paid back, it creates less spending, lower incomes, and lower asset prices, which people don't like. In other words, when someone (a borrower-debtor) borrows money (called principal) at a cost (an interest rate), the borrower-debtor can spend more money than they have in earnings and savings over the near term. **But over the long term, this requires them to pay back the**

principal plus interest, and when they have to pay it back, it requires them to spend less money than they have. This dynamic is why ● *the credit/spending/debt-paying-back dynamic is inherently cyclical.*

THE SHORT-TERM DEBT CYCLE

Everyone who has been around long enough to be affected by it several times should be well-acquainted with the short-term debt cycle. It starts with money and credit being provided readily when economic activity and inflation are lower than desired, and when interest rates are low relative to inflation rates and low in relation to the rates of return on other investments. Those conditions encourage borrowing to spend and invest, which causes asset prices, economic activity, and inflation to pick up until they are higher than desired, at which time money and credit are restrained, and interest rates become relatively high in relation to inflation rates and rates of return on other investments. This leads to less borrowing to spend and invest, which leads to lower asset prices, a slowing of economic activity, and lower inflation, which leads interest rates to come down, money and credit to become easier, and the cycle to begin again. These cycles have typically lasted about six years, give or take three years.

SHORT-TERM DEBT CYCLES ADD UP TO BIG, LONG-TERM DEBT CYCLES

What isn't paid enough attention is the way in which these short-term debt cycles add up to big, long-term debt cycles. Because credit is a stimulant that creates a high, people want more of it, so there is a bias toward creating it. This leads debt to rise over time, which typically leads to most of the short-term cyclical highs and lows in debt to be higher than the ones before. These add up to create the long-term debt cycle, which ends when it becomes

unsustainable. The capacity to take on more debt is different early in the Big Debt Cycle when debt burdens are lower and there is more potential for debt/credit to be able to fund highly profitable endeavors than it is later in the Big Debt Cycle when debt burdens are higher, and lenders have fewer productive options.

In that early stage, it is easy to borrow—even to borrow a lot—and pay it back. These early short-term debt cycles are primarily driven by the previously described availability and economics of borrowing and spending, and also a lingering cautiousness brought about by memories of the pain of the most recent time when money was tight.[2] **Early in the Big Debt Cycle, when debts and total debt service are relatively low in relation to incomes and other assets, increases and decreases in credit, spending, debt, and debt service are primarily determined by the previously described incentives with less risk. But late in the Big Debt Cycle, when debts and debt service costs get high relative to income and the value of other assets that can be used to meet one's debt service obligations, the risks of default are higher.** Also, late in the Big Debt Cycle, when there are a lot of debt assets and liabilities relative to income, the balancing act of trying to keep interest rates high enough to satisfy lender-creditors without having them too high for borrower-debtors becomes more challenging. That's because one person's debts are another's assets and both must be satisfied. **So, while short-term debt cycles end because of the previously described economic considerations, long-term debt cycles end because the debt burdens are too great to be sustained. Said differently, because it is more enjoyable to borrow and spend, if one isn't careful, debt and debt service can grow like a cancer, eating up one's buying power and squeezing out other consumption. This is what makes the long-term Big Debt Cycle.**

Throughout the millennia and across countries, what has driven the Big Debt Cycle and has created the big market and economic

[2] This cautiousness is reflected in market pricing. For example, during the early stages of the cycle, the yields and expected returns of "risky assets" are very high relative to those of "low-risk assets."

problems that go along with it is the creation of unsustainably large amounts of debt assets and debt liabilities relative to the amounts of money, goods, services, and investment assets in existence.

Said more simply, ● ***a debt is a promise to deliver money. A debt crisis occurs when there have been more promises made than there is money to deliver on them. When that happens, the central bank is forced to choose between a) printing a lot of money, which devalues it, and b) not printing a lot of money and having a big debt default crisis. In the end, the central bank always prints and devalues. But either way—either via default or devaluation—the creation of too much debt eventually causes debt assets (e.g., bonds) to be worth less.***

While there are variations in how each of these cases play out, the most important factor is whether the debt is denominated in a currency that the central bank can "print" and whether it is a reserve currency. But no matter the variation, we almost always see that it becomes relatively undesirable to hold the debt assets (e.g., bonds) relative to holding the productive capacity of the economy (e.g., equities) and/or owning other, more stable forms of money (e.g., gold).

To me it is interesting and inappropriate that, when credit rating agencies rate the credit of a central government, they don't rate the riskiness of its debt losing value. They only rate the risk of default on the debt, which gives the misimpression that all higher-rated debt is a safe storehold of value. Said differently, because a central bank can bail out a central government, the riskiness of central government debts is hidden. Creditors would be better served if the rating agencies rated the riskiness of the debt losing value through both default and devaluation. After all, these bonds are supposed to be storeholds of wealth and should be rated as such. As you will see in this study, that is how I look at bonds. For countries with debts denominated in their own currencies (i.e., in a currency they can print), I rate their central governments' debts separately from their central banks' debts to show how risky they are, and I rate the risks of central banks' debts by considering the risk of the devaluation of money to be as, if not more, probable than a default on government debt.

Default or devaluation, I don't care. What I care about is losing my storehold of wealth, which inevitably will happen one way or another.

FOLLOWING THE DEBT CYCLE'S PROGRESSION

The main difference between a short-term debt cycle and a long-term debt cycle has to do with the central bank's ability to turn them around. For the short-term debt cycle, its contraction phase can be reversed with a heavy dose of money and credit that brings the economy up from a depressed disinflationary state because the economy has the capacity to produce another phase of non-inflationary growth. But the long-term debt cycle's contraction phase cannot be reversed by producing more money and credit because existing levels of debt growth and debt assets are unsustainable and holders of debt assets want to get out of them because they believe that, one way or another, they will be poor storeholds of wealth.

Think of the Big Debt Cycle's progression like the progression of a disease or a life cycle through stages that exhibit different symptoms. By identifying these symptoms one can identify approximately where the cycle is in its progression with some expectations of how it is likely to progress from there. Described most simply, the Big Debt Cycle moves from sound/hard money and credit to increasingly loose money and credit to a debt bust that leads to a return to sound/hard money and credit brought about by necessity. More specifically, at first there is healthy borrowing by the private sector that can be paid back; then the private sector overborrows, has losses, and has problems paying it back; then the government sector tries to help, overborrows, has losses, and has problems paying it back; then the central bank tries to help by "printing money" and buying the government debt, and has problems paying it back, which leads it to monetize a lot more debt if it can (i.e., if the debt is denominated in a currency that it can print). Though not all cases progress in exactly the same way, most cases progress through the following five stages.

The Sound Money Stage

When net debt levels are low, money is sound, the country is competitive, and debt growth fuels productivity growth, which creates incomes that are more than enough to pay back the debts. This leads to increases in financial wealth and confidence.

- Credit is the promise to deliver money. Unlike credit, which requires a payment of money at a later date, money settles transactions—i.e., if money is given the transaction is complete, whereas if credit is given money is owed. It's easy to create credit. Anyone can create credit but not anyone can create money. For example, I can create credit by accepting your promise to pay me money even if you don't have the money. As a result, credit easily grows so there is much more credit than there is money. The most effective money is both a medium of exchange and a storehold of wealth that is widely accepted around the world. At the early stage of the Big Debt Cycle, money is "hard," which means that it is a medium of exchange that is also a storehold of wealth that can't easily be increased in supply, such as gold, silver, and more recently Bitcoin. Cryptocurrencies like Bitcoin are now emerging as accepted hard currencies because they are widely accepted around the world and are limited in supply. The biggest, most common risk to money becoming an ineffective storehold of wealth is the risk that a lot of it will be created. Imagine having the ability to create money; who wouldn't be tempted to do a lot of that? Those who can always are. That creates the Big Debt Cycle. In the early part of the Big Debt Cycle, a) money is typically hard and the paper money that circulates is convertible into the "hard money" at a fixed price and b) there isn't a lot of paper money and debt (which is the promise to pay money) outstanding. The Big Debt Cycle consists of the building up of

a) "paper money" and debt assets/liabilities relative to b) "hard money" and real assets (e.g., goods and services) and relative to the income that is required to service the debt. Basically, the Big Debt Cycle works like a Ponzi scheme or musical chairs with investors holding an increasing amount of debt assets in the belief that they can convert them into money that will have buying power to get real things, yet as the amount of the debt assets that are held up by that faith increases relative to the real things, that conversion becomes more obviously impossible until that is realized and the process of selling the debt to get the hard money and real assets begins.

- At the early stage of the debt cycle, private and government debt and debt service ratios are 1) low relative to incomes and/or 2) low relative to liquid assets. For example, government debt and debt service are low relative to government tax revenue and/or low relative to government liquid assets (e.g., reserves and other savings such as sovereign wealth assets) that can easily be converted into money. When the Big Debt Cycle that we are in began in 1945, the ratios of US government debt and US money supply divided by the amount of gold the US government had were equal to 7x and 1.3x, respectively, whereas now these ratios are 37x and 6x, respectively.
- During this early stage in the cycle, debt levels, debt growth, economic growth, and inflation are neither too hot nor too cold and finances are sound.
- At this stage in the cycle, "risky assets" are relatively inexpensive relative to "safe" assets. That is because the memories of the prior period in which there was great damage done affects psychology and pricing. For example, in the late 1940s and early 1950s stock earnings yields were roughly 4x that of bond yields.
- During this stage, there is a healthy economy and good investment returns that lead to the next stage.

The Debt Bubble Stage

When debt and investment growth are greater than can be serviced from the incomes being produced.

- In this stage, money is readily available and cheap, and there is a debt-financed economic expansion and an economic boom. Demands for and prices of goods, services, and investment assets are driven up by a lot of debt-financed buying, sentiment is very bullish, and by most conventional measures, the market is overpriced.
- In this stage, there are typically amazing new inventions that are truly transformative that investors invest in without an ability or care to assess whether the present value of their future cash flows will be greater or less than their costs.
- ***There is always a current most popular meme that just about everyone believes. It is reflected in the price and is bound to be wrong in some way. These memes typically are due to a mix of extrapolating what happened before and emotional considerations. Also, most investors typically don't take into consideration market pricing. In other words, they tend to identify what has been a great investment (e.g., a strongly performing company) as great, and they don't pay enough attention to its pricing, even though its pricing (whether it is cheap or expensive) is the most important thing. At this time, it is typical for almost everyone to be looking to make money by buying assets that they believe will go up (rather betting on them going down), and they quite often use leverage.***
- This dynamic eventually produces a bubble that is reflected in the rates of debt and debt service growth to finance speculation being greater than the income growth rates that are needed to service the debts. In this stage, markets and economies seem great, most everyone believes that they will get better, they are financed by a lot of borrowing, and "wealth" is created out of nothing. By wealth being created out of nothing, I mean that there is greater imagined wealth versus actual

existing wealth. For example, bubble periods are identifiable by extensive periods of debt growth (e.g., three years) that is significantly faster than income growth, high asset prices relative to traditional measures of the present values of likely future cash flows, and many other factors that I measure in my bubble indicator. (You can find an article describing the indicator at economicprinciples.org and in the Principles In Action app.) A contemporary example is the unicorn company that is valued at over $1 billion that has made the owner a "billionaire" on paper but has only raised $50 million in capital because speculative venture capitalists put in the money to get option-like chips in case it does well. Bubbles can go on for a while before the top is made, but they inevitably lead to the next stage.

- Then there comes a time when the debt spiral reaches and goes beyond the point of no return, by which I mean the debt and debt service levels go beyond those that can be prevented from accelerating without great losses to debt investors. This self-reinforcing debt "death spiral" occurs when there is a need to borrow in order to service the debt at a time when interest rates are rising because the risks of holding the debt/currency have become apparent to investors, which leads to a debt crisis.

The Top Stage

When the bubble pops and there is a debt/credit/market/economic contraction.

- The popping of the bubble typically occurs due to a combination of a tightening of money and the prior rate of debt growth being unsustainable. It is just that simple.
- When the bubble pops, a self-reinforcing contraction begins so the debt problems spread very quickly, like an aggressive cancer, so it is very important for policy makers to deal with

it quickly, either to reverse it or to guide the deleveraging to its conclusion. In most cases, the debt contraction can be temporarily reversed by giving the system a heavy dose of what caused the debt problem—i.e., by creating more credit and debt. That continues until it can't continue anymore, at which time a big deleveraging occurs.

The Deleveraging Stage

When there is a painful bringing down of debt and debt service levels to be in line with income levels so that the debt levels are sustainable.

- At the beginning of the last stage of the Big Debt Cycle when there is a big debt crisis, debt problems typically spread from the private sector to the central government and then to the central bank. ● ***Net selling of debt assets, especially net selling of government debt assets, is a big red flag.*** When that happens, conditions deteriorate quickly unless managed very well and very quickly by central governments and central banks. At that time, private holders of debt sell the debt fearing bad returns. That selling takes the form of "runs on banks." By "runs on banks," I mean the turning-in of debt assets to get real money, which lenders/banks don't have enough of. When debt problems become apparent and the holders of the debt assets sell their debt assets, that initially drives interest rates on the debt up. This makes the debt more difficult to service, hence more risky, which drives interest rates higher. At that point, the central bank typically provides money and credit to fill in for the inadequate demand, which reduces the value of money and credit and reduces credit risk.
- The selling of the government's debt leads to a) a free-market-driven tightening of money and credit, which leads to b) a weakening of the economy, c) downward pressure on the

currency, and d) declining reserves as the central bank attempts to defend the currency. Classically, these runs accelerate and feed on themselves as holders of debt assets see that, one way or another (through default or through the devaluation of their money), they will lose the buying power that they had believed was stored in these debt assets, causing great shifts in market values and wealth until debts are defaulted on, restructured, and/or monetized. Because this tightening proves too harmful for the economy, the central bank eventually simultaneously eases credit and allows a devaluation of the currency. The devaluation of money can itself be the reason to sell the debt asset because it becomes a poor storehold of wealth. So, whether there is a tightening of money that leads to debt defaults and a bad economy or an easing of money that produces a devaluation of money and debt assets, it is not good for the debt asset. This dynamic creates what is called a debt "death spiral" because it is a self-reinforcing, debt-contraction dynamic in which the rising interest rates cause problems that creditors see, leading them to sell the debt assets, which leads to even higher interest rates or the need to print more money, which devalues the money and leads to even more selling of the debt assets and the currency and so on until the spiral runs its course. When this happens to government debt, the realization that too much debt is the problem naturally leads to the inclination to cut spending and borrowing. However, because one person's spending is another person's income, cutting spending at such times typically only contributes to increases in debt-to-income ratios. That is typically when policies are shifted to a mix of debt restructurings and debt monetizations, with the mix chosen primarily dependent on how much of the debt is denominated in the country's currency. This defaulting on, restructuring of, and/or monetizing of debt reduces the debt burdens relative to incomes until a new equilibrium is reached. The movement to a stable equilibrium typically takes place via a few painful adjustment spasms because borderline financial soundness is achieved before secure financial soundness.

- Classically, the deleveraging process progresses as follows. Early in this recession/depression phase, central banks bring interest rates down and make credit more available. However, when a) debts are large and a debt contraction is underway, b) interest rates can't be lowered any more (e.g., when they fall to around 0%), c) there is not enough demand for government debt, and d) the monetary easing is not enough to offset the self-reinforcing depressionary pressures, the central bank is forced to switch to new "tools" to stimulate the economy. Classically, to stimulate the economy the central bank must lower interest rates to below nominal economic growth rates, inflation rates, and bond rates, but that is difficult to do when they approach 0%. At the same time, the central government is typically getting itself into a lot more debt because tax revenues are down and spending is up to support the private sector, yet there is not enough private sector demand to buy that debt. The central government experiences a debt squeeze in which the free-market demand for its debt falls short of the supply of it. If there is net selling of the debt, that creates a much worse problem.
- Often in this deleveraging stage of the cycle, there is a "pushing on a string," a phrase coined by policy makers in the 1930s. It occurs late in the long-term debt cycle when central bankers struggle to convert their stimulative policies into increased spending because savers, investors, and businesses fear borrowing and spending and/or there is deflation, so the risk-free interest rate that they are getting is relatively attractive to them. At such times, it is difficult to get people to stop saving in "cash"[3] even when interest rates go to 0% (or even below 0%). This phase is characterized by the economy entering a deflationary, weak, or negative growth period as people and investors hoard

[3] Cash is defined as investor holdings of money earning interest.

low-risk, typically government-guaranteed cash.

- At this stage, central banks must choose between keeping money "hard," which will lead debtors to default on their debts, which will lead to deflationary depressions, or making money "soft" by printing a lot of it, which will devalue both it and the debt. Because paying off debt with hard money causes such severe market and economic downturns, when faced with this choice central banks always eventually choose to print and devalue money. Of course, each country's central bank can only print that country's money, which brings me to my next big point.
- At this stage, if it has the ability to "print money," the central bank creates a substantial amount of money and credit and throws it aggressively at the markets. It typically buys government debt and private sector debt of systemically important entities that are at risk of defaulting (in order to make up for the private sector's inadequate demand for debt and to keep interest rates artificially low), and it sometimes buys equities and creates incentives for people to buy goods, services, and financial assets. At this stage, it is also typically desirable to devalue the currency because that is stimulative to the economy and raises inflation rates, thus negating the deflationary pressures. If the currency is linked to gold, silver, or something else, that link is typically broken and there is a move to a fiat monetary system. If the currency isn't linked—i.e., if the currency is already a fiat currency—devaluing it relative to other storeholds of wealth and other currencies is helpful. In some cases, the central bank's moves can drive nominal interest rates higher, either because the central bank tightens monetary policy to fight inflation or because it doesn't tighten money to fight inflation and holders of the debt don't want to buy the newly issued government debt and/or they want to sell it because it doesn't provide an adequate return. It is important to watch real and nominal interest rates and the supply and demand for debt to understand what is happening.
- At such times, extraordinary policies to get money like

imposing extraordinary taxes and capital controls become common. It has also often been the case that governments will adopt policies that would have previously seemed unimaginable, such as selectively freezing or seizing the assets of "enemy" countries or creating new forms of money. Note that I am not saying that these extraordinary measures always happen; I'm only saying that it is wise to carefully consider the possibility that they will happen.

- This deleveraging stage is typically a painful time when debt burdens are reduced by defaults, restructurings, and/or devaluations. This is when an aggressive mix of debt restructurings and debt monetizations inevitably takes place to reduce the debt and debt service burdens relative to incomes. In a typical deleveraging, the debt-to-income ratio has to be lowered by roughly 50%, give or take about 20%. It can be done well or poorly. When it is done well, which I call a "beautiful deleveraging," central governments and central banks simultaneously do both debt restructurings and monetary stimulations in a balanced way. The restructurings reduce debt burdens and are deflationary, while the monetary stimulations also reduce debt burdens (by providing money and credit to make it easier to buy debt) but are inflationary and stimulative to the economy so, if they get the balance right, positive growth occurs with falling debt burdens and acceptable inflation. Whether done well or poorly, this is the stage of the Big Debt Cycle that reduces a lot of the debt burden and establishes the bottom that can be built on to begin the next Big Debt Cycle.

The Big Debt Crisis Recedes

When a new equilibrium is reached, and a new cycle begins.

- **In order to have a viable debt/credit/money system, it is**

imperative that a) debt/money is sound enough to be a viable storehold of wealth, b) debt and debt service burdens are in line with the incomes to service them so that debt growth is sustainable, c) creditors and debtors both believe that those things will exist, and d) the availability of money and credit and real interest rates begin to fall in line with that which is needed by both lender-creditors and borrower-debtors. There is movement toward these things happening in the late phase of the Big Debt Cycle. It requires both psychological and fundamental adjustments. After a big deleveraging, it is typically difficult to convince lender-creditors to lend because the devaluations/restructurings they experienced in the deleveraging make them risk-averse, so it is imperative that the central government and the central bank take credibility-restoring actions. These generally involve bringing their finances in order by a) the central government earning more money than it spends and/or b) the central bank making money hard again by offering high real yields, raising reserves, and/or linking the currency to something hard like gold or a strong currency. Typically, in this stage, interest rates need to be relatively high in relation to inflation rates and more than high enough to compensate for currency weakness, so it pays to be a lender and is costly to be a borrower. This stage of the cycle can be very attractive for lender-creditors.

The stage that the Big Debt Cycle is in is also reflected in the types of monetary policies being used. As the Big Debt Cycle progresses, central banks have to change how they run monetary policy in order to keep the debt/credit/economic expansion going, so by observing what type of monetary policy they are using, one can surmise what stage the Big Debt Cycle is in. **The phases in monetary policy**

and the conditions that lead to them are as follows:[4]

Phase 1: A Linked (i.e., Hard) Monetary System (MP0). This is the type of monetary policy that existed from 1945 until 1971. This type of monetary policy ends when the debt bubble bursts, and there is the previously described "run on the bank" dynamic, which is a run from credit assets to the hard money, and the limited amount of hard money causes massive defaults. This creates a compelling desire to print money rather than leave the supply of it limited by the supply of the gold or hard money that exists to be exchanged at the promised price.

Phase 2: A Fiat Money, Interest-Rate-Driven Monetary Policy (MP1). During this phase, interest rates, bank reserves, and capital requirements are also controllers of the amounts of debt/credit growth. This fiat monetary policy phase both allows more flexibility and provides less assurance that money printing won't be so large that it will devalue money and debt assets. The US was in this phase from 1971 until 2008. It ends when interest rate changes no longer work (e.g., interest rates hit 0% and there is a need to ease monetary policy) and/or the private market demand for the debt being created falls short of the supply being sold so that, if the central bank did not print the money and buy the debt, money and credit would be tighter and interest rates would be higher than desired.

Phase 3: A Fiat Monetary System with Debt Monetization (MP2). This type of monetary policy is implemented by the central bank using its ability to create money and credit to buy

[4] This explanation of the phases differs slightly from how I have described them in my earlier writings, with the main difference being that I have added a designation for linked (i.e., hard money) currency systems, which I had previously lumped in with fiat ones governed by interest rate changes. Because I think it is important to draw a distinction between linked and fiat systems, in this book, linked/hard money systems will be known as MP0 and the numbering of the other monetary policies will remain the same as in my other writings.

investment assets. It is the go-to alternative when interest rates can no longer be lowered and when private market demand for debt assets (mostly bonds and mortgages, though it can also include other financial assets like equities) is not large enough to buy the supply at an acceptable interest rate. It is good for financial asset prices, so it tends to disproportionately benefit those who have financial assets. It doesn't effectively deliver money into the hands of those who are most stressed financially, and it isn't very targeted. The US was in this phase from 2008 until 2020.

Phase 4: A Fiat Monetary System with a Coordinated Big Fiscal Deficit and Big Debt Monetization Policy (MP3). This type of monetary policy is used when, in order to make the system work well, central government fiscal policy and central bank monetary policy have to be coordinated in order to get money and credit into the hands of the people and entities that need it most. While creating money and credit typically temporarily alleviates the debt problem, it does not rectify the problem.

Phase 5: A Big Deleveraging. This is when there must be a big reduction in debt and debt service payments through a debt restructuring and/or a debt monetization. When managed in the best possible way—what I call a beautiful deleveraging—the deflationary ways of reducing debt burdens (e.g., through debt restructurings) are balanced with the inflationary ways of reducing debt burdens (e.g., by monetizing them), so that the deleveraging occurs without having unacceptable amounts of either deflation or inflation. The Big Debt Cycle sequence to keep in mind is: first the private sector overborrows, has losses, and has problems paying it back (i.e., a debt crisis); then, to help out, the government overborrows, has losses, and has problems paying it back; then, to help out, the central bank buys the government debt and takes losses. To fund those purchases and to fund other debtors in trouble (because it is the "lender of last resort"), the central bank prints a lot of money and buys a lot of debt. Then, at its worst, the central bank loses a lot of money on the debt it bought.

- While it is said that a modern central bank "prints" money to buy the debt, the central bank doesn't literally "print money." Instead, it borrows money (reserves) from commercial banks that it pays a very short-term interest rate on. At this dynamic's most extreme, the central bank can lose money because the interest earnings it gets on the debt it bought are less than the interest that it has to pay out on the money it borrowed. When these amounts become large it can find itself in a self-reinforcing spiral of having to buy debt, which leads it to have losses and negative cash flows, which leads it to need to print more money to service its debt and to need to buy more debt, which ends up having more losses, which requires it to do more of the same. This is the death spiral I mentioned earlier. When done in large amounts, the "printing" devalues the money and creates inflationary recessions or depressions. ● ***If interest rates rise, the central bank loses money on its bond holdings because the interest rate that it has to pay on its liabilities is greater than the interest rate that it receives on the debt assets it bought. This is notable but not a big red flag until the central bank has a very large negative net worth and is forced to "print" more money to cover the negative cash flow that it experiences due to less money coming in on its assets than has to go out to service its liabilities.*** **That is what I mean when I say the central bank goes broke: while the central bank doesn't default on its debts, it can't make its debt service payments without printing money.**
- Eventually the debt restructurings and debt monetizations reduce the size of the debts relative to incomes and the debt cycle runs its course.

Phase 6: The Return to Hard Money. In this phase, the central government takes actions to restore the soundness of its money and debt/credit. This type of monetary policy occurs after the debt has been written down through debt defaults/restructurings and debt monetizations so the debt levels relative to the incomes and amounts of money that are available to service the debts can be brought back into alignment. As previously described, it comes after those who held the debt assets were burned by the defaults and/or inflationary periods, so confidence in holding debt assets has to be rebuilt. At this stage, countries typically go back to MP0 (i.e., a hard-asset-backed monetary policy) or MP1 (an interest rate/money-supply-targeted monetary policy) that is beneficial to lender-creditors via high real interest rates.

- **For great countries with great empires, the end of the Big Debt Cycle has typically meant the end of their prominence.**

A FEW CONCLUDING OBSERVATIONS

● ***Big debt crises are inevitable.*** Throughout history only a very few well-disciplined countries have avoided them. They are inevitable because lending is never done perfectly relative to the incomes that are needed to service it. And it is often done badly because people always want more credit and that turns into debt. Debt levels get beyond that which is sustainable, which leads to the need to bring the debt burdens down, which typically leads to a mixture of debt defaults/restructurings and the creating of money and credit, causing a debt crisis to occur. And people's psychology reinforces the cycle: the bubble period makes people more optimistic, causing them to borrow more, and the bust causes people to be more pessimistic, causing them to cut spending. Even though this progression has happened many times in history, most policy makers and investors think their current circumstances and monetary system won't change. The change is unthinkable—and then it happens suddenly.

● ***It pays to build up savings in the good times so there are savings to draw on in the bad times. There are costs to having too much savings as well as too little savings, and no one gets the balance exactly right.***

● ***The best way to anticipate a debt crisis happening is not by focusing on a single influence or number like debt as a percent of GDP; it is by understanding and focusing on a number of interrelated dynamics.*** We will get into, especially in the next two chapters.

● ***If debts are denominated in a country's own currency, its central bank can and will "print" the money to alleviate the debt crisis.*** This allows the central bank to manage the crisis better than if the central bank can't print the money, but of course it also reduces the value of the money. If the debt is not denominated in a currency that the central bank can print, then it will have debt defaults and deflationary depressions measured in the currency that it owes and can't print.

● ***All debt crises, even big ones, can be managed well by economic policy makers restructuring and monetizing the debt so that the deflationary ways of reducing the debt burdens (i.e., writing off and restructuring debt) and the inflationary ways of reducing debt burdens (i.e., creating money and credit and giving it to the debtors to make it easier for them to service their debts) balance each other. The key is to spread the paying back over time.*** For example, if the debt-to-income ratio needs to fall by about 50% to make it sustainable, a debt restructuring that spreads it out at a rate of 3% or 4% per year would be much less traumatic than one that is about 50% in one year.

● ***Debt crises provide great risks and opportunities that have been shown to both destroy empires and provide great investment***

opportunities for investors if they understand how they work and have good principles for navigating them well.

If you try to focus on debt cycles precisely or focus your attention on the short term you won't see them. It's like comparing two snowflakes and missing that they are pretty much the same because they're not exactly the same.

That's it in a nutshell.

In the rest of this study, I will get into the mechanics in greater depth, show the actual sequences that have played out over 35 cases, look at how the Big Debt Cycle and Overall Big Cycle that includes the other big cycles (for instance, cycles of internal and external order) that started in 1945 and that we are currently in the late stages of have transpired relative to this template, and briefly look at the Chinese and Japanese Big Cycles and a number of other cases. The Japanese case is interesting because Japan is further along in its Big Debt Cycle. Notably, its large debt and debt monetizations have led to the depreciation of its currency and debt, which has led holders of its bonds to have losses of 45% relative to holding US dollar debt since 2013 and losses of 60% relative to holding gold since 2013. **In the final chapters, I will share how I am processing the US relative to this template, how the US could reduce the risk of an acute debt crisis, and how I see the rough outline of future events unfolding.**

CHAPTER 2

THE MECHANICS IN WORDS AND CONCEPTS

This chapter is about how the market and the economy work. It provides some unconventional concepts about the mechanics that have helped me a lot and that I believe would be valuable for professionals and aspiring professionals but may be beyond the interests of others. If you don't have much interest in the mechanics, I suggest just reading the bold material, and if that becomes too much, skipping the rest of this chapter and going to the next one.

Because everything that happens has reasons that make it happen, it appears to me that everything changes like a perpetual motion machine. To understand this machine, one needs to understand its mechanics, and because everything affects everything else, these mechanics are very complex. As a result of breakthroughs in artificial intelligence, I believe that we are on the brink of almost understanding it all, but for now we have to labor along the old-fashioned way, with people studying what happened using contemporary computers to aid them. That's how I created this description of the mechanics of the debt/credit/money/economic dynamic, which is, of course, only one big part of the greater dynamic. In my feeble attempts to understand and describe the most important mechanics that change the world as we know it, I do these in-depth studies and then try to create more simplified explanations of them.5 Keep in mind that this is a very simplified picture.

At the highest level, ● ***the five most important drivers of change that are important to understand are:***

- ***The debt/credit/money/economic cycle***
- ***The internal political order/disorder cycle***
- ***The external geopolitical order/disorder cycle***
- ***Acts of nature (droughts, floods, and pandemics)***
- ***Human inventiveness, most importantly of new technologies***

These are the biggest forces that affect each other to shape the biggest things that happen. I will go into these forces in more detail in Chapter 8, but if you want to understand what I learned from experiencing and studying them in a more complete way than I can cover here, you can read about them in my book *Principles for Dealing with the Changing World Order.*

In this study, we are going to examine the first of those—the debt/credit/money/economic dynamic—focusing most intensely on the late part of the long-term debt cycle when central governments and central banks "go broke." I will start by walking you through some mechanics of how market prices are determined and then look at how the long-term debt cycle works. With that as a background, I will turn to the archetypical sequence that leads to a country hitting the limits of debt and money and central governments and central banks going broke. At the same time, we will explore the other four forces because the interactions of these five forces cannot be overlooked in observing the resulting Overall Big Cycle. From what I can see, we are likely entering the very turbulent stage in the Overall Big Cycle driven by the interactions of these five big forces, and the resulting changes in the world order will be big. I hope this study can

[5] For example, in my book *Principles for Dealing with the Changing World Order,* I looked at and measured at the most important cause/effect relationships that changed the world over the last 500 years and simplified my description of how I see them to consist of the five big forces.

contribute to a better understanding of the dynamics and better decision making to produce the best outcomes possible.

HOW THE MACHINE WORKS

To me, money and credit are the lifeblood of the economy. They circulate nutrients (i.e., spending power) from the parts of the system that have excess amounts of the power to the parts of the system that can best use it. The central government is like the brain that directs how the system works while also taking in and using some of the money and credit (typically about 15-30% of it)[6] to perform its functions (e.g., providing for social programs, defense, etc.). The central bank is like the heart that produces and pumps money and credit through the system. If the exchanges go well, and those who get capital use it productively, then the providers of capital, the users of it, and the economic system as a whole all prosper. If they don't, the system will become ill and experience trauma.

To be clear, viewing the debt dynamic as a cyclical, perpetual motion machine working in essentially the same way through time and across countries doesn't mean that there are not changes over time and differences between countries. It's just that these changes are comparatively unimportant in relation to the timeless and universal mechanics and principles that are far less well understood than they should be. To me, it's invaluable to first see these timeless and universal principles of how the machine works and then focus on the differences and what they are due to because this approach provides a richer understanding of the cause/effect relationships. For that reason, I will start with these most important timeless and universal mechanics and principles. To convey them in brief, I will explain just the major ones in a big-picture, simplified way rather than a detailed and precise way. In this big-picture,

[6] Typically, 35-55% of all spending in developed countries comes from government spending (if you include state and local governments).

simplified model, the following describes the major parts and major players and how they operate together to make the machine work.

THE FIVE MAJOR PARTS AND HOW THEY WORK

There are five major parts of the economic system that make up my simplified model of the machine. They are:

- **Goods, services, and investment assets**
- **Money used to buy these things**
- **Credit issued to buy these things**
- **Debt liabilities that are created when purchases are made with credit**
- **Debt assets (e.g., deposits and bonds), which, since one person's liabilities are another's assets, are the other side of the debt liabilities**

If you can understand the transactions that occur as being made up of these five major parts, you can pretty much understand why there are big debt and economic cycles. To start, I will walk through how I think about transactions and some other important baseline mechanics.

As mentioned, goods, services, and investment assets can be bought with either money or credit.

Money, unlike credit, settles transactions. For example, if you buy a car with money, after the transaction, you and the seller are both done. What constitutes money has changed throughout history and across currencies. For long periods of history, money was a promise to deliver a certain amount of gold or other hard asset. In fiat monetary systems, which we've been in since the US left the gold standard in 1971, money is what central banks print and is more like a form of credit in that it is a promise to deliver buying power, not an actual hard asset. But **money is different from credit as, at this time, it can**

only be created by central banks[7] **and can be created in whatever amounts the central banks choose.**

Credit, unlike money, leaves a lingering obligation to pay, and it can be created by mutual agreement of any willing parties. Credit produces buying power that didn't exist before, without necessarily creating money. It allows borrowers to spend more than they earn, which pushes up the demand and prices for what is being bought over the near term while creating debt that, over the longer term, requires the borrowers, who are now debtors, to spend less than they earn as they pay back their debts. This reduces demand and prices in the future, which contributes to the cyclicality of the system. Because debt is the promise to deliver money and central banks determine the amount of money in existence, central banks have a lot of power. Though not exactly proportional, the more money in existence, the more credit and spending there can be; the less money in existence, the less credit and spending there can be.

Now let's look at how prices are set.

My approach to supply, demand, and price determination is different from the conventional approach in some simple but important ways that have proven invaluable to me.

To explain my approach to understanding prices, I start with the most basic building blocks for understanding all markets and economies, which are transactions, and then build up to the price, and I don't define supply and demand the way conventional economists do. **To me** ● ***all markets and all economies are simply the aggregates of the transactions that make them up,*** and a transaction is simply the buyer giving money (or credit) to a seller and the seller giving a good, a service, or a financial asset to the buyer in exchange. ● ***The price equals the amount of money/credit the buyer gives divided by the quantity of whatever the seller gives in that transaction, and a market is the aggregate of those transactions.*** For example, a transaction to buy wheat occurs when a buyer gives a certain amount of

[7] Bitcoin is an example of an attempt to create a private version of money using blockchain, a distributed ledger technology.

money to a seller in exchange for a certain quantity of wheat, and a market consists of all the buyers and sellers making exchanges for the same things—i.e., the wheat market consists of different people making different transactions for different reasons over time—and these many exchanges are what determine the price. **So. . .**

● ***Price (P) = the amount spent on something ($)/the total quantity of it that is sold (Q)***

Or, more simply

● ***P = $/Q***

In other words, ● ***since the price of any good, service, or financial asset equals the total amount spent by buyers ($) divided by the total quantity sold by sellers (Q), if you know the total spending (total $) and you know the total quantity sold (total Q), you will know the price and everything else you need to know.***

That is indisputably how it is, so it is indisputable that the best way to estimate the price is to estimate the total spending and divide it by the total quantity sold. That is why I estimate these two numbers—the total amount spent and the total quantity sold—to estimate the price. What is the best way to estimate these things? It is to understand the motivations of the buyers and sellers, most importantly the big ones. This approach is invaluable to understanding what is going on with prices and to making money in the markets. All buyers have their own reasons for spending the amount of money they are spending to get the quantity they are buying, and all sellers have their own reasons for selling the quantity they are selling to get the money they're getting. **What I'm saying is conveyed in the conceptual diagram that follows.**

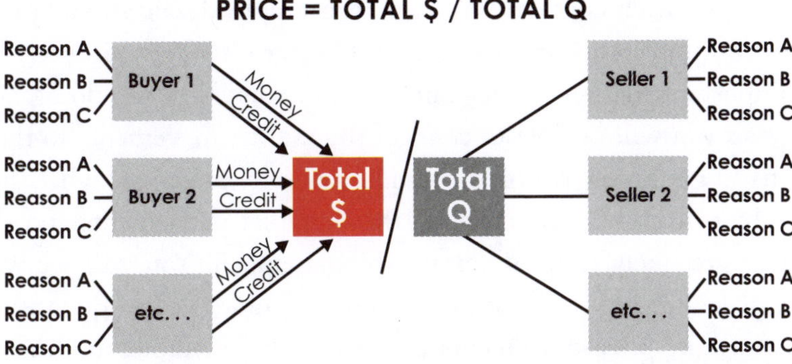

While this might look and sound complicated, it's really not. For each product, the buyers and sellers have their reasons for making those purchases and sales, and it's pretty easy to determine who the main buyers and sellers are and what motivates them. If you can figure out major buyers' reasons for spending and the major sellers' reasons for selling, you can pretty accurately predict their actions, and thus the price.

This way of looking at price determination is very different from how most economists look at it, and it has proven uniquely helpful. The traditional way measures both demand and supply in terms of quantity (i.e., quantity bought and quantity sold), whereas my approach looks at *amount spent to buy* instead of quantity bought. This leads to different ways of explaining why prices change. The conventional approach describes price changes as occurring because the quantity demanded and/or the quantity supplied changes. How these changes occur is called price elasticity. The conventional way of looking at the market implies that there is one price elasticity across time and that a change in supply will always have the same effect on price. This is obviously not true.

If you instead look at it my way, you will see that the conventional approach doesn't makes sense because it assumes that a change in supply will always have the same effect on price (i.e.,

elasticity), which isn't true. You will see supply, demand, and price determination in a very different and better way. You will see who the important market participants are and what they are doing and why, and you will be able to connect the market movements to their actions to get a very real understanding of why prices are what they are, why prices change, and what these market participants and the markets are likely to do if certain things happen. You will see why more or less money is spent on an item and more or less quantity is sold and how price movements are explicable for numerous reasons that previously escaped your attention and are escaping most others' attention. By seeing that prices change because of the total amount spent and the total quantity sold and by working hard to estimate these two numbers, you will be able to make pretty good estimates of price. You will also see that prices change not because of a return to some equilibrium level as most people believe.

If you pursue this approach, you will see that nowadays, with so much great data and computer power available, you will be able to watch this price determination model move with the price practically in real time, and that is fascinating to watch. I discovered this approach when I estimated livestock, grain, and oilseed and oilseed product prices back in the 1970s and found that it worked for all kinds of asset prices, including financial asset prices, so I have been pursuing and benefiting from it for a long time. I now use this approach to model entire economies, not just how specific markets work, but that's a subject for another time.

As for the debt dynamic, an example of how this transaction-based approach has been valuably different from conventional economic thinking is that most people mistakenly think that debt busts and depressions are primarily psychological and that if confidence is built the debt bust and the depression won't happen, and they overlook the mechanics behind them. I ran into this issue with policy makers prior to both the 2008 debt crisis in the US and the 2010-12 debt crisis in Europe, and I am running into it again now. In the two prior cases, I showed policy makers why the rate of change in buying debt would inevitably slow because the buying was being financed by financial institutions (most importantly banks) leveraging up their balance sheets and that would have to slow as they reached their regulatory leverage limits, so the pace of buying would slow at the same time as the supply of debt to be sold was projected to increase, so with less buying and more selling we were headed for a crisis. Until that actually happened, they assured me that they would give the markets confidence so that the buyers would keep buying, so everything would be fine, and refused to look at the supply-and-demand calculations. This is the sort of thinking that is now most popular. For example, I hear policy makers say that if we get control of the budget deficits in out-years investors will see the new calculations and have confidence and the bond market will be fine. That's naïve because it fails to look at the motivations of the bond buyers to calculate who will buy and sell what amounts of bonds in the way I described.

If you play with the previously shown formula/model a bit, you will see that prices change when there are changes in the rates of spending and/or quantities sold. For example, if the rate of buying goes from (X) to (X minus 10%), and all else stays the same, the price will fall by 10%. So ● ***by identifying rates of unsustainable buying and/or rates of unsustainable selling you can identify unsustainable prices and unsustainable economic conditions.*** **You can also calculate what a return to a more normal level of buying/selling would look like and you can calculate the approximate price change that is needed and likely. I have made a lot of money and have reduced a lot of risk by doing that.**

There are a number of other implications for how this different approach leads to unique perspectives on how economies and markets really work. For example, it shows how these debt/credit/money/market/economic cycles are driven more by the creation of money and credit that leads to changes in spending ($) than by the changes in the quantity sold (Q), and it makes clear that most goods, services, and investment assets are produced to satisfy demand (i.e., in response to increased [$]). One can also see very clearly that:

● ***When a) more money and credit are created (so there is more spending) and b) producers have the capacity to produce more quantity, then c) there can be more non-inflationary growth because both spending ($) and the quantity sold (Q) increase.***

Whereas

● ***When a) more money and credit are created (so there is more spending), but b) there is little or no capacity so producers can't produce much more, then c) there is little real growth and a lot more inflation.***

These principles explain why the early stage of the cycle (when there is plenty of excess capacity and central banks are stimulative) is characterized by strong growth and little inflation and the late stage of the cycle typically has weak growth and big price rises. That is what cyclical inflation and growth look like. Later in this study, we will go through this in more detail and explore what monetary inflations and inflationary depressions look like.

How does productivity fit into this discussion? If productivity growth is high, producers can produce more quantity (Q) as more money and credit are produced, so it allows non-inflationary growth to continue for longer. Of course, productivity can be hard to measure directly, as productivity can also show up as products improving in quality, or the marginal cost of producing something falling all the way to zero (e.g., as has happened for producing photos and electronic books).

Now let's look more closely at the reasons buyers spend and sellers sell the quantities they sell. Instead of doing that for all the individual items, I will look at the big categories to convey the principles that affect them all.

● ***People buy goods and services to use and buy investments to make money (i.e., as storeholds of wealth).*** How much they spend on goods and services versus investments depends on **what the goods and services they want to use cost relative to the amount of money and credit they have to spend, and the relative appeal of spending on goods and services compared to that of spending on financial assets.** And of course, they have their own reasons for choosing which goods and services and which financial assets they buy. If you understand these things, you will truly understand the markets.

● ***What people choose to spend their money and credit on is based on the relative appeal of the items.*** People are constantly making comparisons in two dimensions: 1) one item for another (e.g., stocks versus bonds, beef versus chicken, one currency versus another versus gold) and 2) the same item for delivery at different points in time (e.g., a commodity or a currency for delivery today versus for delivery a year in the future) based on their preferences. As a result, there is an enormous array of relative-appeal assessments and arbitrages to be made. Arbitrages and relatively sure bets are the most powerful types of bets in determining relative pricing. It pays for you to understand them.

● ***Currencies are mediums of exchange and storeholds of wealth (in debt assets).*** **In other words, they facilitate both transactions and investing.**

● ***Investments are exchanges of money and credit today for money and credit in the future.***

● ***All investment markets derive their value by providing money in two ways: through their yields and through their price changes. Together they make the total return. So, for all investments, total return = yield + price change.***

● ***By and large, all investment markets compete with each other on the basis of the total returns they provide. That is because a) most***

investors care more about the total returns they get than they care about whether it comes in the form of yield or price appreciation[8] and b) there is an ability to arbitrage investments based on their total returns.[9] To show how that works, let's look at how investing in bonds would be compared with investing in gold to determine the price relationship. Because gold has no yield and a US Treasury bond has a yield of X% (e.g., 5%), it would be illogical for anyone to buy gold unless the price is expected to go up by more than X% per year (e.g., 5% per year). Said differently, the market is priced for the gold price to rise by 5% relative to the price of Treasuries. Investors form their views about what will determine the price of gold (e.g., one big factor is the amount of inflation based on the amount of money and credit that is produced), and they look at the relative attractiveness of the 5% yield that the bonds are offering and the extent to which the gold price would appreciate due to the depreciation in the value of money. If they think that gold will rise by less than 5%, they can buy bonds and sell gold, and if they think gold will go up more than 5%, they can do the reverse. In either case, they'll make money if they're right. On top of this simple price analysis, there is a lot of financial engineering (e.g., leveraging and hedging) that turns one thing into the equivalent of another to make relative-value bets and arbitrages that create a whole matrix of market prices.

An enormous amount of money is allocated in this way, and it would be easy to make a lot of money if the choices between options were easy. But because we know it's not easy to make money in the markets, we can assume that the markets do a pretty good job of making these estimates and pricing assets correctly. At the same time, because I and others who have been successful at investing couldn't have

[8] While it's by and large true that all investments compete on a total return basis, it's not totally true because different investors have different objectives and considerations, so that at some times these different objectives and the differences in the supplies of investments to meet demands can lead to some investments having more attractive returns than others. However, because there is a profit to be made by shorting the asset that has the lower risk-adjusted return to fund the one that has the higher risk-adjusted return, there is a strong tendency for these differences to shrink to be rather small.

[9] I can make money by buying an investment that has a higher total return while selling an investment that has a lower total return.

been successful at investing if the markets were perfect, we can assume that it's not perfectly done and there are opportunities to make money in the markets if you have a better understanding than other people do. Anyway, my main point is that this is how to determine how markets are priced, which you will soon see is helpful in understanding the debt/credit/money/economic dynamic.

● ***The expected rates of return on investment assets relative to the rate of inflation (i.e., the expected real returns of investments) will influence how much money goes into each of these.*** By and large, an investment's inflation-adjusted ("real") returns are more important than its non-inflation-adjusted ("nominal") returns because a) investments are made to be storeholds of wealth so buying power matters most and b) there are arbitrages and relative-value bets between real assets and financial assets that drive their relative prices. In other words, the expected returns of putting money into financial investments are compared with the expected returns of putting money into real assets (e.g., real estate, precious metals, commodities, art, etc.), so the returns of all investments, especially the returns of government bonds (because their returns are so well-known since the yield is set and there is virtually no risk of default for bonds denominated in a country's own currency), are compared with the inflation rate, so when bond yields are low relative to inflation, bonds will be sold and inflation assets will be bought, and vice versa. Also, because the decline in the value of money and credit that arises from central banks creating lots of both causes the prices of goods, services, and most financial assets to rise, when central banks create a lot of money and credit, that tends to lead investors to favor inflation-hedge assets.

● ***Prices are linked by certain determinants that one must understand in order to understand relative pricing.*** When most non-professional investors think about the price, they usually think about the price for delivery of the item today, which is called the spot price. Most markets also have prices for deliveries sometime in the future, which are called forward (or futures) prices, and there are arbitrages or relative-value bets that one can make that determine the price relationship of the same items at different delivery dates.[10] The same sort of analysis of the relative appeal of financial assets (e.g., short-term government debt and long-term government debt) takes place (e.g., a big factor determining that is the projected pace at which the central bank will increase or decrease interest rates).

DEBT IS CURRENCY AND CURRENCY IS DEBT

● ***Since a debt asset is the promise to receive a specified amount of currency at a future date, debt and currency are essentially the same thing.*** **If you don't like the currency, you must not like the debt asset (e.g., bonds), and if you don't like the bonds, you must not like the currency, if you take into consideration their relative yields. (In other words, if you don't like one you must not like the other.)** Let's look again at the gold/bond price comparison process of looking at the relative yields + the expected price changes = the relative total returns. This sets the spot and futures prices for bonds and gold, and it works the same for assessing the value of different currencies and different debt assets of different countries. That assessment drives capital flows in important ways that are very relevant to the debt issue at hand.

More specifically:

Let's say the government interest rate (which is widely considered default-risk-free because government central banks can print money to make payments) in one country is below that in another country by X% per year. If that's the case, then the expected appreciation in that currency must be at the same percentage rate. Otherwise, it would be easy to make virtually risk-free profits (by owning the bonds with the higher interest rate). Instead, the difference in the interest rates is

[10] For example, for items that can be stored, the price premium of the forward (or futures) price over the spot price won't be more than the cost of storing it (including the interest expense on the money tied up with it in inventory). For items that will be stored (e.g., gold), the spot price will be determined by the expected future price minus the storage cost, rather than the future price being determined by the spot price plus the storage cost.

expected to be eaten up by the higher-interest-rate currency falling compared to the lower-interest-rate currency.

But what if that currency change is not expected to offset the interest rate difference? For example, if the 10-year interest rate in Country A is lower (e.g., 3% lower) than that in Country B's currency-denominated bond, you'd ordinarily expect Country A's currency to rise (to eat up the difference from the higher interest rate). What if, instead, Country A's currency is expected to fall (e.g., by 2% per year)? In that case, there is virtually risk-free profit to be made. Investors will flock into the trade, selling the lower-yielding debt/currency. That will produce one of two adjustments (or a combination of them):

1. the spot currency will have to fall (by 40% in this example[11]), or
2. the 10-year interest rate will have to rise by 5%, which will send the bond prices down by about 40%.[12]

Or if those adjustments can't happen (say there are capital controls or the like)—if the interest stays 3% less and the currency falls by 2%—then the loss relative to holding Country B's bonds will be 5% per year, which over the 10 years will compound to 40%.

Any way you cut it, the bond return in Country A's currency will be very bad.[13] If the nominal bond returns are not bad (i.e., the bonds do not depreciate and debt burdens are not reduced in nominal terms) because neither a) the price of the bonds falls in the local currency because the interest rates rise to provide an appropriate return in light

[11] Here's the math: If a currency is expected to depreciate by 2% per year, that means the forward price is 82% of the current price (2% depreciation compounded for 10 years). The spot needs to be priced to appreciate by 3% each year until it reaches the current 10-year forward price of 82%. A spot price of 0.61 x 1.03^10 = 0.82. So, the spot must fall from 1 to 0.61 (which is a ~40% move).

[12] Here's the (somewhat simpler) math: The price impact of an interest rate move on bonds is the change in yield x the duration. The duration of 10-year government bonds is 7-8 years, depending on the country: 8 x 5% = 40%.

[13] From a central banker's perspective, currency weakness and inflation can be good because they reduce the debt burden, which happens when the nominal interest rate is below the nominal growth rate, and especially when the nominal interest rate is below the inflation rate (i.e., when real interest rates are negative).

of the declining value of the currency nor b) the currency declines to a level that makes it cheap enough to provide adequate price appreciation to make up for the interest rates being too low, then the bad return of the bond will come about because c) the annual interest rate and weakness in the currency will not compensate for the inflation.[14]

Now that we understand how the mechanics of these major parts work, and how transactions are driven by the motivations of players in dealing with those parts, you can understand how the machine works and what is likely to happen next, so let's get into that.

THE MAJOR TYPES OF PLAYERS AND HOW THEY BEHAVE TO DRIVE WHAT HAPPENS

● ***There are five major types of players that drive money and debt cycles. They are:***

- ***Those that borrow and become debtors that I call "borrower-debtors," which can be private or government entities***
- ***Those that lend and become creditors that I call "lender-creditors," which can be private or government entities***
- ***Those that intermediate the money and credit transactions between the lender-creditors and the borrower-debtors, which are commonly called banks***
- ***Central governments***
- ***Government-controlled central banks, which can create money and credit in the country's currency and influence the cost of money and credit***

● ***Debt/credit expansions can only take place when both***

[14] Keep in mind that the different inflation rates in the different countries are typically more due to the differences in the rates of change in the values of their money/currencies (which are more due to the changing supplies of money and credit) than they are due to the changing values of the items being bought and sold when measured in a common currency.

borrower-debtors and lender-creditors are willing to borrow and lend, so the deal must be good for both. Said differently, because one person's debts are another's assets, for the system to work, it takes both borrower-debtors and lender-creditors to want to enter into these transactions. **However, what is good for one is quite often bad for the other.** For example, for borrower-debtors to do well, interest rates can't be too high, while for lender-creditors to do well, interest rates can't be too low. **If interest rates are too high for borrower-debtors, they will have to slash spending or sell assets to service their debts, or they might not be able to pay them back, which will lead markets and the economy to fall. At the same time, if interest rates are too low to compensate lender-creditors, they won't lend and will sell their debt assets, causing interest rates to rise or central banks to print a lot of money and buy debt in an attempt to hold interest rates down. This printing of money/buying of debt will create inflation, causing a contraction in wealth and economic activity.**

Over time, environments shift between those that are good and bad for lender-creditors and borrower-debtors. To be effective, it is critical that anyone who is involved in any way in markets and economies knows how to tell the difference. This balancing act and the swings between the two environments take place naturally, and sometimes conditions make it impossible to achieve a good balance. That causes big debt, market, and economic risks. Before I describe the conditions that produce these risks, I want to first explain the other players' motivations and how they try to act on them.

Private sector banks[15] are the intermediaries between lender-creditors and borrower-debtors, so their motivations and how they work are important, too. In all countries for thousands of years, banks have done essentially the same thing, which is to try to make profits by borrowing money from some and lending it to others, earning money on the spread. How they do this creates the debt/credit/

[15] For simplicity, I am using the word "banks" to describe all financial intermediaries that take on financial liabilities to get higher returns on financial assets.

money cycles, most importantly the unsustainable bubbles and big debt crises. **How are these bubbles and crises created? By the banks lending out a lot more money than they have, which they do by repeatedly borrowing at a cost that is lower than the return they take in from lending. That works well for the society and is profitable for the banks when those who are lent money use it productively enough to pay back their loans—and when those the banks borrowed from don't want their money back in amounts that are greater than what the banks actually have. But debt crises happen when the loans aren't adequately paid back or when the banks' creditors want to get back more of the money they lent to the banks than the banks are able to give them.**

- ***Over the long run, debts can't rise faster than the incomes that are needed to service them, and interest rates can't be too high for borrower-debtors or too low for lender-creditors for very long.*** If debts keep rising faster than incomes and/or interest rates are too high for borrower-debtors or too low for lender-creditors for too long, the imbalance will cause a big market and economic crisis. For that reason, it pays to watch these ratios.

- ***Big debt crises come about when the amounts of debt assets and debt liabilities become too large relative to the amount of money in existence and/or the amounts of goods and services in existence.***

Central banks either directly or indirectly create money and credit, which is buying power. Buying power determines the total amount of spending on goods, services, and investment assets. Whatever amount of money and credit is created must be put into goods, services, and financial assets (i.e., investments). So, **the total amount of money and credit created determines the total amount of spending on goods, services, and financial assets**. As a result, goods, services, and financial assets tend to rise and decline together with the ebb and flow of money and credit, like all boats tend to rise and fall with the ebb and flow of the sea. **What this money and credit go into and the quantities of goods, services, and financial assets that are produced are mostly determined by the choices made by**

thousands or millions of market participants.

Central banks came into existence to smooth these cycles, most importantly by handling big debt crises. Until relatively recently (e.g., 1913 in the United States), there weren't central banks in most countries, and money that was in private banks was typically either physical gold or silver or paper certificates to get gold and silver. Throughout those times, there were boom/bust cycles because borrower-debtors, lender-creditors, and banks went through the debt/credit cycles I just described. **These cycles turned into big debt and economic busts when too many debt assets and liabilities led to lender-creditor "runs" to get money from borrower-debtors, most importantly the banks. These runs produced debt/market/economic collapses that eventually led governments to create central banks to lend money to banks and others when these big debt crises happened. Central banks can also smooth the cycles by varying interest rates and the amount of money and credit in the system to change the behaviors of borrower-debtors and lender-creditors.** Where do central banks get their money from? They "print" it (physically and digitally), which, when done in large amounts, alleviates the debt problems because it provides money and credit to those who desperately need it and wouldn't have had it otherwise. But doing so also reduces the buying power of money and debt assets and raises inflation from what it would have been.

- ***Central banks want to keep debt and economic growth and inflation at acceptable levels. In other words, they don't want debt and demand to grow much faster or slower than is sustainable and they don't want inflation to be so high or so low that it is harmful.*** To influence these things, they raise interest rates and tighten the availability of money or they lower interest rates and ease the availability of money, which influences lender-creditors and borrower-debtors who are striving to be profitable.

- ***Central governments are political organizations with those who run them serving at the pleasure of elected officials who are elected by the people, so they want to give the people what they want.*** This is typically done without paying for it, which typically leads to central government borrowing, which reinforces the cycle of creating greater amounts of credit stimulation early and debt depressants later. When central governments do their jobs well, they tax and spend in ways that provide broad-based productivity and prosperity, sometimes borrowing more than they are earning and sometimes paying it back, and when central banks do their jobs well, they keep the credit, debt, and capital markets in relative balance, which produces less disruptive big swings. However, for the previously mentioned reasons, the bias to create more ups in economies and markets through credit stimulation leads to long-term uptrends in debt and debt service relative to incomes until they become too large a percentage of income to be sustainable.

● ***The greater the size of the debt assets and debt liabilities relative to the real incomes being produced, the more difficult is the balancing act of having interest rates high enough to satisfy lender-creditors without having them be so high that they will hurt borrower-debtors, so the greater the likelihood of a debt-caused downturn in the markets and economy.***

Because borrower-debtors, lender-creditors, banks, central governments, and central banks are the biggest players and drivers of these cycles, and because they each have obvious incentives affecting their behaviors, it is pretty easy to anticipate what they are likely to do and what is likely to happen next. When debt growth is slow, economies are weak, and inflation is low, central bankers will lower interest rates and create more money and credit, which will incentivize more borrowing and spending on goods, services, and investment assets, which will drive the markets for these things and the economy up. At such times, it is good to be a borrower-debtor and bad to be a lender-creditor. When debt growth and economic growth are unsustainably fast and inflation is unacceptably high, central bankers will raise interest rates and limit money and credit, which will incentivize more saving and less spending on goods, services, and investment assets. This will drive the markets and economy down because it's then better to be a lender-creditor-saver than

a borrower-debtor-spender. This dynamic leads to two interrelated cycles—a short-term one that has averaged about six years in length, give or take three years, and a long-term one that has averaged about 80 years, give or take 25 years—which evolve around an upward trend line in productivity that is due to humanity's inventiveness.

I'll now briefly review how these cycles transpire.

THE SHORT- AND LONG-TERM (BIG) DEBT CYCLES

By "short-term debt cycle," I mean the cycle of 1) recessions that lead to 2) central banks providing a lot of credit cheaply, which creates a lot of debt that initially leads to 3) market and economic booms, which lead to 4) bubbles and inflations, which lead to 5) central bankers tightening credit, which leads to 6) market and economic weakening. This cycle typically lasts about six years, give or take about three. As of this writing in March 2025, there have been 12 complete cycles in the US since 1945 and we are about two-thirds through the 13th. Each short-term debt cycle typically ends with higher levels of debt than the previous cycle because policy makers try to end recessions by lowering interest rates enough to get borrowing going again.

By "long-term (big) debt cycle," I mean the cycle of building up debt assets and debt liabilities over long periods of time (i.e., successive short-term debt cycles) to amounts that eventually become unmanageable. This leads to a combination of big debt restructurings and big debt monetizations that produce a period of big market and economic turbulence.

● ***The short-term debt cycles add up to the long-term (big) debt cycle, which I call the Big Debt Cycle.***

These cycles move markets and economies around an upward-sloping trend line of rising living standards that is due to people's inventiveness and the increases in productivity that come from it. The incline of its upward slope in productivity is primarily driven by the inventiveness of practical people (e.g., entrepreneurs) who are given adequate resources (e.g., capital) and work well with others (their coworkers, government officials, lawyers, etc.) to make productivity improvements.

Over a short period of time (i.e., 1-10 years), the short-term debt cycle is dominant. Over a long period of time (i.e., 10 years and beyond), the long-term debt cycle and the upward-sloping trend line in productivity have much bigger effects. Conceptually, this is how I see the dynamic transpiring:

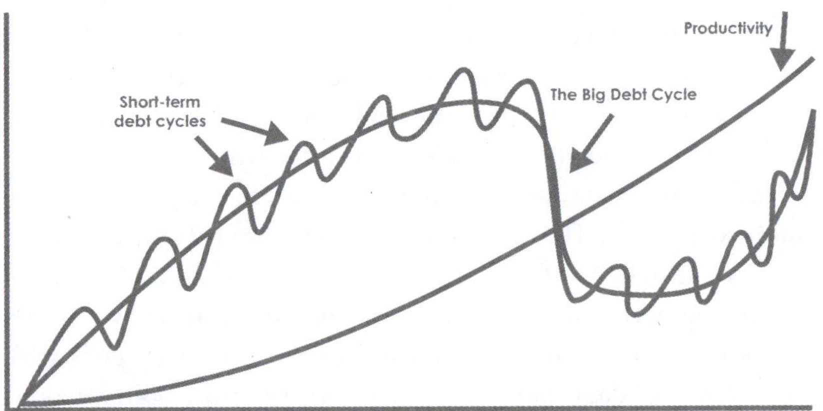

● ***What separates a sustainable debt cycle from an unsustainable one is whether the debt creates sufficient income to pay for the debt service. If incomes fail to grow as quickly as debt and debt service, the ratio of debts to incomes will mechanically grow, which will require increased borrowing to service debt as well as to spend.*** The cycle goes from low to high to unsustainably high debt and debt service relative to incomes. ● ***A sure sign of moving toward a debt crisis is when there is a large and rising amount of borrowing that is being used to pay for debt service.***

Why don't central bankers do a better job in smoothing out these debt cycles by better containing debt so it doesn't reach dangerous levels? There are four reasons:

1. Most everyone, including central bankers, wants the markets and economy to go up because that's rewarding and they don't worry much about the pain of paying back debts, so they push the limits, including becoming leveraged to long assets until that can't continue because they have reached the point that the debts are so burdensome that they have to be restructured to be reduced relative to incomes.
2. It is not clear exactly what risky debt levels are because it's not clear what will happen that will determine future incomes.
3. There are opportunity costs and risks to not providing credit that creates debt.
4. Debt crises, even big ones, can usually be managed to reduce the pain they cause to acceptable levels.

● ***Debt isn't always bad, even when it's not economic. Too little debt/credit growth can create economic problems as bad or worse than too much, with the costs coming in the form of unrealized opportunities. That is because 1) credit can be used to create great improvements that aren't profitable that would have been forgone without it and 2) the losses from the debt problems can be spread out to be not intolerably painful if the government is in control of the debt restructuring process and the debt is in the currency that the central bank can print.*** However, to avoid a debt crisis, the debt must raise incomes enough to service the debt.

● ***Over time, from one cycle to the next, debt liabilities and debt assets have virtually always increased to produce the long-term debt cycle expansion. In virtually all cases, that has continued until the debt burdens have become unsustainably large or the debt assets have become intolerably low-returning.***

When there are a lot of debt assets and debt liabilities relative to incomes, it is difficult for central bankers to keep interest rates high enough to satisfy lender-creditors without having them so high that they unacceptably hurt borrower-debtors, and it is difficult for

central banks to run monetary policy to balance growth and inflation well. And because holders of debt assets want to sell the debt, one way or another debt is going to have a bad return. That puts central bankers in the position of having to choose between:

1. **Not printing money and buying debt (i.e., not monetizing debt)** and letting interest rates rise enough to cut credit demand and economic activity enough to reach the indifference-equilibrium level that will balance the buying and selling of the bonds. This will make cash very valuable, devalue most other assets like stocks and hard assets, cause deflation, lead to debt defaults and restructurings, and depress economic activity. This typically happens first and is intolerable, which leads central banks to start. . .
2. **Printing money and buying debt (i.e., monetizing debt) to make up for the shortfall in demand**, which will make money readily available and reduce its value thus raising inflation, raise the value of most other assets like stocks and hard assets, minimize debt defaults, and stimulate economic activity. This typically happens eventually.

At that part of the Big Debt Cycle, there need to be big reductions in debt liabilities and debt assets. These are the big debt crisis periods. These big debt restructurings and debt monetizations end the prior Big Debt Cycle by reducing debt burdens and eliminating the prior monetary order, leading to the next Big Debt Cycle and monetary order. They take place much like big changes in domestic political orders and big changes in world orders—like seismic shifts due to the old order breaking down. **There are four types of levers that policy makers can pull to reduce the debt burdens:**

1. **Austerity (i.e., spending less)**
2. **Debt defaults/restructurings**
3. **The central bank "printing money" and making purchases**

(or providing guarantees)
4. **Transfers of money and credit from those who have more than they need to those who have less**

Policy makers typically try austerity first because that's the obvious thing to do, and it's natural to want to let those who got themselves and others into trouble bear the costs. This is a big mistake. Austerity doesn't bring debt and incomes back into balance. Cutting debts cuts investors' assets and makes them "poorer," and because one person's spending is another person's income, cutting spending cuts incomes. For that reason, cuts in debts and spending cause a commensurate cut in net worths and incomes, which is very painful. Also, as the economy contracts, government revenues typically fall at the same time as demands on the government increase, which leads deficits to increase. Seeking to be fiscally responsible at this point, governments tend to raise taxes, which is also a mistake because it further squeezes people and companies. More simply said, **when there is spending that's greater than revenues and liquid liabilities that are greater than liquid assets, that produces the need to borrow and sell debt assets,** which, if there's not enough demand, will produce one kind of crisis or another (e.g., either deflationary or inflationary).

As touched on earlier, the best way for policy makers to reduce debt burdens without causing a big economic crisis is to engineer what I call a beautiful deleveraging, which is when policy makers both 1) restructure the debts so debt service payments are spread out over more time or disposed of (which is deflationary and depressing) and 2) have central banks print money and buy debt (which is inflationary and stimulating). Doing these two things in balanced amounts spreads out and reduces debt burdens and produces nominal economic growth (inflation plus real growth) that is greater than nominal interest rates, so debt burdens fall relative to incomes.

If done well, there is a balance between the deflationary and depressing reduction of debt payments and the inflationary and stimulating printing of money and buying of debt by the central banks.

In the countries I studied, most big debt crises that occurred with the debts denominated in a country's own currency were restructured quickly, typically in one to three years. These restructuring periods are times of great risk and opportunity. If you want to learn more about these periods and processes, they are explained more completely in *Principles for Navigating Big Debt Crises.*

THE BIG DEBT CYCLE, ITS RISKS, AND HOW TO DEAL WITH IT NEED TO BE BETTER UNDERSTOOD

As explained earlier, because the really big debt crises that take the form of debt restructurings and devaluations that come at the ends of Big Debt Cycles happen roughly once in a lifetime, they are not well-understood relative to the short-term cycles. Said differently, what ends long-term debt cycles is different from what ends short-term debt cycles, so most people don't know about or acknowledge long-term debt cycles or worry about long-term debt cycles ending even though they're much bigger deals than short-term debt cycles ending. That's dangerous. It's like eating fatty foods and having cholesterol accumulate in the arteries and saying that it doesn't seem to be causing trouble while it is increasing the probability of a heart attack.

Let's remember what is healthy, which is 1) having private sector lenders give their credit in exchange for debt that works well for them and creditors because the uses of the funds are profitable and 2) for government borrowings to be used in ways that produce productivity gains (e.g., by investing in better infrastructure, education, etc.) that can be paid for via tax revenue, or for the government to sometimes borrow and spend more than it takes in when the economy needs stimulation and pay it back when conditions are strong. And let's remember what isn't healthy, which is 1) the central bank chronically printing money and buying debt to make up for the shortage in demand for the debt and 2) the central government chronically having large deficits that result in debt and debt service levels rising faster than the incomes (in the government's case, tax revenue) that are required to service them.

In summary and to reiterate:

- ***Goods, services, and investment assets can be produced, bought, and sold with money and credit.***

- ***Central banks can produce money and can influence the amount of credit in whatever quantities they want.***

- ***Borrower-debtors ultimately require enough money and low enough interest rates for them to be able to borrow and service their debts.***

- ***Lender-creditors require high enough interest rates and low enough default rates from the borrower-debtors in order for them to get adequate returns to lend and be creditors.***

- ***This balancing act becomes progressively more difficult as the sizes of the debt assets and debt liabilities both increase relative to incomes. Eventually they need to be reduced, so a deleveraging happens.***

- ***The best type of deleveraging is what I call a beautiful deleveraging, which can be engineered by central governments and central banks to reduce debt burdens if the debts are in their own currencies. If the debts are denominated in a foreign currency, the deleveraging is quite ugly. I will explain these later.***

- ***Over the long term, being productive and having healthy income statements (i.e., earning more than one is spending) and healthy balance sheets (i.e., having more assets than liabilities) are the markers of financial health.***

- ***If you know where in the debt/credit cycle each country is and how the players are likely to behave, you should be able to navigate these cycles well.***

- ***The past is prologue.***

Important takeaways:

- ***Debt crises are inevitable. Throughout history only a very few well-disciplined countries have avoided debt crises. That's because lending is never done perfectly and is often done poorly due to how the cycle affects people's psychology to produce bubbles and busts.***

- ***Most debt crises, even big ones, can be managed well if economic policy makers spread out their negative impacts.***

- ***All debt crises provide investment opportunities if Investors understand how they work and have good principles for navigating them well.***

- ***Inevitably, at the beginning of the end of the Big Debt Cycle when there is a lot of debt, it is difficult to keep real interest rates high enough to satisfy lender-creditors without them being too high for borrower-debtors, and central banks try to navigate between these choices. Typically during these times, both the tight-money economic contraction and the loose-money inflation occur, and the only question is in what order. In any case, owning the debt/currency of overly indebted governments at such times is a bad investment.***

- ***Central banks have to choose between keeping money "hard," which will lead debtors to default on their debts, which will lead to deflationary depressions, and making money***

"soft" by printing a lot of it, which will devalue both it and the debt. Because paying off debt with hard money causes such severe market and economic downturns, when faced with this choice central banks always choose to print and devalue money eventually. For the case studies, see Part II of Principles for Navigating Big Debt Crises. Of course, each country's central bank can only print that country's money, which brings me to my next big point.

- ***If debts are denominated in a country's own currency, its central bank can and will "print" the money to alleviate the debt crisis. This allows them to manage it better than if they couldn't print the money, but of course it also reduces the value of the money.***

THE FOUR OTHER BIG FORCES AFFECT HOW THIS DEBT CYCLE TRANSPIRES JUST AS THIS DEBT CYCLE AFFECTS HOW THE FOUR OTHER FORCES TRANSPIRE TOGETHER

One can't be a successful global macro investor by just focusing on the markets. One also has to focus on the forces that affect markets.

Thus far, I have just spoken about debt cycles because that is the subject of this study. However, many factors interact to determine what happens, so I couldn't ignore them and do my job well. They were covered extensively in my book *Principles for Dealing with the Changing World Order*. While I showed 18 measures of the major drivers of conditions in that book, **the big five that explain almost everything are: 1) the debt/credit/money/markets/economic cycle, 2) the cycle of social and political order and disorder that takes place within countries, 3) the cycle of order and disorder that is manifest in the peace and war cycle that takes place between countries, 4) acts-of-nature shocks such as droughts, floods, and pandemics, and 5) human inventiveness, especially of new technologies that increase productivity. The interactions between these forces drive**

how conditions change. They tend to reinforce each other both upwardly and downwardly. For example, periods of financial and economic crisis raise the odds of having periods of internal conflict, and periods of internal conflict worsen financial and economic conditions. Similarly, periods of internal financial problems and internal political conflicts both weaken the country that they are happening in and, if they are global, increase the likelihood of international conflicts. Together these forces create the Big Cycles of ups and downs, peace and wars, that occur in countries and between countries and that lead to big changes in domestic and world orders.

These big rises and declines are easy to see by monitoring the 18 forces (particularly the big five) that I have shared with you. For example, you can see the big evolutionary decline of great powers and their monies reflected in 1) the unwavering rises of indebtedness accompanied by the steady weakening of the types of monetary systems used to restrain credit-and-debt-growth-motivated attempts to raise credit and economic growth and 2) the decline of many indicators of health, such as the quality of education, infrastructure, law and order, civility, and government effectiveness, relative to those of other world powers.

Chapter 8 provides a more detailed explanation of these Big Cycle forces and how they are interrelated. But before I get to them, I will first delve into a deeper description of the Big Debt Cycle in both numbers and equations, trying to describe it in an easy-to-understand way.

CHAPTER 3

THE MECHANICS IN NUMBERS AND EQUATIONS

This chapter gets into debt mechanics, including some simple equations that are helpful in calculating what is likely to happen related to the limitations of debt. I believe this material will be valuable for professionals and aspiring professionals but will be beyond the interests of others. I suggest that you give it a scan to grab the important concepts and then decide if you want to delve deeper into this material or skip it.

While in Chapter 2 I described in words how central governments and central banks typically get into financial trouble, in this chapter I will show numbers and equations that can be used to anticipate these financial troubles, including a few formulaic examples to illustrate how high debt burdens compound and create problems.

I will start by showing you the key drivers of debt sustainability and how they interact. Before I do, I will lay out what an "unsustainable" debt burden is. Ultimately, it's simple: ● ***an "unsustainable" debt burden exists when the amount of money that comes in is less than the money that goes out, either because a) the amount in storage (i.e., savings) goes down and/or b) the amount borrowed goes up until one runs out of savings and/or one can't borrow more, at which time***

***a debt failure occurs.* Think of this money flow as being like the flow of blood and think of income statements and balance sheets as the reports that show it. A healthy condition is when the amount that comes in from earning is equal to or greater than the amount that goes out from spending and debts don't build up faster than incomes. This isn't to say that debt growth is necessarily bad. If debts build up, but the money borrowed leads to incomes rising faster than the rate of debt service rises, that will lead to more money coming in than going out, which will be healthy. When debts grow faster than incomes, think of it like plaque building up in the arteries because it reduces the amount of income flow that can be used for spending or saving. That is because it leads to increased debt service payments that reduce the amount of income that can go toward spending. If the money flow is constrained too much, there is a default, which is the economic equivalent to a heart attack.** Interest rates matter a lot because they have a lot of influence on the amounts that have to be paid. They also influence the willingness of lender-creditors to hold and buy the debt assets. As debt service becomes large relative to the amount of income and savings, a squeeze develops, which is when a debt problem occurs.

We can measure debt burdens in the following ways, and we know that as they become high and/or rise quickly, the risks of defaults and/or devaluations also become high. **While there are about 35 indicators that I look at to assess debt risks, the four most important indicators are:**

1. **Debts relative to income.** As debts get larger relative to incomes, all else equal, the debtor will have higher interest and rollover payments each year. There are two problems with high debts relative to income: 1) there is a greater risk that the large amount of existing debt won't be rolled over by creditors and 2) it creates higher debt service payments as a percent of income, which reduces the amount of money that can go to spending, all else equal. That brings me to the next measure.

2. **Debt service relative to income.** Debt service is the amount a debtor must pay in interest and principal payments to not default on their debts each year. As total debt service gets higher and higher relative to income, it leads investors to expect credit problems ahead and choose not to lend more and/or to sell the debt assets they already own, which causes credit problems to come about. To help estimate how debts and debt service will build up, I look at the rate of interest relative to the rate of income growth.
3. **Nominal interest rates relative to a) inflation rates and b) nominal income growth rates (i.e., inflation plus real growth).** I look at these for two reasons:
    a. They show me how debt and debt service are likely to grow relative to incomes. For example, if someone has debts of 100% of income, the nominal interest rate is 5%, and the nominal income growth rate is 3%, they will owe about 102% of income next year (assuming their spending is equal to their income).[16]
    b. They show me how attractive credit conditions are for lenders relative to borrowers. If nominal interest rates are high relative to nominal growth rates and inflation rates, that is an indicator that conditions are relatively favorable for lenders and unfavorable for borrowers, which will encourage lending and discourage borrowing/spending (i.e., it reflects greater risk of debt problems among more indebted debtors that can't print money to pay debt). If the reverse is true, conditions are relatively unfavorable for lender-creditors and favorable for borrower-debtors, which will encourage borrowing and discourage lending.
4. **Debt and debt service relative to savings (e.g., reserves).** If

[16] If the amount earned is greater than the amount spent excluding the interest payments, that is called a primary surplus, and if it is less, that is called a primary deficit.

all of the above are not financially healthy but one has large savings to draw down, one won't have a high risk of default because one can draw on the savings (e.g., reserves) to make debt and spending payments.

● ***Inevitably, equilibrium levels of 1) debts relative to incomes, 2) debt service relative to incomes, 3) nominal interest rates relative to inflation rates (i.e., real interest rates) and nominal growth rates, and 4) debts and debt service relative to savings will be approached. If you watch these ratios over time, you will see them go to extreme levels and return to more normal levels one way or another. If you understand the cause/effect relationships that drive these changes, you can understand how to navigate them and how they can be best managed. Most importantly, if you understand the painful deleveraging part, you will understand that it can be handled well (to be less painful) or handled poorly (and be very painful).***

These four indicators are not the only ones that matter. In Chapter 4, I'll show you how a broader set of indicators evolves through the end of the Big Debt Cycle, and in Chapter 17, I'll show you what my indicators suggest for the US today. However, the previously mentioned four are the most important ones to watch. They give us valuable information about how likely a debt squeeze is and how severe it will be when it happens. However, they cannot tell us exactly when the debt problem will occur because different conditions and different people's reactions to them lead to different lead times for the selling of debt assets and other actions that precipitate a crisis. Still, we can measure the level of risk because ● ***countries with very high debt levels, very large deficits, low savings, and very high and very fast-rising interest rates have a very high risk of a debt default or debt devaluation crisis.***

The rest of this chapter goes through a few formulaic examples to illustrate how high debt burdens compound and create problems.

MEASURING DEBT BURDENS IN NUMBERS

What follows are the mathematical relationships for measuring these indicators. These are just the commonsense constraints on the amount of debt an entity can have, expressed in equations that are the same constraints that can be expressed in words. To help you understand them, you might relate to them the same way you relate to your own debt constraints. I will explain the rules and include a few helpful guidelines. The pages that follow will explain each of these with examples. Not only can these relationships help one to identify debt problems, but they can be used to help policy makers see how to fix them and help market participants position themselves well. Feel free to skip this and come back if it's more helpful to see examples first and then the math.

1. ***Future debts relative to future income.*** The formula to estimate this is:

$$\frac{\text{Future Debt}}{\text{Future Revenue}} =$$

$$\frac{(\text{Future Expenses Excluding Interest} - \text{Future Revenue}) + \text{Current Debt} * (1 + \text{Interest Rate})}{\text{Current Revenue} * (1 + \text{Growth Rate})}$$

In words: Future debt relative to revenue is a function of 1) spending more or less than one makes in revenue, 2) the "compounding" of one's existing debts, and 3) revenue growth. As one's expenses grow relative to one's revenue, one is forced to borrow more to finance the spending, which increases new borrowing (first numerator term). As interest rates rise, existing debts grow faster (second numerator term). As revenues grow, incomes grow relative to debts, so the ratio of debt to revenue falls (denominator term).[17]

Note that I am looking at debt-to-revenue rather than debt-to-GDP. That is because GDP doesn't matter for the government's—or for that matter, for any entity's—finances unless it is tapped into because what matters are its actual cash flows.

Debt-to-income is a good indicator of risk because the larger it is, the riskier and the more burdensome the debt is, all else equal. For example, the more debt there is, the more risk there is that the debt won't be rolled over and the more difficult it is for the central bank to keep interest rates low enough to satisfy the borrower-debtors without having them too high for the lender-creditor. You can probably already see that, in addition to the level of debt-to-income mattering, the interest rate, income growth rate, and primary deficit (expenses excluding interest versus revenue) matter a lot to how debt burdens evolve.

This formula can also be configured to solve for ways to keep the debt-to-income ratio the same. I will show a few different examples of this at the end of this chapter.

2. ***Future debt service relative to future income.*** The formula to estimate this is:

[17] This relationship is also often represented as follows, where *g* refers to the income growth rate, *i* refers to the interest rate, and *t* is the time or year in question.

$$\frac{Debt}{Income_t} - \frac{Debt}{Income_{t-1}} = (i_t - g_t)\frac{Debt}{Income_{t-1}} + \left(\frac{Primary\ Deficit}{Income}\right)_t$$

One implication of this is that to keep debts constant relative to incomes, primary deficits as a share of income must equal the difference between growth rates and interest rates multiplied by the current ratio of debt to income.

$$\frac{Primary\ Deficit}{Income} = (g - i)\frac{Debt}{Income}$$

$$\frac{\text{Future Debt Service}}{\text{Future Revenue}} = \frac{(\text{Future Interest Costs} + \text{Future Principal Payments})}{\text{Current Revenue} * (1 + \text{Growth Rate})}$$

$$\text{Future Interest Costs} = \text{Future Debt Level} * \text{Average Effective Interest Rate on Debt}$$

$$\text{Future Principal Payments} = \text{Future Debt Level} * \text{Share of Debts Coming Due}$$

In words: Future debt service relative to revenue is a function of future interest costs and principal payments, relative to how much revenue grows. If revenue grows a lot, debt service will fall relative to incomes, all else equal.

Future interest costs are a function of the debt level and the average interest rate on the debt. If interest rates shoot up, it generally will not make the interest costs for a debtor go up immediately because, on longer-term bonds, the interest rate will be locked at the interest rate at the time of issuance. As the bonds "roll"—i.e., come due and are reissued at the new interest rate—the bonds will gradually get to have higher interest rates on them, and interest costs will rise.

Principal payments are the amount of debt that is coming due each year that must be paid back, typically via issuing new debt to pay back the old debt that comes due. A rough way to estimate principal payments is by calculating the average maturity—or time until debts must be paid back—on existing debts. When debtors are stressed, creditors typically will not want to lend to them for as long, so we often see the maturity of debts falling as creditors become more stressed, which means principal payments go up for the same level of debts.

3. ***Nominal interest rates relative to a) inflation rates and b) nominal income growth rates (i.e., inflation plus real growth):*** The expected level of nominal interest rates relative to nominal growth rates tells us how debt and debt service are likely to grow or shrink. Here, I show the formula for the interest rate that would keep debt levels and debt service flat relative to revenue. Note that this is based on the first formula, but configured to give us the required interest rate to keep debts flat relative to revenue.

$$\text{Interest Rate Required to Keep Debt Flat} = \text{Revenue Growth Rate} - \frac{(\text{Future Expenses Excluding Interest} - \text{Future Revenue})}{\text{Starting Debt Level}}$$

In words: If the primary deficit is zero (i.e., current expenses before interest = current revenue), debts will stay flat if the interest rate is equal to the revenue growth rate. If the primary deficit is 5% of the current debt level, interest rates would need to be 5% below the revenue growth rate.

The intuition here is that if the interest rates are equal to revenue growth, debts will compound at the same rate that income is growing. If the government is also borrowing, debts need to compound slower than income, so interest rates need to be below revenue growth rates.

As interest rates rise relative to revenue growth rates, debts will grow relative to incomes because existing debts will compound faster than revenue is growing, and debt service costs will grow even faster because both the debt level will grow and the interest rate will rise, and interest costs are the product of these two inputs. Similarly, as interest rates fall, debt levels will grow less quickly and debt service costs will grow even less or shrink. (This is, for instance, what has happened in Japan over the last 20 years. I will show this in more detail in Chapter 16.)

You can probably see that, just as you can solve for the interest rate required to keep debts flat, you can also solve for the deficit or surplus required, revenue growth required, and so on. If you flip to the end of this chapter, I show you what these numbers look like for the US today.

4. ***Debts and debt service relative to savings (e.g., reserves):*** Just as we can estimate debt burdens relative to income, we can estimate them relative to savings—simply by looking at the level and change in savings rather than the level and change in incomes. The formula to estimate this is as follows:[18]

$$\frac{\text{Future Debt}}{\text{Future Savings}} = \frac{(\text{Current Expenses Excluding Interest} - \text{Current Revenue}) + \text{Current Debt} * (1 + \text{Interest Rate})}{\text{Current Savings} + \text{Expected Savings}}$$

$$\frac{\text{Future Debt Service}}{\text{Future Savings}} = \frac{(\text{Future Interest Costs} + \text{Future Principal Payments})}{\text{Current Savings} + \text{Expected Savings}}$$

These formulas are very similar to (1) and (2), so I will not fully walk through them in words. The difference is that we are looking at debts and debt service relative to savings. If one has large debts but very large savings, it is less likely that the debt burdens are concerning because one can pay the debt service and pay back part of the debts using the savings. It creates a buffer.

[18] This equation is inexact because a government could use a surplus to either accumulate reserves/savings or to pay down existing debts, which would show up via expenses being lower than revenue. Depending on what choice a government made, the surplus could show up as future debt falling or as future savings increasing. Either way, the ratio would improve but the effect would be slightly different based on the choices of the government.

If one is consistently running deficits, and the expected surplus is negative, debts and debt service will quickly grow relative to savings, creating a more concerning setup.

A few rules of thumb that help to convey how these equations play out:

- ***If nominal interest rates are at the same level as nominal income growth and a government is running no primary deficit (i.e., revenue = spending excluding interest), the debts will stay the same relative to the incomes. But if interest rates are higher than income growth, then the debt burdens of existing debts will increase.*** This is probably the single most important variable in the calculation. For example, a bad but plausible period of nominal interest rates relative to nominal growth would be interest rates being higher than income growth by 2%. This would cause the debt-to-income ratio to increase by around 50% over 20 years, even without primary deficits, leading to more borrowing and debt. This means that if you start with debts of 50% of income, they'll go to 75%, but if you start with debts of 400%, they'll go to 600%.

- ***Debt service expenses accumulating is like plaque in the arteries accumulating in that it squeezes out the desired flow of nutrients to the economy.***

- ***The main effect of high debt levels is making the debtor vulnerable to not being able to roll it forward.***

These mathematical relationships can provide us with good estimates of the magnitudes of debt service squeezes that will occur if the existing levels of debt are rolled over. However, they don't show the dynamic that happens when holders of debt assets want to sell the debt they are holding. In the following examples, I will explain all these things.

Example 1: Debts Relative to Incomes (Levels and Changes)

As starting debt levels grow, and as deficits (i.e., borrowings) grow, future debt levels, debt service, and interest costs all grow. The next set of tables shows a range of outcomes. The debt-to-GDP ratio, which is more commonly quoted, is not as relevant to the government's debt service picture as its debt-to-income ratio. That is because **for any debtor, including central governments, what matters most is the amount of money that goes out (in this case, in debt service) relative to the amount of money that comes in because that is what creates the debt squeeze**; the size of GDP is only partially related.[19] Both are only rough indicators of the capacity of the economy to bear the debt burden.

For reference, the US government's expenditures excluding interest are projected to average ~112% of income over the next decade, so the primary deficit—the difference between these—is ~12% of income.[20] The US is also borrowing ~20% of its income each year to cover interest expenses on the existing debt.

The US government's debt to money coming in (mostly tax income) is, as of this writing, about 580%. If we assume that interest rates equal income growth but use the actual projected primary deficit for the US (i.e., the 12% actual gap between non-interest expenses and income), the US government's debt-to-income is projected to rise by about 120%, from 580% to 700%, over the next 10 years. This would also lead to a proportional increase in the interest expense and debt service burden.

The first table that follows shows debt levels 10 years forward for

[19] GDP can be an indicator of the size of the economy that can be taxed by governments to make debt payments.

[20] Throughout this study, I am using projections from the Congressional Budget Office (CBO) where possible as a baseline estimate. These projections are based on settled law so they assume that expiring fiscal measures (i.e., the Trump tax cuts) roll off as implemented in current law. If these tax cuts are extended, the CBO estimates they would represent additional annual spending of 1.5% of GDP or 8% of government revenue, which would substantially worsen the fiscal trajectory versus the CBO's baseline projection.

various starting debt levels and deficits. The second table shows the change relative to the starting debt level. You can see that as the starting debt level rises, and as deficits become larger, the expected debt level at the end gets higher.

DEBT-TO-INCOME AFTER 10 YEARS

Government Primary Deficit (% Govt Revenue)

Starting Debt-to-Income	0%	5%	10%	15%	20%	25%	30%
0%	0%	50%	100%	150%	200%	250%	300%
100%	100%	150%	200%	250%	300%	350%	400%
200%	200%	250%	300%	350%	400%	450%	500%
300%	300%	350%	400%	450%	500%	550%	600%
400%	400%	450%	500%	550%	600%	650%	700%
500%	500%	550%	600%	650%	700%	750%	800%
600%	600%	650%	700%	750%	800%	850%	900%
700%	700%	750%	800%	850%	900%	950%	1000%

☐ = US Trajectory Today

Assuming Nominal Interest Rate = Nominal Growth

10YR CHANGE IN DEBT (% INCOME)

Government Primary Deficit (% Govt Revenue)

Starting Debt-to-Income	0%	5%	10%	15%	20%	25%	30%
0%	0%	50%	100%	150%	200%	250%	300%
100%	0%	50%	100%	150%	200%	250%	300%
200%	0%	50%	100%	150%	200%	250%	300%
300%	0%	50%	100%	150%	200%	250%	300%
400%	0%	50%	100%	150%	200%	250%	300%
500%	0%	50%	100%	150%	200%	250%	300%
600%	0%	50%	100%	150%	200%	250%	300%
700%	0%	50%	100%	150%	200%	250%	300%

Assuming Nominal Interest Rate = Nominal Growth

When going through these numbers, you might keep in mind that at the time of this writing, the US, Japanese, Chinese, French, German, and UK numbers are approximately as follows:

	CENTRAL GOVERNMENT DEBT LEVELS		CENTRAL GOVERNMENT DEFICIT		CENTRAL GOVERNMENT REVENUE
	% GDP	% GOVT REVENUE	% GDP	% GOVT REVENUE	% GDP
USA	100%	583%	6%	37%	17%
JPN	215%	1376%	4%	26%	16%
CHN	90%	321%	5%	16%	28%
FRA	86%	478%	6%	31%	18%
DEU	44%	340%	2%	17%	13%
GBR	92%	256%	6%	16%	36%

China extensively raises financing at the local level, so I am including revenues, spending, and debt from local governments and related entities in these figures.

Example 2: The Effects of Nominal Interest Rates Minus Nominal Income Growth Rates on Debt-to-Income Ratios

When interest rates are higher than income growth rates, the existing debt grows relative to incomes because the debt compounds faster than incomes grow.

The following tables illustrate how this works. Previously, I showed how debt grows for different starting debt levels and deficits. This time, I am assuming a starting deficit of 32% of income (using the Congressional Budget Office's projected deficit over the next decade).[21] The rows are still different starting debt levels. The columns now show the nominal interest rate minus the nominal income growth rate. The CBO projects that, over the next decade, effective interest rates will average 3.45% and the US will have 3.9% nominal growth. The difference is about -0.4%, so this would leave the US around the red-boxed area.

[21] As noted previously, the CBO projections use settled law so they assume that expiring fiscal measures (i.e., the Trump tax cuts) roll off as implemented in current law. If these tax cuts are extended, the CBO estimates it would represent additional annual spending of 1.5% of GDP or 8% of government revenue.

The first table shows the levels of debt to income 10 years from now based on these assumptions, and the second table shows the change in debt to income over the next 10 years. **As interest rates get higher than growth, debt levels grow faster. Also, as debts get higher, the impact of high interest rates gets worse much faster.**

DEBT-TO-INCOME AFTER 10 YEARS

Nominal Interest Rate - Nominal Growth

Starting Debt-to-Income	-3%	-2%	-1%	0%	1%	2%	3%
0%	106%	110%	115%	120%	125%	131%	137%
100%	180%	192%	206%	250%	235%	252%	270%
200%	255%	275%	296%	350%	345%	373%	403%
300%	329%	357%	387%	420%	455%	494%	536%
400%	404%	439%	478%	520%	566%	615%	669%
500%	479%	522%	569%	620%	676%	736%	801%
600%	553%	604%	660%	720%	786%	857%	934%
700%	628%	686%	750%	820%	896%	978%	1067%

☐ = US Trajectory Today
Assuming a Constant Primary Deficit of 12% (CBO Projection over the Next 10 Years).

10YR CHANGE IN DEBT (% INCOME)

Nominal Interest Rate - Nominal Growth

Starting Debt-to-Income	-3%	-2%	-1%	0%	1%	2%	3%
0%	106%	110%	115%	120%	125%	131%	137%
100%	80%	92%	106%	120%	135%	152%	170%
200%	55%	75%	96%	120%	145%	173%	203%
300%	29%	57%	87%	120%	155%	194%	236%
400%	4%	39%	78%	120%	166%	215%	269%
500%	-21%	22%	69%	120%	176%	236%	301%
600%	-47%	4%	60%	120%	186%	257%	334%
700%	-72%	-14%	50%	120%	196%	278%	367%

Assuming a Constant Primary Deficit of 12% (CBO Projection over the Next 10 Years).

Previously, I forecast that with current debts and deficits, US debt levels will rise from 580% to 700% of income. If I also incorporate projected interest rates relative to nominal growth, I'd expect US debt levels to rise to 650% of income. You get the idea.

Since interest rates are projected to be slightly below nominal growth, this adjustment doesn't change our debt outlook much for the US today. But you can see that if the central bank wanted to help the central government keep its debt burdens more manageable, it could push interest rates to further below nominal growth by buying the government bonds, which would cause debt burdens to grow much slower, all else equal. Of course, that wouldn't be good for the lender-creditors holding the debt assets because they would get a lower nominal interest rate and a lower real interest rate than they would have gotten. I suspect that you are beginning to get the picture of how this dynamic works and has worked in the past—i.e., why central banks created such low nominal rates (near 0%) and such negative real interest rates by printing money and buying government debt—and what is most likely to take place in the future if the current path isn't altered. More specifically, if debt growth remains as projected, central banks will have to push real interest rates lower, which will make debt assets less attractive for lender-creditors.

In an economy, there are many interrelated drivers that change interdependently. It's like a Rubik's Cube, in which changing one part of the cube—one driver in the grids shown previously—causes changes to the other parts. It gets complicated to understand how these drivers interrelate and to project scenarios. To help illustrate this, I created a simple model to walk through one scenario for the next decade.

Example 3: Interest Rates Spiral Upward to Keep Buyers in the Debt Assets

In this example, I consider a government that has numbers similar to the US government now. Let's say nominal income is growing at 3.9% a year, interest rates are 3.5%, and debt levels start at 580% of government income. In this example, we'll assume that the government spends 32% more than it collects in income, including interest payments.

Since this government is running a 12% primary deficit (i.e., excluding interest payments), it collects $5.4 trillion in revenue and spends $6 trillion in Year 1. It must pay $1 trillion in interest because it started with debts at 580% of government income, and interest rates are about 3.5%. Let's assume that about 35% of the existing debt is coming due this year (which is about how much US government debt matures every year) and will need to be rolled over—so $10.5 trillion of existing debt will come due this year and will need to be paid back. **In total, this government needs to sell $12.2 trillion of debt in Year 1. What happens if the public is no longer willing to buy this debt, or is a seller at current interest rates?**

Markets must clear, so this means that interest rates will go up until someone is willing to buy these bonds. But as the interest rates go up, that makes the government's borrowing even more expensive, meaning the problems get even worse, creating a greater desire to sell the bonds, which creates even more upward pressure on interest rates. **A spiral of rising interest rates leading to worsening credit risk, leading to less demand for the debt, leading to higher interest rates is a classic debt "death spiral." In the next table, you can see how this works. In this example, I show interest rates going up by 0.5% a year while nominal growth stays flat.**

If interest rates stayed flat, the government would have ended Year 10 with debts at 650% of income and interest at 22% of income. Here, relative to income, we end with debts at 865%, interest at 67%, and total debt service (including principal payments) of 342%. **Of course, if interest rates are going up because the debts are unsustainable, they'll only go up more as debts rise and become even more unsustainable.** And at the same time, the high interest rates are likely constricting income growth, increasing the challenge of debt sustainability. Of course, the worst-case scenario is one where a significant additional amount of debt assets must be sold (e.g., to fund a war or social benefits in a recession), which would drive interest rates up a lot more.

A TOY MODEL: INTEREST RATES SPIRAL HIGHER

INTEREST RATES RISE BY 50BPS/YEAR

Income Growth Rate	3.9%
Spending excl Interest (% Inc)	112%
Starting Debt	30.1
Starting Interest Rate	3.5%
Share of Debt Maturing Each Year	35%

Year	0	1	2	3	4	5	6	7	8	9	10
Government											
Nominal Income (USD, Tln)	5.2	5.4	5.6	5.8	6.0	6.3	6.5	6.8	7.0	7.3	7.6
Nominal Spending (USD, Tln)	-	6.0	6.2	6.5	6.7	7.0	7.3	7.6	7.9	8.2	8.5
Debt Service	-	11.7	12.6	13.6	14.8	16.0	17.5	19.2	21.1	23.4	25.9
Principal	-	10.5	11.2	11.9	12.8	13.7	14.8	16.0	17.4	19.0	20.8
Interest	-	1.2	1.4	1.7	2.0	2.3	2.7	3.2	3.7	4.3	5.1
Nominal Govt Interest Rate	-	4.0%	4.5%	5.0%	5.5%	6.0%	6.5%	7.0%	7.5%	8.0%	8.5%
Borrowing	-	12.4	13.3	14.3	15.5	16.8	18.3	20.0	22.0	24.2	26.8
Ending Debt Level	30.1	31.9	34.0	36.4	39.2	42.2	45.8	49.8	54.3	59.5	65.5
Sustainability Ratios											
Debt/Income	583%	595%	611%	629%	651%	676%	704%	737%	775%	**817%**	**865%**
Debt Service/Income		217%	226%	235%	245%	257%	270%	285%	301%	**320%**	**342%**
Interest/Income		22%	26%	29%	33%	37%	42%	47%	53%	**60%**	**67%**

A government can prevent this spiral of rising rates by reducing its debt burdens. I outlined this in the prior chapter and laid it out in more detail in my book *Principles for Navigating Big Debt Crises*, but, to reiterate, there are four ways to reduce debt burdens for a government:

- **Austerity** (i.e., spending less), which doesn't work because one person's spending is another person's earnings, so austerity causes a self-reinforcing deflationary contraction.
- **Debt defaults/restructurings**, which reduce debt burdens and are deflationary because one person's debts are another's assets.
- **The central bank printing money and making purchases of debt**, which reduces debt burdens because it provides the money to pay the debts and is inflationary.
- **Transfers of money and credit from private market players who have money to the government via taxes, which is then transferred to other private market players.**

When I looked at historical cases of private debt problems, I typically saw a mix of these levers being pulled, with a strong bias to print money and buy debt (i.e., to monetize debt) when the debt squeeze is big. I also saw the fight over increased taxes as well as big conflicts between those of the political left and those of the political right. That all occurs for logical reasons. When central governments are squeezed, it's a big deal because central governments are typically the largest part of the economy and the only part of the economy to pay for large amounts of non-economic social expenses, which are critically important when economic conditions are bad. If governments are slow in providing spending and financial support, it's likely that that will create a larger economic downturn, which counterintuitively worsens debt burdens by reducing income growth and net worths and can lead to social turmoil. At a result, at such times it is self-damagingly painful for overly indebted governments to cut their spending to deal with their debt problems. Then the question is: where does the government get its money from?

● ***The easiest path, though not the best path for the long-term health of the system, is for governments to resolve their debt problems***

and spend as they would like to spend by having the central bank print money and purchase the bonds, thereby holding interest rates down at tolerable levels and putting money into the system. That is what they will unfailingly do when the debts are denominated in their own currencies. Let's look at an example of how this works.

Example 4: The Central Bank Steps In Because Private Players Are Unwilling to Hold the Desired Amount of Government Bonds to Keep Interest Rates at the Desired Level for Acceptable Economic Growth

Thus far, we looked at how the starting debt-to-income ratio, the income growth rate, the spending growth rate, the interest rate, and the maturity of the government debt affects future debt burdens. Also, as mentioned, the demand for the debt matters a lot, and the central bank can, and typically does, print money and buy (i.e., monetize) debt. Let's now look at how this last piece works.

There are many factors that determine the private market's demand for government debt. As previously explained, these include the expected real return of bonds relative to the projected real returns of other assets, the total amount of money and credit in the system, the sense of impending risk of a debt/currency crisis, etc.

While these factors are measurable, they are much harder to project than the previously described determinants. However, they are observable, most importantly in the form of either a) interest rates going up while the economy and the currency are weak (due to the supply-and-demand imbalance worsening) or b) central banks spending reserves and/or printing money and creating debt to buy government debt to try to lower real and nominal interest rates by increasing the demand to eliminate the imbalance. In the next chapter, you will see how this typically happens and the signals for the transition to the debt/currency crisis.

Before we move on, I want to show you how it works for the central bank to step in and absorb excess debt supply in order to maintain interest rates and liquidity at a desired level. Let's start with our previous example and modify it slightly. Let's assume that in Year 1 the government has $10.5 trillion of debt expiring and is issuing $12.2 trillion of new debt to replace the expiring bonds, pay interest, and cover spending.

Rather than allowing interest rates to spiral upward to generate sufficient demand for these debt assets, let's assume the central bank steps in and buys all the excess issuance, so that the private sector continues to hold no more than 600% of government income in debt, and interest rates stay flat at 3.5%. In this example, in Year 2, the central bank will have to buy $0.1 trillion of those debt assets. In subsequent years, these purchases get larger and larger.

Mechanically, to purchase these debt assets—i.e., to monetize the government debt—the central bank prints money (by creating new reserves/cash) and gives private players that money in exchange for the bonds. This increases the money supply (M0). In this example, let's assume that the money supply starts at $5.7 trillion—so 110% of the starting government income—roughly where it is today in the United States. **In our example, as the central bank prints more and more to cover government shortfalls, the money supply balloons.**

THE CENTRAL BANK STEPS IN

CENTRAL BANK BUYS BONDS

Income Growth Rate	3.9%
Spending excl Interest (% Inc)	112%
Starting Debt	30.1
Starting Interest Rate	3.5%
Share of Debt Maturing Each Year	35%

Year	0	1	2	3	4	5	6	7	8	9	10
Government											
Nominal Income (USD, Tln)	5.2	5.4	5.6	5.8	6.0	6.3	6.5	6.8	7.0	7.3	7.6
Nominal Spending (USD, Tln)	-	6.0	6.2	6.5	6.7	7.0	7.3	7.6	7.9	8.2	8.5
Debt Service	-	11.6	12.2	12.9	13.6	14.4	15.2	16.0	16.9	17.8	18.7
Principal	-	10.5	11.1	11.7	12.4	13.1	13.8	14.6	15.3	16.2	17.0
Interest	-	1.0	1.1	1.2	1.2	1.3	1.4	1.4	1.5	1.6	1.7
Borrowing	-	12.2	12.9	13.6	14.4	15.1	16.0	16.8	17.7	18.7	19.6
Ending Debt Level	30.1	31.8	33.6	35.4	37.4	39.4	41.6	43.8	46.2	48.7	51.3
Bond Holdings & Money Stock											
Central Bank Bond Purchases		-	0.1	0.6	0.6	0.6	0.7	0.7	0.8	0.8	0.9
Bonds Held by Central Bank		-	0.1	0.7	1.3	1.9	2.6	3.3	4.1	5.0	5.9
Money Stock (M0)	5.7	5.9	6.0	6.8	7.2	7.8	8.5	9.2	10.0	10.9	11.8
Bonds Held by Pvt Sector	30.1	31.8	33.4	34.8	36.1	37.5	39.0	40.5	42.1	43.7	45.4
Sustainability Ratios											
Debt/Income	583%	593%	602%	612%	621%	631%	640%	650%	659%	**668%**	**677%**
Debt Service/Income		216%	219%	223%	227%	230%	234%	237%	241%	**244%**	**247%**
Interest/Income		19.5%	19.9%	20.2%	20.5%	20.8%	21.1%	21.4%	21.8%	**22.1%**	**22.4%**

This is a rough example, but you can see the general contours of how this works for real economies. As an economy needs lower and lower interest rates to keep debt burdens manageable, there is less and less private demand for the debt at those lower interest rates, which requires the central bank to step in. The more the central bank steps in, the more it is forced to increase the money supply, which devalues the money and makes holding debt less desirable.

That is because, **all else equal, central bank money and credit creation lowers the value of money, which increases inflation and currency weakness.** The relationship is not precise and depends on how exactly the printed money is transmitted through the economy. Lowering interest rates and increasing the supply of money lowers the attractiveness of the currency, which makes holding the debt denominated in that currency unattractive.

In the following tables, I will give you a sense of how much money gets printed and how it affects the currency.

In the first table, the rows represent different starting debt-to-income levels for a government, and the columns represent how many bonds private players are willing to purchase at current interest rates. **As a government has more of a debt problem, and as private players are willing to hold less of the debt, the money stock increases more.** The red box reflects the scenario laid out earlier, where the central bank buys $6 trillion of bonds, increasing the money stock from $5.7 trillion to $11.8 trillion.

10YR CHANGE IN MONEY STOCK (M0) (% GOVT INCOME)

Starting Debt-to-Income	Max Private Bond Holdings (% Govt Income) 700%	600%	500%	400%	300%	200%	100%
0%	-	-	-	-	-	-	10%
100%	-	-	-	-	-	6%	79%
200%	-	-	-	-	6%	75%	175%
300%	-	-	-	2%	71%	171%	271%
400%	-	-	-	67%	167%	267%	367%
500%	-	-	63%	163%	263%	363%	463%
600%	-	59%	159%	259%	359%	459%	559%
700%	55%	155%	255%	355%	455%	555%	655%

□ = Range Corresponds to Current Example
Assuming Primary Deficit = 12%; Starting M0 = 110% of Govt Income

● ***Buying up bonds and increasing the money supply are stimulative and put downward pressure on the currency.***

Mechanically, pushing down interest rates usually causes the currency to sell off. Why? To spell out the mechanics:

- Usually, all else equal, lowering an interest rate won't change investors' long-term expectations of the value of a currency. The 10-year forward currency doesn't move as much.
- If you are getting less interest in the meantime because interest rates fell, the new deal is strictly worse.
- The way to make the new deal fair again is for the spot currency to fall. That way, you'll earn more through currency appreciation (as it reaches the same expected 10-year forward point) to make up for less in interest.

My next point will be too technical for some and helpfully technical for others, so if you want to skip the technical stuff, skip it. Mechanically, pushing down interest rates pushes up the currency forward—e.g., a rise in one country's 10-year risk-free bond yield relative to another country's 10-year risk-free bond yield will raise the

10-year forward currency—so if the value to investors of the currency in the 10-year future were to stay the same, the spot currency would have to sell off by the present value of the 10-year interest rate differences to keep the 10-year currency forward flat. Said more precisely and more simply: as explained in Chapter 2, the difference in sovereign interest rates in two countries will be offset by the forward currency premium—e.g., if the interest rate in Country A is 2% above the interest rate in Country B, then the forward currency of Country A will be at a 2% per year annual discount to Country B, so if interest rates in Country A were lowered by 1% from that level and the forward currency stays the same, the currency would weaken by a corresponding amount.

Also, the printed money can directly flow out of the currency, creating a selling pressure in the currency. That is, as a central bank buys bonds and gives other players cash, there is a chance that they use that cash to buy other currencies, rather than holding it or buying assets/spending in the same economy.

In the next table, I show a range of outcomes for how this might work. The columns again reflect different willingness to lend by private players (as you go to the right, private players are less willing to lend to the government). The rows reflect how sensitive the currency is to the money supply. As the market sees a currency as a worse and worse storehold of value, we'd expect the currency to become more sensitive to the money supply because other players will be less willing to hold it. For example, let's assume that printing 1% of GDP in money led to ~1% currency weakness, then in this example, we'd expect a ~10% currency depreciation. **As the currency becomes more sensitive to the amount of money (i.e., M0), and as the private sector becomes less willing to lend, we'd expect to see more and more currency weakness.**

10YR EXPECTED CHANGE IN FX

Max Private Bond Holdings (% Govt Income)

Expected Move in FX for 1% Increase in M0 (% GDP)	700%	600%	500%	400%	300%	200%	100%
0.0%	0%	0%	0%	0%	0%	0%	0%
0.5%	0%	-5%	-13%	-21%	-28%	-34%	-40%
1.0%	0%	-10%	-25%	-38%	**-49%**	**-58%**	**-65%**
1.5%	0%	-15%	-35%	**-52%**	**-64%**	**-73%**	**-81%**
2.0%	0%	-19%	**-44%**	**-62%**	**-75%**	**-84%**	**-89%**

☐ = Range Corresponds to Current Example
Assuming Primary Deficit = 12%; Starting M0 = 110% of Govt Income; Starting Debt-to-Income of 5.8x

What level of interest rates can make debt burdens affordable for a country?

In these examples, we looked at how debts can compound to become unsustainable. I also want to show you the numbers around how debts can be managed sustainably.

In countries that have a lot of debt and high deficits, debts and debt service costs will be a big issue and how much they will increase over time will be determined by the interest rate relative to income growth and inflation, as shown in my calculations. A central bank can prevent debt service costs from rising or cause them to decrease relative to inflation and incomes by pushing down nominal interest rates to below nominal growth rates. What I am referring to are the impacts these things will have on the central government's and the central bank's financial conditions. (Of course, they will also have a ripple effect on all parts of the economy, but let's skip that for now.)

Given that, we can look at a government's debt level and projected deficit and calculate what interest rate will be needed to produce any specified level of debt and debt service relative to incomes—e.g., to keep the debt burden the same, to have it decline, etc.—given estimates of future revenue and expenses.

If I were setting policy for the Fed, I would want to look at what the deficit and debt levels are and likely will be and set an interest rate so that debt burdens won't become too great over time. For example, I would probably want to look at what interest rate would keep debt service payments the same. That would affect my interest rate policy.

I would also want to calculate what level of interest rate would be needed for the Fed not to have big losses on my balance sheet.

Let's look at these things and also look at how they would have worked in the past.

FORMULA FOR DETERMINING FUTURE DEBT BURDENS

As a reminder, this equation shows the drivers of future levels of debt and debt service relative to incomes. This was more fully explained at the start of the chapter.

$$\frac{\text{Future Debt}}{\text{Future Revenue}} = \frac{(\text{Future Expenses Excluding Interest} - \text{Future Revenue}) + \text{Current Debt} * (1 + \text{Interest Rate})}{\text{Current Revenue} * (1 + \text{Growth Rate})}$$

In the following table, I use this formula to estimate what interest rates would stabilize debt burdens relative to incomes for the US today. I also show how each of the other available levers would have to change in order to stabilize debt burdens. You can see that to stabilize government debt burdens, the US would either need to see nominal interest fall to about 1%, see nominal economic growth average about 6.5% (~2.5% additional inflation above the 3.9% nominal growth projected by the CBO), or raise government revenue (i.e., raising taxes) by 11%. Of course, each one of these paths would be intolerably too large so it would take the right combination of lesser amounts of these to successfully achieve the goal. In Chapter 18, "My 3% 3-Part Solution," I show what I believe would be the best combinations to achieve the goal of limiting debt burdens and risks in a very tolerable way.

HOW THE US CAN STABILIZE DEBT-TO-INCOME IN THE NEXT 10 YEARS

Central Government Debt Today (% GDP)	**100%**
Central Government Debt Today (% Revenue)	**583%**
Proj Debt in 2035 (% GDP, CBO)	**118%**
Proj Debt in 2035 (% Revenue, CBO)	**648%**
Proj Nominal Growth Rate (CBO)	**3.9%**
Proj Real Growth	**1.9%**
Proj Inflation	**2.0%**
Proj Effective Nominal Interest Rates (CBO)	**3.5%**
Current Interest Rate (Avg 3M and 10Yr)	**4.5%**
If Lower Interest Rates Were the Only Lever. . .	
Interest Rate Required to Stabilize Debt	1.0%
Change in Interest Rates vs Current Interest Rate	-3.5%
Change in Interest Rates vs CBO's Proj Avg Interest Rate	-2.5%
If Higher Inflation Were the Only Lever. . .	
Required Inflation Rate to Stabilize Debt	4.5%
Change in Inflation Required (vs Current Proj Inflation)	2.5%
If Cutting Expenses Were the Only Lever. . .	
% Spending Cut Required to Stabilize Debt	12%
% of Discretionary Spending	47%
If Raising Tax Revenue Were the Only Lever. . .	
% Revenue Increase Required to Stabilize Debt	11%

PART II

THE ARCHETYPICAL SEQUENCE LEADING TO CENTRAL GOVERNMENTS AND CENTRAL BANKS GOING BROKE

The same basic sequence of events that leads central governments and central banks to go broke has happened repeatedly throughout history and it isn't well-understood. The purpose of Part II is to describe it so that it is well-understood. In it, I provide a template of the typical case and the most important reasons for the two major types of cases: 1) those in which the debt is denominated in currency that the country's central bank can print and 2) those in which the debt is denominated in currency that the central bank can't print. Then I devote Chapter 8 to providing an overview of the five forces that make up what I call the Big Cycle, which drives all major changes in monetary systems, domestic political orders, and global geopolitical orders. After I make that clear, in Part III, I will review how this Big Cycle, starting in 1865 and continuing until now, has transpired relative to the archetypical timeless and universal template.

CHAPTER 4

THE ARCHETYPICAL SEQUENCE

From my experiences in the markets and from examining 35 major debt crises over the last 100 years in which central governments and/or central banks went broke, I have come to understand pretty well how Big Debt Cycles transpire. What follows is the archetypical process, zooming in to the granular mechanics of what typically happens both leading up to central governments and central banks going broke and after. While I think this chapter is valuable for policy makers and investors because it provides a template for dealing with such crises, it is possibly too much for the casual reader. I suggest you read what is in bold and decide if you want to dive into the greater detail or exit and move on.

There is one important determinant that I'd like to explain that affects how the cases transpire. That is between cases with hard money versus fiat money.

HARD MONEY VERSUS FIAT MONEY

The cases I am about to describe come in two broad types that typically behave differently in ways that you should understand. The two big types are the hard currency cases and fiat currency cases. In brief, the way the hard currency cases work is that the governments have made promises to deliver money that they can't print (e.g., gold, silver, or another currency that the parties view as relatively hard, like the dollar). Throughout history, when coming up with these hard currencies that they can't print to pay debts becomes tough, the governments almost always renege on their promises to pay in the currency that they can't print, and the value of their money and the debt payments denominated in it tumble at the moment the promise is broken.

After governments break their promise by not going back to having a hard currency, they have what is called a fiat monetary system. In these cases, the currency's value is based on the faith and incentives that the central banks provide. The most recent shift of most currencies from being hard to being fiat started on August 15, 1971. I remember it well because I was clerking on the floor of the New York Stock Exchange at the time and was surprised by it; then I studied history and found that the exact same thing happened in April 1933, and I learned how they worked.

In fiat monetary systems, central banks primarily use interest rates, their ability to monetize debt, and the tightness of money to provide the incentives for lender-creditors to lend and hold debt assets. And throughout history they, like central governments and central bankers operating in hard currency regimes, have created too much debt (which are claims that people believe they can turn in to get money, which they expect they can use to buy things), so there are the same types of debt/credit dynamics at work—i.e., the governments create and allow their private sectors to create too much debt to be paid back, which leads to printing money to make it easier to pay back the debts, which devalues money and makes the prices of things go up—except in fiat currency cases, the devaluations don't happen all at once at the moment the government breaks its promise to convert the paper money into the hard money storehold of wealth. They happen more gradually.

For example, we have seen this clearly in the Bank of Japan's policies of aggressively monetizing a lot of debt and keeping real and nominal interest rates extremely low, which has resulted in its currency and the debt denominated in its currency being devalued. Since the start of 2013, the holders of Japanese government bonds have lost 60% versus gold, 45% versus US dollar debt, and 6% in domestic purchasing power (as average inflation was 1%). The devaluation came gradually rather than abruptly because the yen is a fiat currency, but it came for the same reasons it would have come if Japan had a hard currency—i.e., too much debt that needed to be monetized.

In the charts in this part, you will see three lines—the blue line shows the average of all cases, the red line shows the average of the fixed exchange rate cases, and the green line shows the average of fiat/variable exchange rate cases. For simplicity, I will explain the dynamic by referring to just the aggregate line.

By the way, the Big Debt Cycles through history have typically included currency regimes going back and forth between being hard and fiat because they each led to extreme consequences and required movements to the opposite—the hard currency regimes broke down with big devaluations because the governments couldn't maintain debt growth in line with their monetary constraints, and the fiat monetary systems broke down because of the loss of faith in the debt/money being a safe storehold of wealth.

NINE STAGES OF THE FINAL CRISIS

In the introduction to this book, I summarized the whole archetypical debt cycle. I am now going to focus on the final phase of the Big Debt Cycle, when the central government and the central bank both go broke. This final phase typically transpires in nine steps. While this sequence is the archetypical one, there are very big variations in what happens and when it happens, and the stages don't necessarily transpire in the exact sequence I describe. So, the things I am referring to here can be viewed as the unhealthy things that lead to the crisis and the steps that are classically taken to get out of the crisis. The more of these unhealthy things exist, the greater the risk of a "heart attack" where the central government and the central bank go broke. Said differently, there are many reasons a country goes broke—e.g., chronic overspending and debt accumulations; costly wars; costly shocks like droughts, floods, and pandemics; some mix of these things; etc. Whatever the causes, this checklist adds up to a risk gauge because the more of the unhealthy things that exist, the higher the probability of a debt/currency crisis. **Here is the sequence of unhealthy conditions that typifies the last stages of the Big Debt Cycle:**

1. **The private sector and government get deep in debt.**
2. **The private sector suffers a debt crisis, and the central government gets deeper in debt to help the private sector.**
3. **The central government experiences a debt squeeze in which the free-market demand for its debt falls short of the supply of it.** That creates a debt problem. At that time, there is either a) a shift in monetary and fiscal policy that brings the supply and demand for money and credit back into balance or b) a self-reinforcing net selling of the debt, which creates a severe debt liquidation crisis that runs its course and reduces the size of debt and debt service levels relative to incomes. Big net selling of the debt is the big red flag.
4. **The selling of government debt leads to a simultaneous a) free-market-driven tightening of money and credit, which leads to b) a weakening of the economy, c) declining reserves, and d) downward pressure on the currency. Because this tightening is too harmful for the economy, the central bank typically also eases credit and experiences a devaluation of the currency.**

That stage is easy to see in the market action via interest rates rising, led by long-term rates (bond yields) rising faster than short rates and the currency weakening simultaneously.

5. **When there is a debt crisis and interest rates can't be lowered (e.g., they hit 0% or long rates limit the decline of short rates), the central bank "prints" (creates) money and buys bonds to try to keep long rates down and to ease credit to make it easier to service debt.** It doesn't literally print money; it essentially borrows reserves from commercial banks that it pays a very short-term interest rate on. This creates problems for the central bank if this debt selling and interest rate rising continue.
6. **If the selling continues and interest rates continue to rise, the central bank loses money because the interest rate that it has to pay on its liabilities is greater than the interest rate it receives on the debt assets it bought. When that happens, that is notable but not a big red flag until the central bank has a significant negative net worth and is forced to print more money to cover the negative cash flow that it experiences due to less money coming in on its assets than has to go out to service its debt liabilities. That is a big red flag because it signals the central bank's death spiral (i.e., the dynamic in which the rising interest rates cause problems that creditors see, which lead them not to hold the debt assets, which leads to higher interest rates or the need to print more money, which devalues the money, which leads to more selling of the debt assets and the currency, and so on).** That is what I mean when I say the central bank goes broke. I call this "going broke" because the central bank can't make its debt service payments, though it doesn't default on its debts because it prints money. When done in large amounts, that devalues the money and creates inflationary recessions or depressions.
7. **Debts are restructured and devalued. When managed in the best possible way, the government controllers of fiscal and monetary policy execute what I call a "beautiful**

deleveraging," in which the deflationary ways of reducing debt burdens (e.g., through debt restructurings) are balanced with the inflationary ways of reducing debt burdens (e.g., by monetizing them) so that the deleveraging occurs without having unacceptable amounts of either deflation or inflation.

8. **At such times, extraordinary policies like extraordinary taxes and capital controls are commonly imposed.**
9. **The deleveraging process inevitably reduces the debt burdens and creates the return to equilibrium. One way or another, the debt and debt service levels are brought back in line with the incomes that exist to service the debts.** Quite often, there are inflationary depressions so the debt is devalued at the end of the cycle, government reserves are raised through asset sales, and a strictly enforced transition from a rapidly declining currency to a relatively stable currency is simultaneously achieved by the central bank linking the currency to a hard currency or a hard asset (e.g., gold) and central government and private sector finances being brought back in line to a sustainable level. At the early stage of this phase, it is imperative that the rewards of holding the currency and the debt denominated in it, and the penalties of owing money, are great in order to re-establish the creditability of the money and credit by rewarding the lender-creditors and penalizing the borrower-debtors. In this phase of the cycle, there is very tight money and a very high real interest rate, which is very painful but required for a while. If it persists, the supply and demand for money, credit, debt, spending, and savings will inevitably fall back into line. How exactly this happens largely depends on whether the debt is denominated in a currency that the central bank can create and whether the debtors and creditors are primarily domestic so that the central government and the central bank have more flexibility and control over the process. If so, that makes the process less painful, and, if not, it is inevitably much more painful. Also, whether the currency is a widely used reserve currency matters a lot

> because when it is there will be greater marginal inclinations to buy it and the debt that it is stored in. Having said that, it should be noted that throughout history there has been a strong tendency for governments with such currencies to abuse that privilege by doing more than enough borrowing to lose that privilege, which makes their decline more abrupt and painful.

In the next few chapters, I will show you all this happening in charts.

CHAPTER 5

THE PRIVATE SECTOR AND CENTRAL GOVERNMENT DEBT CRISIS (STAGES 1-4)

In Chapter 4, I laid out the archetypical sequence that you see across crises. This chapter will take you through the first four of the nine stages in much more detail, showing the specific markers and dynamics I saw when I looked at historical cases. I believe that this is probably very helpful for investment professionals, policy makers, and others who care about the typical sequence, timing, and other particulars of the transition into and through a debt crisis. But it is probably too technical for the casual reader. As most of the chapters in Part II are like this one, if you like this chapter, read them all. And if you don't like it, skip ahead to Chapter 8.

In the pages that follow, I will show the dynamics of the archetypical debt crisis in charts accompanied by brief explanations. In the charts, the blue line shows the average of all cases, the red line shows the average of the fixed exchange rate cases, and the green line shows the average of fiat-variable exchange rate cases. You will note that the timing and the distinctiveness of these events is clearer in the cases where exchange rates are fixed (in which case they more clearly intensify and then break) than in the fiat currency cases (in which the adjustments are more fluid). That is because in fixed rate cases you can see the pressures build up until there is a clear break, whereas in the variable exchange rate cases you will see these changes occur more gradually.

Stage 1: The Private Sector and Government Get Deep in Debt

We see this in classic ways, such as:

- In the years before the crisis, the government classically has **a large and growing stock of debt** as a result of chronic deficit spending. Typically, one sees **a rising share of spending going to consumption/the social safety net and a declining share going to productivity-enhancing investment**, causing debts to increase without a commensurate increase in incomes. Typically, countries become so reliant on a large social safety net that cutting it becomes a political third rail (e.g., today in Brazil or the US).
- **The level of debt is typically high relative to the government's ability to pay it back with tax revenues and the debt service burden is also high relative to the government's incomes**, which starts to crowd out spending on other line items that are considered essential. To cover these costs, more debt needs to be sold than the private sector wants to buy, a source of upward pressure on interest rates (further increasing debt service costs). Note the big differences in what happens in these cases between the floating rate currencies and the fixed rate currencies after the big default/devaluation moment. It reflects the fact that in the fixed exchange rate cases the debt restructuring is more severe and definitive, which sets the stage for a more abrupt and larger rebound. Fiat cases see a gradual increase in debt, as money printing from the central bank allows government spending to continue or even accelerate. In the charts, please note that the numbers in the x-axis represent

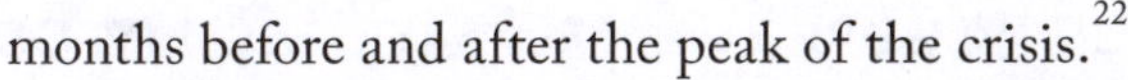

months before and after the peak of the crisis.[22]

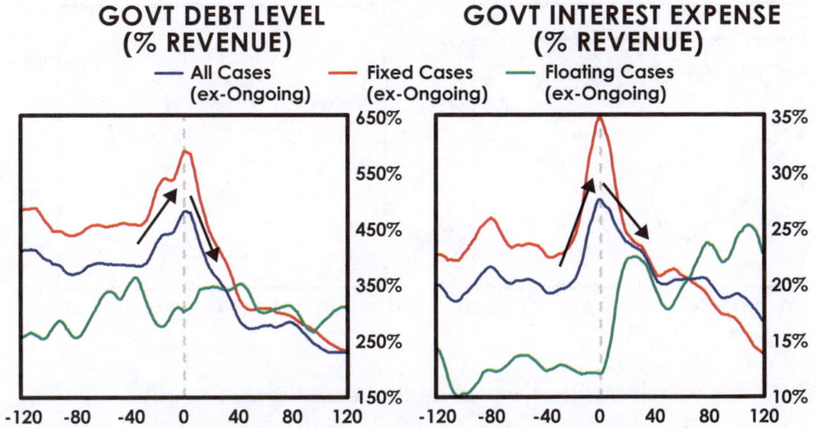

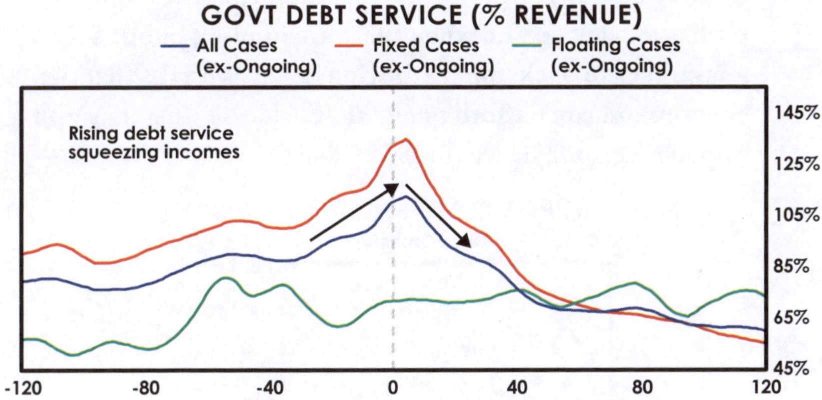

GOVT DEBT LEVEL
(% REVENUE)
GOVT INTEREST EXPENSE
(% REVENUE)
All Cases
(ex-Ongoing)
Fixed Cases
(ex-Ongoing)
Floating Cases
(ex-Ongoing)
650%
550%
450%
350%
250%
150%
-120 -80 -40 0 40 80 120
35%
30%
25%
20%
15%
10%
-120 -80 -40 0 40 80 120

GOVT DEBT SERVICE (% REVENUE)
All Cases
(ex-Ongoing)
Fixed Cases
(ex-Ongoing)
Floating Cases
(ex-Ongoing)
Rising debt service
squeezing incomes
145%
125%
105%
85%
65%
45%
-120 -80 -40 0 40 80 120

- The next charts show the typical amount of government borrowing (in total and excluding borrowing to cover interest payments) that was done in the years leading up to the devaluation. In 31 of the 35 cases I studied, I saw **large, persistent government deficits** going into the crisis.

[22] To show a clearer picture of how the government's balance sheet evolves in the upswing and downswing of the cycle, these charts exclude a handful of recent cases that are still playing out (the US, Europe, the UK, and Japan post-financial crisis).

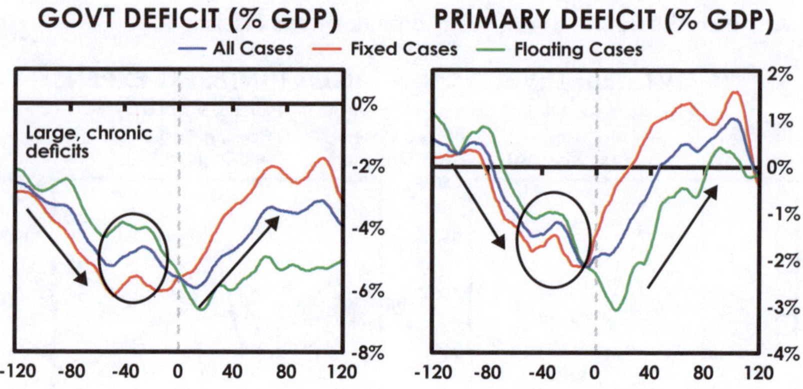

- It's worth noting that on its face sometimes the public sector balance sheet looks less problematic. This is true when **there is heavy borrowing in the private sector that the public sector has to back up and when there are implicit public sector guarantees to backstop institutions such as banks that the government can't afford to let fail**. Such cases might as well be public sector balance sheet problems.

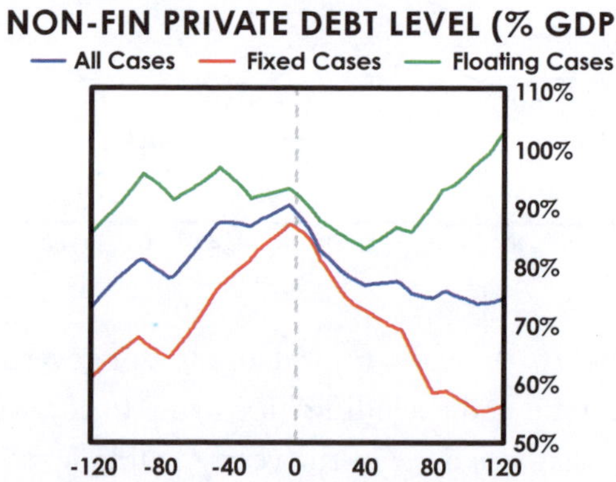

- **The buildup of debts requires large lending from foreigners to finance them.** That lending can be in borrowing the country's currency (which increases the risk of devaluation) or a reserve currency (which increases the risk of default). This increases the country's vulnerability to a pullback in foreign capital. That said, having a current account deficit doesn't necessarily signal problems. It reflects capital coming into the country, which could be indicative of the attractiveness of the country's capital markets. However, in circumstances in which the attractiveness of the country's capital markets gets impaired by the need to issue a lot of debt and money quickly to deal with a crisis, the potential for foreign selling of the country's currency and debt represents an added source of vulnerability. As shown in the next set of charts, steadily increasing current account and twin deficits typically lead the crisis by several years. When the crisis occurs, it takes the form of a big devaluation and a constriction of debt-financed demand (including for imports), which has the effect of reducing these deficits.

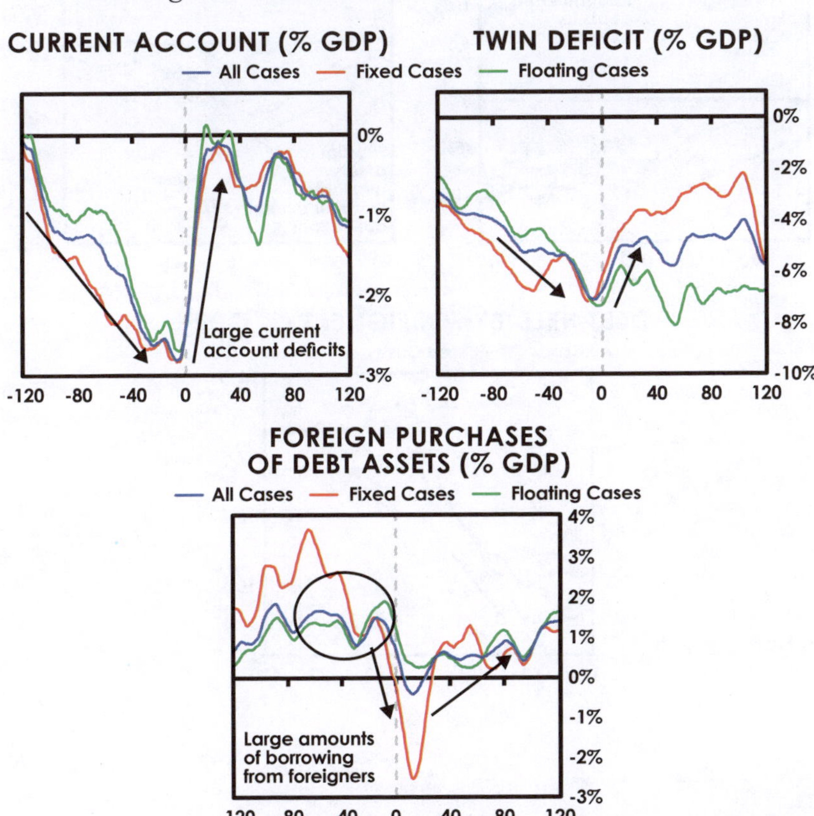

Years of large-scale borrowing from foreigners results in a substantial accumulated debt to foreigners, which increases the country's vulnerability to a pullback in foreign capital. The next set of charts shows, on the left, the total net international investment position (assets owned abroad minus liabilities owed to the rest of the world) and an adjusted version on the right that measures the amount of liquid assets the country has available relative to the external debts it must service. By the time of the devaluation, the country is typically very low in liquid assets it can use to cover external debt service obligations.

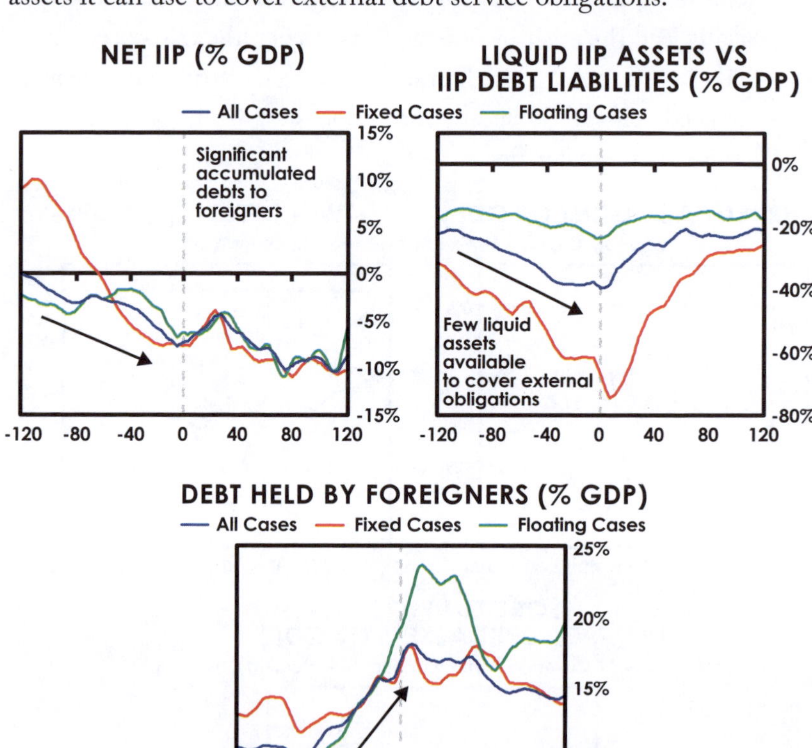

Stage 2: The Private Sector Suffers a Debt Crisis, and the Central Government Gets Deeper in Debt to Help the Private Sector

Typically, this occurs at the stage of the cycle when the government's balance sheet goes from being moderately stretched in the years ahead of the devaluation to extremely stretched when the government is forced to step in to address debt problems that emerge in the private sector. **When the private sector has financial problems, the government typically plays an increased role because it can get money and credit much more easily than the private sector can.** During these difficult times, it is easier for governments to borrow because there is much more willingness to lend to them because everyone knows that their central banks can print money and get it to governments to repay the debt and because governments have the power to tax. Having this greater ability to borrow is especially true for those governments that have the most established reserve currencies because there is high demand to hold that debt/currency.

As a result, when debt conditions deteriorate and governments need to save the day, government debt increases faster than private sector debt. As shown in the following charts, it is typical for the government debt level to soar while the private sector's debt level plunges about a year before the crisis, and for the government debt level to rise a lot relative to the private debt level. In 15 of the 21 cases where I had data on both the government and the private sector balance sheets, I saw this pattern happen. When private debt is falling sharply and government debt is rising sharply, it is a short leading indicator of trouble.

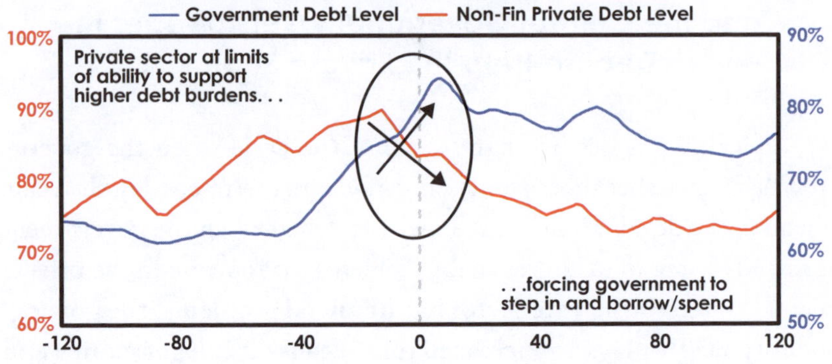

GOVERNMENT DEBT/PRIVATE DEBT

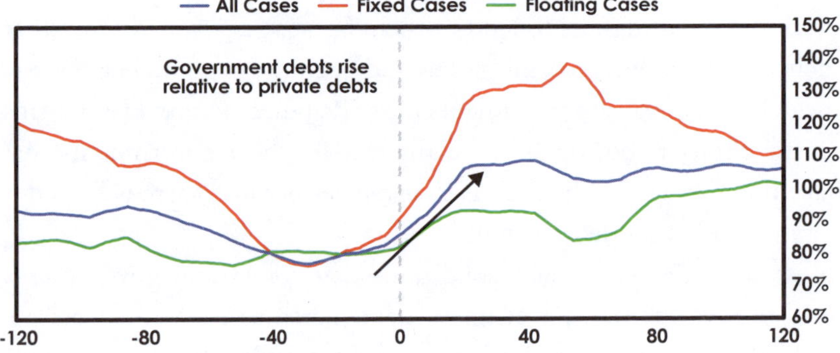

At this time, government debt problems tend to intensify. I will show a few more measures in the following pages.

The stock of government debt grows in relation to 1) its revenues, 2) the hard assets it has available to repay its debts (usually in the form of reserves), and 3) the quantity of money in the economy that is available to finance the debt (until the central bank eventually steps in to provide more money and credit to the government).

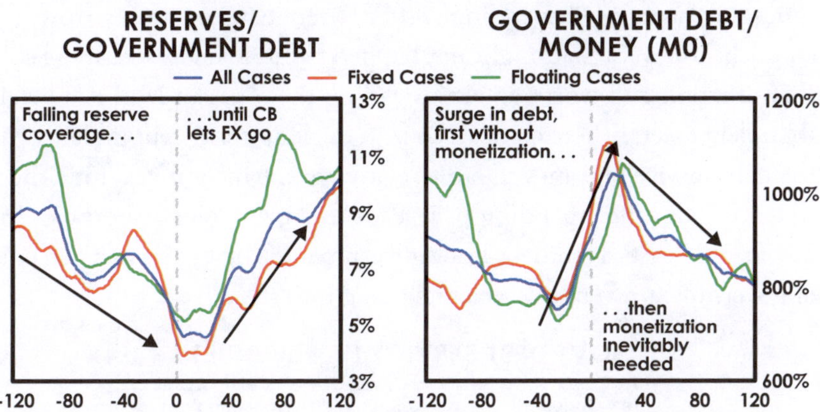

Stage 3: The Central Government Experiences a Debt Squeeze in Which the Free-Market Demand for Its Debt Falls Short of the Supply of It

This squeeze creates a debt problem. If there is net selling of the debt, that creates a much worse problem, so *net selling of the debt is a big red flag.*

The central government gets into financial trouble when 1) its finances are squeezed by debt and debt service expenses that limit its ability to spend on what is essential and 2) the holders of the debt assets created to finance government spending want to sell those assets. This puts upward pressure on interest rates, further increasing the government's financing costs and requiring either painful spending cuts or even more borrowing to cover those costs.

More specifically, when debt service becomes a very high percentage of income (e.g., 100%), it is a red flag because it means that it is a) squeezing out a lot of spending and/or b) requiring a lot of borrowing and debt rollovers that might not happen because lender-creditors see this situation and worry about it, leading them to not lend or to sell their debt assets. There comes a time in the long-term debt cycle when the debt service becomes so large relative to the incomes that it either squeezes out other spending or it leads to a big demand shortage. In 25 of the 35 cases I studied, I saw government debt service as a percent of government revenues accelerate going into the crisis.

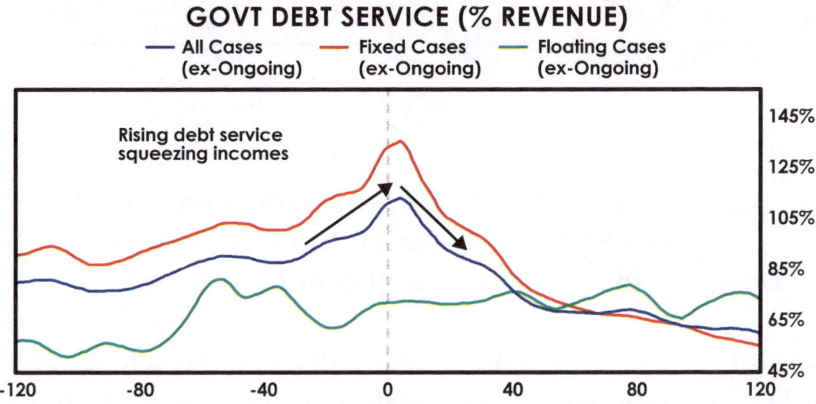

- **Given the debts the government has built up (and the ongoing deficits it is running to compensate for a weak private sector), its debt and debt service burdens are on a path to continue climbing.** The following charts show the average projected path of government debt and interest expense at the time of devaluation across the historical cases. At the time of the eventual devaluation, we can see that the government was typically on a path toward indefinitely increasing debts and debt service absent a devaluation of those debts.

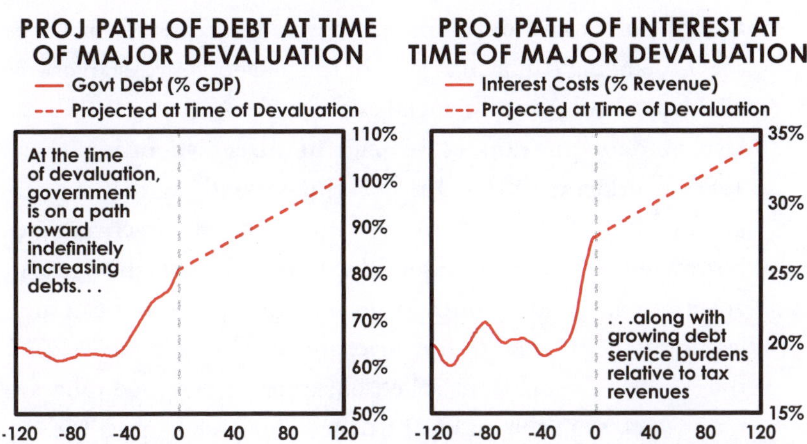

This hasn't happened yet in the US, but it is moving toward happening. As far as Europe, Japan, and China go, government interest service in those places is around half that of the US as a percent of GDP—Europe and China because their government debts are lower (though the debts of other sectors are higher), and Japan because its interest rates have been much lower for a long time. But that can change quickly, especially in Japan, where very high government debts (around 215% of GDP) could become a problem if refinanced at higher rates. As we will see in Chapter 16, the very large government debts, Bank of Japan bond purchases, and the BoJ artificially holding interest rates at extremely low levels led to terrible returns for government debt assets because of both the low yields on the debt and the depreciated value of the currency.

Faced with a large and growing debt burden and financing need, the classic next step is the pursuit of measures to paper over issues and **creative ways to source financing, including accounting tricks**:

1. **Use of policy and development banks** to create off-balance-sheet financing (frequently part of the playbook in Asian crises, e.g., Japan and Asian financial crises).
2. **Use of debt guarantees instead of direct spending** (Peru 1980s, Turkey recently). The government will say that it guarantees losses for a certain type of debt, which encourages borrowing—effectively a subsidy. But it doesn't show up in government spending until losses start to appear, so it can misleadingly seem "free" to the government. For example in 2017, the Turkish government rolled out a loan guarantee program for businesses in the midst of balance of payments pressure.
3. **Requiring or heavily incentivizing domestic players, especially banks, pensions, and insurers, to finance the government** (Turkey and Brazil recently). Sometimes this takes the form of extremely beneficial regulatory treatment of government debt (making a risky instrument seem risk-free), and sometimes manipulation of the yield curve and financing rates to make it attractive (the US during World War II), which is effectively backdoor monetary financing (because it incentivizes banks to lever up at short-term interest rates to lend to the government).
4. **Patriotic campaigns to get people to fund the government** (Turkey recently appealing for people to sell their dollars for lira, World War II appeals for people to buy government bonds, Korea in the 1990s relatively successfully creating a campaign asking people to use their gold to pay back the IMF).
5. **"Paying" for increased spending with future cuts and tax increases that might never come** (Brazil recently, creating a constitutional amendment to limit spending, but creating plenty of outs when needed).
6. **Calling in favors from international creditors and/or making geopolitical deals for financing** (Turkey recently, the UK setting up the Sterling Area after World War II).
7. **Shortening maturities of debt**, since usually borrowers are more willing to lend for short periods than for long periods

(described further later).

8. **Capital controls** to keep money from leaving the country are common in relatively severe situations.

Stage 4: The Selling of the Government's Debt Leads to a) a Free-Market-Driven Tightening of Money and Credit, Which Leads to b) a Weakening of the Economy, c) Downward Pressure on the Currency, and d) Declining Reserves as the Central Bank Attempts to Defend the Currency

Because this tightening is too harmful for the economy, the central bank eventually eases credit and simultaneously allows a devaluation of the currency.

These events typically accelerate investors' and savers' flight from the country's assets, bringing the run on the currency and the debt to a breaking point. Typically, the central bank attempts to defend the currency with monetary tightening and reserve sales but is ultimately forced to change course due to the painful economic effects of tightening and the inadequacy of its reserves.

A relatively large red flag for me is when debts rise relative to the incomes that are necessary to service them to such an extent that smart investors recognize losses are inevitable (i.e., because there must be either a default or a lot of printing of money, currency weakness, and inflation to depreciate the debts in order to avoid a default).

When the lender-creditor loses faith that they will be adequately paid (because the debtor won't be able to afford to pay debt service or because the amount of debt service isn't sufficient—e.g., won't adequately compensate the lender-creditor for inflation), there will be inadequate buying relative to the selling of debt, so the price of debt will have to go down (so the interest rate will have to go up) until there is either less borrowing or more saving.

During times of risks of war or actual war, this is worsened because risks of sanctions (e.g., confiscating debt assets), excessive borrowing, debt default, and devaluation increase. War or not, that is when the doom loop can kick in—i.e., when the upward pressure on interest rates weakens the economy and increases the government's future borrowing needs (or requires big tax increases or spending cuts that would be excessively painful at this juncture), which then creates an even bigger supply-and-demand mismatch in the bond market and puts even more upward pressure on interest rates. That is when central banks have to come in to save the day by "printing money" and buying the debt and we have what is called quantitative easing (QE).

As you will see in the following charts, in these times there is a simultaneous plunge in foreign inflows to buy local government and corporate bonds (left chart), and a spike in real rates (right chart) as there is a classic failed attempt to support the currency via rising interest rates and tightening credit.

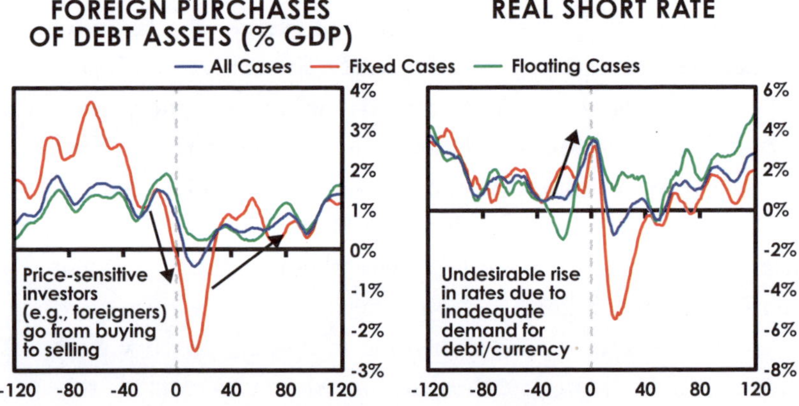

In these periods, we often see the government shorten the maturity of its issuance in order to make the bonds more palatable to the market.

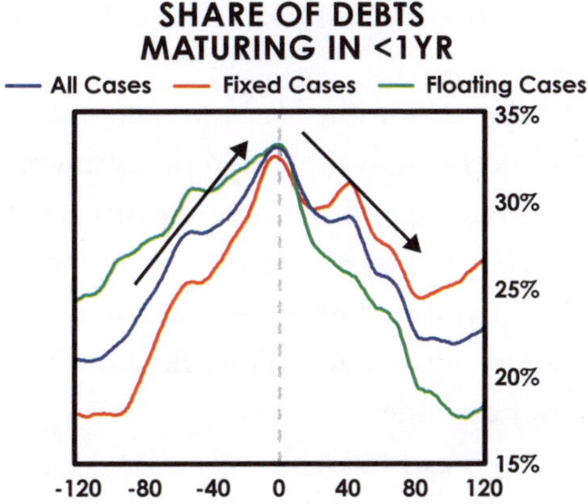

When market participants see that these limitations are being reached, there is selling, which worsens the supply-and-demand balance. When that becomes large, the central bank is faced with the choice of a) allowing interest rates to rise to a level that will curtail borrowing and lead to a greater desire to lend to the government by redirecting money and credit that would have gone to other things (e.g., the purchase of other investments) or b) printing money and buying the debt to make up for the demand shortfall. History shows and logic dictates that the central bank will always choose b) over a), and that the best path is to balance a) and b). When that produces enough selling so that inflation rises when the economy is weak, the central bank is damned if it does print money and buy a lot of debt because it contributes to terrible currency weakness and inflation, and it's damned if it doesn't because it causes extremely tight money, extremely high interest rates, and a very bad economy.

That happens when the debt service squeeze becomes intolerable for the borrower-debtor and/or the lender-creditor doesn't want to hold the debt (typically because it is not providing a high enough real return, the risk of default is perceived as high, and/or the risk of the central bank printing a lot of money, thus devaluing it, is high). When those things happen, a doom loop downward spiral in the value of the government debt occurs until a new equilibrium level is reached when the debt is sufficiently destroyed or devalued so that the debt burdens are no longer excessive.

This hasn't yet happened in the US, Europe, Japan, or China.

Now, we will walk through these dynamics in more detail.

- **There is a tightening and/or currency intervention to defend the currency, but the tightening is abandoned because it's too harmful for the economy and the currency intervention is abandoned because it doesn't work and is too costly, so the debt/currency devalues.**

This situation becomes untenable when investors and savers see what's going on and make the logical decision to abandon the country's assets and currency because there is a high risk that in one way or another they won't get their buying power back. This brings the crisis to a head because it puts more pressure on the central bank to tighten at a time when doing so would likely produce unacceptably bad economic outcomes. **A few of the red flags of this more advanced stage are:**

- **Interest rates rise because there is selling of the country's debt assets and because the central bank typically attempts to tighten to defend the currency.** In the face of such depressed conditions, such an increase in real interest rates is unsustainable as it puts too much pressure on an economy that is already weak and on a government that is facing a debt spiral absent lower interest rates.

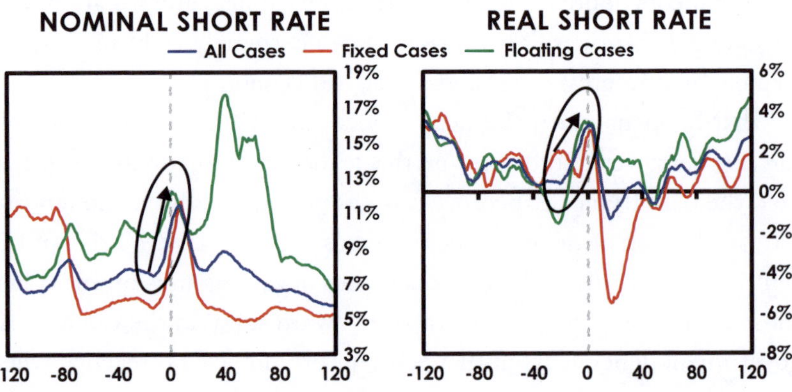

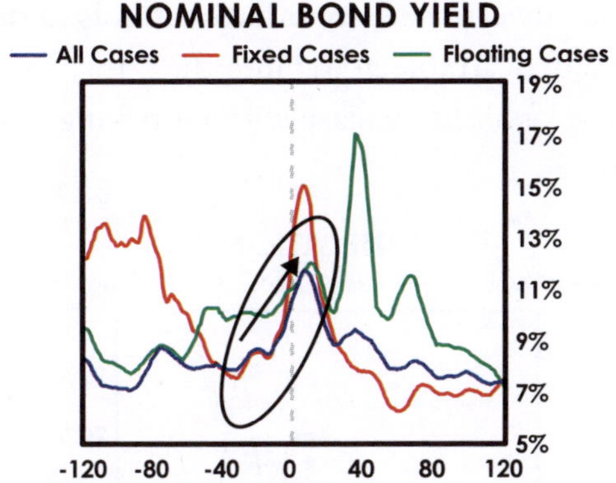

The tightening worsens a weak economy, which ultimately requires the tightening to be abandoned and the devaluation to occur.

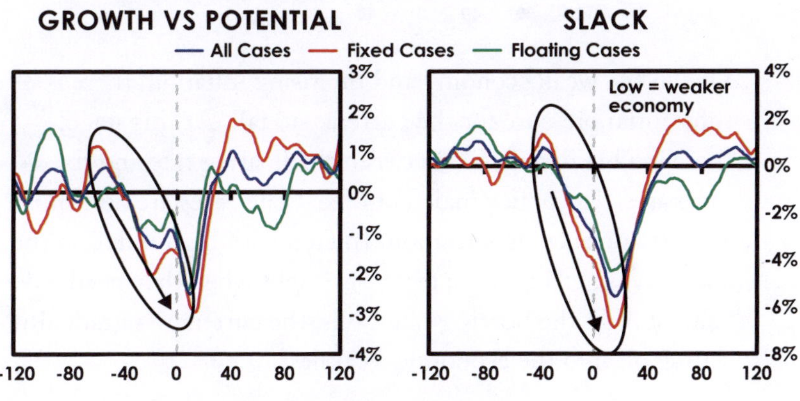

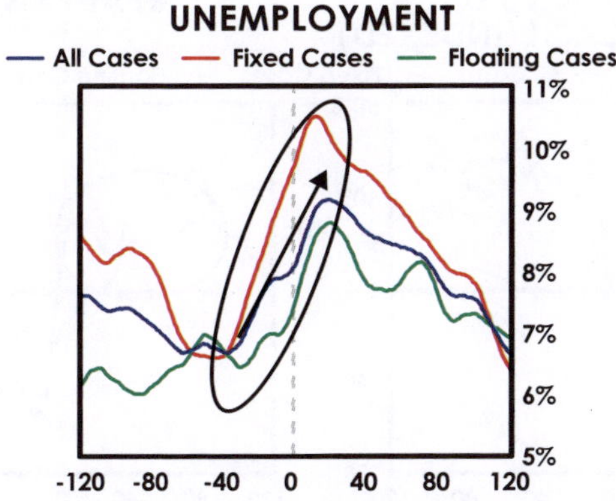

- While not always the case, **inflation tends to rise and become higher than desirable** going into the crisis, constraining the central bank's ability to ease without risking undesirable high inflation.

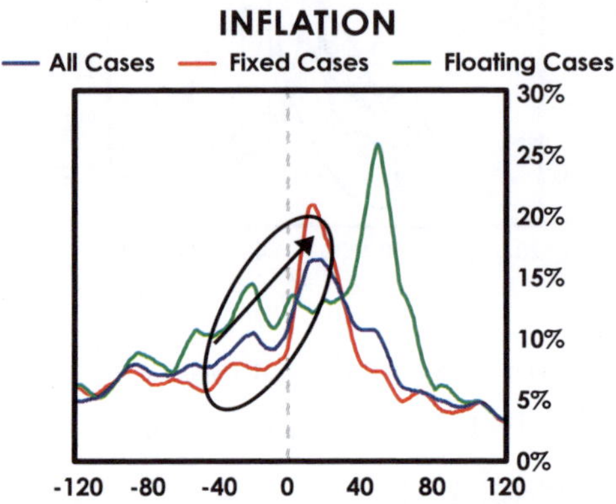

- Due to the weak economy and the rising inflation, there is substantial pressure for the currency to fall. At this stage, there is a big divergence between the floating rate and fixed rate cases. The policy makers in fixed rate cases are fighting against currency depreciation. In fact, with high inflation the currency is getting more expensive right when they need a devaluation. In the floating rate cases, the currency is gradually selling off into the economic weakness.

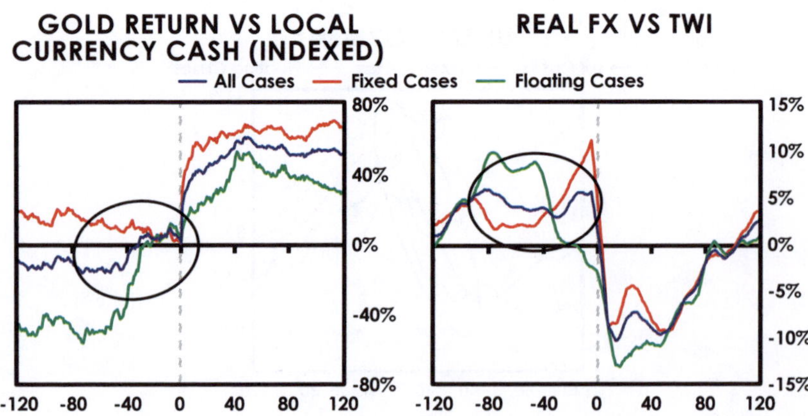

For countries with hard currency debts, **credit spreads rise** as markets price in a greater likelihood of default.

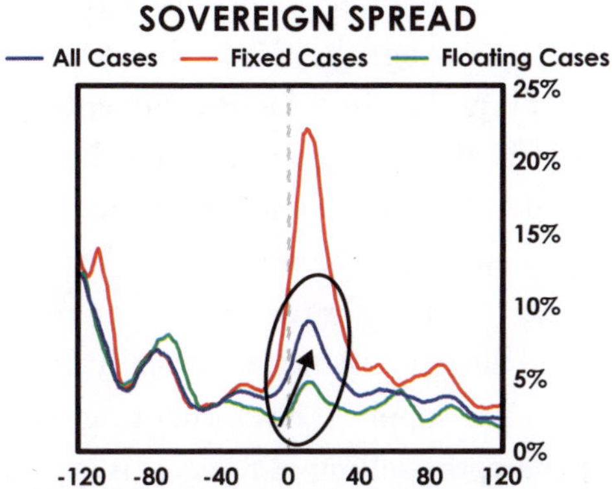

- **Risky assets price in higher risk premiums** (i.e., sell off), adding to the downward pressure on the economy.

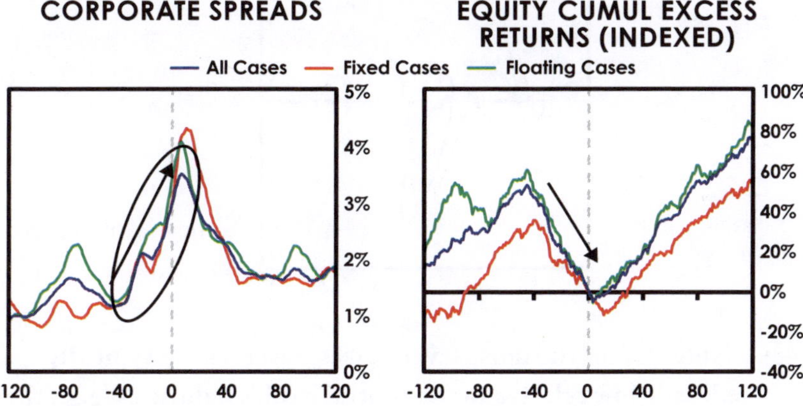

- **At this stage, the central bank typically sells reserves.** Remember that debt works for governments pretty much the same way it works for people and companies except that governments that have the debt denominated in their own currency and have the ability to print their own currency can do so to pay off their debt. Also, as for people and companies, governments can build up savings to help them prevent financial problems when their incomes fall short of their expenses. For that reason, when looking at the riskiness of any debtor, including governments, one should also see what amount of liquid savings they have. Reserves are one of the main forms of liquid savings for governments. So are sovereign wealth funds. Watching their size, how fast they are being drawn down, and how close they are to running out is important to identifying the timing of debt problems. In the process, it pays to watch for the selling of foreign currency and buying of local currency, which is typically done. Because this reduces the money supply, it is a form of tightening. As shown in the next chart, the selling of reserves is typical at this stage of the cycle.

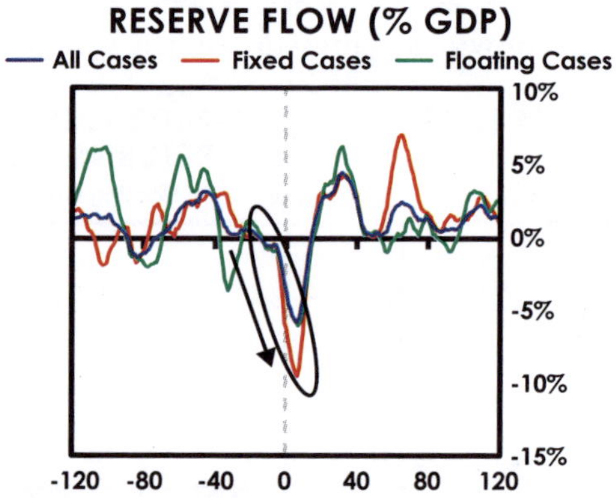

- **Note that in the most severe cases, reserves are typically already low relative to the central bank's liabilities (e.g., the stock of money that savers hold), which gives the central bank little firepower to fight the run on the currency. When that is the case, it becomes apparent that their currency defense will fail, which increases the betting against the currency and the fleeing of debt denominated in it.**

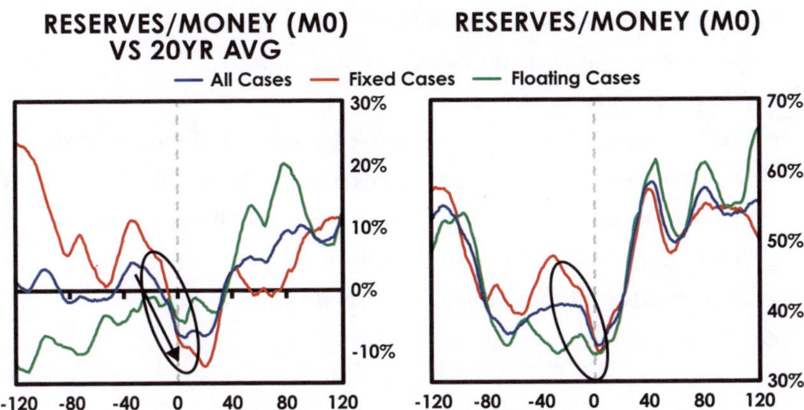

The following table details past interventions of central banks via their reserves across all the cases with meaningful intervention. What you can see is that:

- **Before the central bank intervenes by selling reserves, the country has a modest war chest of reserves** (in the typical case, around 5% of GDP, covering around a tenth of the money supply and government debt outstanding).
- **To stem capital flight and currency weakness, during the intervention phase, the central bank typically spends over half of its reserves in total to defend the currency.** Typically, a lot of this selling is concentrated in a relatively short period of time—for example, in the worst six-month period of intervention, reserves decline by 49% in the median case. Then, the central bank stops spending reserves on trying to hold the currency up because it sees that it will fail at that and the prospect of having no reserves is scarier than the prospect of the currency falling.
- **The currency generally falls during the currency defense**

phase (gold rallies by 42% in the median case)—though in some cases the central bank's intervention is able to temporarily prop up the currency.

- **After a roughly two-year defense (though it of course varies by case)—the central bank gives up.** At this point, the reserves back only about 6% of the money stock and 3% of the government debt. After the central bank stops intervening, the currency sells off (gold rallies another 51% in the median case).

SUMMARY OF CENTRAL BANK INTERVENTIONS VIA SELLING RESERVES ACROSS CASES WITH MEANINGFUL INTERVENTION (1 OF 3)

		Starting Firepower				Intervention Phase						Post-Intervention Phase				
		Reserve Levels Pre-Intervention				Length of FX Defense	Peak 6-Month Intervention		Total Reserve Spend to Defend FX		Gold vs Local FX Excess Return	Reserve Levels Post-Intervention				Gold vs Local FX Excess Return
Case	Fixed vs Floating	% GDP	USD, Bln	% Money Stock (M2)	% Govt Debt	(in Months)	% GDP	% Rsvs at Start of 6m Period	% GDP	% Initial Reserve Level	During Intrven Phase	% GDP	USD, Bln	% Money Stock (M2)	% Govt Debt	Until FX Bottoms
Median (All Cases)		5.1%	6.44	10%	11%	23	-2.6%	-49%	-3.3%	-62%	42%	1.9%	1.66	6%	3%	51%
Fixed		6.1%	4.98	10%	13%	19	-2.7%	-48%	-3.3%	-65%	42%	2.0%	1.66	6%	2%	41%
Floating		4.4%	9.03	14%	11%	29	-1.9%	-57%	-3.8%	-58%	36%	1.7%	1.65	5%	3%	66%
ARG: 1990s Hyperinfl	Fixed	1.3%	5.16	--	3%	6	-2.6%	-50%	-2.6%	-50%	330%	2.0%	2.56	--	2%	--
ARG: 2001 Peg Break	Fixed	8.7%	26.85	43%	25%	19	-6.8%	-47%	-14.1%	-65%	107%	7.9%	9.42	27%	6%	--
BRZ: 1999 Peg Break	Fixed	8.5%	73.62	34%	21%	11	-5.2%	-49%	-6.7%	-56%	52%	5.2%	32.72	21%	10%	--
DEU: Post-WWII	Fixed	0.8%	0.25	2%	0%	64	-0.2%	-46%	-0.6%	-90%	107%	0.1%	0.02	0%	0%	--
FRA: WWII	Fixed	30.9%	2.96	26%	29%	92	-8.2%	-48%	-7.0%	-84%	192%	1.1%	0.48	2%	2%	133%
GBR: Great Depr	Fixed	6.1%	1.34	10%	4%	15	-2.7%	-36%	-3.3%	-43%	40%	5.2%	0.77	7%	3%	3%
GBR: Post-WWII Deval	Fixed	6.2%	2.66	7%	3%	36	-1.0%	-21%	-2.4%	-38%	54%	4.7%	1.66	6%	2%	5%
GBR: WWII	Fixed	14.7%	4.07	22%	11%	37	-3.7%	-66%	-12.8%	-89%	19%	1.5%	0.44	2%	1%	--
JPN: Great Depr	Fixed	4.0%	0.49	9%	15%	26	-3.0%	-55%	-5.1%	-67%	35%	2.7%	0.16	6%	6%	56%
JPN: WWII	Fixed	5.1%	0.37	10%	13%	38	-2.5%	-58%	-2.4%	-81%	10%	0.6%	0.07	1%	1%	>500%

Gold excess return figures are dashed out for cases where the currency bottomed before the reserve intervention stopped. We show "<100%" in cases where the central bank spent more than its entire war chest of reserves (for instance, via a swap line to borrow additional reserves).

SUMMARY OF CENTRAL BANK INTERVENTIONS VIA SELLING RESERVES ACROSS CASES WITH MEANINGFUL INTERVENTION (2 OF 3)

		Starting Firepower				Intervention Phase						Post-Intervention Phase				
		Reserve Levels Pre-Intervention				Length of FX Defense	Peak 6-Month Intervention		Total Reserve Spend to Defend FX		Gold vs Local FX Excess Return	Reserve Levels Post-Intervention				Gold vs Local FX Excess Return
Case	Fixed vs Floating	% GDP	USD, Bln	% Money Stock (M2)	% Govt Debt	(in Months)	% GDP	% Rsvs at Start of 6m Period	% GDP	% Initial Reserve Level	During Intrven Phase	% GDP	USD, Bln	% Money Stock (M2)	% Govt Debt	Until FX Bottoms
MEX: 1982 Default	Fixed	1.6%	4.98	7%	5%	12	-1.8%	-57%	-2.7%	-65%	227%	1.7%	1.76	9%	3%	23%
MEX: Tequila Crisis	Fixed	3.9%	20.89	18%	25%	11	-3.2%	<-100%	-6.4%	-128%	42%	-1.7%	-5.75	-9%	-7%	28%
TUR: 2001 Hyperinfl	Fixed	6.1%	18.44	26%	19%	5	-3.3%	-44%	-4.4%	-50%	27%	4.4%	9.24	19%	14%	16%
USA: 1971 Deval	Fixed	1.8%	18.61	3%	3%	23	-0.2%	-14%	-0.4%	-23%	-6%	1.2%	14.42	2%	2%	150%
USA: Great Depr	Fixed	6.6%	5.15	9%	15%	14	-1.0%	-15%	-1.3%	-18%	-1%	6.1%	4.25	9%	12%	55%
ARG: 2020 Default	Floating	5.9%	36.47	18%	11%	68	-5.0%	<-100%	-12.6%	-135%	163%	-3.2%	-12.93	-11%	-4%	43%
BRZ: 1980s Deval	Floating	2.5%	7.13	18%	5%	6	-1.9%	-55%	-1.9%	-55%	42%	1.4%	3.18	10%	3%	-42%
BRZ: 2002 BoP Crisis	Floating	6.9%	34.88	31%	11%	20	-5.5%	<-100%	-9.5%	-159%	10%	-3.5%	-20.63	-16%	-6%	--
BRZ: 2014 BoP Crisis	Floating	15.9%	371.27	44%	28%	33	-2.9%	-18%	-7.1%	-31%	16%	16.2%	255.62	44%	25%	10%
DEU: Weimar	Floating	6.6%	0.59	7%	5%	63	-1.6%	-39%	-4.8%	-73%	>500%	1.9%	0.12	4%	2%	--
FRA: Early 20s Deval	Floating	4.0%	1.15	7%	4%	77	-0.7%	-19%	-2.8%	-28%	48%	6.3%	0.83	6%	3%	133%
GBR: Late 70s Deval	Floating	4.7%	10.94	11%	11%	25	-1.0%	-29%	-1.9%	-43%	-4%	2.4%	6.21	7%	6%	110%
ITA: Late 70s Deval	Floating	2.9%	6.67	4%	7%	15	-0.8%	-28%	-0.7%	-21%	-26%	2.4%	5.25	3%	5%	94%

Gold excess return figures are dashed out for cases where the currency bottomed before the reserve intervention stopped. We show "<100%" in cases where the central bank spent more than its entire war chest of reserves (for instance, via a swap line to borrow additional reserves).

SUMMARY OF CENTRAL BANK INTERVENTIONS VIA SELLING RESERVES ACROSS CASES WITH MEANINGFUL INTERVENTION (3 OF 3)

		Starting Firepower				Intervention Phase						Post-Intervention Phase				
		Reserve Levels Pre-Intervention				Length of FX Defense	Peak 6-Month Intervention		Total Reserve Spend to Defend FX		Gold vs Local FX Excess Return	Reserve Levels Post-Intervention				Gold vs Local FX Excess Return
Case	Fixed vs Floating	% GDP	USD, Bln	% Money Stock (M2)	% Govt Debt	(in Months)	% GDP	% Rsvs at Start of 6m Period	% GDP	% Initial Reserve Level	During Intrven Phase	% GDP	USD, Bln	% Money Stock (M2)	% Govt Debt	Until FX Bottoms
TUR: 1994 BoP Crisis	Floating	2.6%	6.44	22%	11%	4	-1.9%	-60%	-2.1%	-62%	31%	1.4%	2.47	14%	5%	47%
TUR: 2018 BoP Crisis	Floating	3.8%	30.34	8%	14%	41	-6.5%	<-100%	-10.2%	-293%	108%	-6.8%	-58.67	-15%	-30%	84%

Gold excess return figures are dashed out for cases where the currency bottomed before the reserve intervention stopped. We show "<100%" in cases where the central bank spent more than its entire war chest of reserves (for instance, via a swap line to borrow additional reserves).

At this stage, it becomes relatively clear that the currency is at best highly risky and at worst a very bad deal. This leads to not just investors leaving the debt/currency, but in many cases participants in the economy—most importantly banks, corporations, and households—making prudent/de-risking moves out of the debt and currency. Here are many of the dynamics I saw in the cases I studied that I consider classic signs of being in the late stages of the debt cycle:

Corporate Treasury Actions

1. **Domestic companies decide to keep international revenue offshore principally in foreign FX** (i.e., dollars), not converting it back to local currency like they used to. Seeing their revenues swing in local currency terms even as dollar prices stay more stable, they begin to think of their local currency as the currency to hedge, even though in traditional investing they should hedge the foreign currency.
2. **Domestic corporations decide to increase their amount of hedging of the local currency**, especially those with hard currency debts. Hedging involves a forward contract to sell the local currency and buy foreign currency, which lowers the forward exchange rate and drags down the spot exchange rate.
3. Similarly, **foreign corporations with domestic subsidiaries ensure cash is promptly swept out of the country**.
4. **Companies decide their foreign subsidiaries aren't worth the hassle**—navigating the currency risk, political chaos, and sometimes career risk, for a small expansion opportunity doesn't make a lot of sense. New FDI projects are put on hold.

Domestic Bank Actions

5. **The banks that were forced to buy the debts under government policies have to sell them when liquidity dries up**—accelerating the debt sell-off in the worst of the crisis.
6. **Some of the central bank tactics to keep conditions stimulative (multiple interest rates, capital controls) make it more attractive to keep money offshore than onshore.** Domestic banks and corporations are often the ones best placed to make that market. Even if kept in the same currency, money leaving the domestic banking system often means selling government debt.

International Bank Actions

7. **International lenders close lines of business that are too much of a headache**—trade financing, working capital lines of credit, etc.
8. **Often, they literally sell or give away their bank subsidiaries when it is not worth the exposure to losses** that a small subsidiary has on the broader corporation (let alone the headache of paying attention to this corner of the business).

Large International Investor Actions

9. Ironically, even as borrowing grows, more of it is held by players who can't sell (e.g., banks), and the dollar value of the assets falls. **Liquidity dries up, pushing out large foreign investors who don't like illiquid assets.**
10. **There are moves out of the currency by large government**

reserve holders, often with geopolitical considerations a big part of the decision.

11. Often, big international reserve allocators can't really sell their assets—it would be too disruptive to the market. Instead, **reserve managers start accumulating all new reserves in a different currency**—causing demand to dry up.
12. Relatedly, international investors can't sell their assets (too little liquidity), **but they don't roll the exposures.**

The outflows from foreigners are classic and tend to lead the devaluation.

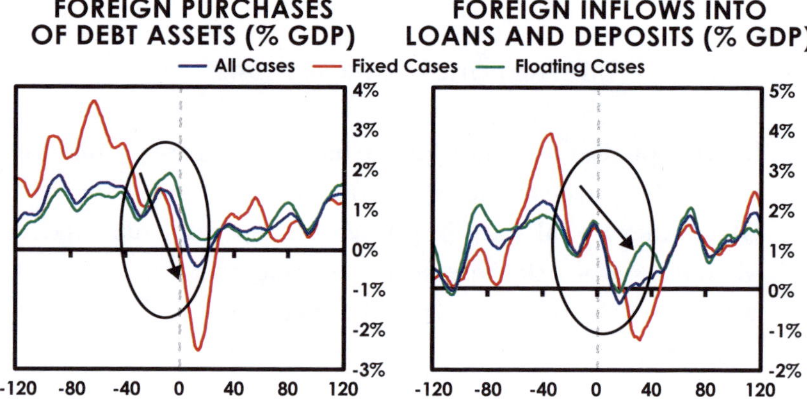

Domestic Saver Actions

13. **Domestic savers decide they want diversification, and to some degree begin betting on inflation-hedge assets, which drives flows in that direction. They convert bank deposits to hard currency**, requiring banks to sell local currency to buy foreign currency.
14. **People buy real goods to get ahead of inflation.** Since imports are a share of these real goods, it creates a currency sale. This of course also fuels inflation and makes matters worse.

15. **High-net-worth individuals, mostly concerned about wealth preservation and rising taxes and wealth confiscation, move money abroad.**
16. **Domestic savers see holding foreign stocks as the more reliable bet.** More products pop up to make that possible.
17. **Opening foreign bank accounts, since domestic banks look troubled, looks like the prudent move.** Those banks make it easy to exchange to other currencies (assuming the government hasn't imposed capital controls; in many cases, the government makes opening foreign bank accounts quite difficult).

More Traditional Speculative Trading

18. **Bond vigilante market action emerges and becomes self-reinforcing.**
19. **Equity investors pull out of the country as the environment deteriorates, which creates a negative currency impact.**

CHAPTER 6

THE CRISIS SPILLS OVER TO THE CENTRAL BANK (STAGES 5-6)

This chapter continues to go through the dynamics I laid out in my archetype of a big debt crisis. Here, we will focus on Stages 5–6, when problems spill over to the central bank.

Stage 5: When There Is a Debt Crisis and Interest Rates Can't Be Lowered (e.g., They Hit 0%), the Central Bank "Prints" (Creates) Money and Buys Bonds to Ease Credit and Make It Easier to Service Debt

The central bank doesn't literally "print money." In doing this, it essentially borrows reserves from commercial banks that it pays a very short-term interest rate on.

Ultimately, the government can't escape the fact that it needs to find much more financing for its spending priorities. But at this stage, it typically experiences financing rates higher than it can afford—often because of the mechanical selling of the currency and debt. Needing financing, the government turns to the central bank. This puts the problem in the central bank's court.

History shows that during such times, central banks typically produce a lot of money and credit to buy the bonds. I view this as a red flag, but not yet a big red flag because of the power of central banks to control the production of money and credit. In the case of central governments and their debts, it will be difficult to avoid the squeeze if the deficits continue because the high debt burdens cause increasing amounts of government spending to be directed to debt service. We will get into an examination of the US government's finances later.

More specifically, the central bank steps in to relieve the pressure on the government's finances (or the finances of other systemically important entities) either through the direct purchase of assets or indirectly through guarantees and backstops. The central bank often takes losses on these assets if they were bought at uneconomical prices in the form of defaults, inflation, and/or rising interest rates. At this stage, the balance sheet hit is transferred from the government to the central bank and the holders of the currency.

As previously explained, **when there isn't enough demand for government debt, the central bank will be faced with the choice between a) having interest rates rise enough to bring supply and demand into balance, which will reduce both the demand for credit and spending and b) printing money and buying debt assets, which will expand the central bank's balance sheet via quantitative easing, which means acquiring a lot of debt assets.** If these things continue for a long time, they should be viewed as early-stage red flags. Also, when governments shorten the maturities of their debt, which typically happens when there isn't enough demand for their long-term debt, that should be viewed as an early-stage red flag, too. And, when both a) the total debt and b) the government debt that is held by the central bank rise because there isn't enough free-market demand to buy the debt, that should be viewed as an early-stage red flag as well. As shown in the following charts, these trends toward greater central bank holdings of bonds and shortening of maturities typically start nearly a decade before the crisis and reverse after it. Notice the acceleration of central bank bond buying and how the maturity of the government debt is rapidly shortening.

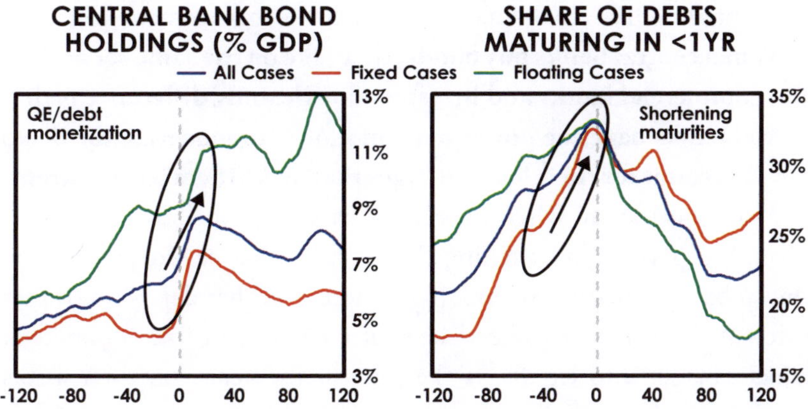

As discussed earlier, when the system is working well, the demand to borrow from borrower-debtors and the willingness to lend by lender-creditors balance. However, when the free-market demand for the debt that is being sold is not adequate, the central government and the central bank take on more of the debt when the private sector can't. The government can do this when the private sector can't because lender-creditors will more readily lend to the government during times of stress as they believe that the central government will pay it back since the central bank has the power to print money to pay debts so there is virtually no risk that it will default. **The risk becomes that the central bank will produce too much money and credit in order to prevent defaults, which will produce a lot of inflation that will make being paid back in devalued money a big risk for the lender-creditor. When this happens, I view it as a red flag, but not a big red flag because history shows that it can happen a lot before the supply-and-demand imbalance becomes a problem.** In the most recent example, this started in 2008. It was previously called debt monetization and has this time around been called quantitative easing. In the United States, it came in four waves that added up to 18% of potential GDP, 5% of total debt, and 16% of government debt. In Europe, it also came in four waves that added up to 30% of potential GDP, 10% of total debt, and 36% of government debt. In Japan, it came in three waves that added up to 95%

of potential GDP, 22% of total debt, and 46% of government debt.

When central banks buy bonds, they take on the same set of risks that commercial banks and investors do. The only difference is that central banks have the power to print money to monetize the debts and to account for their losses in ways that make them less apparent.

More specifically, when the central bank buys the bond (say, from a bank), it pays for it by telling the bank it has a new deposit at the central bank. The central bank pays interest on that deposit (not that different from money you or I keep at a bank). Just like commercial banks can get into trouble if the interest they earn on their assets is below the interest they pay on deposits, it's the same for central banks. If the interest rates the central banks pay on deposits rise above the interest that they are getting on the bonds they own, they will lose money and will have a negative cash flow. If they used mark-to-market accounting, they would have losses on the bonds, and as with banks and investors, if their losses become greater than their capital, they have a negative net worth. In reality, at this stage no one cares much, but for reasons that I will explain, they should.

Stage 6: If Interest Rates Rise, the Central Bank Loses Money Because the Interest Rate That It Has to Pay on Its Liabilities Is Greater than the Interest Rate It Receives on the Debt Assets It Bought

When that happens, that is notable but not a big red flag until the central bank has a significant negative net worth and is forced to print more money to cover the negative cash flow that it experiences due to less money coming in on its assets than has to go out to service its debt liabilities. That is a big red flag because it signals the central bank's death spiral (i.e., the dynamic in which rising interest rates cause problems that creditors see, which leads them not to hold the debt assets, which leads to higher interest rates or the need to print more money, which devalues the money, which leads to more selling of the debt assets and the currency, and so on). That is what I mean when I say the central bank goes broke: it can't make its debt service payments, though it doesn't default on its debts because it prints money. When done in large amounts, that devalues the money and creates inflationary recessions or depressions.

At this stage, the central bank typically ends up in a difficult situation, caught between the need to maintain policy that is at once easy enough to support a weak economy and a fiscally weak government but also tight enough to discourage savers and investors from fleeing the currency. This is a hallmark of an unsustainable situation, and it typically manifests in the following ways:

1. **Central banks have losses and negative net worths.**

After the central bank has bought a lot of debt and interest rates have risen so debt prices have fallen and the central bank's short-term costs of funds are greater than the returns on the debt they bought, central banks have losses that are so big that they lead the central banks to have negative net worths. That is another red flag. Still, all these red flags don't signal the end of the Big Debt Cycle—they just show signs of the fading financial health of the system. It is not the end because central banks can still print plenty of money to provide ample money and credit and to fund their losses. Having said that, it is noteworthy that in some cases where the governments don't want to have flimflam finances, the central government is required to put capital in the central bank to recapitalize it. When that happens, the central government has to get more capital to provide it, which it will do by taxing, cutting spending, and/or borrowing, which adds to the squeeze.

When central banks buy a lot of debt, that lowers the value of the debt because it lowers the value of the money that the debt asset is promised to get. And when the short-term interest rates that they have to pay are high relative to the long-term interest that they get from the debt assets that they own, central banks have losses and

can have a negative net worth. This is a moderate red flag at first—several central banks have negative net equity (or equivalent) today, and it doesn't hinder them much in the way of their operations. But at larger degrees of losses, it could begin a spiral that creates much bigger problems.

The advantage of the central banks doing such buying is that 1) it provides credit that wouldn't have existed to keep interest rates lower than they would have been and 2) when interest rates rise and the bonds have losses, it will be the central bank that has the losses. This raises the question of whether central bank losses matter, and if so why. The answer is that central banks having losses certainly matters less than private sector investors having losses and having to appear to lender-creditors as creditworthy. **When central banks have big losses on their debt, that signifies a step toward a more advanced stage near the end of the Big Debt Cycle so I view it as a flag.** There is typically still no reason for a crisis at this stage because, as stated, small or moderate losses don't matter much for the central bank. However, as these losses move from being small to being very large, they can create cash flow needs for the central bank that can only be met with a lot of money printing, which puts a significant downward pressure on the currency, as the central bank runs up a large interest bill on its liabilities (in an effort to keep savers in the currency) but earns little on its assets (in an effort to support the government) and ends up printing the difference. The following table describes historical cases where these cash flow losses became very large and necessitated a big monetization that contributed to a currency spiral.

HISTORICAL CASES WHERE CENTRAL BANKS TOOK LARGE CASH FLOW LOSSES

Case	Start Date	End Date	Average over Period			Losses Paid By	Propensity to Spend Printed Money	Outcomes of Case		
			CB Balance Sheet (% GDP)	CB Cash Flow Losses (% GDP)	CB Net Reserves (% GDP)			Money Growth (Ann)	Inflation (Ann)	Cumulative FX Move
ARG: Late 80s	Jan-88	Dec-90	31.5%	-3.3%	4.7%	Money Printing	High	107%	4927%	-97%
ARG: Recent	Jan-19	Dec-22	34.0%	-3.5%	1.4%	Money Printing	High	50%	49%	-86%
PER: Late 80s	Jan-85	Dec-88	6.9%	-2.6%	2.5%	Money Printing	High	214%	246%	-100%
Dutch Guilder	1780	1796	5.8%	-3.3%	1.8%	Money Printing	High	27%	22%	-80%
Turkey: Today	Jan-23	Early 2024	17.2%	-2.6%	-2.5%	Money Printing	High	20%	84%	-42%
				Large losses on smaller balance sheets (huge liability costs vs low asset yields)		Losses monetized through printing rather than recapitalization by government	Printed money left the currency as savers had been burned before and were still facing low real rates		Losses were a contributor to massive currency devaluations	

2. **The central bank is forced to print money to monetize losses on its debt and other debts even though it worsens the pressure on the currency.**

Faced with these circumstances, the central bank is ultimately forced to print money to monetize its losses and the losses of others. This can happen explicitly through the direct purchase of assets by the central bank or indirectly through guarantees and backstops. The central bank typically takes losses on these assets (often bought at uneconomical prices) through defaults, inflation, and/or rising interest rates—transferring the balance sheet hit from the government to the central bank and the holders of the currency. **Some of the hallmarks of this stage are:**

- **An expanding central bank balance sheet as money is printed to finance the government or to roll the debts of other stressed entities.** The next chart shows the central bank's purchases of government bonds, but it's worth noting that central bank actions can be much broader than this (up to and including the purchase of private assets like corporate bonds or equities). They can also include measures to guarantee and backstop stressed borrowers that don't always show up on the balance sheet but still represent some transfer of purchasing power to stressed debtors as the central bank and government are on the hook for covering losses (e.g., the Emergency Banking Act of 1933 and the Bank of Amsterdam's backstop of the Dutch East India Company—both of which ultimately required monetization).

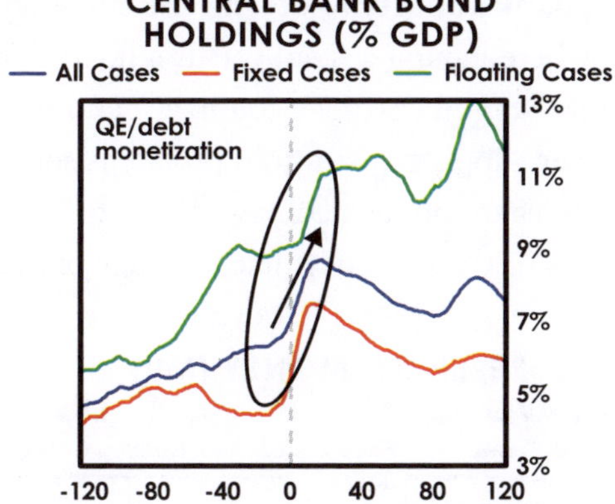

- **The sale of reserves as the central bank tries to defend the currency while simultaneously providing money and credit to those that need it.** The result is that the composition of the central bank's asset holdings shifts from hard assets (gold and FX reserves) to soft assets (claims on the government or financials). This contributes to the run on the currency (particularly when the currency is pegged) as investors see the central bank's resources to defend the currency rapidly decreasing, forcing the central bank to sell reserves even faster until it reaches the point where a defense is no longer feasible. This dynamic is far more pronounced in the fixed rate cases than it is in the floating cases.
- **The monetization of debts combined with the sale of reserves causes the ratio of the central bank's hard assets (reserves) to its liabilities (money) to decline, weakening**

the central bank's ability to defend the currency. This is another case where having a fixed versus a floating rate currency is important. Pegged currency countries tend to have a more backed money supply but run into problems sooner when the ratio of reserves to money declines. They also tend to expend more reserves in the currency defense stage of the cycle.

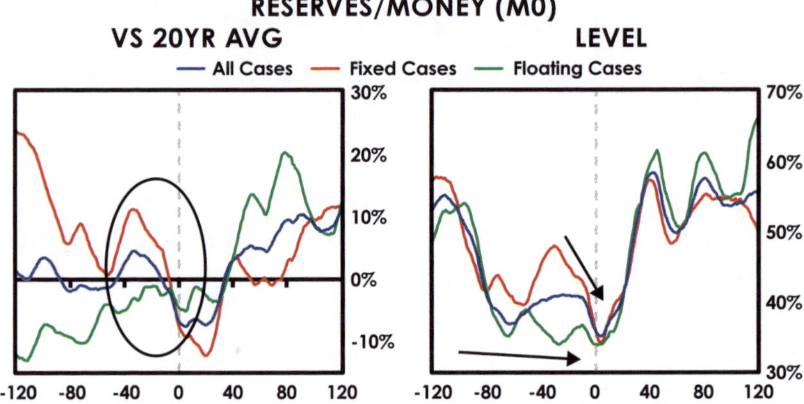

In fixed rate cases, the level of hard assets tends to be higher (closer to 50% backed on average), but begins to decline and is only around a third backed at the time of devaluation

CHAPTER 7

THE PRIOR BIG DEBT CRISIS RECEDES, A NEW EQUILIBRIUM IS REACHED, AND A NEW CYCLE CAN BEGIN (STAGES 7-9)

The cycle ends when a mix of market forces and policy-maker actions create a bottom and an upswing from there. This chapter lays out the dynamics and markers I look for in these times (Stages 7–9 of the archetype I showed in Chapter 4).

Stage 7: Debts Are Restructured and Devalued

When managed in the best possible way (what I call a beautiful deleveraging), the deflationary ways of reducing debt burdens (e.g., through debt restructurings) are balanced with the inflationary ways of reducing debt burdens (e.g., by monetizing them) so that the deleveraging occurs without having unacceptable amounts of either deflation or inflation.

When the debt burdens become too great, a big restructuring and/or devaluation that substantially reduces their size and value will happen, either by itself or with the help of good management.

The currency devalues and the remaining holders of the currency and the debt take big losses in real terms. The loss of purchasing power continues until **a new monetary system is established** with enough credibility to entice investors and savers to hold the currency again. Typically, this involves a substantial write-down and restructuring of the debt.

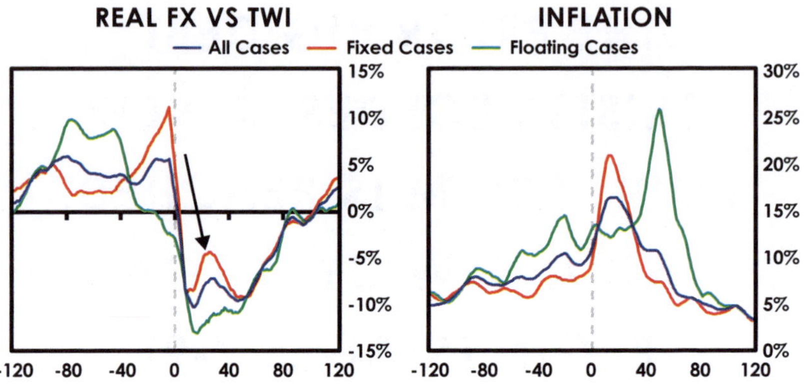

Government debts devalue relative to real assets like gold, stocks, and commodities. Perhaps this time, digital currencies like Bitcoin will benefit. The following charts show the average devaluation of currency and debts across the cases relative to 1) gold, 2) commodities, and 3) equities. **On average, gold outperforms holding the local currency in these cases by roughly 60% from the start of the devaluation until the currency bottoms.** Notice the big difference in what happens in the fixed exchange rate and the variable (fiat) exchange rate cases.

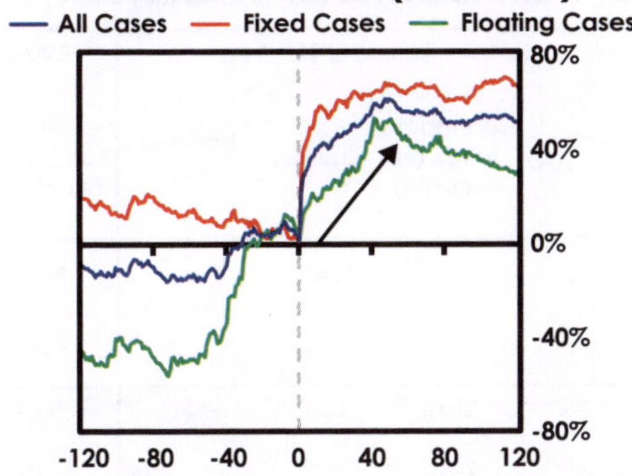

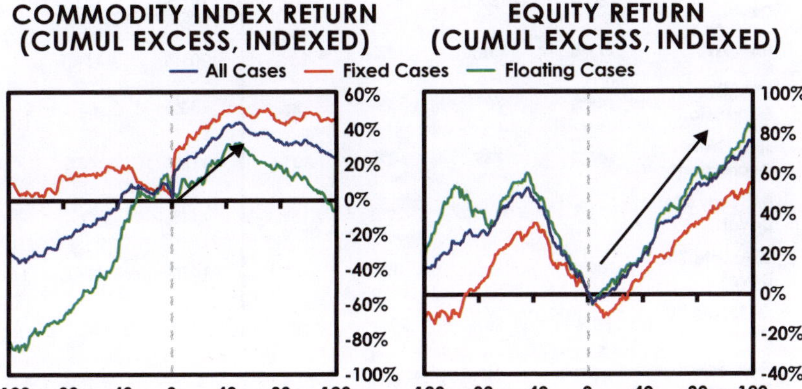

You can see the individual returns of the various assets by case in the following table.

ASSET RETURNS DURING CURRENCY DEVALUATIONS AND DEBT WRITE-DOWNS (EXCESS RETURN) (1 OF 2)

	Individual Assets (at 15% Vol)				Assets vs Debt/FX	
	Gold (in Local FX)	Commodity Index (in Local FX)	Equities	Nominal Bonds	Gold vs Bonds (Vol-Matched)	Equities, Gold, and Cmd vs Bonds (Vol-Matched)
Average Return	81%	55%	34%	-5%	94%	71%
Median Return	66%	49%	3%	-2%	71%	38%
JPN: WWII	282%	203%	100%	-53%	335%	260%
DEU: Weimar Hyperinfl	245%	241%	754%	-99%	501%	516%
USA: 1971 Deval	185%	162%	-44%	-6%	191%	141%
ITA: WWII	173%	156%	92%	-28%	201%	154%
USA: Great Depression	149%	70%	33%	19%	130%	68%
JPN: Great Depression	146%	73%	60%	30%	116%	72%
ITA: Early 20s Deval	126%	105%	-22%	-15%	141%	71%
USA: Late 70s Deval	109%	56%	3%	-33%	143%	104%
GBR: Late 70s Deval	88%	23%	22%	19%	69%	37%
GBR: Great Depression	81%	-4%	-8%	26%	56%	2%
GBR: Post-WWII Deval	75%	57%	11%	19%	57%	38%
ITA: Late 70s Deval	73%	20%	-16%	-42%	114%	79%
FRA: Early 20s Deval	73%	87%	43%	-11%	84%	59%
FRA: WWII	71%	90%	11%	-14%	86%	66%
GBR: 08 Fin Crisis	71%	11%	24%	52%	19%	-4%
GBR: WWII	66%	52%	8%	18%	49%	31%
TUR: 2018 BoP Crisis	66%	40%	63%	-27%	144%	165%

These tables show returns from the moment of devaluation through to the period when the currency has settled at a new equilibrium (e.g., in the US Great Depression, returns are shown from the month of the peg break to shortly after; in cases where the devaluation was more drawn out, returns are shown for the full period of devaluation). We would consider the returns figures in individual cases to be more indicative than exact, because getting returns and volatility adjusting are imprecise in cases with market closures, defaults, and in cases where we have lower-quality data.

ASSET RETURNS DURING CURRENCY DEVALUATIONS AND DEBT WRITE-DOWNS (EXCESS RETURN) (2 OF 2)

	Individual Assets (at 15% Vol)				Assets vs Debt/FX	
	Gold (in Local FX)	Commodity Index (in Local FX)	Equities	Nominal Bonds	Gold vs Bonds (Vol-Matched)	Equities, Gold, and Cmd vs Bonds (Vol-Matched)
USA: 08 Fin Crisis	63%	2%	16%	55%	7%	-27%
MEX: 1982 Default	53%	73%	-27%	-81%	134%	131%
ARG: 1990s Hyperinfl	47%	54%	-	-	-	-
TUR: 1994 BoP Crisis	46%	51%	-1%	-50%	97%	99%
MEX: Tequila Crisis	40%	47%	-18%	-42%	82%	77%
JPN: 08 Crisis + Abenomics	38%	-21%	61%	49%	-11%	-22%
BRZ: 2002 BoP Crisis	31%	33%	-11%	1%	25%	15%
ITA: Euro Debt Crisis	28%	-2%	-16%	11%	17%	-6%
ESP: Euro Debt Crisis	28%	-2%	-15%	39%	-11%	-34%
BRZ: 1999 Peg Break	27%	16%	-3%	-6%	33%	26%
BRZ: 2014 BoP Crisis	25%	-11%	-14%	-2%	49%	24%
JPN: Post-Bubble Deval	23%	64%	6%	48%	-25%	0%
GRC: Euro Debt Crisis	23%	-13%	-50%	-49%	71%	30%
ARG: 2001 Peg Break	20%	14%	-4%	0%	21%	16%
TUR: 2001 Hyperinfl	13%	1%	-13%	22%	-9%	-22%

When debts are restructured and/or devalued, it is typically a terrible time in markets and economies, but this terrible time reduces the debt burdens and establishes the foundation for the improvement. In the archetypical case, debt levels rise significantly relative to the monetary base in the run-up to the crisis, requiring the private sector to absorb a much greater amount of government debt with the same quantity of base money in circulation (which is likely a part of why we see upward pressure on interest rates at first in many of our cases). Eventually, when the pressure becomes too great, the central bank steps in and monetizes the debt, resulting in an expansion of the monetary base and a decline in the debt-to-money ratio.

The ratio of reserves to debt typically falls at first, then rises. Typically, at this stage, we see reserves fall relative to debts—at first because debt levels are increasing quickly, then additionally because reserves are being sold in an attempt to defend the currency. After policy makers give up and let the currency go, we see this ratio improve as the devaluation of the currency mechanically reduces the value of local currency debts relative to hard currency assets and improves the country's competitiveness, helping it to earn more in hard currency terms.

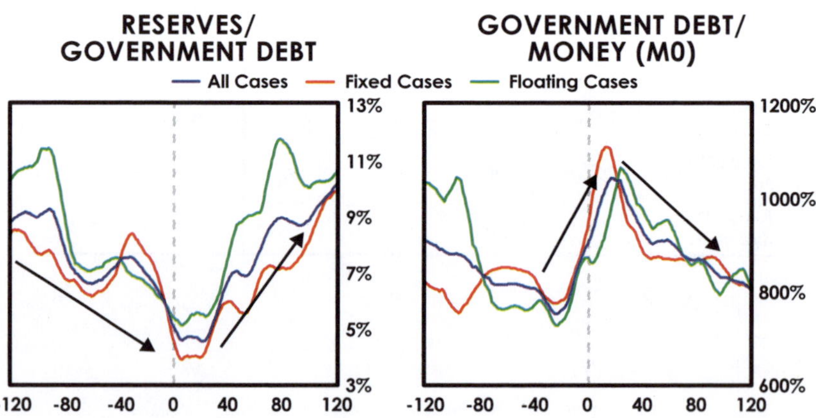

The next charts show how the paths of government debts and the monetary base typically line up. Typically, we see government debt rise first (usually in response to some crisis) while money growth is by and large unchanged (and, in fact, slows at the point of the cycle where the central bank tries to mount a currency defense). The government typically tries to control things through various techniques like foreign exchange controls or managing the currency (e.g., sometimes having an official foreign exchange rate that is different from the market rate). These controls create market distortions and do more harm than good. After the central bank gives up and lets the currency go, the pace of money printing picks up and helps to produce inflation that improves the government's nominal incomes relative to its debts. This dynamic is by and large similar across pegged and non-pegged cases.

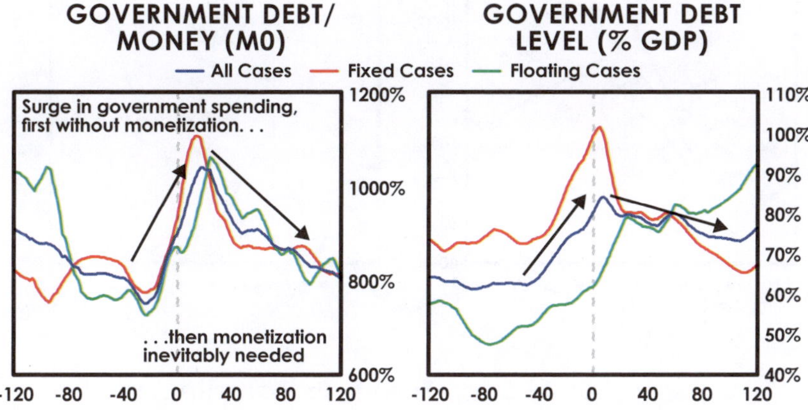

The next three charts show government debt against reserves; the fall in reserves relative to debts is driven mostly by the rise in government debt but also by the selling of reserves late in the cycle to try to fight off the collapse of the currency. After the selling stops and the currency devalues, we typically see an improvement in the ratio as the devaluation lowers the value of local currency government debts relative to any remaining hard currency assets.

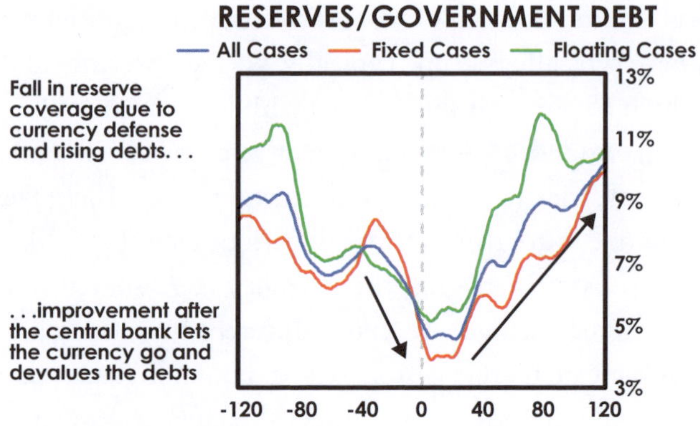

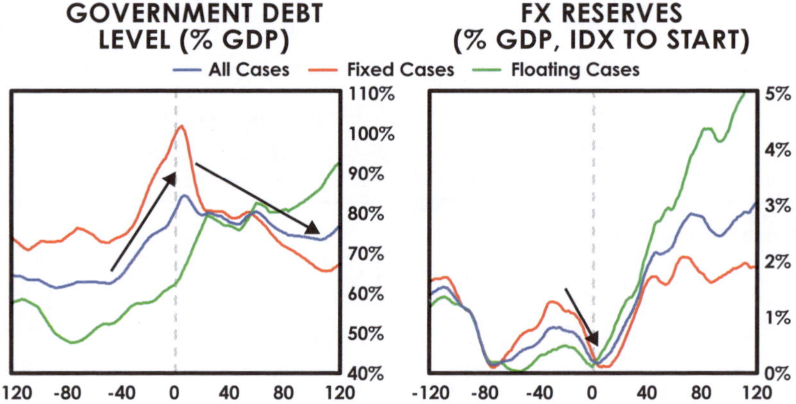

Stage 8: At Such Times, Extraordinary Policies Like Extraordinary Taxes and Capital Controls Are Commonly Imposed

At this point, the government is cash-strapped and typically raises taxes to try to meet its financing need. The prospect of greater taxation puts additional pressure on households and businesses to move what they can out of the country. In response, governments often enact capital controls to try to stem these outflows, though by now the economic pressure to leave the country and the currency is too great for governments to stop the bleeding.

The following charts show a few different perspectives on tax rates across cases. You can see, for example, that both marginal income tax rates for top earners and inheritance tax rates rise by about 10% in the years going into the devaluation.[23]

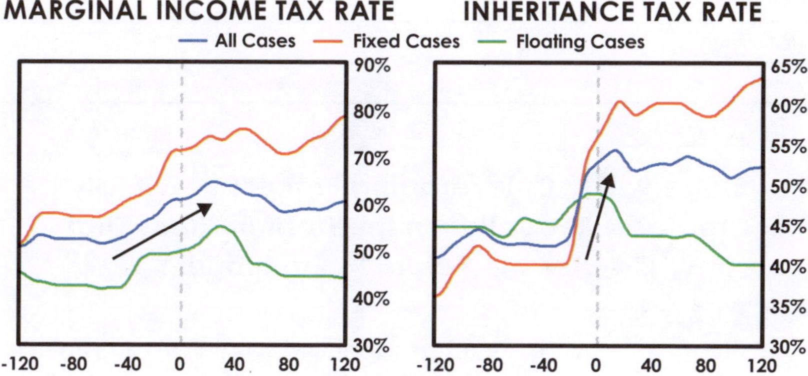

Higher tax rates typically go hand in hand with capital controls in order to try to prohibit money from fleeing the country in response. You can see just how common this is in the following table:

[23] Note that tax rate data only covers the US, the UK, Japan, Germany, and France.

20YR PERIODS OF STRICT/RISING CAPITAL CONTROLS

	1900	1920	1940	1960	1980	2000
UK	Yes	Yes	Yes	Yes		
US	Yes	Yes				
China			Yes	Yes	Yes	
Germany	Yes	Yes	Yes	Yes		
France	Yes			Yes		
Russia	Yes	Yes	Yes	Yes	Yes	Yes
Austria-Hungary	Yes					
Italy		Yes				
Netherlands				Yes		
Japan		Yes		Yes		

[24]

Stage 9: The Deleveraging Process Inevitably Creates a Reduction in the Debt Burdens That Creates the Return to Equilibrium

Quite often, when there are inflationary depressions so the debt is devalued, at the end of the cycle, government reserves are raised through asset sales, and a strictly enforced transition from a rapidly declining currency to a relatively stable currency is achieved by the central bank linking the currency to a hard currency or a hard asset (e.g., gold) while having very tight money and a very high real interest rate, which severely penalizes the borrower-debtors and rewards the lender-creditors, which leads to the buying of the debt/currency, which stabilizes the debt/currency.

At this stage, the currency has been devalued and the remaining holders of the currency and the debt have taken big losses in real terms, which has relieved a lot of the debt burdens of the debtors.

[24] While this diagram is not exhaustive, I include instances where I could find clear evidence of each occurring in the 20-year period shown. Relevant capital controls are defined as meaningful restrictions on investors moving their money to and from other countries and assets (although this does not include targeted measures directed only at single countries, such as sanctions).

Now, it doesn't take much to back up the debt, stabilizing it and the currency. When managed well, the government raises reserves, sometimes by selling government-owned assets, sometimes by getting IMF or other loans requiring sound financial policies including austerity. At this stage, the interest rate is still high—in fact, very high in relation to the prospective inflation rate and the prospective rate of depreciation in the currency, which means that the central bank can make the debt/money an attractive investment again, and debt in that currency very expensive, if they manage the situation well. This is when **a new and more stable monetary system is established** with enough credibility to entice investors and savers to hold the currency again. Typically, this follows a substantial write-down and restructuring of the debt along with a return to some form of hard money. And this typically requires a set of fundamental adjustments that improve the country's balance sheet and income statement.

The five classic steps typically necessary to make the transition are:

1. **A restructuring of the country's debts to manageable levels** where reserve assets can cover a substantial portion of liabilities and the government's debt service no longer exceeds its revenue growth. Typically, defaulting and restructuring foreign currency debts and some local currency debts are required, too.

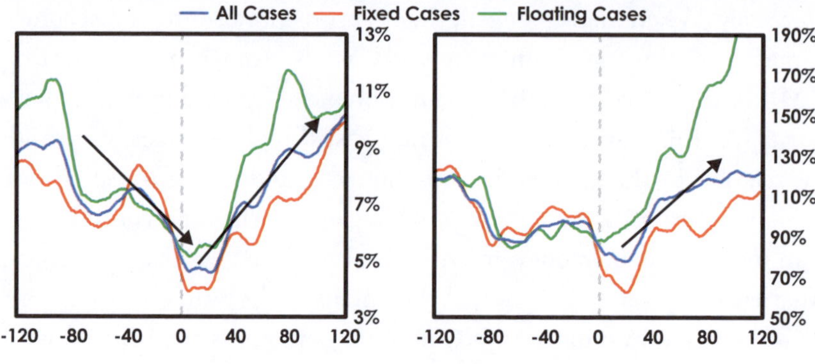

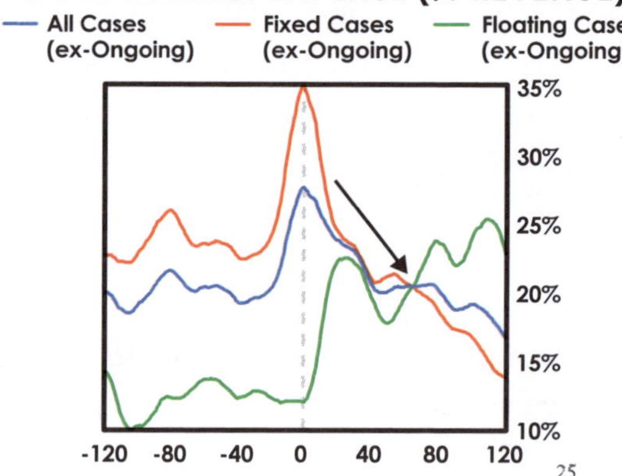

[25]

The next two charts show an attribution of what happens to government debt-to-GDP following the devaluation, on average across the case set. You can see that in the average case, central government debt is at 89% of GDP around the time of the devaluation. The green bars show the factors that work to bring the debt-to-GDP ratio down—on average, 7% comes from central bank purchases, 38% is due to inflation, 26% is due to positive growth in real GDP, 16% is due to primary surpluses, and 8% is due to defaults or restructuring of the debt; the red bar shows what led it to rise—76% driven by

[25] To show a clearer picture of how the government's balance sheet evolves in the upswing and downswing of the cycle, these charts exclude a handful of recent cases (the US, Europe, the UK, and Japan post-financial crisis) that are still playing out.

continued interest payments. The net of these is that in the average case, debt falls from 89% to 70% of GDP and that rising inflation and rising real growth arising from aggressive stimulations are the big forces behind the debt burden reduction. Said differently, governments that have debt in their own currencies 1) make their interest and principal payments by having their central banks create money and credit, raise inflation, and stimulate real growth, and by restructuring debts, which raises nominal income growth relative to debt service payments, and 2) restructure defaulted debts in the amounts shown. While this chart shows all cases, this is especially true in the cases when the currencies are denominated in monies that the central banks can produce. In most such cases, the debt problems never go away as much as they remain a manageable burden handled in the way described. Of course, these are average numbers and the ranges around them are large, though the patterns are pretty consistent.

ATTRIBUTION OF ARCHETYPICAL DECLINE IN GOVERNMENT DEBT-TO-GDP

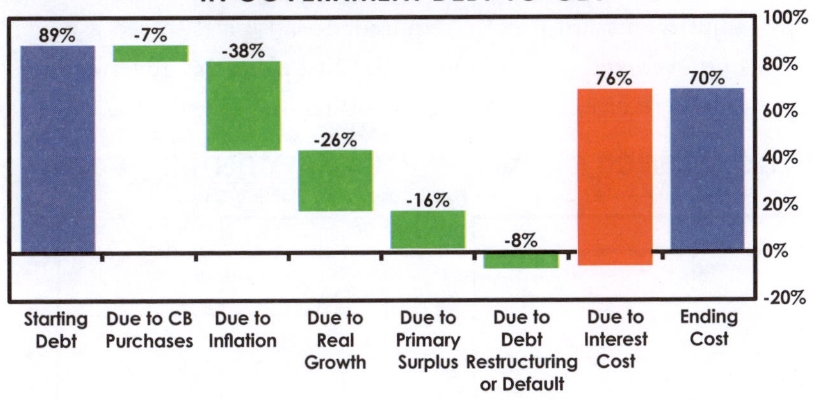

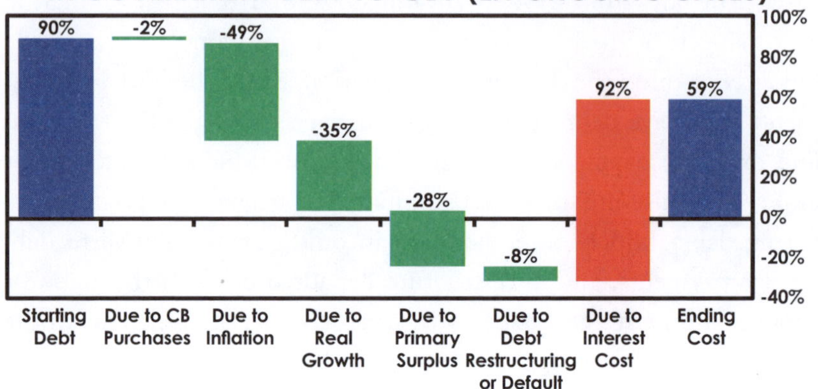

2. **A deep, painful fiscal policy adjustment** to make the country's finances sustainable without requiring the printing of money to monetize the debt. Deep, painful fiscal policy adjustments from the central government and healthy balance of payments adjustments are usually required. It is typical to see a bigger improvement in the primary deficit before the government is able to reduce interest costs by rolling into lower rates.

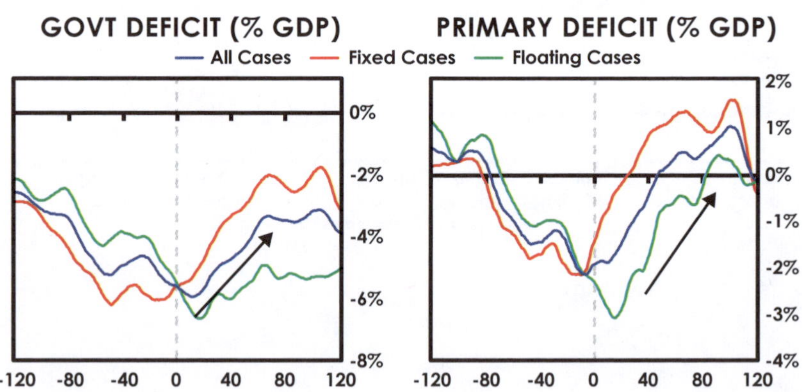

3. **Obtaining sufficient quantities of reserves to defend the currency (or back the new currency if the old, collapsed currency**

is being replaced) is typically part of the process. The devaluation of the currency typically helps with this both because the fall in the exchange rate increases the value of the country's reserves relative to its nominal liabilities and because it improves the country's competitiveness, helping to increase export incomes relative to import costs. In addition, we see a combination of asset sales to build up reserves further and occasional borrowing from official creditors (which at this point are among the few parties still willing to lend). Also, government-owned companies and other assets are typically sold off, which brings in money for reserves and improves efficiencies of these businesses.

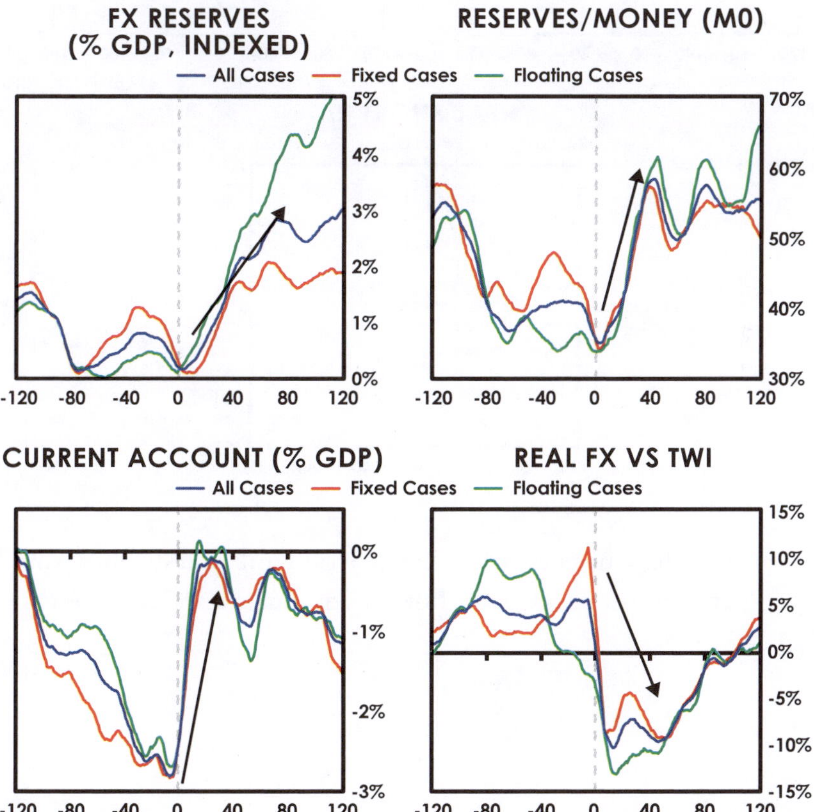

4. **High real interest rates** that more than adequately compensate investors for the risks of holding the currency. These charts show the nominal interest rates on local currency and hard currency debts.

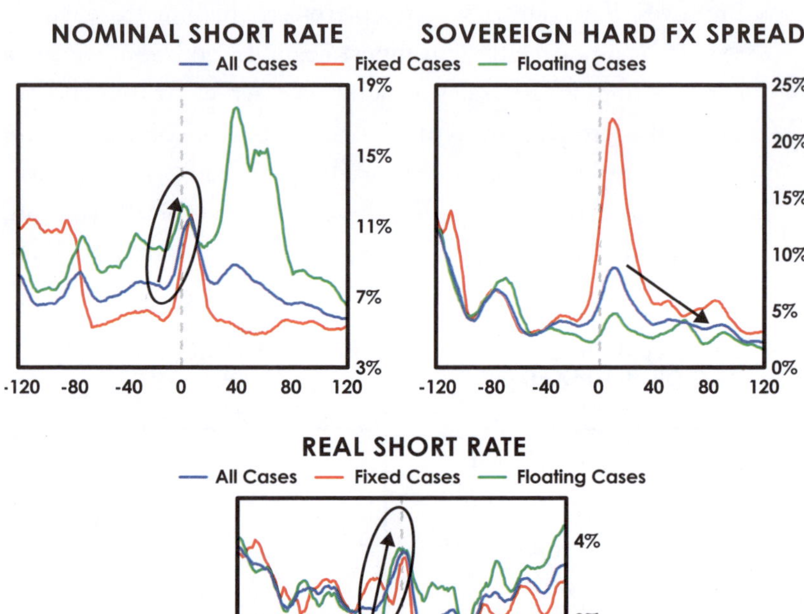

5. **Placing limits on what the central bank can do that would undermine sustainable finances of the new stable money.**

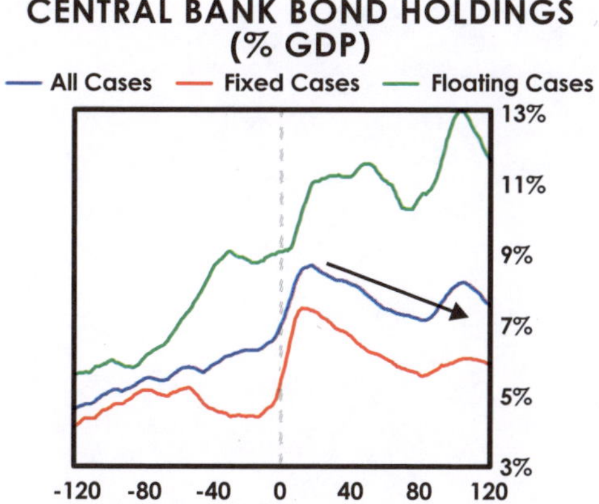

When these conditions are met, these are among the best times to hold the country's currency and debt.

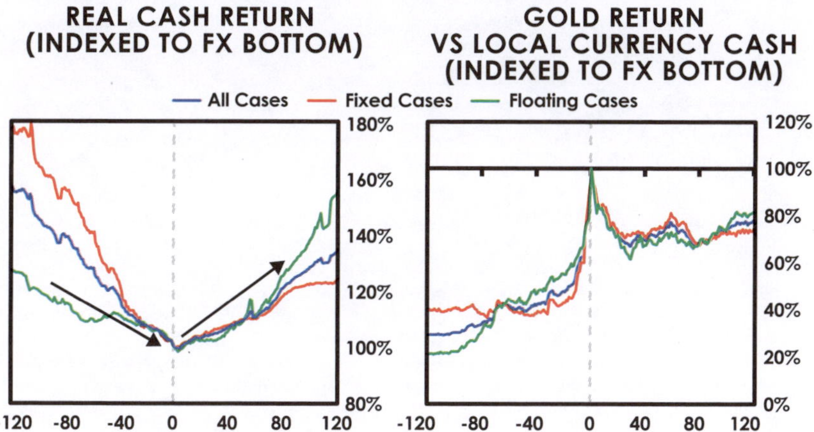

That is what the end stages of the typical Big Debt Cycle look like to me. Let's now return to the very big-picture level and look at how the current Big Debt Cycle has played out over the last 80 years.

not necessarily precisely or in detail. If they fail to explain all the big developments in all time frames and in all countries, that indicates that an important influence is missing and needs to be added to the template/model.

The expert systems I have built are previously developed forms of artificial intelligence. Now, with various breakthroughs in artificial intelligence, I am—and I believe we all are—on the brink of being able to understand all of the cause/effect relationships that drive everything, though for now we still have to labor along the old-fashioned way, with people studying what happened using the computing and AI tools available today. That is why, in my own feeble attempts to understand and describe the most important mechanics that change the world as we know it, I do these in-depth studies and create explanations of them. What I am about to describe is a result of this process. However, because the forces that drive the Big Cycle are so big, it is easy to see and understand them without worrying about the details and the complexities.

Zooming out to the highest level, the five most important drivers of change are:[26]

1. **The debt/credit/money/economic cycle**
2. **The internal order and disorder cycle**
3. **The external geopolitical order and disorder cycle (i.e., the changing world order)**
4. **Acts of nature (droughts, floods, and pandemics)**
5. **Human inventiveness, most importantly of new technologies**

These forces affect each other to shape the biggest things that happen, creating cycles that move markets and economies around an upward-sloping trend line. The incline of its upward slope is primarily

[26] Additionally, there is the demographic force that will certainly lead to a lot of old people who don't work and will be expensive to support (because at that stage in their lives, their healthcare costs will be high), a shrinking workforce in developed countries, large increases in population in less developed countries, and only a small percentage of the people being truly productive.

driven by the inventiveness of practical people (e.g., entrepreneurs) who are given adequate resources (e.g., capital) and work well with others (their coworkers, government officials, lawyers, etc.) to make the inventions and products that create productivity improvements.

Over a short period of time (i.e., 1-10 years), the short-term cycles, especially the debt and political cycles, are dominant. Over a long period of time (i.e., 10 years and beyond), the long-term cycles and the upward-sloping trend line in productivity have much bigger effects. As I explained earlier, conceptually the way this dynamic transpires looks like this to me:

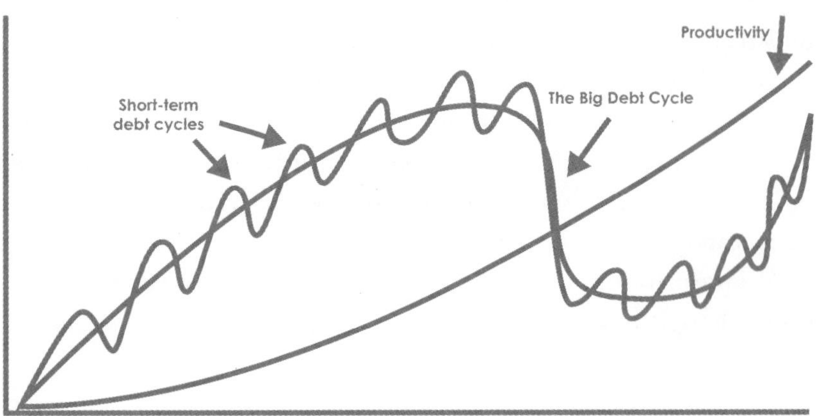

I will now delve into these five forces. While reading about them, please think about how these forces have worked and how they are working now. That will help you see how and why "history rhymes" and better understand what is now happening and what is likely to happen.

HOW THE OVERALL BIG CYCLE WORKS: THE FIVE BIG FORCES

We are now 80 years into the Overall Big Cycle that began at the end of World War II, which is by and large unfolding in the classic ways that will produce dramatic changes that one can only

imagine by visualizing these five forces interacting simultaneously in a historical context.

More specifically:

1. The Debt/Credit/Money/Economic Cycle

Throughout this book, I have described the most important things that influence the Big Debt Cycle (like debt service payments relative to income, the amount of new debt sold relative to the demand for it, the desirability and willingness of debt asset holders to hold their existing debt assets, and other factors explained earlier, etc.).

Because I have already covered this Big Debt Cycle so completely that you are probably sick of hearing about it, I won't say much more. **I will just reiterate the main points I want to get across, which are:**

- **There has always been, and I expect that there will always be, short-term cycles that over time add up to Big Debt Cycles.**
- **The average short-term debt cycle has typically taken about six years, give or take about three (with the duration of that cycle dependent on a number of influences that we can monitor and use to come up with rough estimates of how long each one will last).**
- **The average long-term Big Debt Cycle has typically taken about 80 years, give or take 25 years (with the duration of that cycle also driven by a number of influences that we can monitor and use to come up with rough estimates of how long each one will last).**
- **These debt cycles are influenced by and influence other things, most importantly what I have identified as the four other big forces.**

To summarize the dynamic in a few sentences, what has timelessly and universally (i.e., throughout the millennia and across

countries) driven the Big Debt Cycle changes and has created the big debt and economic problems is the creation of unsustainably large amounts of debt assets and debt liabilities relative to the amounts of money, goods, services, and investment assets in existence. This always has led to big debt crises and runs on banks. By a run, I mean a turning-in of debt assets (that have no intrinsic value—i.e., their only value is to buy things) to banks in order to get real money, which the bank doesn't have enough of to meet the demand. Classically, when the holders of those financial assets actually try to convert them back into money and buy things and see that they can't get the buying power they believe they have stored in their debt assets, the run accelerates and feeds on itself, which causes great shifts in markets' values and wealth until debts are defaulted on, restructured, and/or monetized, reducing the debt burdens relative to incomes, and a new equilibrium is reached. The debts are almost always monetized, by which I mean that it is almost always the case that the central bank creates a lot of money and credit to make it easier to pay back the debt, which devalues the money and debt.

It's worth noting that at times when the debt/money force, the internal order force, and the external order force are late in their cycles (i.e., when there is a lot of debt and a lot of internal and external conflict), it is typically just before big conflicts and revolutionary changes to monetary orders, internal orders, and world orders. **Like a life cycle, the Big Cycle goes through stages. This late-cycle stage, which I call Stage 5, comes just before the depression and war stage that brings about the end of the Big Cycle. For reasons I will explain later, I believe that we are now in this late-cycle stage. It is a time of radical, typically unexpected changes that haven't happened in one's own lifetime but have happened many times throughout history.** At such times, it is extremely valuable to understand these past cases of big changes and consider whether they could happen again.

In *Principles for Dealing with the Changing World Order*, I examined a number of such cases. Since history can be an effective guide for understanding cause/effect relationships and bringing perspective on what is now happening and might happen, we can use these historical cases to think about what's logically likely to happen under the existing circumstances.

So, what are the existing circumstances? At this time, there is great overindebtedness in the US and in all other major countries at the same time as there are increasingly nationalistic and fragmented internal orders in these countries, increasingly contentious relationships between countries, adverse and expensive acts of nature, and amazing new technologies.

Looking at past cases with similar configurations of conditions can help us imagine otherwise unimaginable possible developments. For example, I repeatedly saw, and will show you in the next part of this book, that, when faced with similar conditions of excessive debt, countries (including the US) took the following extraordinary actions:

- **Exerting great pressure on countries to buy the country's debt (as the British did in the past)**
- **Selectively freezing debt and/or taking the assets of "enemy" countries (the way the US did to Japan in 1941 and Russia more recently)**
- **Defaulting on/restructuring debts by extending maturities and/or monetizing them to cut debt burdens (the way Germany did after Hitler came to power)**
- **Imposing confiscatory taxes and capital/foreign exchange controls to prevent assets from leaving the country**
- **Revaluing/managing government assets**
- **Creating new types of money**

To be clear, I am not saying that these sorts of things will happen, and I am hesitant to raise them as possibilities because my doing so could engender exaggerated fears, which could prompt inappropriate and exaggerated actions. However, like a good doctor speaking to a patient suffering from serious conditions, I feel that it would be an irresponsible omission of mine not to convey what past cases tell us about the possibilities that sometimes accompany these conditions.

2. The Internal Order and Disorder Cycle

Within countries, there are both short-term political swings lasting about six years on average, give or take three years, that over time add up to big shifts in domestic orders that last about 80 years, give or take 25 years. To reiterate, I don't mean that these time frames are fixed because they are highly variable in duration, but I do mean that they have always happened and I believe always will happen, with the durations driven by influences that we can monitor and use to come up with rough estimates of how long each one will last.[27] These are the cycles that exist within countries and lead to conflicts and changes in the system of governance, or what I'm calling "orders."

These fights for power work basically the same way in all systems of government, all types of organizations, and even within families because the approaches to fighting them are embedded in human nature.

So, how do they work?

It's simple: nothing lasts forever. That includes the orders built around established leaders and governance systems. **Changes in orders are driven by those who have the greatest power getting to determine what is done. Orders change when those who don't run the existing order acquire more power than those who do and want to change it.** Fights occur when both a) a powerful group wants to change the order and b) it is not clear which side has more power, so only a fight can determine it. Fights don't occur if a) there isn't a powerful group that wants to change the order and/or b) there is a powerful group that wants to change it and is so much stronger than the existing

[27] I explained these more completely in Chapter 5, "The Big Cycle of Internal Order and Disorder," of *Principles for Dealing with the Changing World Order.*

group that the changes will take place with little or no fighting.

In democracies, there is an election cycle that roughly coincides with the economic cycle because bad economic conditions typically lead to political changes. ● ***At the beginning of a new popularly chosen leader coming to power—e.g., in the first 100 days of a new presidency—there is a honeymoon period and great optimism. That is when dreams of great changes and great improvements exist and before realities and criticisms of how the new leader has shaped and handled them set in. As time passes, typically the big promises the leader made to get elected become difficult to deliver and bad things happen so disappointment sets in, critics and enemies become bolder, and support wanes. All this makes fighting to stay in power harder, which often leads to more extreme actions to make that happen.***

These dynamics are at play in the US at my time of writing this book in March 2025. How things go typically depends mostly on the economy, which depends mostly on where the market- and economy-shaping short-term and long-term debt/credit/money/economic cycles are, though exogenous events (like droughts, floods, and pandemics, and big international or domestic conflicts) can also matter.

All governance orders within countries change from one type to another—e.g., from democracies to autocracies and from autocracies to democracies—and each major type of order comes in varying flavors with some managed well and some managed poorly. I will now focus on what happens when democracies fail.

● ***When democracies fail, autocracies come in.***

In my studies of how orders have changed throughout history, I have seen how changes from republic-style representative democracies to autocracies typically happen. These changes are exemplified in how Julius Caesar in ancient Rome (from 49 to 44 BCE), Napoleon Bonaparte in France (from 1799 to 1815), Benito Mussolini in Italy (from 1922 to 1943), Adolf Hitler in Germany (from 1933 to 1945), a consortium of leaders in Japan (from 1931 to 1945), Francisco Franco in Spain (from 1936 to 1975), Recep Tayyip Erdogan in Turkey (from 2016 until now), and many other countries' leaders have shifted to become autocratic leaders. I also read about it in Plato's *Republic*, written around 375 BCE, which is still a valuable description of how democracies become autocracies.

In almost all cases, there are large gaps in wealth and values, bad and worsening conditions, and weak, fragmented leadership in the republic-style representative democracies. These democracies can't fix their problems because democracies intrinsically rely on compromise between opposing factions, and compromise breaks down during such times. So, instead of following the laws and the system of compromise, the opposing sides become willing to fight to win at all costs. Typically, this leads to intensifying populist conflicts between those of the hard right, those of the weak middle, and those of the hard left. Conflicts increase, especially during times of economic stress, which leads to fights for the power to control. How these fights for power take place are largely similar for logical reasons that I will explain.

Plato pointed out, and my study of history showed me, that leaders in democracies typically appeal to their constituents' desires for immediate benefits and temporary relief rather than doing the hard things that address deeper, systemic issues and make their nation strong over the long term. I have seen and read historical accounts of how leadership also typically becomes weak, decadent, and corrupt, especially after periods of great prosperity and few challenges. Plato argued that when democracies become weak and decadent and lose sight of justice and virtue, they pass their peaks and begin their declines. These periods are typically marked by growing corruption, inequality, and a failure of institutions to function effectively. When the system no longer satisfies the needs of a large percentage of the people, it loses legitimacy. Independently, and long before Plato observed this, this dynamic was recognized in China (as far back as 1046 BCE), where it is called "losing the mandate of heaven." It is when and why orders fail.

● ***In times of disorder, financial, political, and military power matter more than laws, and authoritarianism works better than weak, disorganized collectivism.***

Plato called the person who typically leads the revolutionary changes from democracy to autocracy a "demagogue." Demagogues manipulate public opinion, stir up emotions, and use extraordinary means to gain power. They typically rile up populist sentiment, promise easy solutions to complex problems (often at the expense of truth or rational discourse), and use propaganda and bullying to gain and increase power. They are generally of the well-educated class and gather around them others who are powerful. When they are of the political hard right, they and those who support them are typically rich and powerful nobles (in the old days) or capitalists (since the Industrial Revolution) who are allied in their belief and their self-interest that great leadership requires strong leadership and strong partnerships from the top, like strong companies that have to work well together to do great things. When demagogues are of the left, they typically get their support from the unprivileged masses. As these populist leaders, whether they are from the right or the left, gain power, they typically employ tactics such as propaganda, coercion, and the consolidation of power to undermine their enemies and the democratic institutions that support their enemies and/or that support the inefficient bureaucracies that are enabling the problems rather than fixing them. This typically leads to the eventual replacement of democracy with a more centralized, dictatorial form of government.

The approach a strong CEO uses in running a company can be difficult to distinguish from a demagogue's approach. In fact, it can be said that some strong CEOs govern as demagogues, so it should be expected that if they were running governments, they would run them the same way. In both cases, they are people who take control and make radical changes to make radical improvements, and the big questions are what will the controls on them be and how far will they take the autocracy. If looking at a company, one should see if there is strong oversight and a controlling force like a strong board and controls from effective regulators; for governments, such controls come from oversight functions and the separation of powers. The more uncontrolled they are, the more dictatorial the leaders are likely to become. A relevant good principle is ● ***power corrupts and absolute power corrupts absolutely***, a phrase attributed to historian and politician Lord Acton in 1887.

In the new order that emerges, financial and political power matters more than laws, and authoritarianism works better than weak, disorganized collectivism.

In most of these cases, the transfers from the democracies to autocracies take place within the rules of the democracy and become increasingly extreme over a few years, usually around three to five. These leaders typically make radical changes to the monetary, political, and geopolitical orders, and they typically become very nationalistic, militaristic, expansionist, and autocratic. As mentioned, examples include Caesar in Rome, Napoleon in France, Hitler in Germany, and Mussolini in Italy.

In ways that were more thoroughly explained in *Principles for Dealing with the Changing World Order* and that should be apparent to observers who are watching what is happening today, this is now taking place with big political shifts (mostly toward the hard right) for the same reasons that they happened in the past.

3. The International Order and Disorder Cycle (i.e., the Changing World Order)

How countries deal with each other is of paramount importance and it, too, is cyclical.

For the same reason that there are periods of order (i.e., periods of harmony, productivity, and prosperity) and periods of disorder (periods of great conflict, destruction, and depression), and big cyclical swings between these periods within countries, there are periods of order (periods of harmony, productivity, and prosperity) and periods of disorder (periods of great conflict, destruction, and depression) between countries. The periods of disorder take place when there are fights to determine which country or countries will have the power to set what type of order exists. However, because there has never been an effective global governance system, the world order is more prone to disorder and conflict.

As part of the Big Cycle, there have also been big swings between a) unilateralism in which there is fighting for one's self-interest, the strong winning over the weak, and the law of the jungle/the survival of the fittest and b) multilateralism in which there is striving for global harmony, peaceful coexistence, and egalitarianism.

Historically, the only times that multilateralism worked were after wars when people were sick of fighting and there was a dominant power to enforce how things should go. In fact, throughout most of history, brutal and destructive unilateralism was the norm and periods in which there was multilateralism in pursuit of harmony, peaceful coexistence, and the common good were extremely rare and never sustained. Consider that it wasn't until 1648, after the terrible Thirty Years' War, that there was an agreement in Europe (the Peace of Westphalia) establishing that countries have borders and that all countries would pledge to enforce those borders rather than to simply fight one another to get what the other had, which up until then was the norm (though these pledges not to fight have only worked sporadically).

Also consider that it wasn't until after World War I, when Woodrow Wilson, the idealistic academic president of Princeton University who became president of the newly powerful United States in 1913, naïvely aspired to have a world governance system that imitated the US governance system, the League of Nations. It didn't last and failed to prevent World War II, which was followed by the new American world order, which created multilateral organizations like the UN, the IMF, the World Bank, the World Health Organization, the World Trade Organization, the International Court of Justice, the World Intellectual Property Organization, etc. **These organizations aimed to foster global cooperation, economic stability, and collective problem-solving. The US, leveraging its unparalleled economic and military power, became the linchpin of this liberal international order, promoting democracy, free markets, and human rights.**

While not without its flaws, this system maintained a relative stability that has so far prevented another world war.

While we all have lived through a time when multilateralism's striving for harmony, peaceful coexistence, and egalitarianism was of course what we all wanted, **multilateralism is now fading into irrelevance and unilateralism is rising** for reasons that are understandable in the context of history. As a result, the powers of multilateral organizations are declining rapidly and transitioning into the hands of the major powers. I believe that realists must accept the fact that both the aspiration for and the existence of global cooperation are eroding as the pendulum is swinging toward self-interested unilateralism and survival of the fittest. It increasingly becomes the case that ● ***the strong prey on the weak.*** These developments are all typical of the stage of the Big Cycle that we are now in.

While this transition from multilateralism to unilateralism is at first shocking, it quickly becomes normalized. For example, it was only months before this writing that Donald Trump's statements concerning Greenland, Canada, and the Panama Canal would have been considered unimaginable (much like Russia's use of military force to defend what it saw as its interests by invading Ukraine if its interests weren't guaranteed peacefully).

At such times, ● ***alliances often change fast as circumstances change quickly and winning is more important than loyalties.***

To help us imagine the future, we should pay close attention to the lessons from history. Through most of history, without the existence of countries with borders, collections of people with common interests (i.e., tribes) fought to seize wealth from other tribes or defend their own. As those who won got richer and more civilized, they typically got more decadent and weaker and were eventually taken down by stronger barbarians, who were in turn brought down by subsequent generations learning to be stronger. For example, that is the story of the rise of the Roman Empire and its defeat by the Gauls as well as the rises and falls of most dynasties, and with them, the rises and declines of leadership approaches. These alternating ages of barbarianism and civility contributed to periods of war that took down the more advanced civilizations when the barbarians were strong and civilizations were weak.

● ***History has repeatedly shown us that civility when taken too far creates weak decadence that eventually loses to strong barbarism.***

The peaceful and productive, modern-day version of this is the "fighting" that happens in business with the invention of new and effective business ideas/weapons that fuel creative destruction. We love to watch these fights, which are like watching fights in the Roman Colosseum, or better yet we love being in them. Frankly, I love being in them, and I detest impractical idealism (while I love practical idealism above all else). But the destructive version of this same impulse leads to a lack of cooperation and to fighting in politics, geopolitics, dealing with acts of nature (particularly climate change), and new technologies, and I worry a lot about it.

4. Acts of Nature (Droughts, Floods, and Pandemics)

Throughout history, acts of nature have killed more people than wars and toppled more orders than the previously mentioned forces, and an objective view of the data shows that **droughts, floods, and pandemics are increasing and increasingly costly. While why this is happening is debated, that it is happening is not debatable. Nor is it debatable that humanity's polluting and disrupting of nature, higher human population density, closer contact across the world (brought about by more international travel), and closer contact with other species due to land development (leading to animal-human disease transmissions) are all causes.** We regularly see these happening in the news, most recently with the Los Angeles wildfires. **It is also almost certain that these problems will get worse.**

As with the other forces, this force is intertwined with the other big forces to shape what is happening. For example, the migration issues in developed countries (with immigration pressures resulting from changes in climate) and the living conditions issues in underdeveloped countries (where people are struggling to adapt to droughts, floods, and other changes) are obviously worsening due to damaging acts of nature increasing, and given that nearly all nations are facing debt issues, there isn't enough money to be spent on climate mitigation or adaptation.

5. Human Inventiveness, Most Importantly of New Technologies

There are great advances in technology, particularly in artificial intelligence, that will dramatically affect all thinking in all areas for good or for bad.

Throughout history, technological advances have raised living standards and life expectancies, have been used to generate economic and military power, and have been used in wars to create great destructions. They are closely tied to the other four forces. When technological advances are supported by good financial, economic, and social conditions, they advance more quickly than when those conditions are bad. But when their developments are supported by unsustainable credit growth, they tend to cause financial bubbles and busts. For example, the South Sea Bubble in 1720 when the Dutch Empire was beginning to decline, the Railway Mania in the 1830s and 1840s, the electricity and utilities bubbles (the "War of the Currents") in the 1870s and 1890s, and the dot-com bubble and telecoms crash of 1990-2001 are all relevant examples of cases where great advances in major life- and productivity-improving technologies led to debt bubbles and busts, as well as big beneficial changes.

That's enough of the Big Cycle for now—enough to help you better understand the dynamics you'll read about in Part III as you look at the events that have unfolded since our current Big Cycle began in 1945 with the end of World War II. It will also help you understand the perspective I take when I attempt to look into the future in Part IV. But before we move on, it is worth sharing one final principle, which has the biggest impact on how the challenges that arise during the Big Cycle are handled, namely:

- ***The biggest and most important force is how people deal with each other.***

If people deal with their problems and opportunities together rather than fight each other, they can get the best possible results. Unfortunately, while technology has evolved a lot, human nature hasn't changed much, so this is still probably beyond the capabilities of humankind.

PART III

LOOKING BACK

As explained, watching what is now happening is like watching a movie that I have seen many times before but set in different countries at different times because all of these Big Cycles transpire in analogous ways. In the previous chapters, I described how that classic movie typically transpires. In this part of the book, I will show you the most important cases of it transpiring over the last 180 years, which covers two Big Cycles in the US, China, Japan, and the wider world. That way, in just about 100 pages you will be able to get a comprehensive review of roughly the last two centuries, see these Big Cycles transpire, and compare them with the Big Cycle template I previously described in Parts I and II.

In Chapter 9, I will very briefly take you through the 80-year Big Cycle before 1945. Then, in the following chapters, I will show you more completely what has happened from the end of World War II until my writing of this book in March 2025. I conclude Part III with single chapters that cover the same periods and the Big Cycles for China and Japan. After you see all these cases and the Big Cycle changes to monetary, internal governance, and external governance orders, you will have seen the Big Cycle template play out repeatedly so you can join me in using that template to look at what we are now seeing happen and what may be ahead, which we will do in Part IV.

THE PAST IS PROLOGUE

Before I begin my descriptions of history, I will pass along two principles that I think will help you if you keep them in mind:

- ***If you want to see how and why big events have unfolded, be careful not to focus precisely on small events. People who try to see things up close and precisely typically miss the most important big things because they are preoccupied with looking for precision. So, when looking for the big things, pay attention to the big things.***
- ***Everything that happens does so for reasons that make it happen, so we should strive to understand and explain the cause/effect relationships that drive changes and create from them a logical template/model that both explains past changes and aligns with what is actually happening, and if there are discrepancies, we should work to understand and resolve them.***

What I am saying is that in the most fundamental ways, the previously described processes and cycles have happened in all countries over all of time, though none of them have been exactly the same. So, to see the processes and cycles and the template they provide us, you need to pay attention to the biggest and most important changes that have happened, keeping in mind the reasons for the big changes and the big differences.

To emphasize the importance of the big things, I describe them in a simplified way, so it's easy for some people to say, "That's not exactly right!" and be correct. I am intentionally conveying this template in a non-exact way in order to draw attention to the most important things.

As you read these descriptions of history, please remember that this timeless and universal template has been working in essentially the same way for thousands of years in all countries, driven by the same basic and logical cause/effect relationships that will be clear to you if you don't get too focused on the details.

THE PAST IS PROLOGUE

CHAPTER 9

FROM 1865 TO 1945 IN A TINY NUTSHELL

This very brief, eight-page chapter begins a series of chapters that explain how the Big Cycle has played out in the past. It describes the 80 years from 1865 to 1945. By reading it, you will gain a great perspective on what happened and how well my template explains it. In this chapter and those that follow, you will see the classic Big Debt Cycles and the classic domestic and international cycles that changed the monetary, internal political, and international geopolitical orders, starting and ending with wars. You will see how the wars were followed by periods of great inventiveness and productivity early in the post-war periods, leading to great debt-financed speculations, big increases in wealth differences, and then bubbles and busts that created new fights over wealth and power that led to new internal and international wars, produced new winners and losers, and created new orders and the next Big Cycles.

Starting in the US, 80 years before 1945 brings us back to the end of the US Civil War. That is a good time to begin this review of what happened, given that Big Cycles typically start after a war.

FROM 1865 TO 1918

The US Civil War was over the usual issues—i.e., who got to say what would happen related to economic, political, and social issues—e.g., slavery in this case. As is typical of such conflicts, it was very costly and financed by debt that grew too great to be paid back. The US government's debt went from 2% of GDP to 40% of GDP and interest payments alone ate up over half of the budget, not including the debts of the losing Confederate states, which defaulted after the war. At the start of the war, the dollar was linked to gold at a price of $20.67 per ounce. During the war, the US government defaulted on its promise to pay its debts by not letting holders of dollars turn them in for gold. It printed paper money that wasn't backed by gold (called greenbacks), so the value of money plunged, the value of gold in this new printed currency soared to roughly $250 per ounce, and the inflation rate in this new currency rose to 80% in 1865.

A timeless and universal principle to keep in mind is:

● ***During times when there is too much debt relative to the quantity of money that is needed to service debts, the need to either increase the amount of money that exists and/or cut the amount of debt there is leads governments to break their promises and do some combination of a) raising the amount of money and credit, b) reducing the amount of debt (e.g., by restructuring it), and/or c) preventing the free-market ownership and movement of the hard money (e.g., gold). At such times, there is a run away from bad money to good money that the government wants to stop. This often leads to prohibiting good money from being freely held and freely moved.***

That devaluation of money, defaults, and monetary stimulations reduced the debt burdens relative to incomes, and when the civil war ended, it was followed by a period of great productivity and leveraging up that created the next bubble and bust, which I will soon describe.

It was all classic.

From 1870 to 1914, with the war over and debt burdens reduced, the Second Industrial Revolution productivity miracle began.

Classically, debt- and equity-financed great technological investment booms led to great economic advances, big wealth and values gaps, and then bubbles and busts that led to great internal conflicts. At the same time, similar conditions around the world led to newly powerful countries challenging both the established powers and the established world order, which eventually led to war.

The technological advances that accompanied this great productivity boom were in railroads that opened up and linked the Western and Eastern US; steel production that was used to build bridges, skyscrapers, and railroads; electricity (e.g., Thomas Edison's invention of the light bulb and revolutionary improvements in electricity distribution); Alexander Graham Bell's invention of the telephone; oil production that fueled these advances; and the invention and broad distribution of the automobile. As always, big wealth gaps appeared as **the great new inventions that were turned into great new products made those who came up with them and commercialized them very rich. The rich were increasingly resented (they were then called "robber barons") for their business tactics and their lavishness (this era was called the Gilded Age), which led to classic left/right class conflicts developing in the early 20th century.**

During this time, there was no central bank, and the dollar was fixed to gold by commercial banks. As a result, when there were debt busts, there was no printing of money to ease them, so some of the busts were very big and long-lasting. For example, a big debt bust led to the Panic of 1873, which marked the start of the Long Depression and several national and regional panics that lasted until 1896. There were similar debt-bust panics in 1893 and 1907. Sticking to the gold standard became a major political issue that led presidential candidate William Jennings Bryan to famously declare, "You shall not crucify mankind upon a cross of gold." **Eventually, the severity of these booms and busts, especially the Panic of 1907, prompted the government to create the Federal Reserve central banking system in 1913 in order to better manage monetary policy for dealing with these boom/bust cycles.**

In the 1900 to 1914 period, all the classic late Big Cycle symptoms emerged. There was overindebtedness and internal political conflicts between rich business elites/capitalists of the right and the low-earning workers and socialist/anarchists on the left. Capitalism versus Marxism was the economic/ideological conflict in both the US and Europe, and many extremist followers on both sides were willing to fight to the death rather than compromise.

In the US, there was a move toward the left with progressive Theodore Roosevelt becoming president after President William McKinley was assassinated by an anarchist. Anarchists assassinated several world leaders around this time. In Europe, the rising power of Germany and its allies challenged the more established power of the UK and its allies (most importantly, France). In Asia, Japan went to war with and defeated Russia, making Japan the leading imperial power in the region. The world was much less connected in this era and foreign countries seemed much farther away, so what happened in one's own region was much more important than what happened on the other side of the world. But by the early 20th century, the world was starting to come closer together, and the United States increasingly became a world power.

Then in 1914, Archduke Franz Ferdinand from Austria-Hungary was assassinated and **World War I began.**

I won't go into the blow-by-blow of it, but I will say that it led to the world order changing in the classic big and important ways previously described, including the emergence of the United States as the world's richest and largest creditor nation. The US became the world's leading financial power because it played a big role in financing the war and manufacturing and selling things for the war, and it didn't have major spending or war destruction costs because it entered the war late. While the US profited from the war, the other winners—the UK and France—were weakened and indebted by it, and the war's losers were devastated by it. Germany became terribly indebted, and both Austria-Hungary and the Ottoman Empire were completely destroyed and broken up. Germany was in debt both to those who lent it money to finance the war (which it immediately defaulted on) and to the winners of the war through the imposition of reparations. Germany's economy was burdened by these obligations until Hitler defaulted on them in 1933.

In Russia, the World War I period brought conflict between the rich monarchy (who wanted to keep its wealth and privileges) and the poor masses (who were angry and wanted more). This led to civil war and the dramatic change in the domestic order to become Marxist-communist. Russia then created the Soviet Union in 1922 by taking over Ukraine, Belarus, and parts of central Asia. Japan, which had allied itself with the winners of the war, became the leading power in Asia.

At the end of the war in 1918, a big pandemic happened.

After all that, the winners got together to determine what the new world order would look like. In this case, it was clear that the world was becoming more interconnected due to advances in transportation and communications. World War I was the first truly global versus regional war, so naturally the question of how world governance should work arose for the first time. As described in the last chapter, President Wilson aspired to create an orderly world that would in some ways replicate a US style of representative governance. That led to the formation of the League of Nations, which failed at preventing the next major war. We still haven't figured out how world governance could advance beyond fighting to determine who gets what they want.

FROM 1918 TO 1945

Then, from 1918 until around 1930, in the West, there was another classic period of peace, great inventiveness, and productivity due to entrepreneurs coming up with great new products that were financed by debt and equity investments/speculations that produced big increases in wealth differences and bubbles.

More specifically, the 1920s became known as the Roaring '20s because of the rapid economic growth and technological

innovations that, early on, produced great productivity and productive lending in which incomes were more than large enough to fuel advances and provide good returns. The great inventions that were converted into mass production and greatly advanced the world included automobiles, airplanes, radios, televisions, talking movies, refrigerators, drugs and medications, and many other items. As always, what started as productive lending and investment grew into a big bubble. When it burst in 1929 with debt defaults and a stock market crash, it was followed by a depression. When the crash happened, the debt/money/economic force greatly impacted the domestic political and international geopolitical forces and changed the monetary, political, and geopolitical orders.

Seeing this debt/stock market/economic bust, what principle should jump to mind? The same one I mentioned a few pages ago:

● ***During times when there is too much debt relative to the quantity of money that is needed to service debts, the need to either increase the amount of money that exists and/or cut the amount of debt there is leads governments to break their promises and do some combination of a) raising the amount of money and credit, b) reducing the amount of debt (e.g., by restructuring it), and/or c) preventing the free-market ownership and movement of the hard money (e.g., gold). At such times, there is a run away from bad money to good money that the government wants to stop. This often leads to prohibiting good money from being freely held and freely moved.***

Through a series of actions, President Franklin D. Roosevelt outlawed the private ownership of gold, defaulted on the promise to allow holders of paper money to turn it in for gold, and changed the official exchange rate of $1 for 1/20.67th of an ounce of gold to $1 for 1/35th of an ounce—devaluing money by about 40%. He also imposed strict foreign exchange controls that prevented Americans from taking their money abroad and restricted Americans' abilities to have foreign bank accounts.

This wasn't the only significant change in monetary policy or radical approach to a debt issue that occurred during the period covered in this chapter. Many more countries went broke (i.e., defaulted on or significantly devalued their debts in the ways I've reviewed) between 1865 and 1945 than I can describe here, but I can give you a partial list:

- The US leaving the gold standard during and devaluing money after the civil war
- Several countries, in addition to the US, leaving the gold standard and devaluing money in the Great Depression
- Weimar Germany restructuring its Treaty of Versailles debts
- China and Russia repudiating past debts
- China abandoning the silver standard in favor of paper currency in 1935
- Greece debasing its coinage, causing it to be expelled from an early European currency union (1908)

As is classic, in the 1930s there were those of the hard right (fascists) and those of the hard left (communists) who fought in their own ways for control within their countries. In the 1920s and 1930s, several inefficiently run, conflict-ridden representative governments (Spain, Italy, Japan, and Germany) turned to demagogic leaders and autocracies of the right (fascism) to bring order to the chaos. Just as we are now seeing in the US and several other countries, this turn toward more rightist governments led to a squaring-off against leftists, and there was a marked move away from attempts at multilateralism, a breaking of agreements, and the rise of strongman unilateralism. For example, Hitler broke out of the Treaty of Versailles by choosing to default on the debt that Germany had agreed to pay. Germany and Japan both became more nationalistic and expansionistic, seizing territories in Europe, Africa, and Asia (more detail on Japan during this time can be found in Chapter 16). These ascending powers largely rose at the expense of the prior leading world powers—the UK, France, and the Netherlands—that had all become overextended and unable to defend their colonies around the world. As a principle, ● ***when countries are weak, opposing countries take advantage of their weaknesses to obtain gains***. All these dynamics set the stage for increased conflict between nations, eventually leading to World War II, after which there was the beginning of the next world order, which is the one we are now in the late stages of.

As previously explained and covered much more completely in *Principles for Dealing with the Changing World Order* and elsewhere in my writings, in the period leading up to World War II, nations around the world employed all the classic maneuvers and developments that precede military wars. These include economic warfare, freezing of financial assets, and military buildups. Once the war began (with Germany's attack on Poland in 1939 and Japan's attack on Pearl Harbor in 1941), all the usual war developments unfolded, such as using conventional weapons and the secret development and then usage of powerful new weapons that won the war. Then the unconditional surrenders of the losers led to meetings of the winners and new monetary, internal political, and external geopolitical orders. The spoils of war went to the winning Allies and the penalties of losing were handed out to the Axis powers as laid out in the Treaty of Versailles. As always, these decisions reshaped the world order and had implications for decades to come.

We will next look in greater detail at what happened after the end of World War II until my writing of this book in March 2025. While I will frame the evolution of the cycle in the context of the Big Debt Cycle, showing how the Big Debt Cycle went through its various monetary regimes, I will also show how it combined with the other four forces to shape the Overall Big Cycle.

CHAPTER 10

A BRIEF REVIEW OF THE BIG DEBT CYCLE FROM 1945 TO NOW

This chapter is a very brief overview of the Big Debt Cycle that began in 1945. In it, I explain how the cycle has transpired as a function of the earlier-described template based on mechanical cause/effect relationships. If you are interested in the relationships that drive the markets and the economy and how they have moved in the post-1945 period, this chapter will probably interest you. If you're not interested in such things, you may want to skip it and move on to Chapters 11–14, in which I walk through the monetary policy phases of our current Big Debt Cycle.

Because I was born in 1949 and have been a global macro investor for most of my life, I have both experienced and studied most of what I am going to describe, so I am going to share some personal descriptions to help enrich the picture and pass along some lessons that I learned from going through these experiences, especially through my painful mistakes, which stick in my mind much more than my winning decisions. As you watch the story of the last 80 years unfold, observe the almost in-unison swings in the five forces from one extreme to the other. Note that they were so extreme that each decade was more likely to be more opposite than similar to the decade before it, yet at the end of each, markets and investor psychology expected more of the same, so those were the key times to understand the fundamentals well and bet against the crowd on the unexpected developments that were logically probable.

Let's now look at what has happened since the end of World War II when the new world order began. While I will be putting what happened in the context of the Big Debt Cycle, you will see that the other four forces also swung greatly and interacted with the debt cycles to shape what happened. You will see all five forces flow like waves, sometimes small ones and sometimes big ones, sometimes reinforcing each other and sometimes negating each other, and sometimes with big ones coming together to create perfect storms. As for the debt cycle force, to repeat, the main thing to keep in mind is:

● ***Normally, when central banks want to be stimulative, they lower interest rates and/or create a lot more money and credit, which creates a lot more spending and debt. This stimulation both extends the expansion phase of the cycle and raises debt assets and liabilities relative to incomes, which makes the debt asset and debt liability balance more precarious. History shows us that when central banks can't lower interest rates anymore and want to be stimulative, they print money and buy debt, especially government debt. That gives debtors, most importantly governments, money and credit to prevent them from defaulting and allows them to continue to borrow in order to spend more than they are earning until the debt assets and liabilities become too great to balance, which is when a debt restructuring and/or debt monetization must occur.***

THE CURRENT BIG DEBT CYCLE IN BRIEF

Before I get into what happened, I'd like to show you the Big Debt Cycle in a few charts, starting in 1900 with the United States. Showing the whole period from then to the present will give you a greater perspective. I have focused on the US dollar debt charts because the world money/debt market has been a US dollar debt market during this Big Cycle, even though it is the case that other countries have also had their own Big Cycles.

In the US, between 1945 and 2024 there have been 12 complete short-term debt cycles and we are about two-thirds through the 13th). They averaged about six years in length and added up to one Big Debt Cycle that brought the central government's debt-to-income ratio up and worsened the central bank's balance sheet in the ways shown in the charts that follow. Said differently, the US and its credit markets have been in the leveraging-up phase of the long-term debt cycle, and they haven't yet entered the deleveraging part of the long-term debt cycle, though there have been some brief deleveragings along the way. These charts show the big picture. Most people overlook this big-picture arc because they are focused on the short-term wiggles, which don't even show up in these charts.

This first chart shows US private debt relative to GDP since 1900. The current Big Debt Cycle beginning in 1945 is obvious. Note the peak in private debt (as a percent of GDP) in 2008 and the slight decline since then. The decline happened as the US central government and US central bank stepped in in a big way to help the private sector, which is shown in the next two charts. As previously explained, this is typical of the beginning of the Big Cycle's late stage.

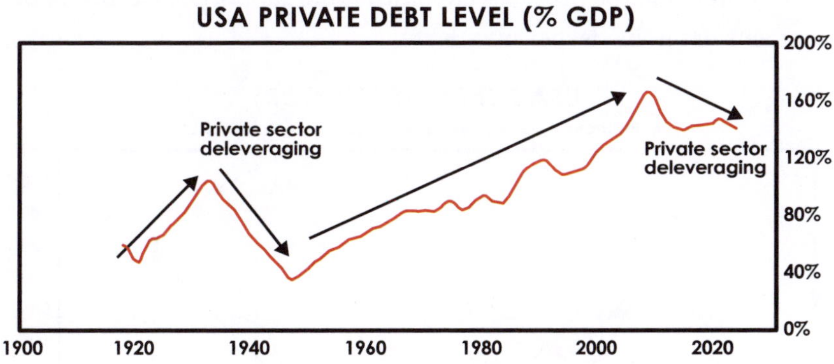

The next chart shows US government debt relative to GDP, with the dots signifying projections by the CBO in 10 and 20 years. As

shown, it is evolving in a Big Cycle way, is now at the highest level since 1946 (around the end of World War II), and is projected to be much higher in the future.

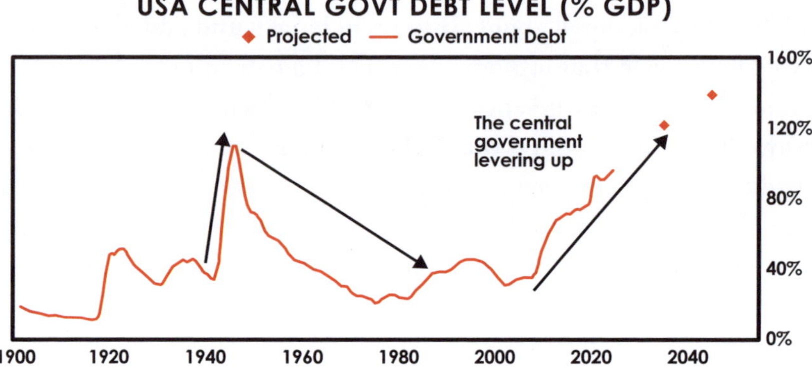

Now I will combine the last two charts into one chart so you can see how they relate to each other. You can see how private and public sector debt levels have been related: most importantly, how the government has tended to acquire more debt when the private sector is acquiring less. For example, you can see how the government's debt as a share of GDP has increased dramatically since 2008, while the private sector's debt-to-GDP has gone down. That is because in order to provide the private sector with more support, the central government has gone deeper into debt.

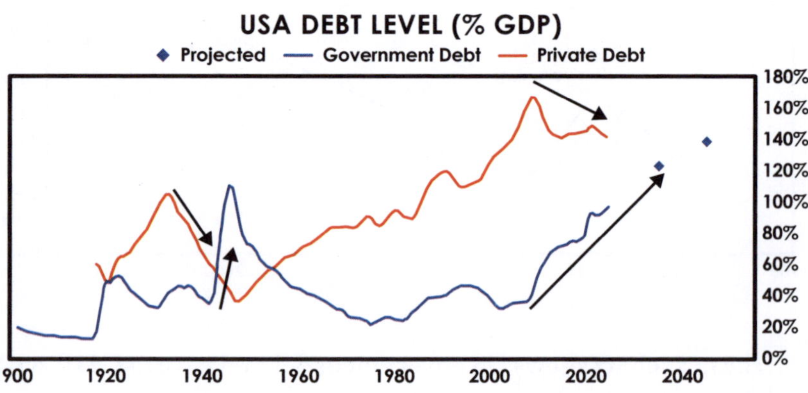

The next chart shows central government debt service as a percentage of government revenue. As shown, it is now at about 100% and it is projected to rise to about 150% in 15 years. To visualize what that means, imagine that the amount of money you had to pay in debt service each year was 50% greater than what you earned each year. It's unthinkable. So, what would one have to believe to think this would work? One would need to believe that the government will be able to 1) roll over the debt that is coming due, 2) sell the new debt that it needs to borrow to fund the deficit, and 3) have holders of the existing debt not sell it (i.e., that those who are lending to the government decide that they want to continue lending to the government because it's not too risky).

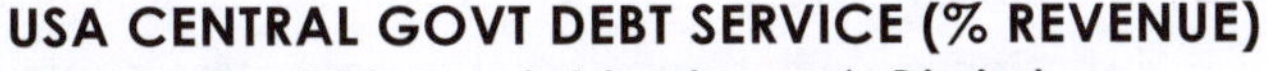

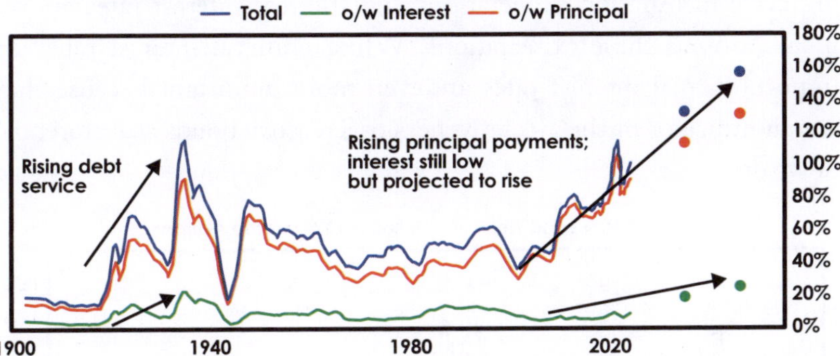

Because everything that happens does so because of reasons that make it happen, if one looks at and thinks about them, one can see indicators of the cause/effect relationships, watch them unfolding, and use them as indicators of what is likely to happen. To help paint the picture, I will pass along a few more of these indicators.

The next chart shows the 10-year Treasury bond rate and a three-year moving average of the inflation rate. ● ***The relationship between interest rates and the inflation rate is important because when interest rates are high relative to the inflation rate there is an incentive to save and earn the interest rate, and when interest rates are low relative to the inflation rate there is an incentive to borrow and hold assets that***

benefit from inflation and the growth that low interest rates foster.

The bond yield consists of two parts—the expected inflation rate and the expected real bond yield. Both are important in affecting the value of money and debt as a storehold of wealth and as a cost of funds. Note that on the upswing of this Big Cycle, all short-term cyclical swings in bond yields (i.e., those that took place in the cycles of recessions, stimulations, strong growth, and rising inflation periods that led to tightening money and credit that then led to recessions and falling bond yields) and all the cyclical declines in bond yields were higher than the ones before them until 1981. Also note that each of the short-term cyclical swings in bond yields from 1981 until 2020 was lower than the ones before until nominal interest rates nearly hit 0% and real interest rates were significantly negative. That reflects the big cycle in inflation expectations and the real interest rates' movements around these expectations. While nominal interest rates are important, real interest rates are even more important because they are an indicator of the attractiveness of Treasury bonds as a storehold of wealth.

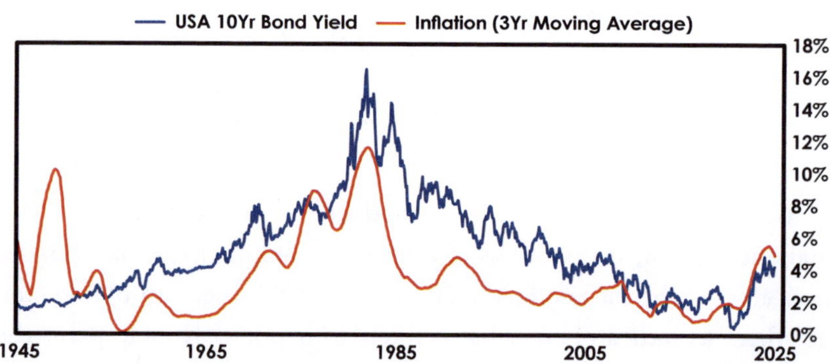

In the next chart, you can see the real 10-year bond yield. In the years after 1997, I am using the real yield on a 10-year Treasury inflation-protected bond. In my opinion, the real bond yield is the most important number to watch in the financial world. That is because it shows what real return you can certainly get on your wealth (i.e., free of inflation risk and default risk),[28] which is the most foundational rate for all capital markets. To earn more than that rate, one has to do so through cleverness. Even more importantly, **it is the single best indicator of whether it is better to be a borrower-debtor or a lender-creditor**—e.g., when real interest rates are low, it is much easier to borrow money and convert it into profits than when real interest rates are high. As such, it is a great tool for central banks to use to modulate credit and economic activity. As shown, the real bond yield has averaged about 2% over the last 100 years, which is a rate that is neither too low for borrower-debtors nor too high for lender-creditors. Periods of great differences from this 2% were times of excessively cheap or excessively expensive credit/debt that contributed greatly to the big swings in the Big Debt Cycle.

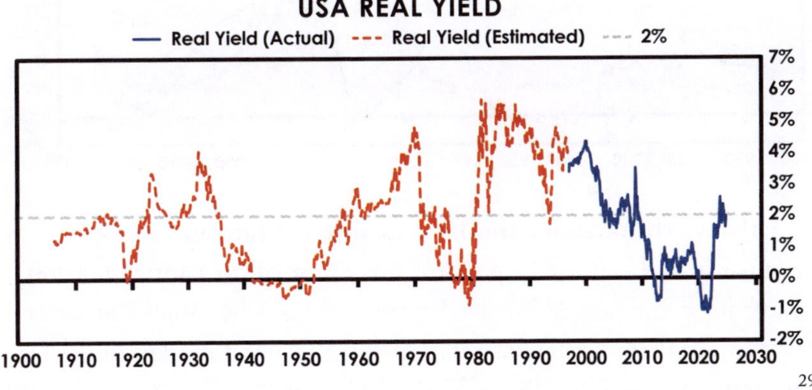

29

When looking at nominal bond yields relative to inflation-indexed bonds' real yields, I can also see the breakeven inflation rate, which is the inflation rate that the market is betting on. Since one can make money betting against that rate if one thinks inflation will be higher or lower than the market believes, and the markets are pretty tough to beat, one can use that inflation rate as a naïve but pretty good estimate

[28] If it were free of tax risk, it would be a perfect estimation of the real return you can certainly get.

[29] We show rough estimates of the real yield and breakeven inflation rate (using surveyed inflation expectations and recent inflation) for periods when those were unobservable because inflation-linked bond markets did not exist.

if one doesn't have a market-beating way to make a better estimate. Because I can see in the market pricing both the "discounted" (i.e., market-expected) inflation rate and the discounted real interest rate that I can lock in, I see the bond yield and price as consisting of these two important drivers. I am always watching them rather than just the Treasury bond interest rate, and I often think of and trade the two pieces—i.e., the inflation rate and the real interest rate—separately. Their historical estimated pricing is shown in the next chart.

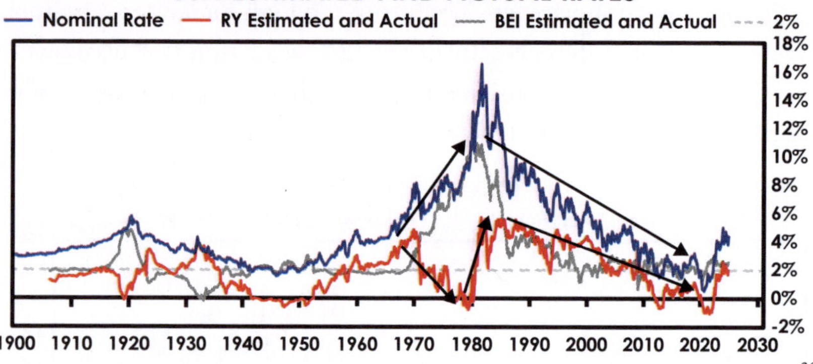

30

I always think about the 10-year interest rate and its two parts because it is the most important governor of all capital markets. I have been intimately involved with it for a long time. For several years, when there wasn't an inflation-indexed bond market in the US, I invested in non-US inflation-indexed bonds that I currency-hedged to create a synthetic equivalent of a US inflation-indexed bond. That came about because a great investor, David White of the Rockefeller Foundation, explained that he had to give away 5% a year and asked me what I thought was the surest way of investing to fund that, which prompted me to think about leveraging and hedging non-US inflation-indexed bonds. That led Bridgewater to become the largest global inflation-indexed bond manager in the world, and I was invited

30 We show rough estimates of the real yield and breakeven inflation rate (using surveyed inflation expectations and recent inflation) for periods when those were unobservable because inflation-linked bond markets did not exist.

to work on the design of the Treasury Inflation-Protected Security (TIPS) market with Larry Summers when he ran the US Treasury. Since then, we have had a real market showing real bond yields both to look at for guidance and to invest in, which has been foundational to all my investment thinking. I believe that the inflation-indexed bond markets that exist around the world are much underappreciated and underused relative to their potential. I watch them as indicators and use them as storeholds of wealth.

● ***The relationship between short-term rates and long-term rates (i.e., the yield curve) is very important because when short-term interest rates are high relative to long-term rates that indicates money is tight and encourages the holding and lending of cash, which becomes more attractive than borrowing and investing in other assets.*** Movements in the attractiveness of different assets affect the nominal interest rate yield curve—i.e., the difference between the 10-year nominal bond yield and the nominal short rate[31]—reflecting the changing tightness of money and the changing incentives to hold cash relative to bonds.[32] That is because a higher interest rate is normally required by lender-creditors to hold longer-term debt and because long-term interest rates higher than cash rates provide a reward/inducement for lending. When the central bank wants to slow credit growth and economic demand, it raises short-term rates relative to long-term rates, and when it wants to stimulate, it does the opposite. When both 1) real yields are high and 2) the yield curve is nearly flat or inverted, money and credit are tight, which is typically a good environment for lender-creditors and a bad environment for borrower-debtors, and when 3) real yields are low and 4) the yield curve is relatively positive, that is typically a good environment for borrower-debtors and a bad environment for lender-creditors. When central banks shift these things extremely, that leads to extremely good or extremely bad envi-

[31] I look at both the short rate minus the long rate and the short rate divided by the long rate as measures of the yield curve.

[32] The yield curve is typically upward-sloping, with short rates about 1% below long rates and about 70% of long rates.

ronments and a lot of volatility for both borrower-debtors and lender-creditors, which is also disruptive to economies and causes pain and inefficiencies.

I think the Fed should not be as extreme and volatile as it has been in its use of interest rates to influence monetary policy. If I were running monetary policy, my goal would be to keep the long-term real interest rate relatively stable at a rate that balances the needs of both borrower-debtors and lender-creditors and doesn't contribute to the making of debt bubbles and busts. That would mean seeking to have the real Treasury bond yield around 2%, varying that target by something like 1%, and targeting the yield curve slope so that a) the short-term rate is about 1% below the long-term rate and b) the short-term rate divided by the long-term rate is about 70%, give or take about 2% and about 50%, respectively.

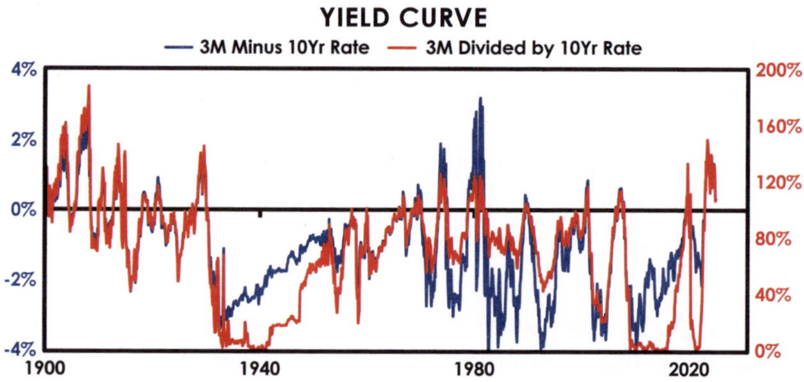

Setting policy in a way that produces fewer big and volatile swings in real interest rates and yield curves would lead to less volatility. In turn, that would lead to less harm to borrower-debtors and lender-creditors (and everything else they affect in the economy), and it would allow them to plan better. In other words, with a more consistent policy, borrower-debtors and lender-creditors would know that they could expect a reasonable real rate, which should be acceptable to both of them so they could plan their activities accordingly. With that relatively certain borrowing rate, lending and economic conditions would adapt to that reasonable interest rate. Also, setting that rate would help provide both borrower-debtors and lender-creditors more stable cost of funds and real returns, which would make for more stable capital markets and yield more stable economic conditions, which would improve efficiencies that would enhance the running of capital markets and the economy. But let's get back to exploring rates and how they impact the economy.

Thus far I have just shown you the big picture of the Treasury interest rate, but that isn't the rate that people, companies, and local governments borrow at. For that reason, watching credit spreads is helpful. Next is a chart that shows an average credit spread (for Baa corporate bonds) since 1920.

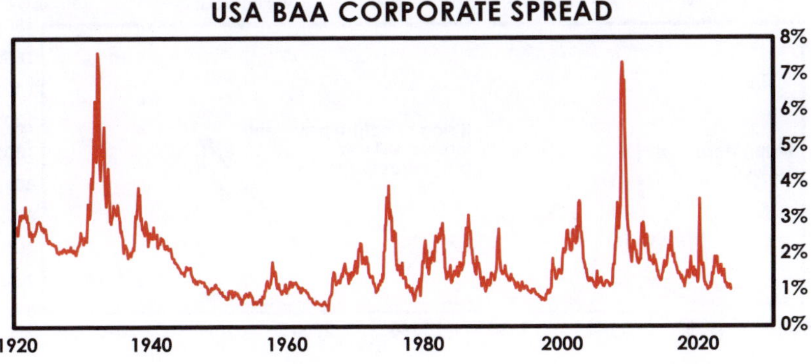

The amount of interest owed on a debt is determined by the amount borrowed and the interest rate, which, together with the amount of principal to be paid back, is the amount of debt service.

Let's revisit the chart shared earlier that shows total debt service (principal payments plus interest payments) for the US central government relative to its revenues and how much of that comes from principal payments and how much comes from interest payments. Note that debt service was roughly flat from 1950 to 2000; that is because government debt levels were roughly flat or falling slightly relative to revenue over that period, so principal payments were also roughly flat to slightly falling. Interest payments rose slightly from

1950 to 1990, as the average interest rate on government debt slowly rose, then fell from 1990 to roughly 2022, as the average interest rate on government debt slowly fell.

I am using dots to show how this is projected to grow, based on the CBO's estimates, for the next 10 and 20 years. The projected picture is very different from the recent past because the central government's debt levels are high and projected to rise fast and the interest rate on these high debts is also projected to rise, which will cause a big increase in government debt service relative to government revenue, which will produce a significant squeeze on spending unless there is a lot more borrowing, most likely financed by the central bank. Therein lies the problem.

USA CENTRAL GOVT DEBT SERVICE (% REVENUE)

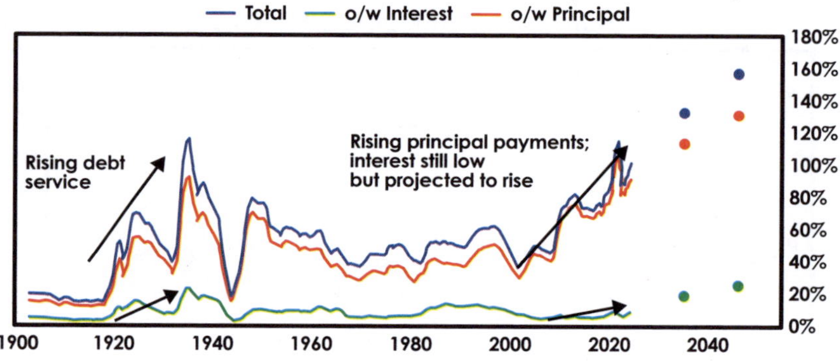

Who did the central government borrow the money from? It borrowed a lot of it from the central bank. It also borrowed a lot from commercial banks and, for about a third of it, from foreign investors. These commercial and foreign buyers/holders of US debt have had losses in it as interest rates have risen, they have more US debt as a percentage of their holdings than makes sense on a financial basis alone, and some of them are worried that the US government won't pay them the way it didn't pay Japan in the years before World War II so they have become sellers. In the case of the biggest foreign holders of US government bonds, they acquired so much because they wanted to store buying power in the most widely used and accepted currency of the greatest and most credible world power—said differently, because the dollar is the leading reserve currency of the leading world power. Looking ahead, given the increased supply of US government dollar debt that is coming (as shown in the last chart) relative to the desired demand for it, it is hard to imagine that these big buyers/holders are likely in the future to buy the huge amounts of US Treasuries that they did in the past, especially if any of the key underpinnings of that demand weaken—e.g., a) if the US government irresponsibly handles its debt and its domestic and foreign policy issues, b) if the US government threatens to sanction them by withholding payments on the debt, c) if the returns from holding the debt are bad, and/or d) if the US loses its economic and geopolitical prominence.

From 1980 until 2008, lowering interest rates was more than enough to keep debt service affordable even as debt levels kept rising. But **when rates nearly hit zero in 2008, as they did in the post-1933 period, private market demand for the bonds was inadequate to meet the supply so the central bank stepped in to print money and buy the bonds, which put downward pressure on longer-term rates. It happened in two major waves—one in response to the 1929-33 debt-crisis-induced Great Depression when interest rates hit 0% in the post-1933 period, and again in response to the 2008 debt-crisis-induced Great Recession when interest rates hit 0%.** (You can see this in the following chart where the small circles indicate the beginning of money printing and interest rates hitting zero.) I wouldn't have known that, and Bridgewater wouldn't have been successful in this period, if we hadn't studied the time frame shown in this chart. This is also what led to my first discovery of how the Big Debt Cycle works.

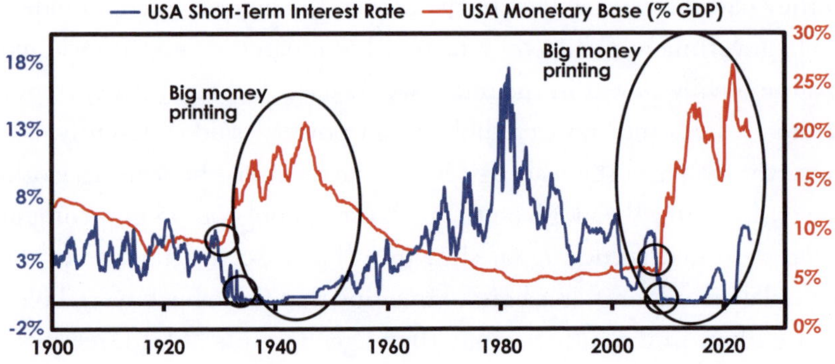

As for the central bank, the Federal Reserve and other central banks' debt assets provide lower returns than the costs required to service their liabilities, so the modest rise in the interest rate that has occurred in this most recent tightening has caused the Fed to take modest operating losses (blue line in the next chart). If the bonds on the Fed balance sheet were marked to market, the Fed's losses would be around $700 billion, or 2.5% of GDP (red line). This sounds significant but it is relatively minor compared to the central bank's capacity to obtain funding. However, it is a red flag and would become a major problem if there was a big selling of US debt, which is what typically happens when that debt is perceived to be a risky asset. As previously explained, for countries like the United States that have the ability to print their own money, that would lead to either a) a big and intolerable rise in nominal and real interest rates, which would contract credit and lead to a severe economic contraction, or b) a big central bank printing of money and buying of debt and providing of credit, which would lead to the devaluation of debt and money. The big central bank losses and bad conditions would also increase the likelihood that the central bank's independence would be called into question. For those countries that have debt denominated in a reserve currency that is not their own, conditions would be much worse.

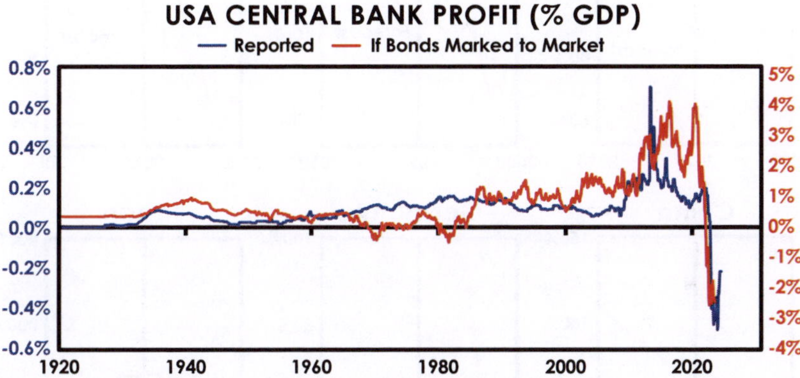

DEBT BURDENS WILL INCREASE GLOBALLY

In this overview chapter, I have focused on the debt picture for the US. You can see in the charts that follow that this is not only a US issue. Debt burdens are projected to grow substantially across the developed world over the coming decades. It is crucial to understand how these dynamics will play out in order to understand how to make policy and how to trade in markets in the years ahead.

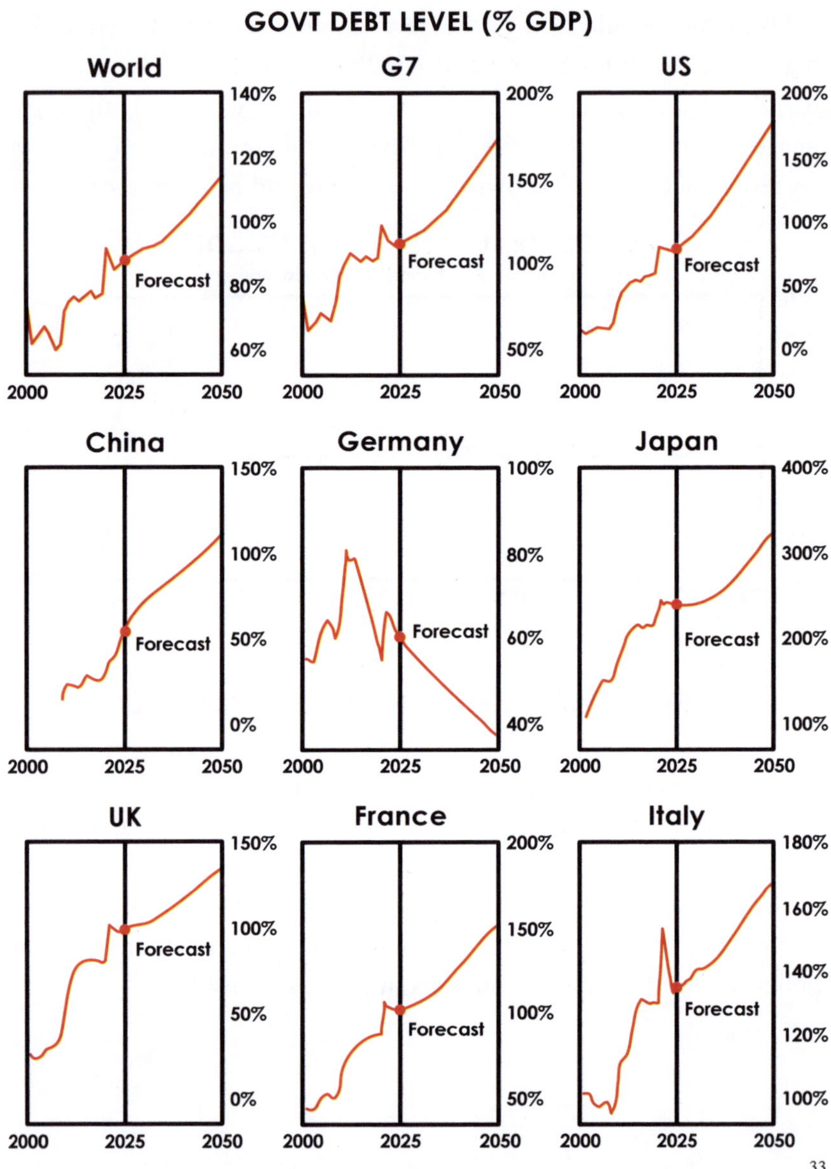

[33]

In the rest of Part III, I am going to take you through the complete Big Debt Cycle for the US since 1945 because the US dollar was and

[33] Source: Bloomberg Economics. Note: Debt is shown as a proportion of gross domestic product.

still is the dominant reserve currency that most transactions were and still are denominated in and most savings are in, before diving into China's and Japan's Big Debt Cycles in Chapters 15 and 16. To me, the US over the last 80 years, Japan after its bubble bursting, and the other cases I have looked at are all classic Big Debt Cycles that are operating in the previously described ways that are important for investors and policy makers in all countries to understand. This is especially true now that some of them are encountering the late stages of Big Debt Cycles in their own countries and they will likely experience serious consequences from their own Big Debt Cycles, as well as the US's Big Debt Cycle and its implications for US dollar assets and liabilities.

We will now look at what has happened through the phases of the long-term debt cycle. To make clear how events have transpired relative to the previously explained debt/credit template, I will divide the post-1945 period into four phases signifying the four main monetary regimes that have driven the debt/credit dynamic since 1945. We will begin in 1945 because that is when the new monetary, geopolitical, and, in many cases, domestic political orders began.

CHAPTER 11

1945 TO 1971—A LINKED (I.E., HARD) MONETARY SYSTEM

I urge you to read this and the following three chapters, which will take you from the beginning of the current monetary, domestic, and international orders in 1945 up to now. I believe we are near the end of these orders and our current Big Cycle. I would be surprised if, after reading these chapters, the rhymes of history don't ring loudly in your ears and you don't feel that you have a good sense of the rhythms of the Big Cycle. With that, we will then be prepared to look ahead.

As explained, World War II ended the prior world order and caused the transition to the world order that we are now in. As always, the biggest winners of the war—in this case, the US, the UK, and their allies, as well as the Soviet Union and its allies—determined the rules of the new world order including the new world monetary system, though right from the start there was a split between the US and its allies and the Soviet Union and its allies. In 1944, the US, the UK, and their allies created what is called the Bretton Woods system (because it was created in Bretton Woods, New Hampshire). This type of system was a gold-linked (i.e., hard) monetary system. I call this type of monetary system Monetary Policy 0 to signify that it is the first type in a sequence of monetary systems/

approaches to deal with the Big Debt Cycle's evolving conditions.

A Monetary Policy 0 system looks like most prior monetary systems that existed throughout the millennia with "paper" money being linked to the real money (gold), which was held in banks (in this case, central banks). In an MP0 system, currency can be used to buy a designated hard asset (most often gold) at a set price, and because of that ability, the supply of the currency is supposedly limited. That is because if the supply of the currency becomes too large, its price should fall. This is because if there is too much currency relative to the item the currency is backed by (e.g., gold), people will exchange their money for that item, worsening the imbalance between the amount of money and the amount of the hard asset the money is backed by. The fear of this doom loop is intended to limit money creation and therefore support the value of the money. The problem with this system is that it has never worked in the long term because, even with the link to a hard asset, governments still create more money and allow more debt growth than they should, which leads to many more claims on the asset (e.g., gold) than there is money that can be converted into it at the specified price. The consequences of this are almost always a "run on the bank," with people rushing to make the conversion, and the breaking of the promise to deliver the hard asset.

The gold-linked MP0 system set up at Bretton Woods lasted until 1971, during which time dollars, which were then considered like checks with no intrinsic value, were exchangeable for gold, which was considered the real money, at a fixed exchange rate. Other currencies were exchangeable for dollars at agreed-upon and changeable rates. During this 27-year period, there were five short-term debt/economic cycles, which were wiggles around an uptrend in debt relative to incomes during this period. I will now describe how this period unfolded, including what happened with all five of the big forces.

Like all prior monetary systems, the system set up at Bretton Woods had its own particular characteristics. In this case, because the US had about two-thirds of the world's gold, which was held by the

US Treasury, the dollar became the world's reserve currency. Other countries had their own currencies, so to get gold from the US central bank, they had to buy dollars and then use those dollars to buy the gold. Only countries' central banks were allowed to buy gold; individuals were prohibited from buying gold with their paper money. In fact, in the US and most other countries, it was illegal for citizens to own gold because governments wanted people to save in debt assets in order to build the credit system and they didn't want debt assets to have to compete with gold.

This system was created for the United States and the countries that wanted to join it, and the US wanted to let others in. The UK became a subordinate power in this new world order because its financial and other powers were weakened by the war, while the United States became much richer because it entered the war late. The Soviet Union opted out of Bretton Woods agreement and had its own monetary system and ways of doing things that were independent of the US-dominated system.

The main geopolitical competition was between the US (which was a capitalist democracy) and the Soviet Union (which was a communist autocracy). The United States was much stronger economically and militarily than the Soviet Union, so it was able to provide financial support programs like the Marshall Plan to help rebuild its allies, especially in Europe. These programs were done to enhance alliances, which was especially important at the time of the Cold War. Because the US was rich, had the world's reserve currency, and accounted for about half of world GDP, it could easily afford to provide this support to allies. Having the world's reserve currency, which other countries wanted to save in, gave it great buying power that it eventually abused.

At that time, China, which was allied with the winning powers against the Japanese in the war, was a destroyed and powerless country having suffered what it calls the "Century of Humiliation," in which foreign powers took over different parts of China, conditions deteriorated terribly, and the whole system of government

collapsed. This roughly 100-year period began in 1839 and ended with the end of World War II. During this period, Japan took over Taiwan in 1895, which was given back to China by the winning powers at the end of the war. **Between 1945 and 1949, China had its version of a classic civil war between the hard-right Kuomintang party and the hard-left Chinese Communist Party. That led to the communists driving the Kuomintang out to Taiwan, Chinese communists siding with Russian communists, and the United States alienating China.** At that time, both parties to the civil war agreed that there was only one China and that Taiwan was a part of it, and the argument was over who would control both. Arguments about this issue have festered for a long time and are intensifying, which is especially important because of the powers the US and China possess and because Taiwan is the center of chip production, which today is even more important than oil production was in the last cycle.

In that early post-war period, inventive people, especially American scientists and entrepreneurs who were financed by the capitalists with government support, continued to come up with great new technologies that would eventually have huge effects. For example, in 1956 "artificial intelligence" was invented, and in 1957 the first satellite was launched. In the mid-1950s the technical foundations of the internet were developed. Of course, there were too many inventions that had big economic, political, geopolitical, and environmental effects for me to delve into here.

Because the UK was heavily indebted and in fast relative decline economically and militarily, it rapidly and persistently had its bonds and money devalued in the classic ways that were described earlier and that are important to keep in mind when looking at the US now. Immediately after the war, the UK had a lot of debt, and it had colonies and military bases in over 40 countries that it couldn't afford to maintain. I won't repeat all the steps, but I will point out that this overextended British Empire had debt problems that led to a managed 30% devaluation of its currency in 1949, which was followed by a series of devaluations in the years that followed, all to relieve its debt burdens at great cost to its debt holders. The decline in the value of the currency and debt was classic. There were debt payment problems and the inevitable losses of the controlled foreign territories that made it obvious to the world that the UK was declining, which reinforced the desire not to hold its debt and currency and led to their further declines. Most obviously, when Egypt took over the Suez Canal in 1956, loyal holders of UK bonds sold them. In 1967, another financial crisis led to another major devaluation and abandonment of its debt/money being held as a storehold of wealth, and in 1976 the UK's financial condition got so bad that it had to go to the IMF for financial help. The decline of the British pound and the British Empire is the most recent classic case study of the decline of a reserve currency and is described at length in my book *Principles for Dealing with the Changing World Order.*

In the early 1960s, the US short-term money and credit cycle was expansionary, which was great for the US markets and economy until 1965-66 when inflation rose to 3.8% and the Fed tightened monetary policy, inverting the yield curve for the first time since 1929. These events produced, in 1968, what would be the peak inflation-adjusted price in the S&P 500 for the next 25 years, with that long period of bad performance due to the Big Cycle influences I described earlier in this study. It also led to a recession in 1969-70. That long period of terrible stock and bond market performance and terrific gold and other inflation-hedge asset performance was primarily due to the needed creation and devaluation of money to deal with the debts (i.e., the debtors' obligations to deliver money) being too large relative to the actual amount of real money in existence. That paradigm taught me a lot about the need to be able to make money in all types of market environments and the skills required to do it. It also puts me today in a very different mindset from most investors who haven't been through something like that and have views based just on their experiences and so think that being long only in equity-like assets and ignoring the Big Cycles is the best way to invest.

In the 1960s, there were also some nail-biting political and

geopolitical conflicts that made a big impression on me, most notably when the Cuban Missile Crisis in 1962 brought the world's two most powerful countries to the brink of nuclear war. I was 13 at the time and vividly remember watching John F. Kennedy's address to the country explaining the situation and wondering if there would be nuclear war or which country would back down. I was sure the potential for geopolitical catastrophe would have a big impact on the markets, but over the next few days the stock market didn't behave nearly as badly as I thought it would have. What happened was that the Soviet Union pulled its missiles that were aimed at the US out of Cuba, and the United States pulled its missiles that were aimed at the Soviet Union out of Turkey. This allowed both countries to claim victory without telling their people about the concessions they made.

This episode also gave me my first lesson about how brinkmanship diplomacy really works and how markets behave during such dramas (when the damages that would result from the conflict are unacceptably high). In November 1963, JFK was assassinated, which also had only a brief passing effect on the markets and economy; then came the civil rights movement, and big spending on "guns" (the Vietnam War) and "butter" (US domestic social programs). The fact that these and numerous other seemingly earthshaking events didn't have much effect on markets helped me to realize why they didn't affect the markets more and to sort out what really matters and doesn't matter to market prices and the economy. While I won't delve into all that matters, I will tell you that what matters to markets is the money that investments earn, so big political events like threats of war don't matter much until they start to affect those cash flows. That is why, from an investment perspective, I don't worry about the headline-grabbing events of today, and I suggest that you do the same. Also, I learned that most of these global threats turn out to sound more threatening than they actually are because most countries' leaders will step back from the brink rather than choose to go over it. However, to be clear, there are times when international conflicts have impacts, such as on supply chains and the value of currencies, and there are rare occasions when leaders don't step back and things do blow up, so that these conflicts become very consequential. Because I view protecting myself against these events as being like buying insurance to be protected against an improbable, unacceptable loss, I look for ways to be insured against them even though I don't expect them to happen.

In the 1960s, there was also a big geopolitical swing in the relationship between China and the Soviet Union. They changed from being "friendly" countries to becoming "enemy" countries, which led to a corresponding big geopolitical swing between China and the United States from being "enemies" to being "friends." That led to Henry Kissinger's secret visit to China in 1971 and then President Nixon's visit in early 1972, which set the stage for China's opening up after Mao Zedong died in 1976. These developments, like the earlier-mentioned technology developments, were like small seeds of change being planted that grew into enormous changes that would affect all five forces everywhere. They mattered a lot even though they didn't seem to matter much at the time.

During this 1945-71 period, the US overspent and financed that overspending by borrowing, especially in the 1960s on the Vietnam War and the "war on poverty," so its paper-money promises to give real money (gold) far exceeded what it had in its central bank. That mattered a lot, though it didn't seem to at the time because the bad finances grew slowly until they led to the blowup. You see, early in the 1950s and 1960s, most countries were happy to accept these "paper" dollars in return for their goods and services because they wanted to accumulate dollars as savings. As a result, the US could overspend liberally. Also over those years, other countries, especially Germany and Japan, gradually recovered from their big losses from the war and became competitive economically, which led the US balance of payments to worsen. **In the late 1960s, one could see the US and the UK having runs on their central banks because holders of paper money turned it in to get the real money (gold), so the US central bank's reserves of gold steadily declined.**

You might recall the following principle: ● ***During times when***

there is too much debt relative to the quantity of money that is needed to service debts, the need to either increase the amount of money that exists and/or cut the amount of debt there is leads governments to break their promises and do some combination of a) raising the amount of money and credit, b) reducing the amount of debt (e.g., by restructuring it), and/or c) preventing the free-market ownership and movement of the hard money (e.g., gold). At such times, there is a run away from bad money to good money that the government wants to stop. This often leads to prohibiting good money from being freely held and freely move.

Seeing the US central bank running out of real money (gold), Charles de Gaulle, the French president at the time, openly called for a reform of the monetary system in 1965. Other holders of paper dollars caught on and the run accelerated and the US spending and deficits didn't slow down, so the run on the US central bank ended like most such central bank runs end. For previously described reasons, the selling of the debt drove interest rates up and the currency down at the same time as the economy weakened. **The US central bank did not have enough real money (gold) in the bank to meet its obligations to exchange it for the paper money at the promised price.**

On the night of Sunday, August 15, 1971, President Nixon went on television and announced that the United States was no longer going to allow dollar holders to turn their dollars in for gold. That ended the monetary system, and money, as we knew it. It immediately devalued money, raised inflation, and made it much easier to pay debts for the reasons I previously explained. I was clerking on the floor of the New York Stock Exchange at the time. It was a summer job between college and business school. I figured that ending the monetary system as we knew it and preventing people from getting the real money was a big, bad deal, so I expected the stock market to be down a lot. Instead, that Monday was the best day for the market that year—stocks were up more than 3%.

Because I had never experienced a currency devaluation before, I was ignorant about how they work. That led me to study history, which led me to find out that, in 1933, President Roosevelt had done the exact same thing (default on the promise to allow people with dollars to exchange them for gold at the promised exchange rate) for the exact same reason (the US had created more promises for gold than it had in gold, and it was running out of gold and money during a bank run), which had the exact same effect (the devaluation, big market rallies in stocks and gold). The only real difference from Nixon was that Roosevelt made the announcement on the radio, not television, which wasn't common yet.

In both cases, de-linking the currency meant the central government didn't have to deliver the real money, and it freed central bankers to create a lot of money and credit. This made it easier to handle the debts and stimulate the economy, leading equity, gold, and commodity prices to rise and the economy to pick up. That's when I learned that when central banks create a lot of money and credit, the value of money and credit goes down and the price of most things goes up. I realized that these moves were classic cases of "hard" currency (gold-linked) exchange rate systems breaking down, leading to the devaluations of the money and debt. Once I saw this happen in these two cases, I saw that it happened throughout history in almost all such cases, and I learned the principle that ● ***when there is a big debt problem that is intolerably painful, central banks will "print money" and distribute it to make it easier for debtors to pay their debts, which will devalue the money and debt relative to other assets.*** That helped me make a lot of money and avoid a lot of painful losses.

CHAPTER 12

1971 TO 2008—A FIAT MONEY, INTEREST-RATE-DRIVEN MONETARY POLICY

The August 1971 breakdown of the monetary system changed the value of money and how the system worked—i.e., the gold-linked system was replaced by a fiat monetary system in which central banks stimulated and restrained debt/credit/money growth by changing interest rates. I call this type of monetary system (i.e., one in which fiat currencies are managed via interest rate changes) Monetary Policy 1 (MP1).[34] I make these distinctions between types of monetary policy because they work very differently, and it is important to understand these differences. The most important differences between MP0 and MP1 are that in an MP1 monetary system a) the amount of money and credit provided by lender-creditors to borrower-debtors is primarily driven by the cost of money (i.e., interest rates) and b) it is not restrained by the link to hard currency (e.g., to gold). Because the amount of money and credit was unrestrained and because the world's central banker (the Fed) wanted to accommodate

[34] There are two other types of monetary policy that take place at the later stages of the long-term debt cycle, which I call Monetary Policy 2 (MP2) and Monetary Policy 3 (MP3). I will touch on them later in this study. If you are interested in learning more about them, I describe them in my book *Principles for Navigating Big Debt Crises*, which you can buy in print or find in PDF form at economicprinciples.org.

what happened, this change in policy led to a very classic combination of economic stagnation and inflation, which was called stagflation.

FROM 1971 TO 1982: STAGFLATION AND TIGHTENING AND THE MOVE FROM THE POLITICAL LEFT TO THE POLITICAL RIGHT

The decade from 1971 to 1982 provides a good example of how cycles in the five big forces interrelate to create the Overall Big Cycle. In this period, the Big Debt Cycle was influenced by, and helped drive, big cycles in politics and global conflict.

We'll start by looking at the debt/money/economic cycle. When President Nixon ended the MP0 monetary system and transitioned to the MP1 system, the central bank and the central government took advantage of having fewer constraints and printed money. From 1971 until the end of 1981, the Federal Reserve increased the supply of money by 100%, and the broader measures of money supply that included some bank accounts and cash instruments (called M2) increased by 180%. The prices of goods and services (measured in CPI) went up by about 140%; stocks went up by around 30%, and the price of gold increased about 10x. Stock prices fell by 45% in real terms. Of course, debtors benefited because they could pay their debts with much more available and much cheaper dollars and creditors suffered because the value of the money they were promised dwindled. In that 10-year period, a holder of 10-year Treasury bonds lost around 40% in inflation-adjusted terms, and holders of Baa corporate bonds had slightly negative returns in inflation-adjusted terms. **In other words, starting in 1971 and through the next few years, the Fed dealt with the debt crisis by creating a lot more money and credit, which created great debt relief for debtors and great losses of buying power for creditors, which encouraged borrowing and discouraged lending.** This decade of debt monetization developments made a big impression on me and taught me some invaluable lessons about the need and ability to make money in all kinds of markets. I think that current investors who have only lived in an environment in which equity-like assets have had positive real returns approach investing by only looking to buy equity-like investments to provide great real returns, and that is a mistake.

The most important difference between today's dollars and dollars in the 1945-71 period is that today's money is and has been fiat money since 1971. That means that the Fed (which is essentially the world's central banker because the US dollar is the world's dominant medium of exchange and storehold of wealth) can more freely create money and credit than in the past. Other central banks can do the same, so this affects all mediums of exchange and storeholds of wealth. For previously explained reasons, doing that is the easiest and subtlest way for governments to alleviate debt burdens and confiscate wealth. By the way, fiat monetary systems have existed throughout history, so studying those from the past provides invaluable lessons on how they work that can provide clues for how the one we are in will go as the debt cycle progresses.

While the gold-dollar-based system broke down in 1971, the US remained the dominant world power economically, militarily, and in most other respects, and most world trade and capital transactions were done in dollars, so the dollar remained the world's leading currency that governments, companies, and people wanted to save in, despite the fact that it was such a terrible storehold of wealth in the 1970s.

In the 1971-82 period, it paid to be a borrower-debtor because the big devaluation that started in August 1971 had immediate inflationary effects. At the same time, geopolitical conflicts played a role in shaping the environment.

More specifically, the big easing of monetary policy in 1971 after the de-linking from gold got inflation going. Simultaneously, in 1973, the British Empire and colonialism were breaking down, so there was a big geopolitical shift in the Middle East. With more money chasing limited supply—in this case, of oil—Middle Eastern countries took advantage to create the first "oil shock" that caused

more inflation. It was mostly a fight about money, as it normally is. More specifically, at that time, the colonized countries of the Middle East (and elsewhere) were overthrowing the colonialists that controlled them and nationalizing the colonialist claims on the assets of the colonized. Saudi Arabia, Iran, Iraq, and Libya nationalized most of the oil properties that were owned by the "Seven Sisters" (the seven major oil companies), and in October 1973, war broke out between the Arabs and Israelis. These events led to oil prices rising a lot.

The debt/credit/money/economic cycle played out differently for different countries depending on whether they benefited or suffered from this change in prices. Commodity producers, especially in emerging countries, boomed and experienced debt-financed bubbles while the US created more money and credit to finance its debts.

Naturally, dollars from Europe, the US, and elsewhere began to be lent to commodity-producing emerging economies, creating their debt bubbles. In the early 1970s, a lot of dollars were held in other countries, especially in European countries, so there was the growth of what was called the Eurodollar market. Those dollars had to be lent out. Because there was high inflation in the world due to the previously described currency devaluations, commodity prices were high, so it seemed good to lend to commodity-producing emerging countries. That fueled a boom that created a bubble in those countries, with the lender-creditors to them being US, European, and some Japanese banks. All this investment into commodity extraction eventually contributed to price declines, especially when money became tight in the 1980s.

Early in this period, in 1971-74, money was easy, inflation and economic activity rose, and the oil-exporting countries embargoed oil, which sent oil prices and inflation higher. So, from the end of 1973 to 1974, the Fed tightened money and credit, raising interest rates and inverting the yield curve, which sent the markets and the economy into severe declines. That led to a recession. That completed that short-term debt cycle, and as always, a new cycle began.

This next cycle played out in the same way. The easy money and credit that followed the recession caused economic activity and inflation to pick up, and there was a second oil price shock that was caused by internal political and international geopolitical conflicts. In Iran, the shah's domestic order was overthrown, which led to the US embassy being seized and American hostages being held by those who took power. That began the conflict with Iran that remains with us. This development was both inflationary and humiliating for the United States. The following chart shows the average interest rate (the average of the 90-day Treasury bill rate and the 10-year Treasury bond rate) and the CPI inflation rate from 1971 through 1981. As you can see, in the 1970s interest rates rose more slowly than inflation rates, so real interest rates were low until they were negative (as low as -4% at certain points, compared to the average up to that point of 2%). These artificially low interest rates relative to inflation rates were great for borrower-debtors and terrible for lender-creditors, which encouraged borrowing and buying, which drove inflation rates up and interest rates followed, until inflation became so bad that changes had to be made, which led to the reverse. You can clearly see the two short-term debt cycles reflected in this chart. The vertical lines in these charts represent January 1980.

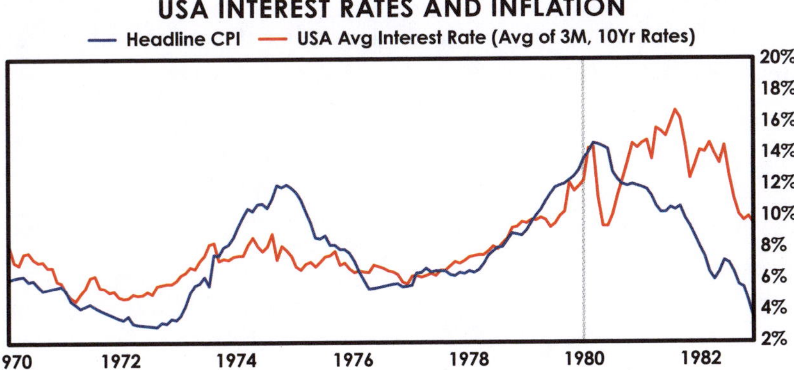

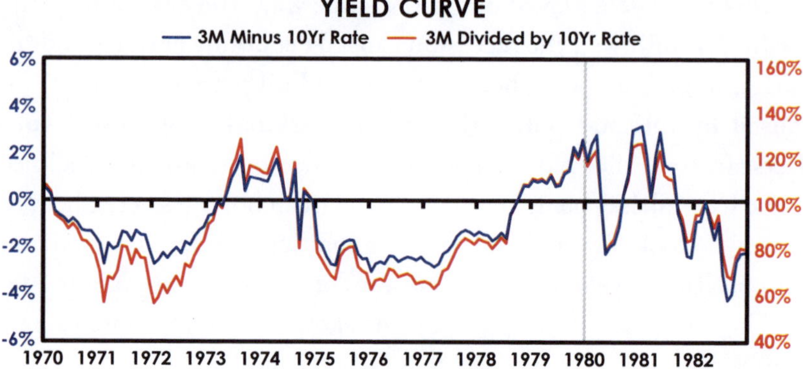

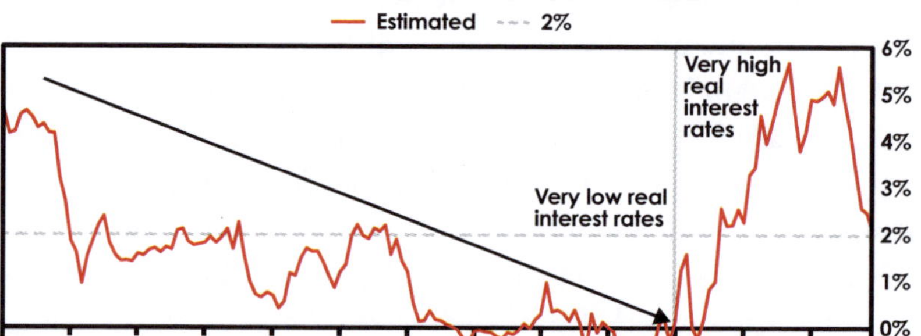

[35]

In the next chart, you can see a few other flavors of real interest rates.

[35] We show rough estimates of the real yield and breakeven inflation rate (using surveyed inflation expectations and recent inflation) for periods when those were unobservable because inflation-linked bond markets did not exist.

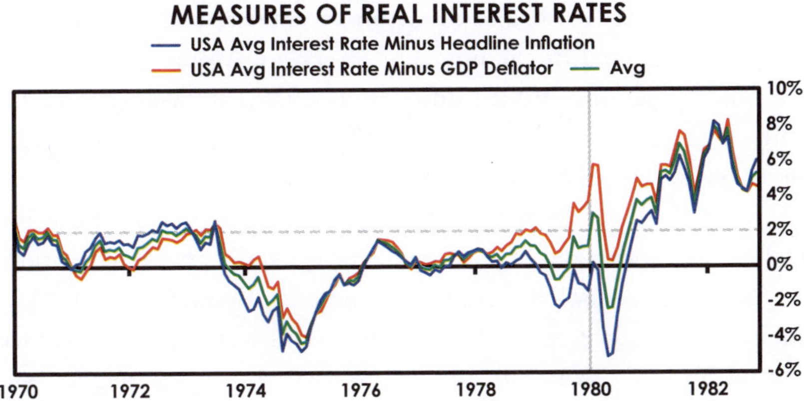

At the same time, workers and labor unions had become stronger, which raised wage inflation and squeezed company profits. As shown in the next chart, labor's share of revenue increased from 68% in 1965 to the US historical high of 74% in 1980. That both reflected and influenced the political cycle that accompanied the debt cycle.

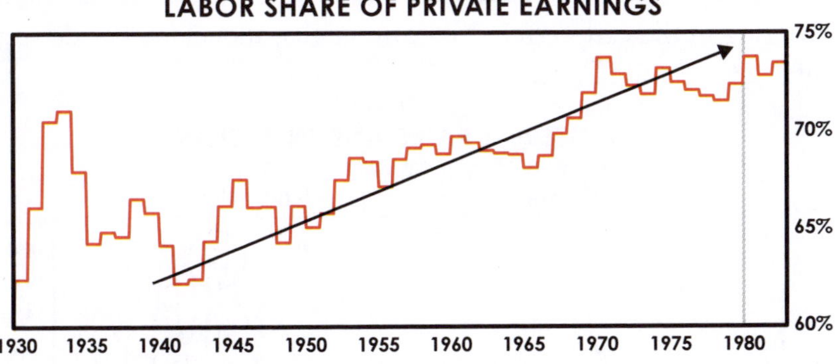

Enough was enough. The combination of high inflation, a weak dollar, bad economic conditions, bad conditions for businesses, and geopolitical crises was intolerable for voters.

The debt/money/economic, domestic-political, and international-geopolitical pendulums/orders had swung to their extremes, so

big changes were made and conditions were reversed. Pretty much everything moved in the opposite direction. More specifically, in reaction to the uncontrolled inflation, in 1979 Paul Volcker was appointed chair of the Federal Reserve to shift monetary policy from very easy to the tightest money and the highest level of interest rates "since the birth of Jesus Christ" (according to German Chancellor Helmut Schmidt), and in reaction to the generally terrible conditions that occurred under left-leaning governments, Ronald Reagan, Margaret Thatcher, Helmut Kohl, and other right-leaning leaders gained control. In other words, there was one of those classic roughly synchronized debt/economic and political swings that typically occurs because the people's discontentment with their conditions causes discontentment with the country's leaders and the party in power.

The following chart shows the CPI inflation rate (as a simple proxy for inflation), the average of the three-month and the 10-year interest rate (as a simple proxy for interest rates), and the yield curve (the three-month rate minus the 10-year rate—as a simple proxy for the tightness of monetary policy). From this chart, you can see the two short-term credit cycles in the 1970s and you can see the next one emerging in the early 1980s. You can see that money was made very tight to fight inflation around 1980.

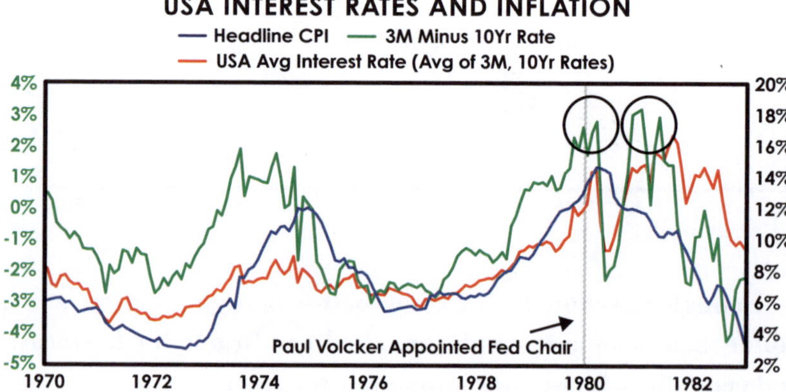

In addition to the monetary tightening, high real rates, and falling inflation, there was a shift from liberal to conservative labor policies. Thatcher in the UK, Reagan in the US, and Kohl in Germany (all moderate conservatives) led strong fights against labor inflation and labor unions that cut labor's share of the revenue pie, which reduced inflation and raised corporate profits. These conservative leaders also cut taxes on income and corporate profits and pursued tougher geopolitical policies.

The new Iranian leadership released the hostages exactly as Reagan took office in response to his threat of severe consequences if they didn't. Thatcher went to war with Argentina and won; the war was over Argentina's attempt to take the Falkland Islands, a group of small, nothing-special, British-controlled colonial islands. And Reagan accelerated the Cold War with the Soviet Union, which eventually ended the Soviet Union.

The strong moves by the American central government and central bank changed the flow of money and power and the direction of most everything. The markets respected strength and loved the combination of falling interest rates, falling inflation rates, high real interest rates, improving profit margins, and falling tax rates. It was a capitalist's delight. I remember the changes in policies and the changes in mood very well, especially the willingness of these leaders to have the fights to do the difficult things, even when doing these difficult things was painful.

As a result of all of these things, the 1980s were more opposite from than similar to the 1970s—i.e., it was a decade of disinflationary growth, strong stock and bond prices in developed countries, and debt bubbles popping, leading to classic inflationary depressions in emerging countries.

Throughout this period, I was deeply involved with these markets and the circumstances that drove them, which gave me the perspective that allowed me to identify great investment opportunities and to describe the mechanics of the process. But that's not to say that I fully understood all the mechanics behind these big moves from the start. In 1982, I was dead wrong because I expected the big debt crisis to cause big debt problems for American banks, the stock market, and the American and world economies. I was wrong because I failed to anticipate how forceful the change in global financial flows away from emerging markets and into American markets would be and how well the Federal Reserve and the regulators would protect the American banks. That failure provided me with great but painful lessons about the need to watch capital flows and how to do it, about how to diversify to reduce my risks without reducing my returns, and about how to be humble. That painful experience, like many others, turned out to be great because it educated me, which radically improved my and Bridgewater's performance over the next 30-plus years.

As you can see, all these big movements in markets and economies that had big effects on politics, geopolitics, and technology development were driven by debt/money/capital flows. For that reason, I decided to become an expert on capital flows.

The decade from 1971-72 to 1981-82 was a very painful and very classic decade of debt restructurings and debt monetizations that played out following the archetypical template previously described. As is quite typical, the decade that followed it was more opposite from than similar to the decade that came before it.

FROM 1982 TO 1990: FALLING INFLATION, STRONG GROWTH, AND LEVERING UP; FROM ONE DEBT CRISIS TO ANOTHER; STILL OPERATING WITH AN MP1 MONETARY SYSTEM

The 1979-82 monetary policy changes shifted the environment from benefiting borrower-debtors, as it had in the early 1970s, to

benefiting lender-creditors, as it did in the 1980s. As shown in the following charts, it lowered the inflation rate, which lowered nominal interest rates while keeping real interest rates relatively high in the 1980s. The following charts update the previous chart, showing interest rates and inflation rates through 1990 so you can see how different the 1980s were from the 1970s. The monetary policy moves that ended the 1970s' decade-long period of rising inflation, rising nominal interest rates, and low real interest rates created the 1980s' period of falling inflation and a relatively high real interest rate environment, which began a long period of falling interest rates. With those things happening and profit margins widening, the 1980s were more opposite from than similar to the 1970s. They were almost ideal for the markets and the economy because strong growth was accompanied by falling inflation, falling interest rates, and big stock and bond market gains in the US and most developed countries. From the early 1980s to the early 1990s, inflation fell a lot and interest rates and the tightness of credit fell even more, thus shifting the environment from one that was great for lender-creditors and terrible for borrower-debtors to one that was slightly good for borrower-debtors and slightly bad for lender-creditors.

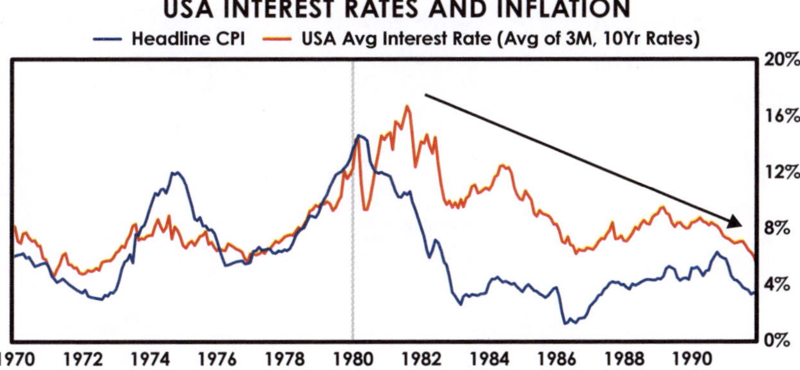

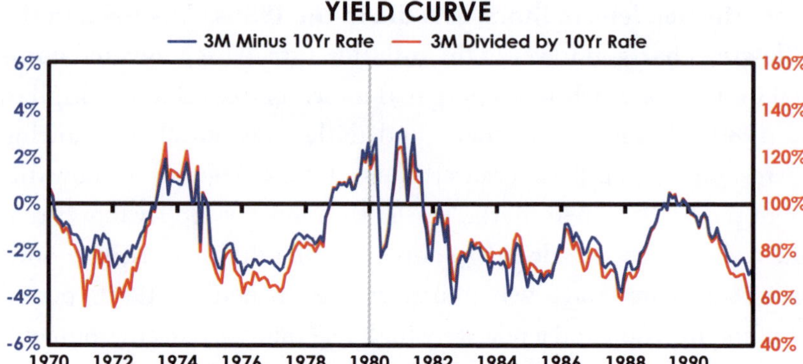

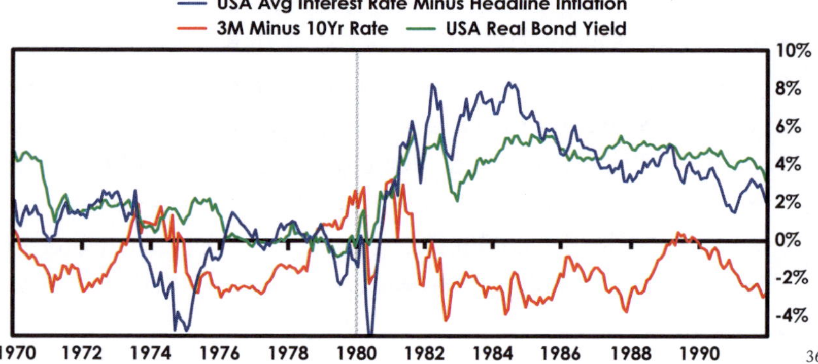

36

[36] We show rough estimates of the real yield and breakeven inflation rate (using surveyed inflation expectations and recent inflation) for periods when those were unobservable because inflation-linked bond markets did not exist.

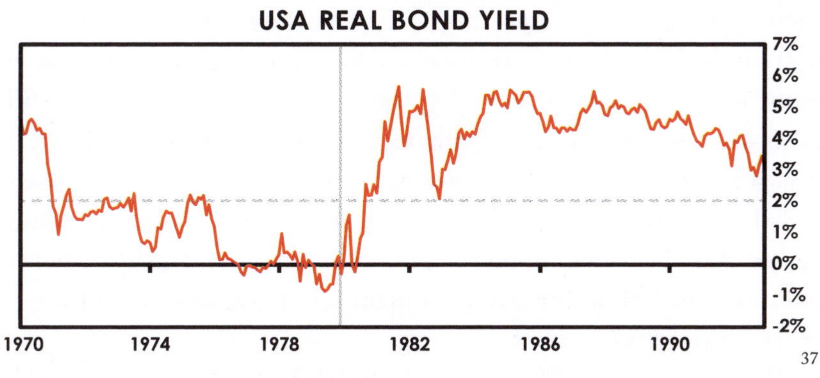

[37]

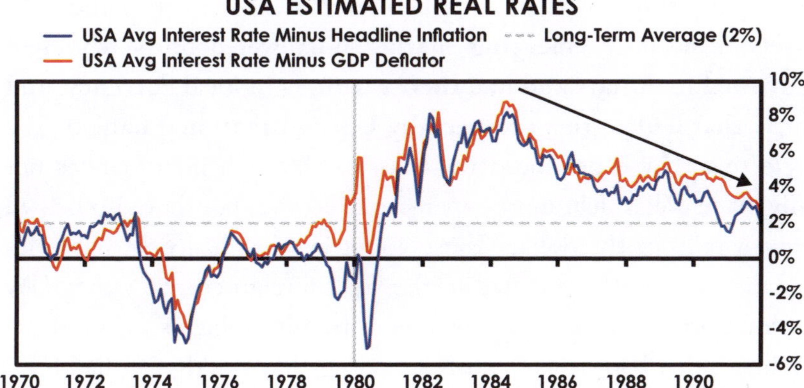

In the 1980s, the previously described tight money and short dollar (debt) conditions drove the dollar higher until 1985 when there was the Plaza Accord, which was an agreement to get the dollar to fall, which it would have done anyway because the large current account deficit and the large demand for dollars were unsustainable.

Throughout these years, there were big swings in interest rates and inflation that felt massive as you lived through them. But the overall dynamic is clear (as seen in the prior chart): in the 1980s, inflation rates fell as a result of the tightness of money in the 1980-82 period,

[37] We show rough estimates of the real yield and breakeven inflation rate (using surveyed inflation expectations and recent inflation) for periods when those were unobservable because inflation-linked bond markets did not exist.

then nominal interest rates also fell, following inflation down but keeping real interest rates relatively high. **Those high real rates were great for lender-creditors and terrible for borrower-debtors. And then when nominal interest rates fell after inflation began to fall, it was great for bond and stock prices because the discount rate used to value future cash flows fell, and the lower rates made borrowing easier. All of this was good for economic activity. And along with declining inflation, it created an ideal set of circumstances for US markets and the economy.**

But where was this transfer of wealth from? It came from the borrower-debtors who held high-interest debt liabilities and debt assets, especially emerging market borrower-debtors who had borrowed in dollars and had their earnings in local currency, and those that lent to them (especially US multinational banks). The cycle that they experienced was classic. The high interest rates not only made dollar debt more expensive to service, but they also helped drive a rally in the dollar. Those countries that had debt liabilities and debt assets denominated in the tight foreign currency that they couldn't print (US dollars) faced debt default problems, while those countries that had debts in currencies that they could print had their currencies plunge in value due to the money printing. In other words, that produced monetary inflation (i.e., inflation in the currencies they could print) and monetary deflations in the currencies that they owed and couldn't print.

The debt bubbles of the late 1970s turned into classic debt busts when there was a big tightening that tortured both sides with an ugly deleveraging in the 1980s. Those countries facing debt busts, including many emerging countries, experienced a classic full debt cycle over these 20-plus years that included inflationary depressions because there were great debt monetizations that depreciated the value of the money and debt denominated in their local currencies while they had deflationary debt default problems in the foreign currency debt that they couldn't monetize. That cycle transpired in accordance with the template laid out in Part II. The debt busts for these countries created a classic "lost decade" with inflationary depressions in these countries and classic debt workouts for the banks that had lent to them. Eventually, in 1991, there was a classic end to the debt bust that occurred in the way described in Part II—i.e., the local currency debt was devalued and the foreign currency debt was restructured. Also, near the end of the cycle, most overly indebted governments sold their government assets to build foreign exchange reserves, and they linked their domestic currencies to the dollar, completing their Big Debt Cycles.

Of course, each country experienced its own cycle and we will explore a few of these cases, notably China and Japan in Chapters 15 and 16, respectively. But there were also important geopolitical shifts during this time that impacted the Big Cycle for all nations in important ways.

During the 1980s, the geopolitical landscape changed as the Soviet Union declined, China rose, and wealth gaps increased. These changes were mostly driven by the Soviet Union's inadequate financial and economic system. More specifically, the United States had much more money and productivity than the Soviet Union and so it outcompeted the Soviet Union in most everything; notably on the military. That led to the Soviet Union's debt, economic, currency, political, and geopolitical collapses, which were manifest in the fall of the Berlin Wall in late 1989 and the official collapse of the Soviet Union in December 1991.

Deng Xiaoping coming to power in China in 1978 brought about big changes in the 1980s that have had big impacts on shaping the changing world order up until now. Deng's ascension ushered in the beginning of China's capitalist-like era and the start of its big debt/credit/money/economic cycle. Before then, there was little debt/credit/savings/economic activity. Deng changed that by creating China's "open door" and "reform" policies, which brought in foreign capitalists with their money and their talent. This swing from pure and extreme communism to market-oriented, capitalism-infused "communism" had a huge impact on China and the rest of the world. That shift unleashed a wave of productivity that led China

to become the greatest trading and manufacturing power ever because it was able to produce many tradable goods at much lower costs than could be produced elsewhere. This also had a huge impact on China and other countries, as we will explore later. Because of my relationships in China and my knowledge of financial markets, I was able to contribute to and watch up close China's big transformation during this period. I will explain China's Big Cycle evolution in much more detail in Chapter 15. Suffice it to say for now that China became extremely productive, to the degree that it swamped the world with attractively priced items, earned a ton of money, and lent a ton of money to Americans and others so they could buy Chinese goods. So, Americans got the goods and the Chinese got Americans' debt and I'm still trying to work out who got the better deal.

In the 1980s, the most important big inventions were laptop computers, lithium-ion batteries, the internet, the digitization of thinking, apps, and DNA profiling, and big advancements were made in GPS, video game consoles, microprocessors, and satellite television. Americans remained the leading inventors and investors while other countries were the leading producers. Most importantly, in the 1980s, the technology development force, in which entrepreneurs were supported by capitalists, led to the internet being developed, which led to the launching of the World Wide Web in 1991 and the dot-com bubble emerging in the 1990s. This led to the dot-com bubble bursting in 2000, when the Fed tightened money to rein in the rapid debt-financed speculation on the dot-com miracle.

FROM 1990 TO 2000: MORE DISINFLATION AND LEVERAGING UP, WHICH LED TO A BUBBLE

In brief, as with all decades, the 1990s brought many developments that seemed giant at the time and are barely memorable in retrospect. I wonder if I am giving you too much detail or not enough. To me, at the time these events were unfolding, every minute seemed

like an eternity; now I struggle to remember them, which led to my principle that ● ***everything seems bigger up close.*** **This has helped me keep things in perspective and navigate changes.**

Looking back, I am happy to see that I did well navigating them, which I know is because of what I learned and am trying to convey in this study. I hope to show you these events in the context of the Big Cycle so you can put things in perspective and see how the five big forces work and are interrelated. In brief, the changes I'd highlight are described here.

In the mid-1980s and early 1990s, tight money and abundant commodity supplies led commodity producers to sell at low prices. More specifically, the investment into commodity production in the 1970s/early 1980s led to a lot more supply at the same time as money was tight and producers that had dollar-denominated debt were squeezed. These factors caused the prices of key commodities to collapse in the mid-1980s and stay relatively low through the 1990s. That caused the flow of money and credit to commodity producers to dry up. As is typical, these big financial/economic changes that came from the debt/credit/money turning down led to big changes in domestic and international orders. For instance, these tight money and strong dollar conditions led to oil prices averaging only around $20 per barrel from 1986 to 1991, and these very low oil prices had a big negative impact on the Soviet Union and contributed to its fall, which greatly changed the world order.

The collapse of the Soviet Union ushered in an era of globalization. Amazing new technologies were developed during this period, most importantly, Wi-Fi, smartphones, and e-commerce, and further big advancements were made in GPS, video games, and perhaps most significantly artificial intelligence. **As in all Big Cycles, these big inventions were financed and accompanied by debt and equity cycles (e.g., the steam engine and the railroads come to mind). In this case, the early development led to excitement that turned into a bubble (in 1995-99), which contributed to an overheating economy and rising inflation, which led the central bank (in this case, the Fed) to tighten monetary policy, which burst the bubble** (in this case, in March 2000), which produced a short-term cyclical downturn in the markets and the economy, which ended when the tighter credit and the downturn reduced inflation, which led the Fed to ease monetary policy in the classic way.

For highly competitive, low-labor-cost countries, especially those in Asia, this era of globalization, combined with the decline in commodity prices, created a boom lasting from the mid-1980s to the mid-1990s. China started the process of joining the World Trade Organization in the 1990s, which would later bring about an era of its inexpensive goods flooding world markets and China becoming very rich and financially and economically powerful. As is classic, the boom produced debt bubbles. In 1997-98, that bubble popped, and there was the Asian financial crisis, which, while concentrated in Thailand, Indonesia, Malaysia, and South Korea, affected all countries in the region in the "Asian Contagion." As is typical, these debt/economic crises led to internal social and political conflicts in all those countries to varying degrees. These crises were all very classic in following the previously described process and exhibiting all the classic leading indicators.

In Europe, the need for countries to operate as an economic unit and to be of a scale that allowed it to compete with other economic blocs—and the need for the European economic bloc to have a coordinated currency policy—led to the major European countries linking their currencies in the Exchange Rate Mechanism (ERM). Because a system of separate currencies held together with separate monetary policies doesn't work, this ERM broke up, which was one of the great trades of the 1990s for those who understood how currencies work, and eventually led to the abandonment of individual currencies and central banks and the making of one currency (the euro) and one central bank (the European Central Bank) in 1999. The major European countries made these choices to unify despite the unimaginable challenge of bringing together such different and independent people who had a long history of fighting because in this globalized world they were not viable economic or geopolitical powers if operating separately as individual nations. The EU remains a highly fragmented union that is declining in competitiveness.

Also in this period, in the US, President Clinton succeeded in transforming a large budget deficit into a budget surplus, so it's one of a number of cases worth remembering to help us think about how to handle things well.

FROM 2000 TO 2008: FROM THE BUBBLE BURSTING TO DELEVERAGING TO RELEVERAGING TO CREATING A NEW BUBBLE THAT POPPED AND LED TO THE GLOBAL FINANCIAL CRISIS AND DEBT MONETIZATION

● ***Investors typically make the mistake of thinking that great companies in great industries are great investments because they don't pay enough attention to the prices that they have to pay to invest in them. Bubbles are made when there is a lot of thinking in that way and a lot of borrowing to lever up those purchases. Bubbles are most typically burst when central banks tighten monetary policies and interest rates rise.*** **That's what happened in 2000. The debt/asset bubble burst in March 2000, with the tech-heavy Nasdaq falling by around 80%. To make things worse, on September 11, 2001, the World Trade Center and the Pentagon were attacked, which began the "war on terror" and wars in Afghanistan and Iraq. Both of these events (though primarily the first) contributed to a contraction in the short-term debt cycle.**

The next charts show this dynamic well. In the bubble (1), unemployment rates fell to quite low levels, and stock prices rose to bubble levels. Both reversed in the early 2000s (2). These things led to a recession, which reduced inflation and led to the next short-term debt cycle easing of credit, which then led to a recovery (3). From 2006 to 2007, another classic bubble developed; while it was most prominent in real estate mortgages, it was also in banks and companies.

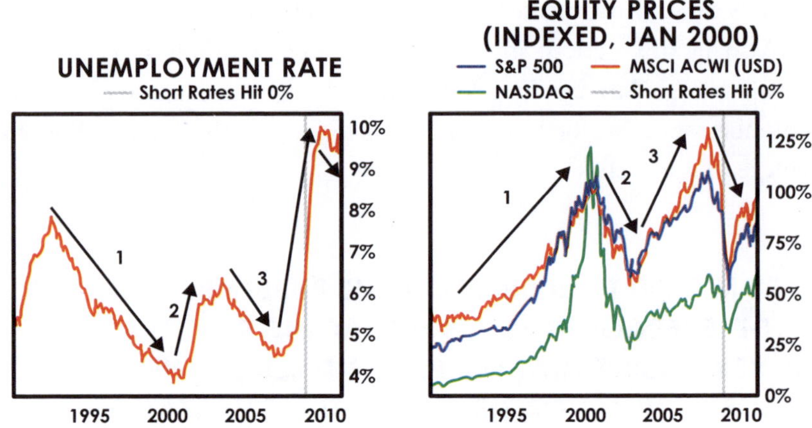

These were the last two short-term debt cycles in the MP1 era. In the 27 years from 1981 (when interest rates hit "the highest levels since the birth of Jesus Christ") to 2008 (when interest rates hit 0%), the Big Cycle consisted of four short-term debt/credit/economic cycles. From 1981 until 2008, every cyclical high and every cyclical low in interest rates was lower than the one before it, until interest rates hit 0%. That ended the MP1 monetary era (in which central banks' monetary policies were implemented with interest rate changes) as it was replaced by quantitative-easing-driven monetary policy (MP2).

Having studied the big cycles from 1918 to 1945, from the end of World War I to the start of the new monetary system that began when World War II ended, we at Bridgewater put into our investment system rules that if there was a debt contraction crisis and short-term Treasury and fed funds interest rates nearly hit 0%, we would bet on a bad contraction until the central government and the central banks became very stimulative in the ways they became stimulative in March 1933. That served us well in 2008 because we understood it, so we were able to navigate the crisis well for our clients. I also saw from my study of history that the declines of real and nominal interest rates shifted conditions from those that benefited lender-creditors back to those that favored borrower-debtors, which allowed debt/income levels to rise. **This downward trend in interest rates and increase in**

debt burdens set the stage for the next major shift in monetary policy, which we will explore in the next chapter.

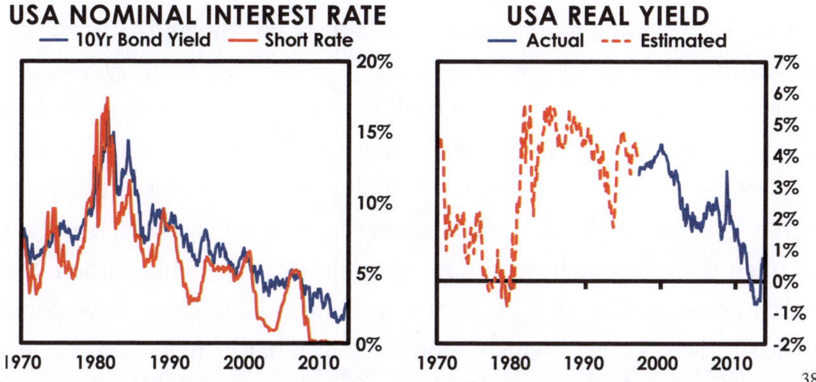

[38]

Before I describe the MP2 era in depth, I will touch on the other big forces at play in the 2000s.

Despite the tech stock bubble bursting in 2000, the internet tech industry and its effects on the world continued to grow and improve rapidly. Social media began in the middle of the 2000s (e.g., Facebook in 2004, YouTube in 2005). The iPhone was released in 2007, which created the "everything device" because of all the things it has on it (phone, camera, and many tools in apps). It was a period in which the internet and computing impacted just about every aspect of life. The US system led these developments far more than others, though around this time China began to copy and compete effectively.

China and other emerging market producers became more competitive in producing most everything, from everyday goods (apparel, toys, appliances, etc.) in the 1990s and 2000s to electric vehicles and high-tech goods now. This was wonderful for the Chinese sellers who earned a lot of money and for the American and other buyers who benefited from good-value purchases, though it put a lot of manufacturing workers in the US and Europe out of work. The US was also

[38] We show rough estimates of the real yield and breakeven inflation rate (using surveyed inflation expectations and recent inflation) for periods when those were unobservable because inflation-linked bond markets did not exist.

helped by the fact that Chinese sellers were lending the money they were making back to the US to fund its deficits. This dynamic worked essentially the same way for the Chinese as it had worked previously for Japanese goods manufacturers and their customers. In this case, it was the Chinese who were earning money by selling to Americans and lending money they earned back to Americans by buying US debt assets. China, like Japan before it, put a sizable amount of its earnings into its foreign exchange reserves, which led it to buy a lot of US Treasuries because the dollar was the world's leading reserve currency. That enabled the US government to ramp up deficits and debts without too much consequence (at least so far) while also helping to keep global goods inflation down, which allowed central banks to keep monetary policy easier and contributed to bull markets in stocks. **This dynamic was good for the capitalists who owned the means of production and not good for the workers who were displaced.**

While there were wars in Iraq and Afghanistan, there weren't big wars between big world powers. But the seeds were being sown for conflict. The European Union and NATO continued to take in more Eastern European countries and move closer to the Russian border. And as China got much richer, it began to rival the US as a geopolitical power, increasing tensions.

Risks from acts of nature increased. Climate change, which had first received significant attention as an area for global policy action in the 1990s, began to bring about destructive weather events, like Hurricane Katrina hitting New Orleans in 2005. These impacts grew more and more costly with time. During this period, global health authorities monitored novel virus outbreaks including SARS in 2002-03 and H1N1 in 2009. Neither turned out to be as disruptive as feared, but they were symptomatic of challenges to come.

Politically in the US during this period, the president was a moderate rightist, George W. Bush. The House and Senate were narrowly controlled by Republicans. Republicans, and members of Congress voted across party lines more often and government was much more bipartisan than it is at the time of this writing.

CHAPTER 13

2008 TO 2020—FIAT MONEY AND DEBT MONETIZATION

In 2008, there was a big deleveraging—the global financial crisis. It was led by the mortgage/real estate sector being financed by a lot of debt, which led to big debt problems that spread quickly to affect almost everyone in all countries, like the Great Depression in the 1930s. The debt crisis that started with the mortgage/real estate sector spread to take down overleveraged banks, companies, and individuals and to knock down financial assets and the real economy. Unemployment hit 10% in late 2009 and major stock indices were down over 50% from their peak in 2007.

In late 2008, the interest-rate-driven monetary system (Monetary Policy 1) could no longer be used to create money and credit anymore because interest rates hit 0%, and because that could not continue, central banks had to make up for inadequate free-market demand to buy these debt assets by printing money and buying the assets themselves. As a result, a new monetary system (MP2)—where central banks buy large quantities of debt and provide credit funded with their balance sheets, which is essentially printing

money, debt monetization, and quantitative easing[39]**—replaced MP1.** In MP2, the central bank creates and provides money and credit to the government and marketplace to make up for an inadequate amount of private market lending. That began in 2008 and was the first time this monetary policy had been used since 1933 (i.e., 75 years earlier). Such moves to monetize debt have occurred throughout history and are symptomatic of being in the late phase of the long-term debt cycle.

During this part of the Big Debt Cycle, the central bank becomes the big buyer and big owner of debt (i.e., the big creditor) rather than private investors. Because the central bank doesn't mind having losses from holding the debt that has reduced in value and because it doesn't worry about getting squeezed, it can continue to prevent a debt crisis by printing money and buying debt. It is willing and able to lose lots of money and have a negative net worth to protect the spending ability of both the government and the private sector even when their finances are bad. One can see this occur via changes in central bank balance sheets by looking at their holdings of debt assets that were acquired by providing those who sold the debt assets to central banks with cash and credit. The central banks of the US, Europe, and Japan own roughly 15%, 30%, and 40% of central government debt, respectively, and roughly 5%, 10%, and 20% of the total debt, respectively. In the charts that follow, you can see how this process unfolded in the US. Note the timing of the hitting of the 0% interest rate bottom and the printing-of-money expansion of the Fed's balance sheet. Because the Fed responded quickly to the problem—much more so than during the Great Depression—the markets and economy rebounded quickly.

[39] Debt monetization and quantitative easing are essentially the same thing, though slightly different. Both are intended to reduce debt problems and stimulate economic activity via the central bank buying government bonds. In the case of quantitative easing (QE) the central bank buys the bonds or other securities from private investors, whereas in the case of debt monetization the central bank buys the bonds directly from the government. That normally doesn't make much of a difference, though it can when the banking system is impaired.

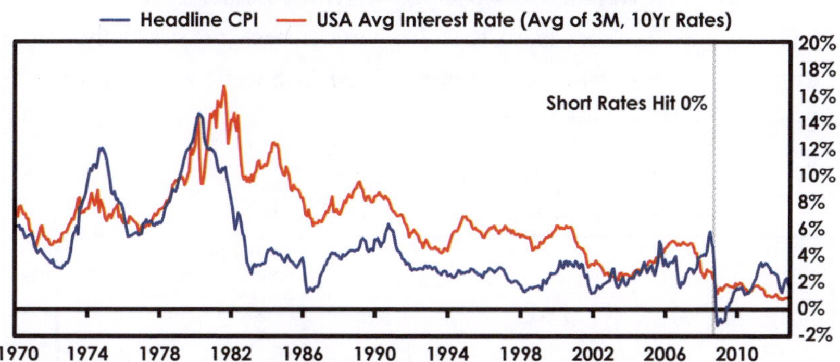

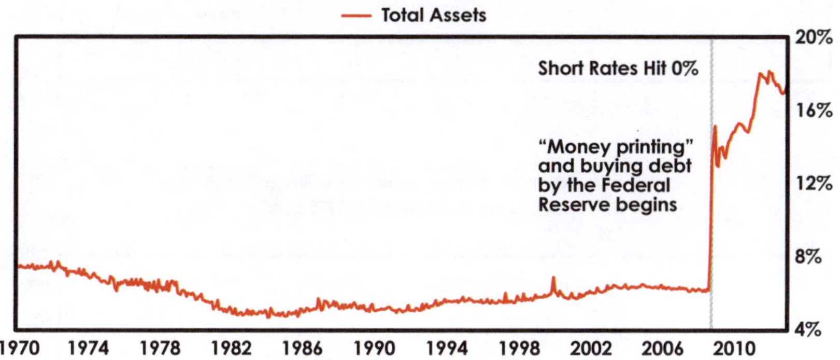

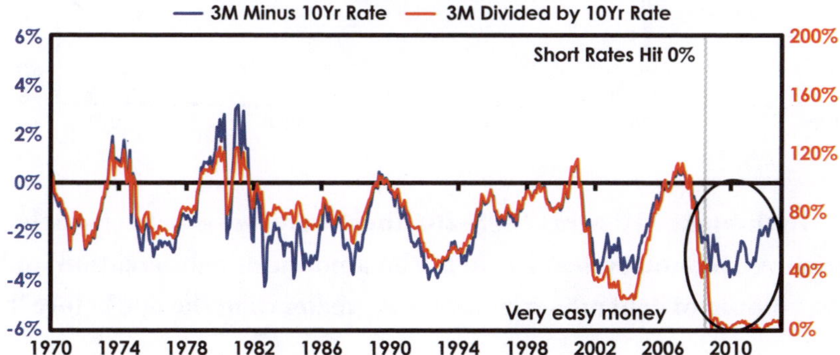

The real bond yield has averaged about 2% over the last 100 years (indicated in the following charts by the dashed line), which is neither too low for borrower-debtors nor too high for lender-creditors. Periods of great differences from this 2% were times of excessively cheap or excessively expensive credit/debt that contributed greatly to the big swings in the Big Debt Cycle.

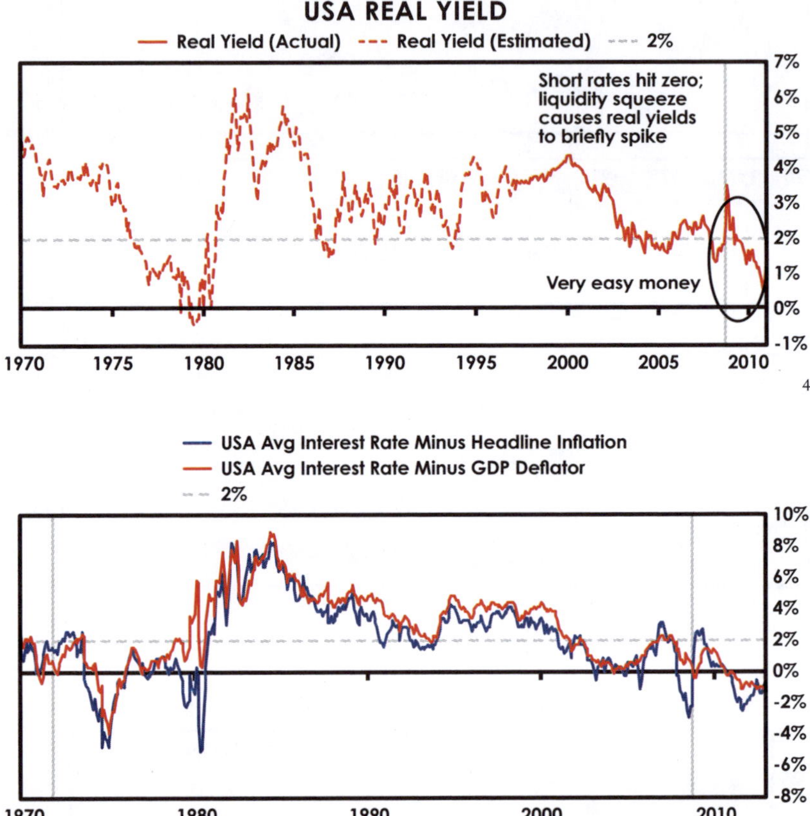

[40]

In this new MP2 era (2008-20), there were two short-term debt/credit/economic cycles. In each, the amount of debt creation and the amount of debt monetization was greater than the one before it.

[40] We show rough estimates of the real yield and breakeven inflation rate (using surveyed inflation expectations and recent inflation) for periods when those were unobservable because inflation-linked bond markets did not exist.

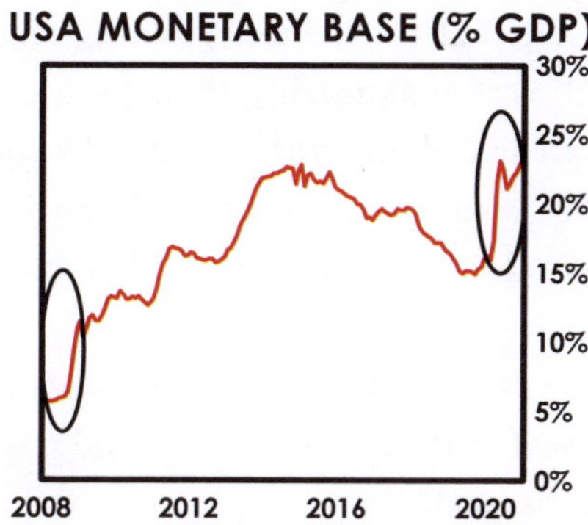

While the 2008 crisis began in the US, it spilled over into a global crisis, and virtually all developed world central banks followed the US and transitioned from MP1 to MP2 (and many emerging market central banks did, too). These actions pushed up the prices of financial assets and pushed down the yields for lender-creditors and created cheap money for borrower-debtors. The stimulative monetary policies that flowed through the system further benefited the rich, who had financial assets. The government bailing out the banks contributed to the perception that the system favored the rich, which heightened animosity toward the rich capitalists, especially those who seemed to cause the problems and got away free and made a lot of money. Ultimately, the US was able to manage its private sector debt problems and engineer an economic recovery, even as public debt kept rising (effectively kicking the can down the road; more on that in Chapter 18).

The continuing increases in imports of Chinese- and other foreign-produced goods took away American jobs at the same time that new technology was taking away jobs. These forces contributed to the hollowing out of the middle class, which increased tensions between the "elites/capitalists" and the "proletariat." China came to hold a lot of US debt assets and the US lost lots of jobs in uncompetitive businesses, which in the US contributed to the creation of large wealth and values differences, anti-China sentiment, and great political and social polarization. People who were hurting economically believed that the "elites" running things and the system they controlled were maximizing their profits at the expense of American workers. That, along with the 2008 debt/economic crisis and the fact that the government bailed out financial institutions and benefited those who held financial assets more than it was perceived to have helped the common man, also had a big impact on domestic conflict. **As a result, the financial crisis led to a shift toward populism of the right (e.g., the Tea Party movement) and populism of the left (e.g., Occupy Wall Street).**

Conflict between the politically and socially right and the politically and socially left became greater in response to growing wealth and values differences in most countries, especially in the United States. In the US, the rise of populism of the right, especially among the non-college-educated, non-urban white population, led to Donald Trump's election in 2016. That changed the American approach to its domestic order and the world order in profound ways that wouldn't be understood for many years (and, at the time of my writing in March 2025, still are not fully understood). I will describe these changes more extensively at the end of Chapter 14. However, said succinctly, **President Trump produced a shift in the domestic, international, economic, political, and geopolitical orders to be much more aggressive, top-down/autocratic, rightist, nationalistic, protectionist, and militaristic. These shifts in policies to ones that are characterized by increased confrontation and reduced levels of cooperation (and that are also reflected in the breakdown of multilateral organizations and increased unilateralism) are analogous to those that occurred many times throughout history, most recently in the periods before World War I and World War II.**

Trump's election led to rightist policies of big tax cuts for companies and individuals, the appointment of three conservative justices to the Supreme Court, big cuts in government regulations, the renegotiation of trade and military support deals with other countries, big tariffs, and immigration restrictions. Cutting income and corporate taxes and reducing regulations helped stock prices rise and the economy grow, so the unemployment rate fell to a 50-year low of 3.5% by the end of 2019. Then COVID, the first major global pandemic since the 1918-20 H1N1 pandemic, came along in early 2020.

For those who are interested, these developments and their outcomes are explained in more detail in *Principles for Dealing with the Changing World Order* and are analogous to those in the early 1930s. They are not unexpected if one understands the Big Cycle.

The big debt, political, and geopolitical cycles and the relationships between them have been unfolding in pretty classic ways so they have been contributors to the Overall Big Cycle transpiring in pretty classic ways. What we saw and are now seeing are these three big cycles transpiring along with big disruptions coming from nature (i.e., the pandemic and climate change) and with big advances in technology, especially artificial intelligence (which should greatly improve productivity and be disruptive in other ways, too).

In Europe, events closely followed the template that I laid out previously, though Europe in 2012 consisted of 17 countries in the Eurozone, some debtors, and some creditors, which made the process more difficult. The overly indebted countries that had their debts denominated in a currency they couldn't print (the euro) suffered in the way I described, and the European Central Bank handled the situation in the typical way. I will use Greece as an example of how the cycle transpired and what happened to the heavily indebted countries that couldn't print their own currency because they were tied to the euro. **To show how the cycle tracked the template, I will restate what typically happens and then show what actually happened.**

1. **The private sector and central government get deep in debt.** In the 10 years prior to the 2008 financial crisis, Greece's total debt as a percent of GDP increased by around 90%, from 160% to 250%. The impetus was Greece joining the euro, making the country's debt assets seem much safer (no devaluation risk, backstop from the ECB). Capital flowed in from across the Eurozone, and debt increased in every sector.

2. **The private sector suffers a debt crisis, and the central government gets deeper in debt to help.** When the 2008 financial crisis hit, the Greek government responded with stimulus and bigger deficits that added to its debt. Because they couldn't monetize debt, this worsened rather than alleviated the debt crisis, so Greece entered a deep depression.
3. **The central government experiences a debt squeeze in which the free-market demand for its debt falls short of the supply of it. That creates a government debt problem.** The debt crisis became an acute public sector debt crisis in late 2009 and the Greek government revealed that it had been substantially underreporting its own debt and deficits.
4. **The selling of the government's debt leads to a) a free-market-driven tightening of money and credit, which leads to b) a weakening of the economy, c) downward pressure on the currency, and d) declining reserves as the central bank attempts to defend the currency.** The obviously crushing debt burdens and the reporting fraud made Greek debt much less desirable to foreign investors, so they became sellers of Greek debt and Greece needed more stimulus to offset its depression-like conditions. Unavoidably, Greece pursued austerity, which caused the depression to get deeper and made government finances worse as tax receipts dried up. The result was a massive sell-off in Greek debt, which raised interest rates even higher and worsened the debt problem. By 2012, short-term interest rates in Greece had spiked to over 70%. Greek debt increased another roughly 70% of GDP, a combination of austerity not working and GDP declining (a dynamic I call an "ugly deleveraging").
5. **When there is a debt crisis and interest rates can't be lowered (e.g., they hit 0%), the central bank "prints" (creates) money and buys bonds to ease credit and make it easier to service debt.** Actually, it doesn't literally print money; it essentially borrows reserves from commercial banks that it pays a very short-term interest rate on. The ECB stepped in with

huge amounts of crisis money printing and buying of debt, and expanded its balance sheet just as the Fed had. But that wasn't nearly enough, and it became politically toxic as the more financially stable European countries decried this bailout of Greece, worrying that one way or another they would have to pay for it.

6. **If interest rates rise, the central bank loses money because the interest rate that it has to pay on its liabilities is greater than the interest rate it receives on the debt assets it bought.** We did not see this dynamic in this case. This typically happens when the central bank has purchased significant government debt at a fixed rate, financed via creating bank reserves that pay floating short rates, and then is forced to raise short rates because of flight from the currency or an inflation problem creating a negative net interest margin for the central bank and forcing the central bank to continue printing money to cover those losses. In the case of the European debt crisis, we saw the central bank purchase significant government debt and finance it via creating bank reserves, but in that period, Europe as a whole did not see an inflation problem or currency flight, so the ECB was not forced to raise interest rates and never had a negative net interest margin problem.
7. **Debts are restructured and devalued, reducing debt burdens.** It became clear that Greece needed a debt restructuring, and the money the ECB was spending on Greece was likely to lead to losses. There was even a chance Greece would leave the euro. Meanwhile, the exceedingly tight credit in Greece was crushing the economy. Ultimately, what was called "the Troika" (the ECB, the IMF, and the European Commission) engineered a debt restructuring paired with a bailout. In 2012, that restructuring reduced debt burdens by about 50% of GDP.
8. **Extraordinary taxes are raised, and capital flees the country and/or capital controls are imposed.** There was a bank run as smart citizens pulled money out of Greek banks. Needing

money, new taxes were introduced, and capital controls were eventually imposed in 2015.

9. **There is a transition from a severely devalued currency to a stable currency.** This restructuring was enough to end the most acute phase of the crisis, and Greece stayed in the euro. Reducing debt through an explicit restructuring is usually the more painful, drawn-out path. Greece took years to recover, but it did recover as all countries eventually do. If Greece and other overly indebted countries could have printed the currencies they owed, they would have gone down the classic path that was previously described for countries in that position.

Here are some other key developments that I'll note briefly but not digress into:

- Regarding international relations, there were big resets economically and geopolitically that led to more allied and enemy geopolitical relationships that were analogous to those that occurred in the 1933-38 period (and numerous prior analogous periods). If you want to get into them, they are covered in *Principles for Dealing with the Changing World Order.*
- Climate change started to get a lot of attention. In 2015, there was the Paris Agreement, which initiated an attempt to keep global temperatures from rising by more than 2 degrees Celsius. Climate change is a big force that is very costly and will reshape what the human and natural worlds look like.
- Regarding new technologies, computer chips rapidly advanced, cryptocurrencies were launched, self-driving-car features started rolling out, movie streaming became more widespread, 4G (and then 5G) wireless began, reusable rocket ships began to be used, and many more advances were made.

CHAPTER 14

SINCE 2020— PANDEMIC AND BIG FISCAL DEFICITS MONETIZED

In 2020, the world was hit with the COVID pandemic. While there is a government financial management principle in the US and in many other countries that monetary policy should be independent of fiscal policy and be targeted to pursue inflation and, in the US case, economic growth goals, because without that independence and that independent mandate there would be the politicization and degradation of the supply and value of money, the truth is that nearly every sacrosanct rule is inevitably tested by reality and starts to break down later in the Big Cycle.

I call that economic-impact-necessitated change in monetary policy Monetary Policy 3 (MP3). MP3 is when there are coordinated moves between the central government and the central bank, where the government runs large deficits and the bank monetizes them. The dynamic inevitably arises when interest rate changes (MP1) and quantitative easing (MP2) are no longer effective at helping conditions for most people and when the free-market capitalist system doesn't get the job done. Naturally, the capitalist system provides capital to those who are financially well-off, hold financial assets, and are able to borrow, and it doesn't provide capital to those who have the least and suffer the most. That is what happened starting in 2008. But, because of the

COVID pandemic, there was a need not just to make money and credit, but also to get it into the hands of specific people and organizations. **Throughout history, MP3 has been used in similar cases when there were very bad economic conditions and big wealth gaps so interest rate changes or quantitative easing alone could not do what was needed. MP3 typically occurred late in the long-term debt cycle. In this case, it came in two big rounds.**

What follows are a few of the previously shown key charts brought up to the time of my writing. They do a good job of painting the big picture both in terms of what has happened since 2020 and in putting what has happened into perspective within the Big Debt Cycle. As you can see, in the context of the big picture shown in the long-term charts going back to 1945, the weekly, monthly, and even annual changes seem trivial. I hope these charts help you to see the more important bigger pictures.

DEBT LEVELS AND DEBT SERVICE

The central government spends a lot and hands out lots of money, getting itself into much more debt while relieving the private sector's debt burdens. In the following charts, the gray vertical lines represent transitions from one type of monetary policy to another.

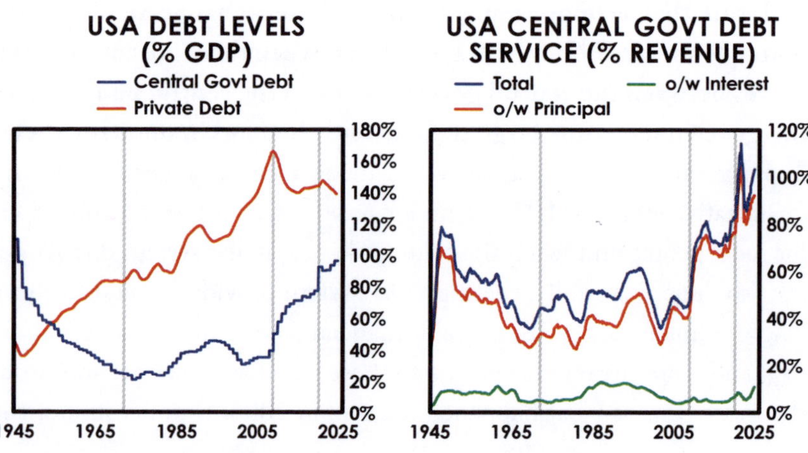

MONETARY POLICY AND CENTRAL BANK HEALTH

The Fed's printing of money and buying of the government's debt increased a lot from 2008 until late 2021, after which the Fed began tightening to fight inflation. That was a pretty classic tightening in response to accelerated inflation. The tightening and higher interest rates led the Fed to lose money on all the bonds it had acquired, as shown in the chart on the right.

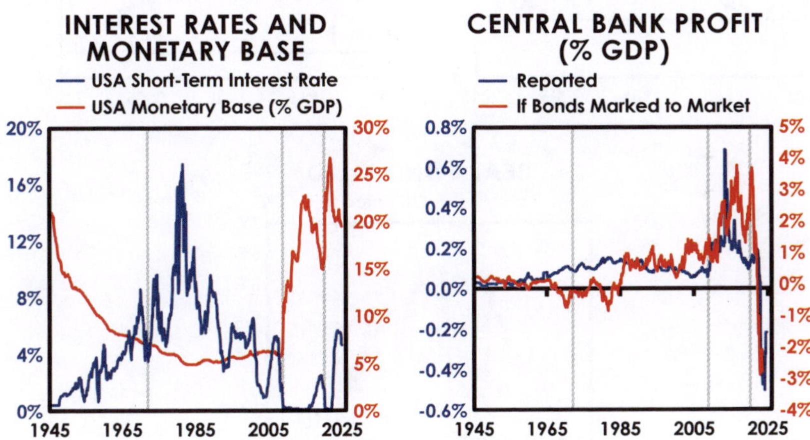

INTEREST RATES

The rise in interest rates, while significant, was less significant than the rise in inflation (the chart on the left), though it brought the real bond yield up to its long-term average of ~2% (the charts on the right and at the bottom).

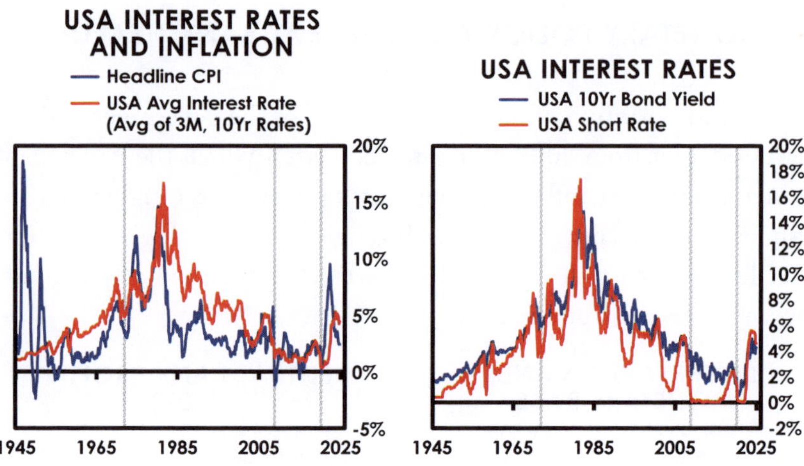

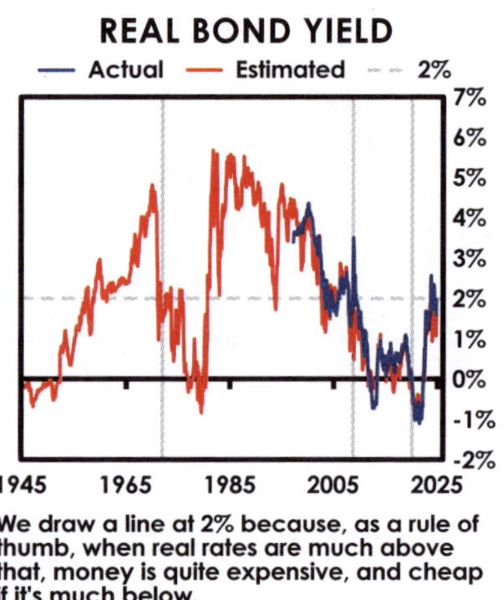

We draw a line at 2% because, as a rule of thumb, when real rates are much above that, money is quite expensive, and cheap if it's much below.

[41]

BREAKDOWN OF INTEREST RATES

The yield curve inverted; the discounted 10-year inflation rate stayed steady at around 2% as the real yield rose to about 2%. These moves reflected the tightening.

[41] We show rough estimates of the real yield and breakeven inflation rate (using surveyed inflation expectations and recent inflation) for periods when those were unobservable because inflation-linked bond markets did not exist.

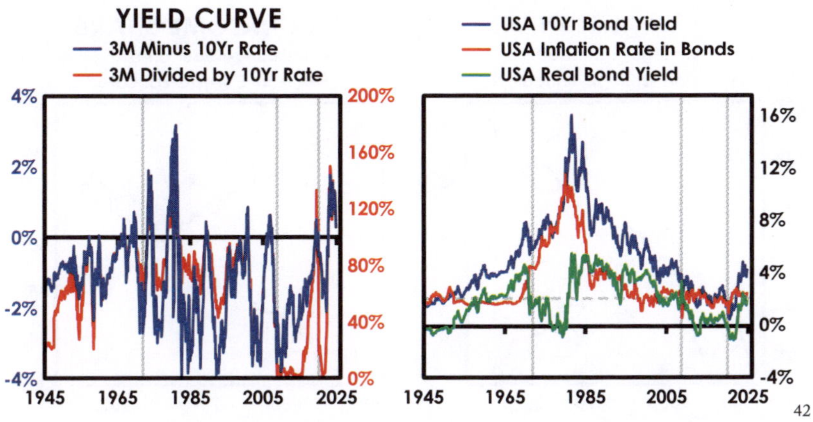

42

THE WEALTH AND INCOME SHIFTS

Labor's share of earnings continued to trend down to the lowest level since the 1950s, and the wealth and income shares of non-college-educated Americans continued to fall, so the wealth and values gap issue grew worse.

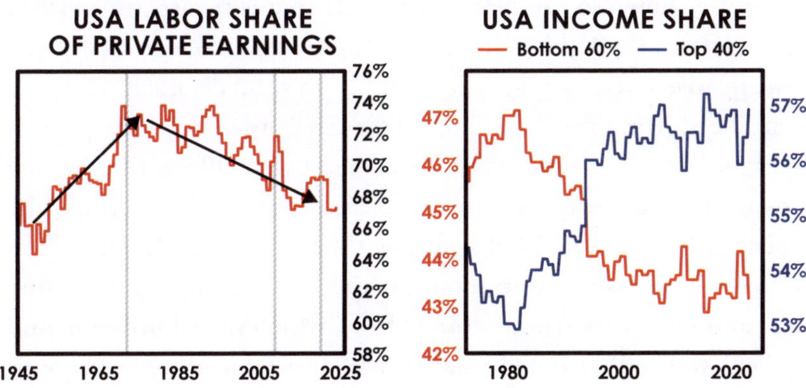

[42] We show rough estimates of the real yield and breakeven inflation rate (using surveyed inflation expectations and recent inflation) for periods when those were unobservable because inflation-linked bond markets did not exist.

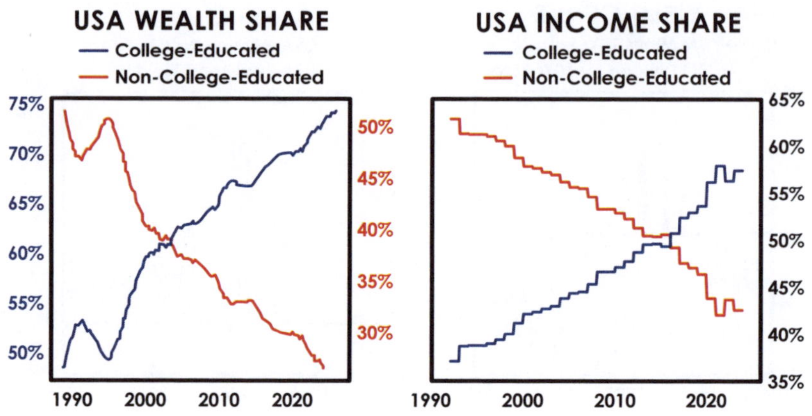

During this period, the US population and political parties became much more divided and more extreme, and there was a change in 2020 in leadership from the Trump-led rightist Republicans to the Biden-led leftist Democrats.

I am now going to look in more detail at what happened between 2020 and the present (i.e., March 2025), shifting from my Big Cycle perspective down to the short-term cycle that is transpiring within the long-term Big Cycle. That shift from the macro of several decades to the relative micro of years and months can seem disorienting. It can seem like shifting from big, important forces to small, unimportant forces, but that is not true as the small short term affects the big long term as much as the big long term affects the small short term. **Most importantly, between 2020 and now there was a pandemic, which led to a big economic contraction, which led to a huge coordinated fiscal and monetary stimulation (MP3), which raised inflation and markets and redistributed wealth, which produced a big surge in inflation, which led to a tightening that helped to bring down inflation, which led to a relatively modest easing. It was a time of continued movement to greater political polarization and the political shift to the right and back to a Trump presidency, which were also accompanied by big changes in climate and technologies.**

More specifically:

- **This short-term debt cycle easing began in 2020 in response to the combination of a) a COVID-induced economic crisis, b) large wealth gaps, and c) political moves to the left via the elections of a Democratic president, a Democratic-controlled House of Representatives, and a Democratic-controlled Senate. The easing took the form of huge government spending increases that led to huge government fiscal deficits and government debt sales that were much greater than free-market lender-creditors would buy, which required central banks, most importantly the Fed, to buy/monetize the debt.** Other entities like banks and Japanese institutional investors also bought a lot of US Treasury debt. That stimulation increased the amount of debt/credit/money/spending by a lot. This massive MP3-type of coordination of fiscal and monetary policies that allows the government to borrow and direct money as it chooses because the central bank buys its debt with printed money is explained more completely in *Principles for Navigating Big Debt Crises*, if you're interested in knowing more and seeing past cases, which you can download at economicprinciples.org. That is what happened in 2020-21; as mentioned, it has happened repeatedly for similar reasons throughout history though not in our lifetime.
- **The 2020-21 debt monetization was the fourth[43] and the largest big debt monetization since the original big debt monetization/QE in 2008 (which was the first since 1933).** From the start of the easing cycle of 2008, the nominal Treasury bond yield was pushed down from 3.7% to only 0.5%, the real Treasury bond yield was pushed from 1.4% to -1%, and the non-government nominal and real bond yields fell a lot more (because credit spreads narrowed). **Money and**

[43] Counting QE1, QE2, QE3, and then this QE during COVID lockdowns.

credit became essentially free and plentiful, so the environment became great for borrower-debtors and terrible for lender-creditors and led to an orgy of borrowing and new bubbles forming. My bubble indicator, which was at only 18% in 2010, rose to 75% at the end of 2020, showing the bubbles in companies and assets that had little or no profits and were funded by selling equity and/or borrowing money based on promises of doing well in the future and speculative buying fever. It was analogous to the Nifty Fifty bubble in the 1970-72 period, the Japan bubble of 1989-90, and the dot-com bubble of 1999-2000. The decline in interest rates in the years following 2008 took them so low that they couldn't continue to fall and it benefited stocks a lot. I estimate that the interest rate decline raised stock prices about 75% more than they would have risen without that decline (compared to the pre-financial-crisis peak). In addition, profit margins roughly doubled on average as a result of advances in technology and globalization, which also boosted profits and profit margins. Corporate and personal taxes declined, which also helped asset prices. **From the post-crisis lows of 2009 through the second quarter of 2024, the nominal value of US household wealth in financial assets (i.e., "paper wealth") rose from $32 trillion to $99 trillion, so there was a tripling of paper wealth.**[44]

- **That debt/credit/money surge in 2020 produced a big increase in inflation, which was exacerbated by supply chain problems and external conflicts (the third of the five major forces that I will touch on at the end of this chapter).**
- **That big increase in inflation led to the short-term debt cycle tightening by the Fed and the contraction in the balance sheet by having maturing debt roll off rather than buying more of it. As a result of the Fed (and other central banks)**

[44] Household wealth here is the difference between total household financial assets and total household liabilities (using data from the Federal Reserve).

changing their short-term debt cycle mode from easing to tightening, nominal and real interest rates went from levels that were overwhelmingly favorable to borrower-debtors and detrimental to lender-creditors to levels that were more normal (e.g., a 2% real bond yield). Once the tightening began, US Treasury bond nominal yields rose from 0.5% to over 4% and real yields rose from about -1.1% to about 2.5%, which hurt most asset prices, particularly those with weak or negative profits and/or needs for new equity funding. Naturally, that shift especially hurt the prices of assets that were in bubbles. My bubble indicator fell from 75% (in a significant bubble) to 35% (not in a bubble) and the bubble stocks in the index fell an average of 75%. **As a result, the nominal value of wealth in stocks and bonds fell by ~12% in the US and the real value of wealth fell by nearly 18%, which were the largest declines since 2009.** As cash (i.e., investing in short-term cash instruments like T-Bills) went from "trash" to "attractive," and both short-term nominal and real interest rates were brought to levels that were more attractive than they were for lender-creditors and more unattractive than they were for borrower-debtors, and the yield curve inverted, these changes had the very classic effect of lowering the present values of most investment assets' future cash flows and strengthening the dollar relative to the currencies of other countries whose central bankers were slower to tighten. In other words, the Fed's quick movement brought US dollar-denominated cash to relatively attractive levels in relation to most assets, cash denominated in other currencies, and gold. This, as usual, hurt interest-rate-sensitive sectors like commercial and residential real estate, as well as low or negative cash flow bubble companies, both public and private, though public more so. For example, the then-hot "FAANG" stocks and the tech-heavy Nasdaq fell from their peaks by around 45% and 33%, respectively. Non-public-market assets—private equity, venture capital, and real estate assets—were not marked down commensurately as there was a great reluctance to accept the markdowns. Write-downs and having down fundraising rounds became too painful for both the companies and the venture capital and private equity managers in these markets, so there has been, to this day, a stand-off in which sellers and buyers can't agree on prices and transaction volumes have plunged. It did not, however, weaken the economy as much as it typically would have because it was the central government that got into more debt rather than the private sector and it was the central bank that bought the debt and had the losses from holding it rather than the private sector. Also, the inflation was in wages and other compensation being earned as well as in goods and services being bought.

- **Then inflation fell but prices stayed high, and the Fed and other central banks eased their monetary policies, which supported asset prices generally. Artificial intelligence and artificial intelligence companies became the new hot things and are expected to improve the economy and life hugely like the new hot things that produced the industrial and digital revolutions and led to financial bubbles. With these changes came great differences in which stocks, companies, and countries did well.** Also, the world capital markets changed with new types of investment products, though in the same sort of ways we saw before. For example, we are seeing new types of lending, like the development of the private credit market, which is the modern-day version of the junk bond market of the late 1970s and early 1980s (though more customized, not securitized, more illiquid, and inclusive of early-stage companies). The large amount of money entering this type of lending helped to keep credit spreads down and fund more speculative activities.
- **Regarding the internal conflicts over wealth and values between the populists of the right and the populists of the left,**

the intensity increased in most democracies, most importantly in the US. In the US, the divide between the political right and the political left became more extreme and the big rises in prices that came from the earlier-described big fiscal and monetary stimulations by the US central government and central bank led to big price increases in goods, services, and financial assets. **In the 2024 election, this inflation and other factors, such as President Biden's impaired acuity, helped a) the rightist/capitalist/social conservative Donald Trump and the Republican Party to a decisive win over b) the leftist/socialist/social liberal Kamala Harris and the Democratic Party, giving Trump a mandate to undertake a big renovation of the central government and the country as a whole and prepare for some type of war with China and its allies.** The potential great conflict that would have likely occurred if there was a close Trump loss was averted and huge changes to the US domestic order began.
- **Climate changes continued unabated.**
- **Technological advances, most notably in artificial intelligence but in several other areas as well, led to big shifts in wealth and power.**

That brings us up to where we now are.

THE FIVE BIG FORCES: DEBT, CIVIL WAR, INTERNATIONAL WAR, ACTS OF NATURE, AND TECHNOLOGY

Every day we see news about these five forces. If you connect the dots from the past to the present, you can see them evolving along the lines of the Big Cycle template that was comprehensively explained in my book as well as my 40-minute and five-minute videos about the changing world order, on economicprinciples.org. Government debt is obviously a big and growing issue. The thus-far nonviolent civil war between the rightists/capitalists/MAGAs and the leftists/socialists/communists/woke is continuing to intensify, though in the last US election the rightists clearly beat the leftists. This shift has brought the big domestic order/disorder cycle to the same stage it last was in the 1930s. Simultaneously and relatedly, the international great power conflict, particularly between the United States and its allies and China and its allies, is intensifying. Similarly, the acts of nature force, most importantly climate change, is intensifying, while technology, especially AI, will have a big impact, both good and bad, that we won't be able to imagine. As always, these five big, interrelated forces are moving the Big Cycle forward. Most importantly, the internal fight within the US and the external fight between the US and China is and increasingly will be affected by the technology war and the economic war (e.g., the need to raise military spending). For previously explained reasons, this looks quite like the 1930s period.

Because of the importance of China, I will now briefly review its whole Big Cycle starting in 1945 (when the new world order began) and 1949 (when its new domestic order began). Then I will look at Japan's Big Cycle, focusing most on how its Big Debt Cycle unfolded because it provides another good case study for gaining the valuable lessons it offers.

CHAPTER 15

CHINA'S BIG CYCLE FROM 1945-49 UNTIL NOW IN A TINY NUTSHELL

This chapter explains how the Big Cycle has played out in China, bringing you right up to the present. It will take you about 15 minutes to read. Having spent a lot of time in China and having had very close relationships there for over 40 years, including with some of the leaders, I have seen much of it unfold from up close, so China's Big Cycle is as vivid to me as the US's Big Cycle. I think this chapter is well worth your time to read.

To put China's history in the context of its Big Cycle, I will summarize what has happened since the start of the new world order and China's domestic order in the 1945-49 period with a very brief look at what happened before then.

BEFORE 1945

I will start by directing your attention to the following chart that shows the Big Cycles of China back to the year 600. This measure shows the estimated relative strength of China using many measures of strength as described in *Principles for Dealing with the Changing World Order*. It shows the biggest Big Cycle waves in Chinese history.

Having studied these cycles, I have found them to be consistent with the Big Cycle template that I am touching on in this study and that I comprehensively explained in that book and the animation of the same title.

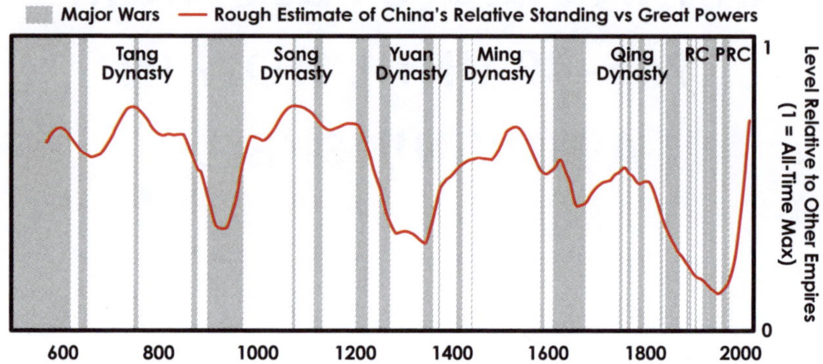

In the following chart, you can see China's Big Debt Cycles since 1865, which is 26 years after the Century of Humiliation began, until now. This 110-year period of humiliation (as the Chinese call it) was the period in which foreign powers humiliated and exploited China, starting in 1839 with the First Opium War and ending in 1949 with Mao and the Chinese Communist Party coming to power and the founding of the People's Republic of China. As you can see, big debts were built up, wiped out, and built up again. As is typical, the debt wipeout corresponded with internal and external wars (in 1945-49); then there was a new order, and debts were built up again. Through most of these years, Chinese money and debt were not considered a good storehold of wealth so it was difficult to build credit and other capital markets. Then in 1989, with the development of the stock market and the beginnings of the bond market, they started building their capital markets. Because I was closely involved with this, I can tell you all about it.

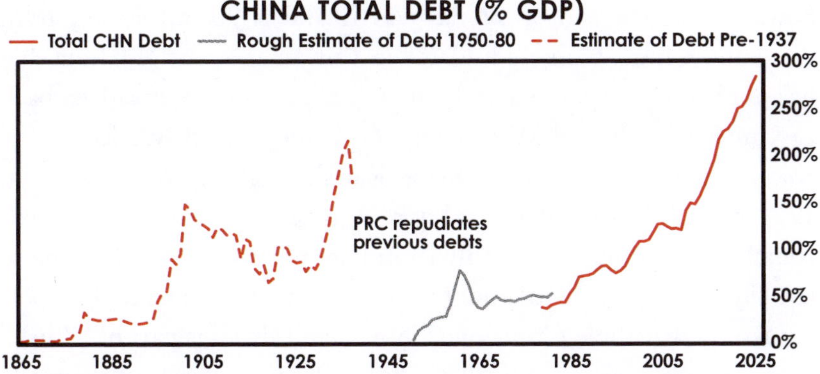

While I will not delve into a detailed discussion of China's prior Big Cycle, which encompassed the Century of Humiliation, I will touch on it because it profoundly affected Chinese leaders' perspectives on foreign powers and what is now going on domestically. That part of China's history is deeply embedded in Chinese leaders' psyche and has led to a belief that the way foreign powers are now fighting for their interests is broadly analogous to the way they did during the Century of Humiliation. They feel, above all else, that China must have the economic and military power to take care of its people and not be abused by other powers. More specifically, China's leaders see the US as operating as a hegemon trying to control the world order to serve its self-interests and trying to contain China in an area of the world that the US is not part of. I am not saying that the Chinese perspective is more true than the American one. I am simply describing what happened and touching on both perspectives.

China's leaders now see America's handling of Taiwan as being even more intrusive than Americans saw Russia's influence in Cuba in the 1960s because from their perspective Taiwan has been "indisputably and consistently" recognized as part of China by all the world's powers since the end of World War II and is 90 miles away from mainland China. Chinese leaders see Taiwan as a part of China that has not been incorporated back into China, because it was given back to China after World War II but the Chinese civil war led to the Kuomintang and its leader Chiang Kai-shek taking control of it. In 1971, the UN General Assembly recognized the mainland People's Republic of China as "the only legitimate representative of China to the United Nations" and reinforced the "One China" policy. That policy asserts that there is only one China and Taiwan is part of China.

So, there is no question that Chinese leaders expect to eventually take control of Taiwan and parts of the South China Sea. In contrast, most Americans see China as a big and growing threat to the United States and the existing US-led world order, and they see the Chinese as being ideologically threatening communists who autocratically control their people and who are in a great ideological war with its capitalist/democratic/Abrahamic (i.e., Jewish/Christian/Islamic) approach. Some in both Washington and Beijing see this conflict as being the last and biggest great cultural/religious/economic and possibly military war. Of course, this relationship is complicated and there are at least two sides to this story, which I won't go into because it would be too large of a digression. I just wanted to make clear Chinese leaders' perspective, which has a big effect on how they think and what they do. Additionally, I want to point out that because of the very long history of the Chinese civilization, which the leaders know very well, they are very aware of the Big Cycle.

The most important things to know are that China has had a strengthening over the last 50 years that has been greater in magnitude than any other country's in history. This has led to it becoming a great power that is approaching the power of the United States, and as a result, the United States and China have entered into a classic period of great power conflict. The next two charts show my aggregate readings of relative powers since 1825 and my US-China conflict gauge since 1963. As you can see in the first chart, China's relative power fell a lot during the Century of Humiliation and then rose a lot thereafter, so that it is now close to rivaling the US. This is leading to a classic great power conflict between the US, China, and their respective allies.[45]

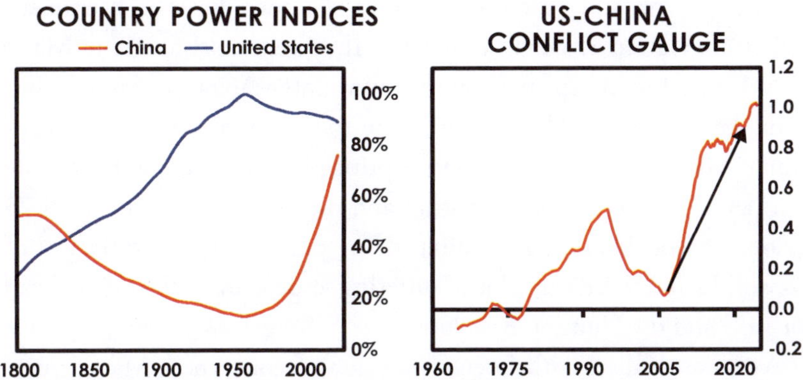

SINCE 1945

Here is my very brief description of what has happened in China since 1945.

The end of World War II led to the creation of the new and current world order, and in 1949, China's civil war ended, which led to the creation of the new and current domestic order.

From 1949 until the 1970s, China was a strictly isolated communist country run by the revolutionary leader Mao Zedong and his chief administrator, Zhou Enlai. During those years, China recovered slowly from World War II and its civil war because it was encumbered by rigid and unproductive communist economic policies that didn't reward hard work and didn't allow savings and wealth creation, and imposed draconian controls that ensured that Mao and the Chinese Communist Party remained in power, and created isolation from the rest of the world that prevented China from benefiting from what the world had to offer. In Big Cycles it is typical for those who win political power in a civil war

[45] On my website, economicprinciples.org, you can see much more detail on the measures that led to this reading for China.

to suppress the opposition in order to consolidate and solidify their power over the opposition due to fears that they will be overthrown. In Chinese dynasties, secret and violent overthrows of leaders have been frequent so they are viewed as a constant threat. That went on throughout Mao's life. Mao had many enemies, most importantly capitalists from within China and the Soviet Union (starting in the late 1950s) from outside of China. Marxist-Leninist communist principles and isolation from "foreign devils" shaped what China did and didn't do during the 1949-76 period. During Mao's reign, China's development fell behind the rest of the world's and there was a lot of suffering, especially in the Great Leap Forward and the Cultural Revolution.

As far as dealing with foreign powers was concerned, Mao's greatest fear was the Soviet Union, which became increasingly threatening in the 1960s and especially in the 1970s. As has typically been the case throughout history and is conveyed in the adage "the enemy of my enemy is my friend," the common enemy brings countries together, which was true in this case, with the common enemy of the United States and China being the Soviet Union. That is what led to the visits to China first by Henry Kissinger and soon after by President Nixon. Because I knew both Henry Kissinger and Ji Chaozhu, who were both participants in those discussions, I heard firsthand about the thinking and the discussions that took place and can assure you that the common enemy perspective was top of mind for both sides in motivating the initiating of their "friendship" in 1972.

Mao and Zhou died in 1976.

As described in Chapter 12, Deng Xiaoping came to power in 1978 and changed just about everything with his "reform" and "open door" policies, which introduced a much freer, market-based economic system that brought in foreign talent and foreign capital to enable the Chinese to seize new opportunities. He distinguished the new way with statements like "to get rich is glorious" and when asked about his move to a more market-capitalist direction, he said,

"It doesn't matter whether a cat is black or white as long as it catches mice." This was the recognition that the market-capitalist systems can "catch mice" (i.e., make riches) and that it is best to get rich and powerful first and then work toward "common prosperity." **These policies led to China having huge economic advances that changed not just China but the whole world. China went from being a poor, weak country to being a very strong one that was more capitalist.**

I saw all this up close from 1984 until now and, through my contact with China, got to see things through Chinese leaders' eyes as we became friends working on the development of markets and the economy in China.

I started going to China in 1984 as a guest of CITIC, which was the only "window company" (so-called because it could deal with the outside world in a capitalist way). They asked me to teach them about the world's capital markets. China hardly had any money at the time so I didn't go there to make money or be involved with their markets; I went at first because I was curious, and I've kept going until now because I love the people and culture, and I could have a good impact on the country's markets and economic development. That has given me an invaluable education as well as lots of enjoyment, so much so that I don't dare describe it entirely because it would be too great a digression. What I am now going to describe is through the lens of my experiences. **I watched that combination of powerful economic reform and opening up to the outside world take China from:**

1. **a classic unproductive communist country to**
2. **an effective "socialist market economy" to**
3. **the development of its capital markets and its version of capitalism to**
4. **the forming of a classic debt bubble that led to**
5. **a classic debt bust of the type that those who have their debt denominated in their own currency and have most of the debtors and creditors as their own citizens have to**
6. **a classic great power conflict.**

More specifically, China experienced a classic upward swing in the Big Cycle that took China's people from terrible poverty to much-improved living standards, with many people and the country as a whole gaining great riches and powers. At the same time, there were big increases in indebtedness and developments in the capital markets that created big wealth gaps and a bubble. **I witnessed up close China go from grappling with its poverty and its geopolitical weaknesses to creating its market/debt reform and open-door policies, which created great increases in its riches and geopolitical power, to grappling with these greater wealth and geopolitical powers because with them came big wealth and opportunity gaps and big domestic and international conflicts.**

In the Deng era, I saw the Big Cycle unfold up close as follows:

- **China's inexpensive labor and high productivity gains provided the world with attractively priced manufactured goods.**
- **The US and most of the world liked getting attractively priced manufactured goods on good terms, especially because China used a lot of the money it earned to lend money to Americans who bought the merchandise.**
- **China's income, wealth, and power increased greatly. At the same time, the US overborrowed and started to decline.**

In 2008, the US had a big debt crisis that put China in the position of not knowing if a large portion of its debt assets would be paid back and questioning the United States' financial strength. I was in the midst of that situation and must say that the Chinese side handled the debt crisis with grace and understanding.

In 2008, the Group of 20 (G20) countries, which was formed to be a more realistically representative group of powerful countries than the G7 given the shifts in world power, had its first summit to deal with the global financial crisis. They agreed to be very stimulative, so China and virtually all countries increased the credit they

made available, which improved conditions, increased wealth gaps, and raised debt levels relative to income levels. As explained earlier, in the US the widening wealth gaps and economic suffering of those left behind created a change in sentiment to blame the Chinese for their job-loss problems. Those American workers who were most adversely affected were the non-college-educated men who Donald Trump later appealed to. **At the same time, American companies complained that they were not allowed to fairly compete in China and that the Chinese were stealing Americans' intellectual property.**

China's skills and powers continued to grow, which gave China the resources to develop its military, geopolitical influence, and technological powers, which led it to become more assertive and seemingly threatening. In 2009, pointing to an old map that demarcated the South China Sea boundary, China asserted that the proper boundaries of its territory were far beyond what other countries claimed they were. Although in 2016 the Permanent Court of Arbitration ruled against China's claim, the dispute continues today.

President Xi Jinping and the new leadership team came to power in 2012. Their main goals were to reform the economy and eliminate corruption. Because of my expertise and my long and trusted relationships, I was able to participate in the discussions about these things in the third plenum (the new government's big planning meeting after the top people are appointed). I experienced a very open and collaborative environment in which key issues were discussed, and we exchanged thoughts about them openly. I found the quality of those discussions about how to eliminate corruption and make reforms to be sincere and excellent. There was a great desire and enthusiasm from the new strong leaders to improve China and I was thrilled to be of help. **Reforming the economy meant modernizing it to be more market-driven.** For example, back then five major banks lent money to state-owned enterprises that were implicitly guaranteed by the government, which had the printing press to guarantee them, and there was little lending to small- and medium-size enterprises. The leadership wanted to change that, so they sought to develop capital markets that improved access to borrowing, lending, and investing. I was closely involved with that, so I saw how those responsible for it thought about it and what they did. I found that for most of Xi's first five-year term, there was a) an openness to outside thinking, b) a strong desire to further reform the economy by making it more market-driven and taking actions to build and reform the capital markets, and c) strong action taken to eliminate corruption. The senior leaders chosen were the ones who were inclined to do those things. Of course, how to do these things was debated, and some people benefited from the changes while others were hurt by them, which created divisions. **After coming to power, Xi immediately purged a strong rival (Bo Xilai) and moved strongly to make big changes to eliminate corruption and reform the economy.**

Late in Xi's first term there was a movement to consolidate political power around him via a move to "core leadership." If you think politics in the United States is brutal, you should see politics in China. This became most clear in the leadership changes that accompanied the shift from the first to the second five-year term under Xi.

Up until then, there were remarkable accomplishments—by many measures the greatest in human history. In the years since I first started going to China in 1984, China's per capita income increased 20x, the average life expectancy increased by 12 years, and the poverty rate fell from 81% to less than 1%.

In 2014, Russia annexed the Crimean Peninsula from Ukraine, which is a whole other story to be discussed at another time. Suffice it to say that at the time, though the Russians and the Chinese had a dislike and distrust for each other, they were drawn together by the common enemy and saw that they could have a symbiotic economic relationship.

In 2015, Xi put out his 2025 plan, which described the need for China to rise and dominate certain industries. This was viewed as aspirational by the Chinese and threatening by the Americans. China could no longer "hide power." Also, China became more threatening to other countries as it grew a lot in world trade, as its riches grew, as it asserted itself more geopolitically, and as it "stole" intellectual property. **At this time, Americans began to blame China for their economic problems and viewed China as a greater threat.**

Due to middle-class job losses in the US, which were attributed to Chinese imports and China's greater assertiveness internationally, the pendulum of sentiment toward China swung from positive to negative. When President Trump came to power in 2017 and President Xi began his second term in 2018, the great power conflict began in earnest, starting with trade negotiations that evolved into tests of power and a type of cold war. At the time, it became clear to Chinese leaders that the classic great power conflict was emerging. I was assured by a Chinese senior leader that the Chinese leadership didn't want to change the multilateral world order with respect to multinational organizations like the UN, the World Trade Organization, the World Health Organization, the World Bank, and the IMF. This senior leader argued that the changes to the world order and threats to multilateralism were instead the result of the Trump administration's move toward a unilateral, "America First" approach, which put US interests ahead of the global community's, and made containing China its top priority. By this time, Russia and China increasingly viewed the United States as the common threat, so they became more aligned.

Then in 2019-20, COVID emerged. At the same time, China's debt bubble and wealth gaps grew, and relations with the US worsened, so there was a classic convergence of big debt/financial, internal order, external order, and acts of nature forces into a risky mix. Also, the Taiwan issue was (and still is) a very big, contentious issue because China expected the One China unification promise to be delivered on while instead there seemed to be movement toward more independence. This has been intensified because most of the advanced computer chips in the world were (and still are) produced in Taiwan, and whichever country controls them controls the most powerful technology in the world. Seeing all those contentious domestic and international issues evolve, in addition to his understanding of history, led Xi to convey that there is a big 100-year storm on the horizon.

In 2018, Xi began his second five-year term with more consolidated power around him as the head of the core with four of the seven members of the Standing Committee of the Politburo as his close allies.

In 2020, much of China was shut down due to COVID, which raised some internal ire about how it was being handled. And then in 2021, a bit more than halfway through Xi's second term, China's domestic debt bubble burst. Xi emphasized the importance of "common prosperity" and did not like how rich business leaders were arrogantly seeking to exert influence over how China was being run, so the government took some seemingly arbitrary actions that were not consistent with the type of rule of law and traditional property protections that investors thought were important. The leadership also knocked back some billionaire business leaders and their businesses to put them in their place.

At the beginning of Xi's third term in October 2022, China's leadership shifted from reform-minded globalists to loyal, patriotic communists with tighter controls over possible opposition, and it shifted from being highly free-market-oriented with capital markets flourishing to being more Mao-like communist as internal conflict and the international great power conflict intensified.

China is now a country that is 1) experiencing a big debt crisis at the same time as it is also turning to more traditional communist economic policies, while 2) there is increased internal conflict that is being eliminated by more strict, autocratic policies directed by the president/chairman, while 3) there is increased international conflict with the United States and great changes in the world, which China is increasingly playing a leading role in shaping, while 4) climate change is happening and is likely to have a big effect on China, while 5) China is in a technology war that neither it nor the United States can afford to lose. Simultaneously, it is making great advances in many areas, especially in technology-enabled manufacturing that it sells very inexpensively, with emerging countries that account for 85% of the world's population being China's big new target market.

At the time of my writing this in March 2025, the second Trump administration has recently come into power in the US and has to deal with 1) the big debt issue, while 2) internal conflict is leading it to employ more strict, semi-autocratic policies to overpower the opposition and its leftist policies, while 3) there is increased international conflict with China, countries aligned with it, and great changes in the world order with the US under Trump shifting from being a global leader to becoming an "America First" nationalistic participant in the changing world order, while 4) climate change is likely to have a big effect, while 5) the US is in a technology war that neither it nor China can afford to lose. The under-the-surface attacks on each other have been vicious.

So, we are now seeing a squaring-off of these two great powers, along with their allies lining up behind them and their ideologies, which looks a lot like what we saw in the 1930s when the world was at a similar stage in the Big Cycle. At the same time, there is a rapprochement of the US toward China as President Trump has described President Xi as a "great leader" who "controls 1.4 billion people with an iron fist." What will happen in the US and China and the world will be another test of the relative strengths of these two great powers and their two very different approaches and systems. These two great powers are now in a war that fortunately for the world hasn't yet turned into a military confrontation. This is shaping up to be the greatest great power conflict ever. Many years ago, a very senior Chinese leader explained how differently these two sides fight war; he explained to me how Western countries follow a Mediterranean approach to war, which is head-on, while the Chinese use a much subtler, deceptive approach along the lines of what was described in *The Art of War* by Sun Tzu, which was written about 2,500 years ago. Over my many years and through my close contacts in China, I have learned about the power of such timeless principles that affect Chinese leaders' approaches to dealing with the Chinese people and the outside world.[46]

CHINA AND THE FIVE BIG FORCES

In this ultra-brief summary, I will look at what has happened in China vis-à-vis my Five Big Forces template:

---

[46] A timeless guiding principle is *da* (which means big/grand) *tong* (which means unity, harmony, and coordination), which dates back to ancient China (around the time of Confucius). It describes how good things should be shared by all, leaderships should operate for the public good rather than for their own interests or the interests of any group, resources should be distributed equitably, and people should live in harmony. These are essential things that they will strive to get at all costs. How do they strive for them? The approaches are conveyed in 1) Confucianism (which is a series of ways of operating to have harmony through clear hierarchy and moral leadership in which the leaders put the society's well-being ahead of their self-interest and put education, meritocracy, family, quality relationships, and paternalistic governance as priorities; it was formed around 500 BCE) and 2) legalism (which emphasizes very strict rule of law and pragmatism over morality; it was formed around 250 BCE). I learned that running China as a hierarchical family is important (e.g., the word "country" in Chinese is made up of two characters that are "state" and "family"). Of some but lesser influence are Taoism, which emphasizes harmony and the nature of all things, and Buddhism, which emphasizes harmony among people and all things, the acceptance of how things are, and materialism's lack of value. By understanding such principles and how deeply rooted they are, I could understand the leaderships' perspectives and their system better than if I didn't understand such things. For example, I could understand why they are inclined toward Marxism (which to them represents common prosperity), autocratic leadership, and the desirability of people in the society to know their place and to faithfully follow the leader (which they believe is required for order to exist), unless the leader fails them, which will be shown in great disorder that will lead the leader/emperor to lose "the mandate of heaven" and be overthrown, which will change the dynasty/order. And I can understand how they can find capitalism and individualism antithetical to their beliefs because they see both as selfishness that will fragment people and lead to disharmony and disorder. I am not commenting on what I think of Chinese approaches versus American or more generally Western approaches other than to say that it seems to me that humanity has struggled with their relative merits (i.e., the relative merits of capitalist self-interest and democracy and communist common interest and dictatorship) and has swung back and forth between different versions of them for all recorded history. I also think that the Chinese core values about how people should be with each other are more similar to the core values that Christianity espouses than is generally recognized and that both of these are quite different from those of capitalism when capitalism is taken to an extreme. I also know that capitalism has been a far more effective approach in producing prosperity, including broad-based prosperity, than the other approaches, though that approach has tended to operate in the Big Cycle way that has produced the booms and busts that we are looking at comprehensively in this study.

1. **The debt/economic force** led to China's debt rising relative to incomes, though not relative to liquid assets until 2009 (coming out of the global financial crisis). Then debt—especially local government, corporate, and real estate debt—started to grow into a bubble that burst in 2021, which began a deleveraging. Like Japan's, most of China's debt is denominated in its local currency, which allows it to engineer a "beautiful deleveraging," which Japan failed to do. We don't yet know whether China will manage this well, though it now appears to me that China has been slow to deal with it and is in the late part of the Big Debt Cycle that is most analogous to Japan in the 1990s. At the same time, China has highly competitive innovative sectors that are not at all encumbered by debts.
2. **The internal conflict and internal politics force** led the government to tighten controls, leading to an environment of more fear, which has slowed decision making, which has chilled the economy and hurt capital and people flows, which has contributed to economic slowness in China. It has moved about halfway back toward Maoist-Marxist communist policies. At the same time, Chinese policies have been known to swing a lot as a way of creating fear, cleaning things out, and then rebuilding.
3. **The external conflict force** led to the classic great power conflict with the United States, which has hurt flows of trade, capital, and people and led to greater military preparation and risk.
4. **The acts of nature force** took the form of the COVID pandemic problem that started in late 2019 and continued through 2022, which strained the population's satisfaction for how the leadership was handling it, which contributed to the government increasing controls. China also used its remarkable inventiveness, its government-directed economic policies, and its advanced manufacturing capabilities to make such great strides in solar and wind power that it has become the world's most cost-effective producer of these items, which is another story that I won't digress into.

5. **The technology force** led both China and the US to make advances in a number of new technologies, most importantly in advanced AI, with China seemingly having fallen behind the US in the development of the most advanced chips while at the same time excelling in inexpensive AI and advanced manufacturing, especially in robotics. China is very competitive in a number of technology areas.

So, in brief, in recent years four out of the five major forces (i.e., debt/economic, internal conflict, international conflict, and acts of nature) have become increasingly threatening to China, and the fifth, the technology force, appears to be a mixed picture of great advances and falling behind and leaping ahead of the US in different ways. In Part IV, I will tell you what I think about the future.

APPENDIX: CHINA'S BIG DEBT CYCLE IN A FEW CHARTS

I am now going to show you a bunch of charts that do a good job of painting China's debt picture, but I won't get into an analysis with a commentary because a more complete proper analysis would be too much of a digression for now. Also, notably not all the debts are properly accounted for, so these charts are meant to just be broadly indicative.

As shown, China is in the part of the Big Debt Cycle in which non-central-government debt burdens have become excessive and a problem so that the central government and the central bank will have to help manage it. Fortunately, most of the debt is denominated in local currency and most of the debtors and creditors are domestic so that the central government and the central bank have much greater ability to manage this situation than if they weren't. However, China's currency (the renminbi) is not a widely held reserve currency, so it isn't an effective storehold of wealth. Ideally, Chinese policy makers would have both the ability and the courage to swiftly engineer a beautiful deleveraging. However, as previously explained, such adjustments are initially painful because they cause great shifts in wealth and, if not balanced properly, can just shift the debt burdens, worsen the long-term central government debt burdens, and/or so severely undermine the value of the currency as to do great damage to the capital markets and through it to the economy. The Japanese case, and the next chapter on it, provides some valuable lessons for Chinese policy makers (as well as for other policy makers, investors, and businesspeople).

As shown, China's debts are reaching new highs, even as its economy is weaker than desired. That's been the dynamic in Japan over recent decades as well.

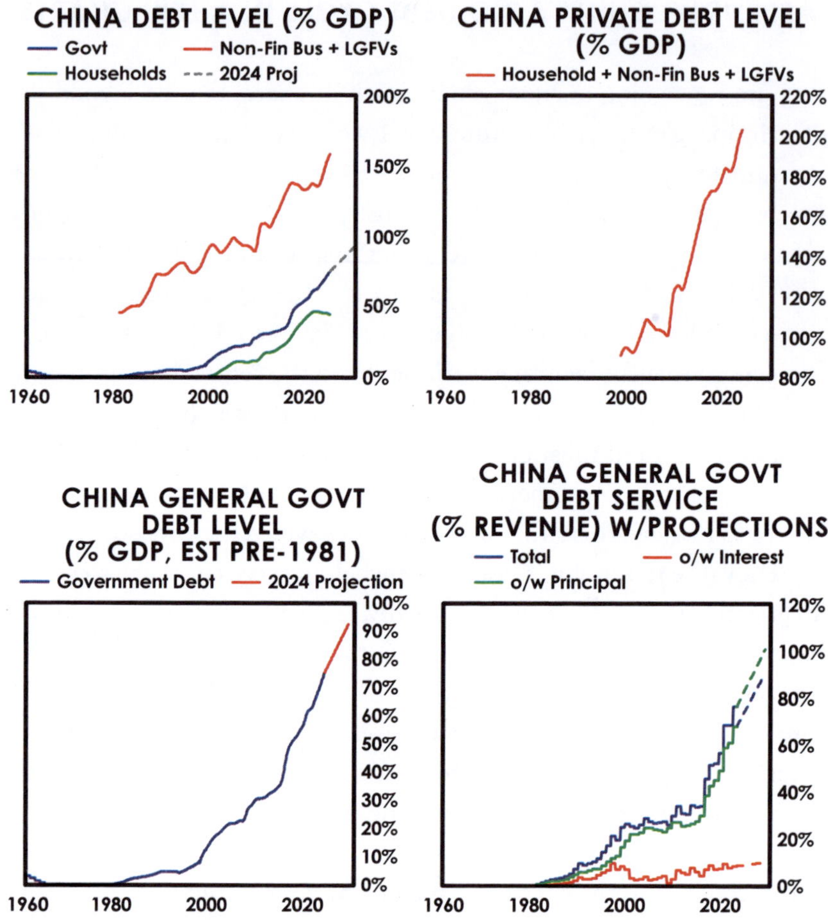

Next, the chart on the left shows the levels of 10-year bond yields relative to the stated one-year and three-year average headline inflation numbers. Actual deflation in both items and in investments held has been worse than shown here. Also, as shown in the chart on the right, real bond yields are about 0.5%, so a) they are relatively unattractive in a normal environment but b) still relatively attractive in relation to a deflating economy with falling asset prices and also c) relatively unattractive relative to other countries', especially the US dollar bond market's interest rates.[47] As shown in the last chart in this group, nominal government bond rates are approaching zero, so other "non-conventional" fiscal and monetary policies will likely have to be used.

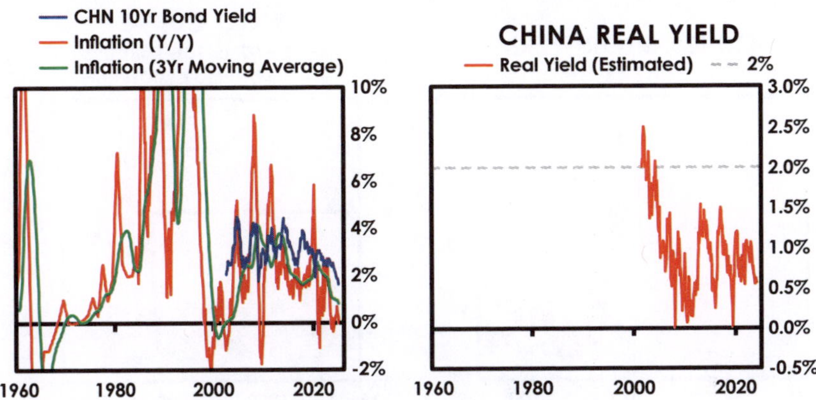

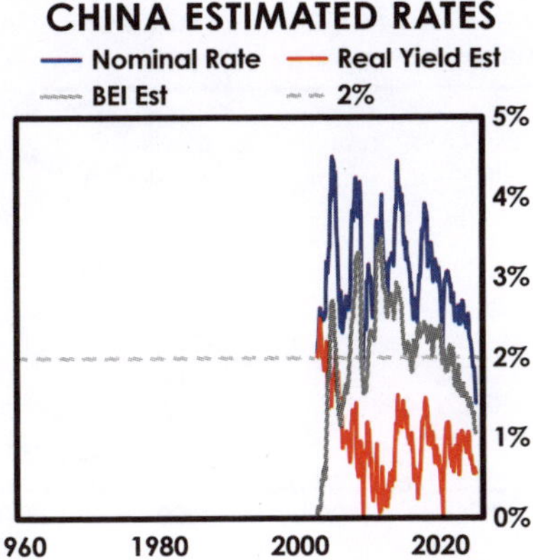

As shown in the following charts, the yield curve (as of late February 2025) is inverted, which makes cash relatively attractive at a time when that encourages a holding of cash, which leads to a "pushing on a string" issue. I previously conveyed my thinking about this in Chapter 1 so I won't repeat it. Also as shown, various measures of

[47] China does not have inflation-linked bonds, so I am showing an estimate of real yields based on nominal yields and an estimate of market 10-year inflation expectations.

liquidity (e.g., total social financing, money supply, total loans from the financial sector) continue to rise without producing a rebound in real economic activity—another sign of "pushing on a string."

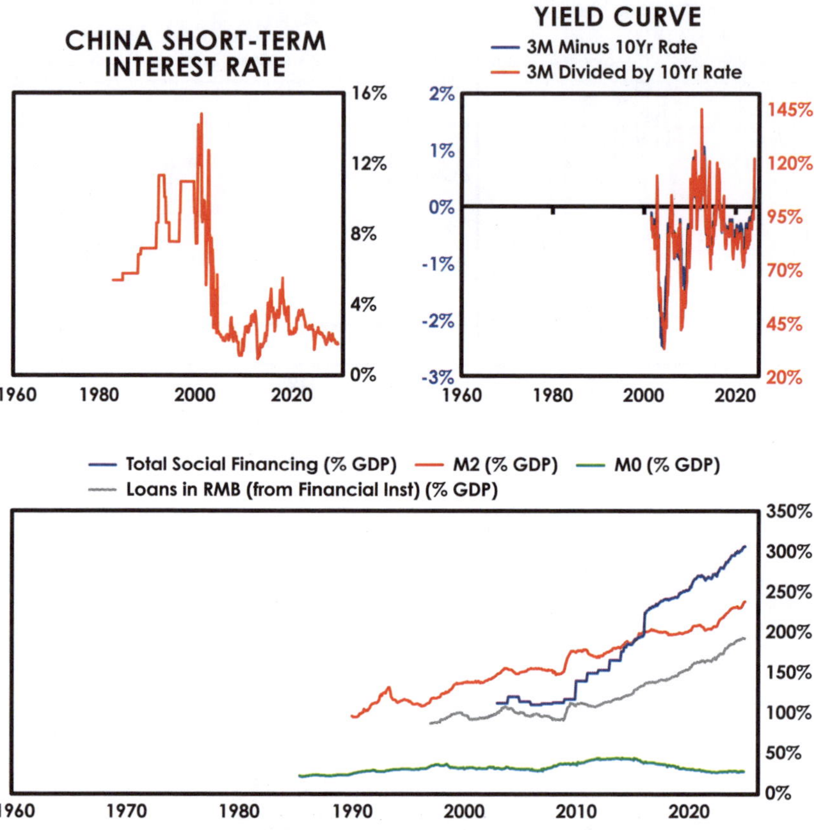

While the previous charts focused on the debt issue in China, I want to conclude this chapter by making the following clear:

While the debt issue is a big, important issue that could be a terrible burden for the Chinese economy as it was for the Japanese economy if Chinese policy makers don't handle it well—i.e., if the leaders don't engineer a beautiful deleveraging, which they have the ability to do because their debts are denominated in their own currency and most debtors and creditors are their own citizens.

However, I want to reiterate that there are important non-debt-burdened parts of the economy that are innovating and flourishing that will certainly be viable both in and out of China in the years to come and that Chinese assets are now very cheap. Chinese policy makers would be well-served to read the next chapter on the Japanese case and the lessons it provides, as would the rest of us.

CHAPTER 16

THE JAPANESE CASE AND THE LESSONS IT PROVIDES

This chapter shows how a heavily indebted reserve currency country, Japan, handled its debts with reference to the earlier-described template. It shows the Big Debt Cycle transpiring in the very classic way, with the cause/effect relationships working as I described, but it is especially interesting because for more than two decades Japanese policy makers did the exact opposite of what should be done to execute a beautiful deleveraging—i.e., they did not restructure the debts for nine years and they didn't drive interest rates below inflation rates and nominal growth rates for 23 years. While this Japanese case study tells a very interesting story for those who are interested in seeing how the economic machine works, it does get a little technical. Those who don't want the technical details can skip them by just reading the highlights in bold, which will take only about 10 minutes.

Japan's story, like China's story, is a very interesting one that extends back to its Big Cycle prior to the one that began in 1945. To put Japan's history into the clear context of its Big Cycle, I will summarize what has happened since the beginning of the new world and domestic orders starting in 1945 and take a very brief look at what happened before 1945. I'm doing that because, as with China's story, Japan's story since 1945 would be greatly lacking in context if we didn't at least briefly touch on the Big Cycle dynamics of the 100 years before.

BEFORE 1945

I will briefly recount Japan's history in the roughly 100 years prior to 1945. Besides using it to help you understand what has happened since then, be sure to observe how the classic Big Cycle of ups and downs repeated in that period before going on to observe how it continued from 1945 up until now.

In brief, like China, Japan had an elevated civilization that was happily isolated from the rest of the world until foreign powers came and demanded to "trade" with Japan and then threatened and exploited Japan. This led to a period in Japan similar to China's Century of Humiliation and the collapse of Japan's internal order, which affected the world order.

In Japan's case, it started with US Commodore Matthew Perry and his American fleet arriving in 1853 and led to the fall of Japan's 250-year-old domestic order under the Tokugawa family shogunate. Because the foreign powers clearly had greater powers than the Japanese, their obvious military superiority led to the collapse of the then-existing domestic order and then-existing monetary order, which were replaced by new ones. **As the Japanese realized that the foreign, more modern approaches were better, the Japanese government was replaced by a new government in 1868, which largely copied the Western powers' approaches.**

The new domestic order was a constitutional monarchy, which had a parliament and a new emperor (Meiji). That led to the modernization of Japan, which was achieved largely by following Western styles for education, the economy, and the military. (Puccini's magnificent *Madama Butterfly* plays out during this Meiji era.) These policies of reform and opening up led to Japan becoming a great power in a way similar to what happened in China when Deng

Xiaoping did a similar reform and opening up about a hundred years later. Under this new order, Japan fought and defeated its two rival regional powers—China in 1894-95 and Russia in 1904-05—and conquered and annexed Korea in 1910. During World War I, it allied itself with the British and took advantage of Germany's fighting in Europe to take over German territories in Asia, as well as some Chinese territories. At the end of World War I, since it was on the winning side, Japan was given formal control of the German territories and the Shandong province in China.

From 1912 to 1926, Japan's domestic order was a parliamentary democracy. But when economic problems began, the classic combination of a debt/economic crisis and the dysfunction of its democracy led to a collapse of public trust and a classic hard-right takeover, characterized by rising nationalism, militarism, and expansionism to secure economic resources and territory. In 1921, Japan's prime minister was assassinated by a young nationalist. After the crash of 1929, the nationalistic military seized control. To consolidate power, the new regime treated opponents as threats and used laws to silence leftists and democratic activists (e.g., the 1925 "Peace Preservation Law"). **The Great Depression made the economic situation worse and from 1937 to 1940 all political parties were dissolved, and there was increasing autocratic control that left the power exclusively in the hands of the military. In other words, events followed the classic script.**

Geopolitically, this newly nationalistic and militaristic Japan invaded and took over China's Manchuria region (in 1931) and more of China (in 1937). Then it got into a conflict with the United States, which led the US to impose trade sanctions, similar to what's happening with the US-China conflict today. The US, the UK, and the Netherlands imposed export restrictions that hurt the Japanese economy and Japanese security by freezing Japanese assets and cutting off oil exports to Japan. This led to Japan attacking the US naval fleet at Pearl Harbor, which led to a war with the United States that Japan lost due to the United States secretly

inventing a powerful technology that could be used for both peace and war—nuclear power. Because of Japan losing World War II, all Japanese money and debt were destroyed, and Japan was occupied and reconstructed by the United States from 1945 until 1952.

The following chart shows the total debt-to-GDP ratio going back to 1870. It shows both the Big Debt Cycle prior to 1945 and the one since. As you can see, there was the big run-up in debt in the 1930-45 period before and during the war, the debt wipeout that brought it down to low levels until 1970, the big debt bubble leading to the debt bust in 1989-90, and the rise in that ratio until recently. That is what the Big Debt Cycles have looked like since 1870. As is normal when looking at the Big Debt Cycles, the short-term debt and economic cycles are imperceptible.

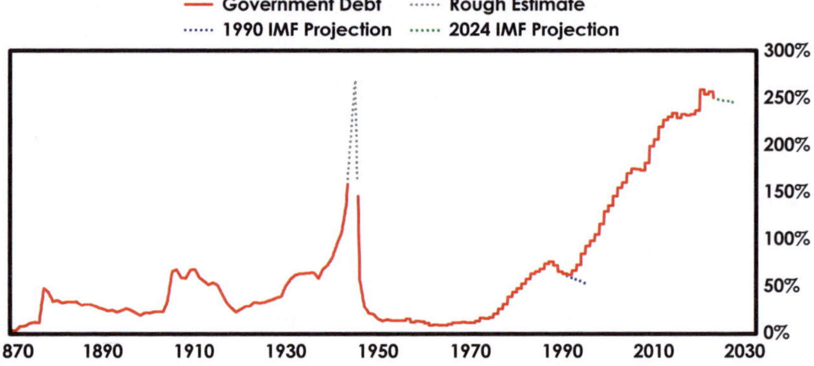

SINCE 1945

In brief, from 1945 through 1990, Japan rebuilt itself to become the second-greatest economic power in the world and in the process built up a huge debt burden that funded a bubble that burst in 1989-90, which has had a huge weakening effect on Japan ever since. I will now look at the time from the debt bubble bursting until today because that is the most relevant period to understanding the part of the Big Debt Cycle that this study is focused on. The lessons that examining this part of the Big Debt Cycle provides in helping us understand other cases—most importantly the current cases in the United States, China, and Europe—are very valuable. Since I am focused on the deleveraging part of the Big Cycle, I won't cover the 1945-90 period and will focus on the post-1990 period.

THE BIG DEBT CYCLE SINCE 1990

The Japanese government's handling of its debt problem from 1990 until 2013 exemplified exactly what not to do. It was the exact opposite of what I described should be done to execute a beautiful deleveraging even though Japan had the capacity to execute a beautiful deleveraging because almost all of its debt was denominated in its local currency and almost all of the difficult debtor-creditor relationships were between Japanese parties, plus it was a net creditor to the rest of the world. More specifically, policy makers did not restructure their debts so the debt burdens lingered on bank and company balance sheets making them "zombie institutions," they held to employment and cost policies that were rigid so that they couldn't effectively cut costs and adapt, they didn't make interest rates low in relation to both nominal growth rates and inflation, and they did not meaningfully monetize their debts until after there was deflation and interest rates were near zero in 1995. For nearly two decades, the amount of fiscal and free-market policy adjustments and the amounts of monetary stimulus and debt purchases were woefully insufficient to engineer a beautiful deleveraging. As a result, until mid-2013, Japan had continuous deflation and economic stagnation as companies and people didn't have the previously described financial conditions to get this debt burden crisis behind them. The Japanese government did not deal with its non-performing-loan problem until 1999 (so for nine years after the debt bubble popped) when the government finally forced the banking system to restructure its debts and injected huge amounts of capital into the banks, and it didn't monetize debt and bring interest rates significantly below nominal growth and inflation rates until 2013. Additionally, Japan's aging population was a headwind (e.g., in 1990, 12% of the population was over 65 and 69% of the population was working-age while now 29% of the population is over 65 and only 59% is working-age).

Fiscal and monetary policies changed greatly and appropriately when Bank of Japan Governor Kuroda and Prime Minister Abe came to power in late 2012/early 2013 and initiated their "three arrows" policy to 1) increase the money supply, 2) boost central government spending, and 3) enact economic and regulatory reforms to make the Japanese economy more competitive, which, as previously described, are classically the best policies to negate deflationary, depressionary forces. As a result, from 2013 through 2019, there was no deflation and there was low positive growth (0.9% per year) and the beginning of a healing period, though the deflationary and depressing psychological conditions lingered. The psychological overhang of 23 years of debt depression has had lasting negative effects on the strength and vibrancy that characterized Japan prior to 1990 and many times throughout history.

During this period, extremely large debt monetization and fiscal deficit stimulus (5% of GDP deficits on average) and extremely large central bank buying of Japanese yen debt (the BoJ now holds government bonds worth more than 90% of GDP) took place, which pushed interest rates 0.9% below the nominal growth rate and 1% below the inflation rate on average, and depreciated the yen, all of which were very stimulative. The combined lower interest rates and currency depreciation led to Japanese government bonds being a terrible storehold of wealth, losing 45% relative to US bonds and 60% relative to gold. These and other actions provided an average interest rate that was about 2.2% below the US rate and depreciated the currency by an average rate of 5.5% per year in real terms versus the dollar. More specifically, the -45% cumulative return of a Japanese government bond versus a US government bond was almost entirely attributable to currency depreciation, since the lower carry/accrual from Japanese bonds was entirely offset by price gains (roughly 20%) due to falling Japanese yields. At the same time, Japanese inflation averaged only 1.1% per year relative to US inflation of 2.7% per year because of domestic deflationary pressures. The principle should resonate: ● ***don't own government bonds when there are extreme amounts of debt monetization.***

Let's look at what happened more closely.

While there has been modest inflation of 0.8% per year in average worker compensation in yen terms since 2013, the big yen depreciations—along with greater wage gains in other nations—made them more competitive. For example, there has been a total decline of 58% in the cost of a Japanese worker relative to an American worker since 2013. Similarly, other domestic items in Japan have fallen a lot in cost relative to the costs in other countries. Both have helped to make Japan more competitive. These changes are shown in the following charts.

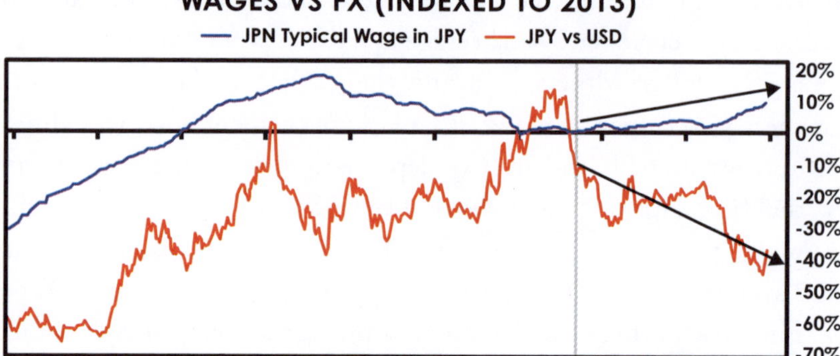

Low interest rates reduced debt service costs a lot—since 2013, Japanese interest debt service has fallen over 50% (and has fallen over 65% since 2001), making it much easier to service the debt.

Still, the Japanese debt relative to the size of the economy has increased by almost 10%. To neutralize its effects, the Bank of Japan bought over half of all the government debt and absorbed the debt service costs, which it monetized. The declines in interest rates engineered by the BoJ also contributed to the debt relief (though more of that benefit occurred even before Governor Kuroda took the helm, as short rates had already hit zero).

HOW JAPAN MANAGED BIG INCREASES IN TOTAL GOVT DEBT AND BIG DECLINES IN INTEREST PAYMENTS

	2001	2013 (Pre-QE)	Today	% Chg	
Govt Debt (% GDP)	99%	197%	215%	9%	Debt increased by ~10%. . .
ex-CB Holdings	93%	178%	123%	-31%	. . .but the CB monetized enough to push ex-CB debt down ~30%.
Average Interest Rate on Govt Debt	2.3%	0.9%	0.6%	-40%	Meanwhile, average interest rates fell 40%. . .
ex-CB Govt Interest Service (% GDP)	2.1%	1.7%	0.7%	-56%	. . .and the interest govt pays to the public is down >50%.

The following charts show these trends. The bottom-left chart shows the substantial declines in the interest service actually paid by the government to the public, and the other charts show how Japan got there: through central bank purchases and large declines in interest and principal payments.

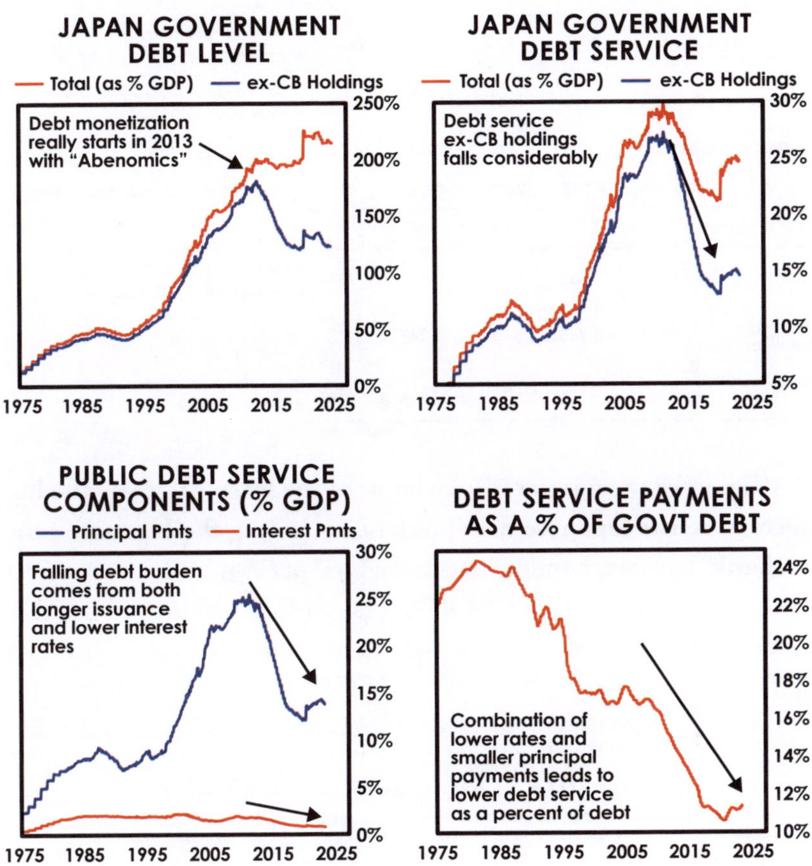

Remarkably, the massive increase in debt that occurred in this period was concurrent with an improvement in Japan's central government balance sheet. Net assets (government assets minus government liabilities) are now 20% better in dollar terms compared to 2013 because the Bank of Japan accumulated dollar reserves (primarily in the 2001-12 period) and Japan's debts as measured in dollars are not up as much due to the yen depreciation.

HOW JAPAN MANAGED BIG INCREASES IN GOVT DEBT AND BIG IMPROVEMENTS IN ITS BALANCE SHEET

	2001	2013 (Pre-QE)	Today	Change (Since '01)	
Total Debt (% GDP)	99%	197%	215%	116%	Total govt debt more than doubled. . .
Debt ex-CB (% GDP)	93%	178%	123%	33%	. . .while debt held by public is only up ~30%.
Debt ex-CB (JPY, Tln)	504	893	748	49%	Up a lot in yen terms. . .
Debt ex-CB (USD, Bln)	4,322	9,734	4,650	8%	. . .but not as much in dollar terms.
USD/JPY Spot	117	92	144	23%	
Reserves (USD, Bln)	358	1,371	1,408	293%	Reserves up in dollar terms because of accumulation
Assets (Reserves) - Liabilities (Debt)	-3,965	-8,363	-3,242	18%	
Assets - Liabilities (% GDP)	-85%	-153%	-76%	9%	Improvement in "net worth" of government

Who were the winners and who were the losers? Clearly the big losers were the Japanese debt holders, including the Japanese central bank. Japanese bond holders lost a total of 6% in real terms (as real yields were generally negative), 45% versus if they had instead held US bonds, and 60% relative to the old "hard money" of gold. Next is a chart of the real return of just holding JGBs as a Japanese investor (in local currency) and their performance relative to US bonds and gold.

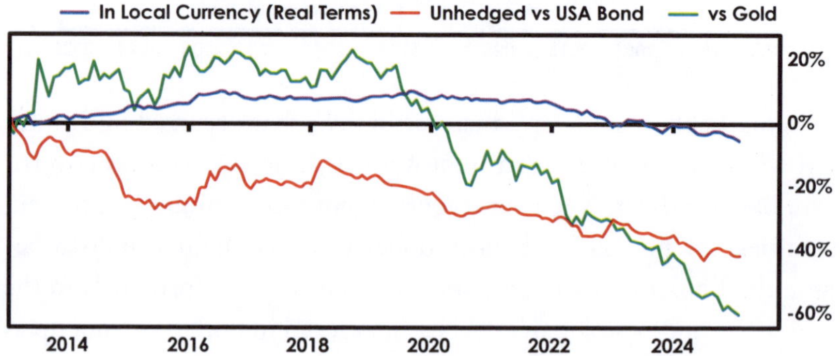

During this period, there was also a big deterioration in the BoJ's balance sheet. These losses will be very large if Japanese real and nominal bond yields rise to more reasonable levels (e.g., 2% and 3%, respectively).

For example, if Japan were to have a 3% rise in real interest rates (from -0.3% to 2.7%), then:

- The BoJ would experience about a 30% of GDP mark-to-market loss on its bond holdings and would be in a seriously negative cash flow situation of around -2.5% of GDP.
- The government would see the deficit widen from roughly 4% of GDP to around 8% of GDP over the next 10 years due to the increase in interest costs (not including any outlays to cover central bank losses). The government debt level would surpass its post-WWII peak, rising from 220% to 300% over the next 20 years.

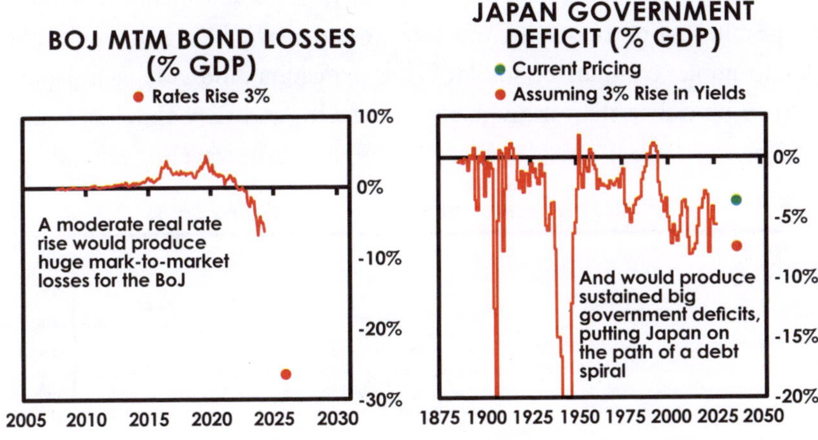

- **The combined cash flow need across the central bank and the central government would be around 5-6% of GDP per year, which is huge.** That would have to be handled through debt issuance, money printing, and/or deficit reduction. If it were financed by central bank printing, this would be the equivalent of another round of QE in terms of expansion of the money stock, not including any additional printing needed to offset selling by the private sector.

- **Resolving it would require even greater write-downs in debt and devaluations of the currency**—with the Japanese people becoming relatively poorer in the process—until Japan is competitive enough to begin a new cycle.

Key non-tradable goods—local wages, local services, local housing—have seen essentially no price increases in yen terms and significant deflation in global currency terms since 2000. The affordability of rent (rent compared to wages) has barely moved. This is despite tradable goods and commodities being way up because of the currency's depreciation. And Japanese workers are more competitive than ever.

That said, Japan has seen dramatically lower dollar incomes, meaning purchases on imports are much more expensive. Using the most apples-to-apples comparison (dollar GDP per capita), individuals in Japan used to be richer than individuals in the US, and now they are some 60% poorer. This is obvious to any Japanese person traveling abroad.

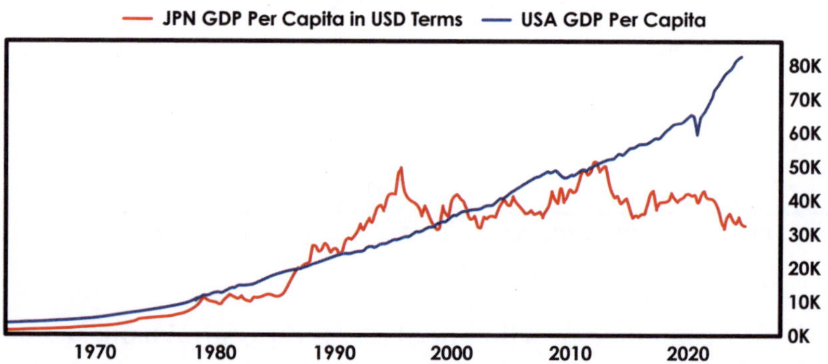

For a different angle of who the winners and losers were, it's helpful to take a look at how prices have changed in Japan at a very granular level because it provides a window into what it's like to earn, spend, and save there. The following table provides a lot of details, but to summarize:

- Since 2000, the yen is down 30%. If you were a US investor who kept their money in yen versus dollars earning the dollar interest rate, you'd be down 84%.
  - Your returns for holding unhedged Japanese bonds versus US bonds were slightly better (but still very bad, down roughly 70%) and slightly better (but still very bad) for unhedged Japanese equities versus US equities (down around 67%).
- Meanwhile, prices in Japan (aggregate CPI) are up 10%—much less than in the US, where prices are up 90%.
- At the same time, all fiat currencies have devalued versus goods. The dollar has depreciated about 50% in the last 25 years.
- **Whereas total average inflation is similar across major categories, the composition of inflation is very different. In Japan, there has been deflation in non-tradables—housing and labor especially—while prices of tradable goods (i.e., things you can purchase from abroad like electronics, toys, oil, etc.) have soared with some key tradable commodities up more than 3x in yen terms.**
  - Non-tradables are about flat in price while tradable commodities are up 2-10x (3x on average).

	JPY			USD		
	Price in 2000	Price Today	% Chg in FX Buying Power	Price in 2000	Price Today	% Chg in FX Buying Power
FX vs USD	107	156	-31%	-	-	-
Aggregate CPI	1	1.11	-10%	1	1.95	-49%
Non-Tradables						
Housing	1	0.98	2%	1	2.14	-53%
Services	1	1.07	-6%	1	2.08	-52%
Tradables						
Goods (CPI Indices)						
Food/Beverage	1	1.32	-24%	1	1.84	-46%
HH Durables	1	0.86	16%	1	1.16	-14%
Clothes/Footwear	1	1.14	-12%	1	1.04	-4%
Commodities						
Soybeans	52,318	174,594	-70%	488	1,122	-57%
Wheat	27,650	85,725	-68%	258	551	-53%
Oil	2,933	12,637	-77%	27	81	-66%
Natural Gas	288	328	-12%	3	2	28%
Coal	2,254	20,961	-89%	21	135	-84%
Aluminum	184,000	353,235	-48%	1,715	2,270	-24%
Copper	194,410	1,395,822	-86%	1,812	8,970	-80%
Lean Hogs	6,375	13,971	-54%	59	90	-34%
Live Cattle	7,390	30,137	-75%	69	194	-64%
Gold	30,436	377,104	-92%	284	2,423	-88%
Silver	568	4,561	-88%	5	29	-82%
Avg of CMDs	1	3.2	-69%	1	2.23	-55%

Return of Holding Yen in a Bank, Converting at End: -29%
Return of Holding Yen Financed with Borrowed USD, Converting at End: -84%

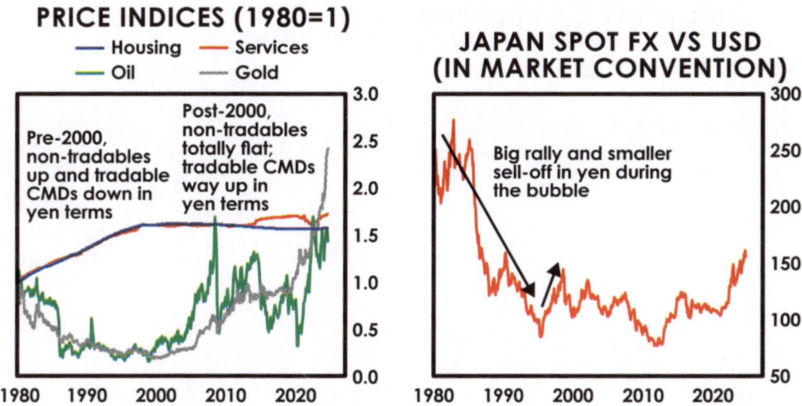

- All of this is largely the inverse of what happened in the lead-up to the bubble (1980-90), when overheating growth and strong capital inflows led to both significant non-tradables inflation (+40%) and yen strength (+70%). These changes reflect the changes in the Big Cycle in Japan.

The following charts convey the picture for a Japanese worker. As shown, in the past 25 years, typical worker wages were relatively flat in yen terms, just shy of 400,000 yen a month, but fell significantly in dollar and world currency terms. In other words, while the average Japanese worker used to make the equivalent of $3,500 a month, they now make about $2,500. In gold terms, they used to earn 13 ounces of gold-equivalent a month; now it's 1 ounce.

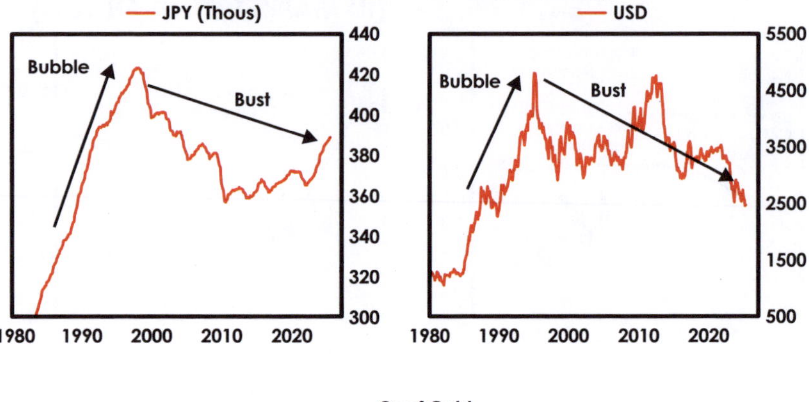

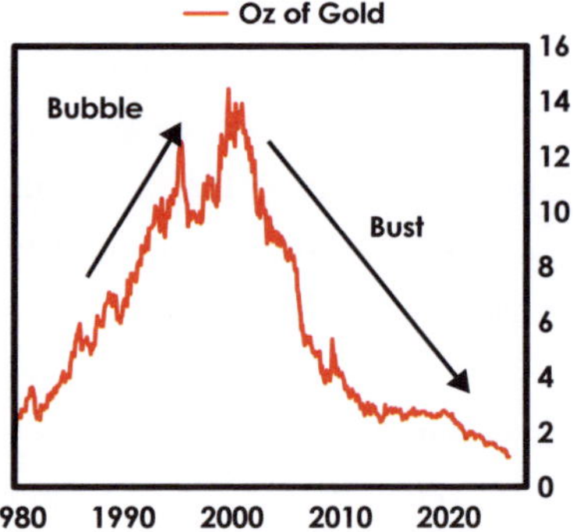

For the Japanese people, the relevant question is how much of their labor it takes to afford what they purchase, and the fact that non-tradable essentials stayed affordable was important. The rent on a typical apartment—maybe the purest non-tradable—has stayed almost flat in hours-of-work terms, at 0.6 months of labor (though it's way less expensive in dollar terms).

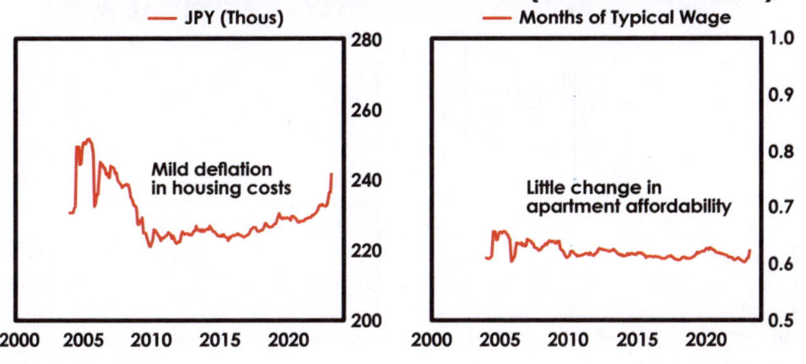

Source: ARES JP

You can also see the impact by looking at some real prices of items that mix commodities with heavy doses of domestic labor. The data on costs of vehicles tends to wiggle a lot, but roughly speaking a domestically made car used to cost eight months of labor, and now it's nine months. A convenience store boxed lunch used to take 10 minutes of work to afford, now it's 16 minutes (up more than 60%). Going to a theme park used to cost a third of a day of labor, now it's a half a day.

TYPICAL CONVENIENCE STORE BOXED LUNCH (EST)—HOURS OF TYPICAL WAGE

Bubble
Bust
0.45
0.40
0.35
0.30
0.25
0.20
0.15
0.10
1980
1990
2000
2010
2020

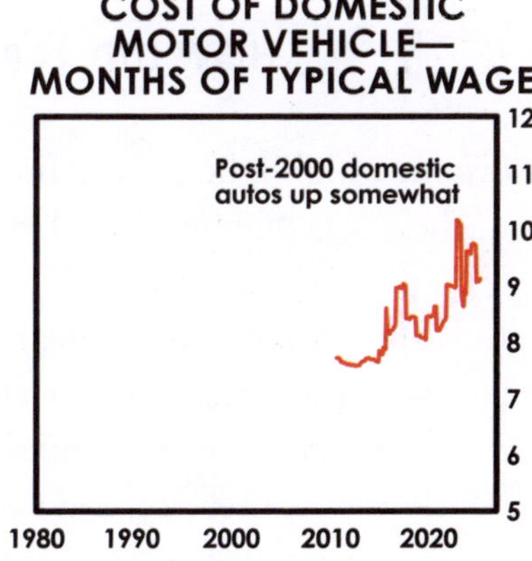

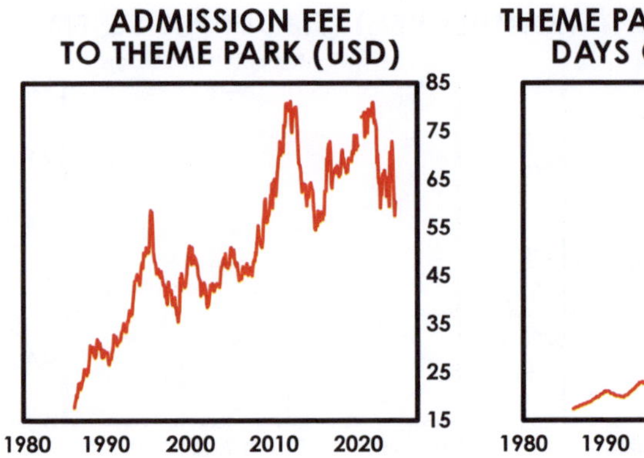

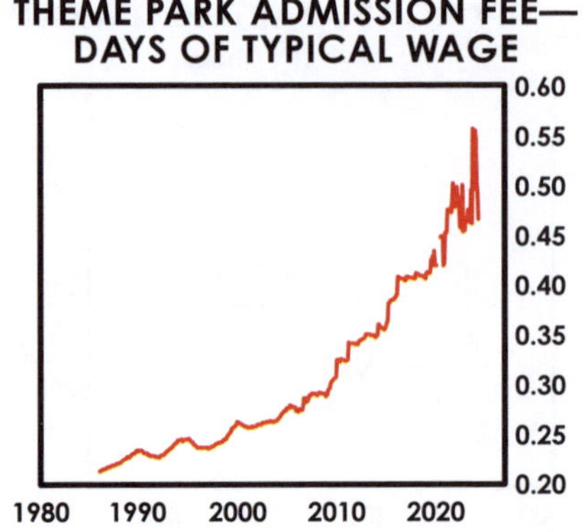

The charts reflect the dramatic changes that took place and are likely to continue to take place due to the previously described typical mechanical process of the Big Debt Cycle in which the country has a lot of debt denominated in its own currency and it is a reserve currency country.

Remarkably during this period, there were no really big internal or external conflicts, though Japan is now preparing for war with China (though it doesn't want it) as the United States' most important ally in the region.

HOW DID JAPAN GET HERE?

I want to highlight five dynamics at play in Japan that helped bring about these sets of winners and losers. Here is what happened:

1. The government's deficit spending floods the private sector with cash, aiding in private sector deleveraging.
2. The central bank monetizes the debt to keep long rates low, lower debt service, and boost demand. The government's debt burden minus central bank holdings begins to fall as a percent of GDP.
3. The resulting currency depreciation acts as a sort of tax on foreign investors holding unhedged domestic bonds and

domestic investors who didn't invest outside the country, while it lowers the government debt burden as that falls in value when measured in foreign FX and gold.

4. Domestic savers are similarly taxed, though to a lesser degree because, even though their buying power abroad decreases, that fall in buying power isn't as much domestically.
5. The country gets more competitive as both assets and factors of production get cheaper.

More specifically it happened in the following way.

Dynamic 1: Public sector deficit spending floods the private sector with cash, helping the private sector delever.

The following chart shows that dynamic, with public sector debt rising from roughly 1990 to 2020, during the period of private sector deleveraging. After that government leveraging, Japan was left with the highest government debt levels of any major country. There are many historical cases of other governments struggling to deal with their debt burdens. Japan was able to manage it because of the second dynamic.

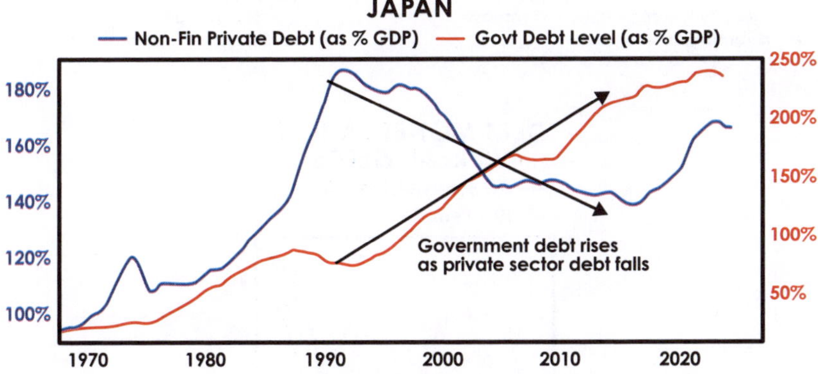

Dynamic 2: The central bank monetizes the debt to keep long rates low, lower debt service, and boost demand. The government's debt burden minus central bank holdings begins to fall as a percent of GDP.

The following table shows how Japan's debt service (interest and principal repayment) in yen effectively fell by around 7% during a period in which debts rose by nearly 30%. About half of that was because of lower interest rates (shown in the second chart) and debt being termed out. The other half was because of BoJ purchases of the debt.

JAPAN CHANGE IN PUBLIC DEBT SERVICE AS A % GDP SINCE 2013

Metric	Contribution	Level (2013)	Level (2023)
Δ in Debt Service as % GDP	-11%	26%	15%
Δ in Debt Service (Yen)	-7%	128 Tln	85 Tln
Δ in ex-CB Govt Debt	-3%	898 Tln	748 Tln
Δ in Total Govt Debt	6%	997 Tln	1270 Tln
Δ in CB Holdings	-9%	99 Tln	522 Tln
Δ in Debt Service as % Govt Debt	-4%	14%	11%
Δ in Avg Interest Rate	-1%	0.9%	0.6%
Δ in Principal Payments	-4%	13%	11%
Δ in GDP (Yen)	-4%	497 Tln	583 Tln
Δ in Price Level	-2%	-	-
Δ in Real GDP	-2%	-	-

Lower interest rate and longer-maturity issuance helped decrease debt service costs

Expansion of CB balance sheet largely offset additional government debt

DEBT MONETIZATION VS REAL YIELDS

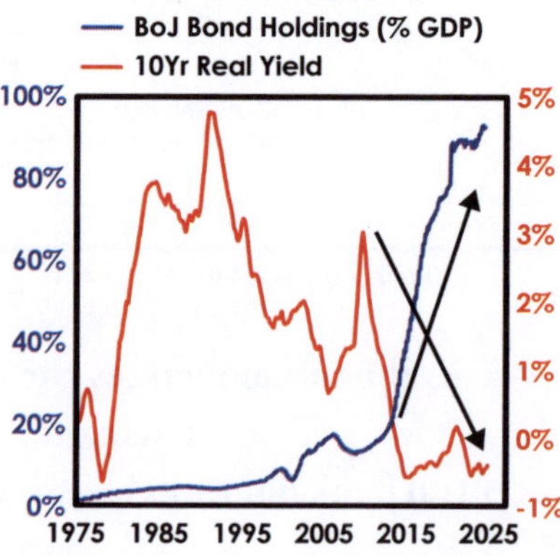

Dynamic 3: The resulting currency depreciation acts as a sort of tax on foreign investors holding unhedged domestic bonds and lowers the government debt burden in foreign FX and gold.

BoJ actions significantly contributed to declines in the yen, as shown in this chart.

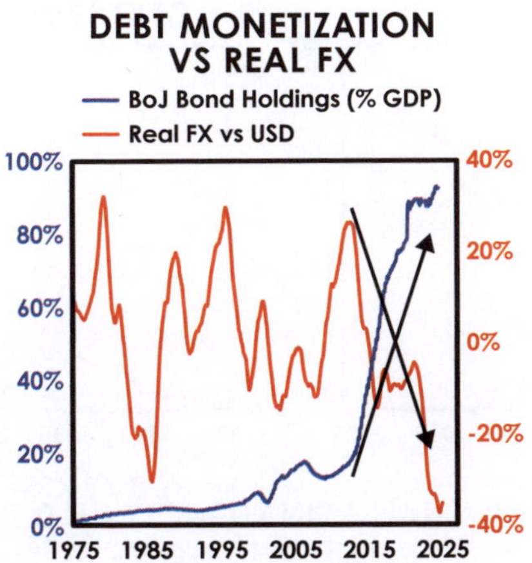

This meant that holders of yen-denominated assets saw their holdings lose a significant amount of value. The following charts compare the returns of yen bonds to dollar bonds, and yen currency to USD currency. In both cases, yen holdings lost more than half of the value. This is not dissimilar to a default.

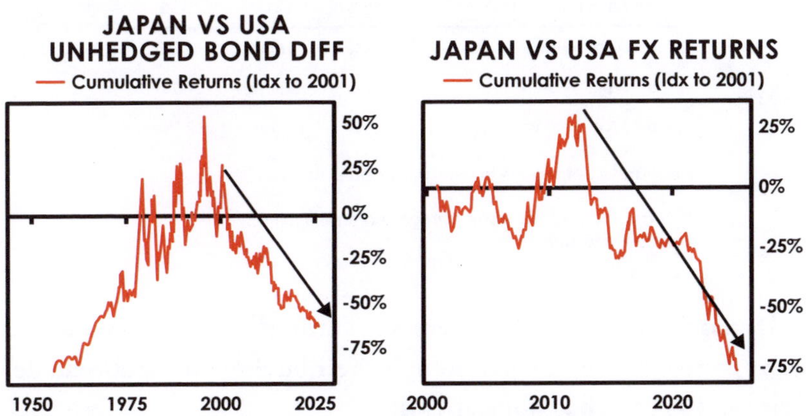

This also has produced a deleveraging of Japanese government debt as measured in other currencies. Measured in dollars, debt service is down since 2001, a period with rapid government borrowing. Measured in gold, debt levels are down some 80%.

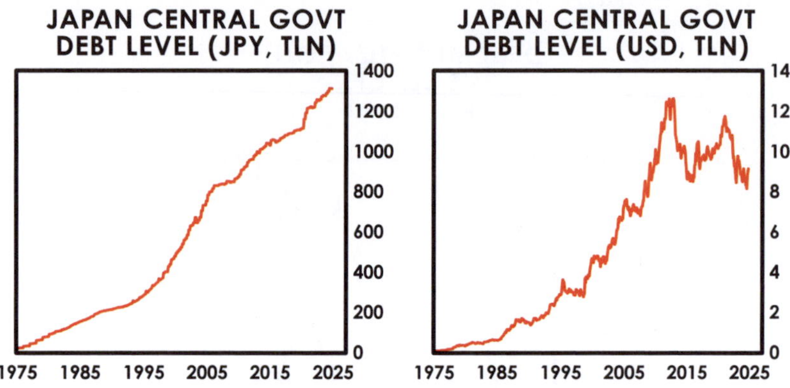

JAPAN CHANGE IN PUBLICLY HELD DEBT IN USD AND GOLD

Metric	% Change Since 2001	Level (2001)	Level (2023)
Δ in Total Debt (USD)	30%	4.3 Tln	5.6 Tln
o/w Δ in Debt (JPY)	48%	504 Tln	748 Tln
o/w Δ in Spot vs USD	-12%	117	133
Δ in Debt Service (USD)	-16%	0.8 Tln	0.6 Tln
o/w Δ in Debt Service (JPY)	-4%	88 Tln	85 Tln
o/w Δ in Spot vs USD	-12%	117	133
Δ Total Debt (Gold)	-82%	16 Bln	3 Bln
o/w Δ in Debt (JPY)	48%	504 Tln	748 Tln
o/w Δ in Spot vs Gold	-88%	31 Thous	262 Thous

Debt and debt service in foreign FX and gold falls

Sub-components for each category are multiplicative, i.e., sum geometrically

Dynamic 4: Domestic savers are similarly taxed, though to a lesser degree because, even though their buying power abroad decreases, it's not as bad domestically.

We'll look at this point through two lenses:

- Holders of Japanese government debt without the currency exposure have done OK, even while the assets have done quite badly in dollar terms.

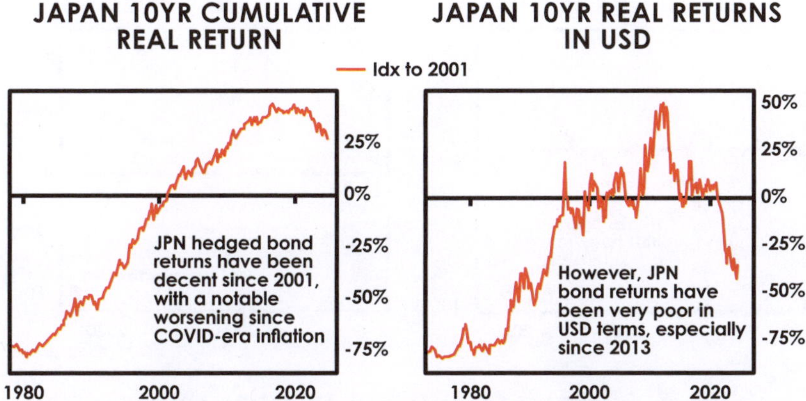

- Japanese households have seen muted inflation over the period (discussed in more depth previously). The weak economy has kept the currency declines from translating into much domestic inflation.

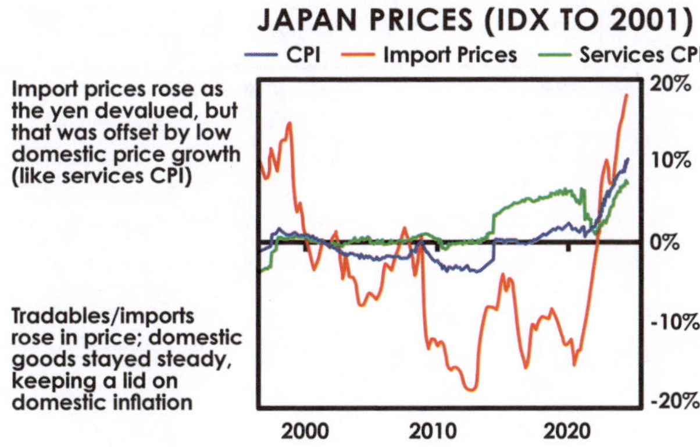

Dynamic 5: The country gets more competitive as both assets and factors of production get cheaper.

In the next charts, note how just about everything in Japan became much cheaper and how that attracted FDI inflows.

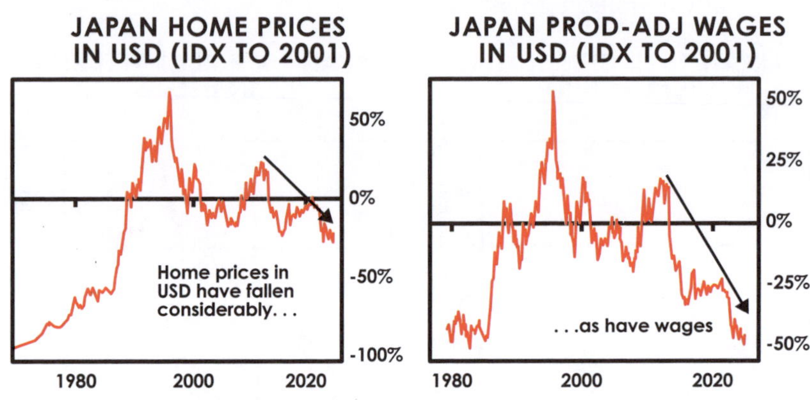

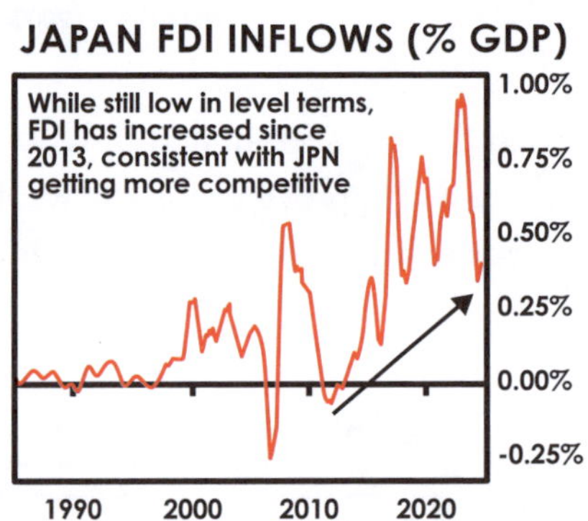

Asset valuations have mirrored this as well. Japan went from one of the more overvalued markets (at least as measured by imperfect statistics like P/Es) to inexpensive relative to the US.

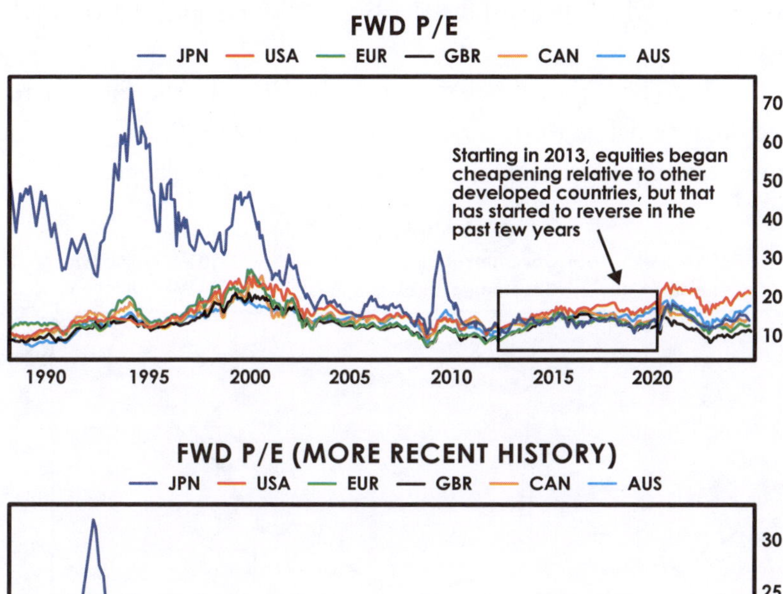

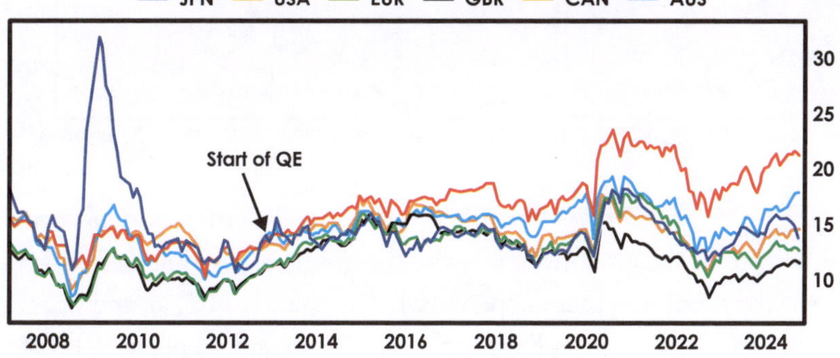

APPENDIX: JAPAN'S BIG DEBT CYCLE IN A FEW CHARTS

As with China, we'll end this chapter with charts that are more zoomed out, which helps show the Big Cycle transpiring over many decades.

The first chart shows Japan's Big Debt Cycle in the form of the government's debt-to-GDP ratio going back to 1900; that way you can see two Big Cycles, though we will focus on the second.

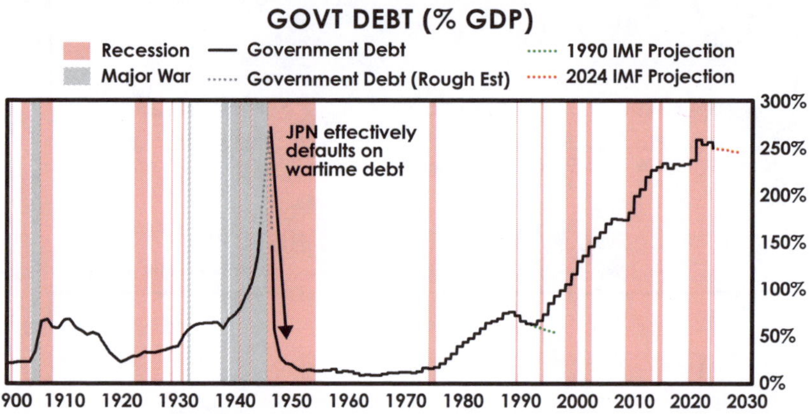

The next chart shows the amount of central government debt service as a percent of the amount of revenue the government took in. In it, you can see the debt busts that happened when it exceeded 150%, and you can see how, in recent years, it has risen toward—but stayed below—150%.

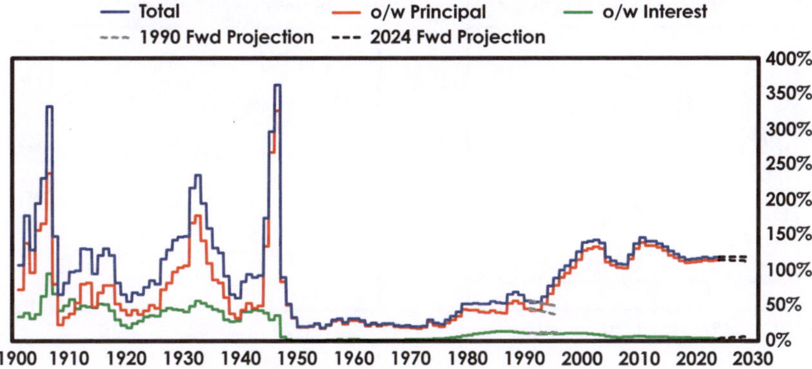

I will now shift to a post-1950 perspective. Through these charts, you can see how the last couple of decades are best characterized by "pushing on a string," with nominal rates falling below 0%, real rates a bit negative,[48] large amounts of money printing, and the yield curve just slightly upward-sloping. Corporate spreads have stayed low (for perspective, as of this writing, they are around 1% in the US and 0.6% in Japan for Baa-rated companies). All of these are characteristics of very stimulative monetary policy, especially in the last decade or so. Despite the stimulative policy, inflation has remained much lower than policy makers have generally desired, slipping in and out of deflation.

[48] I am showing real yields since the creation of the Japanese inflation-linked bond market in 2004. Prior to this, I am showing an estimate of real yields based on nominal yields and an estimate of market 10-year inflation expectations.

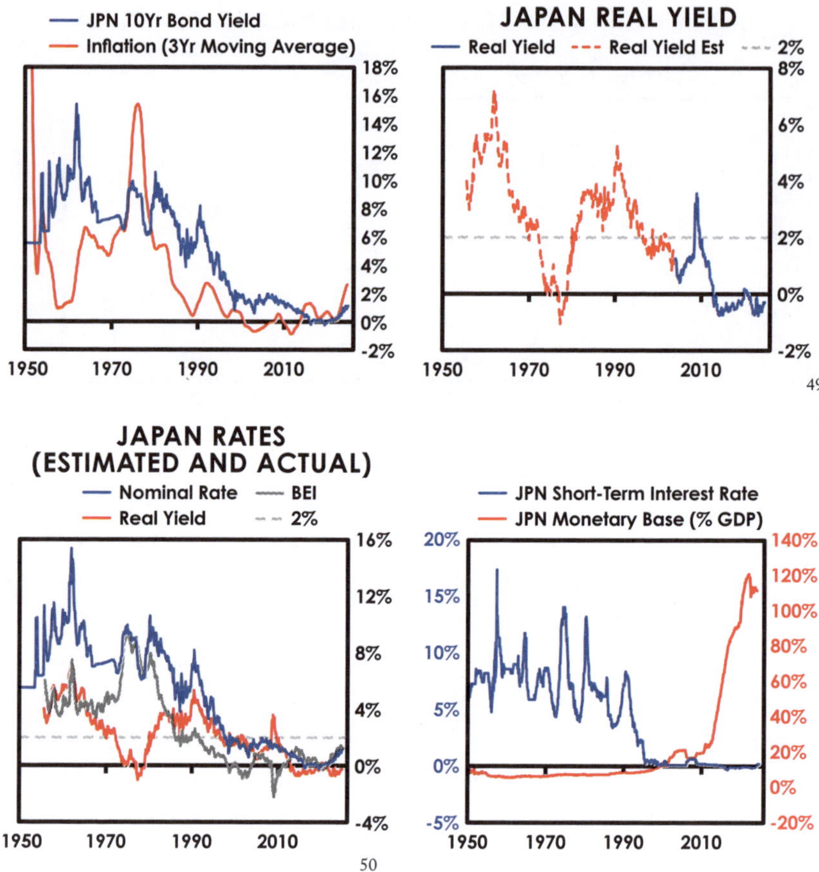

[49] [50]

[49] We show rough estimates of the real yield and breakeven inflation rate (using surveyed inflation expectations and recent inflation) for periods when those were unobservable because inflation-linked bond markets did not exist.

[50] *Id.*

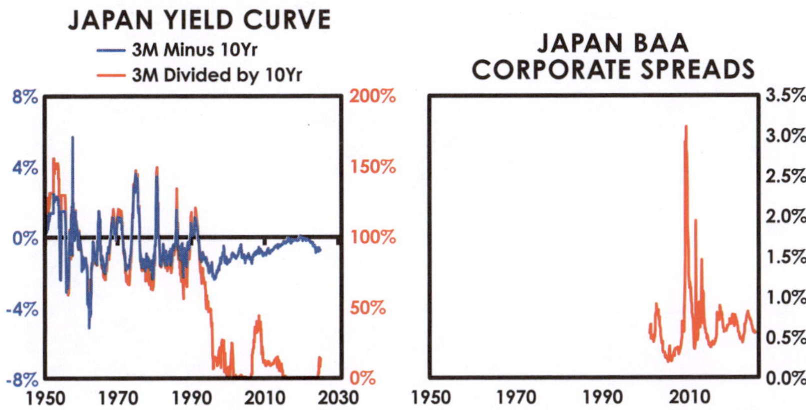

Highly stimulative policy comes with risks. So far, the BoJ has remained profitable: the bonds it's bought (with printed money) haven't seen big sell-offs, and the interest it's had to pay on excess reserves has remained quite low (because of low short-term interest rates). But if rates rise, the BoJ will become significantly unprofitable, fast. That recently happened to the Federal Reserve, producing moderate but manageable losses—up to 0.5% of GDP. But with the BoJ's monetary base at around 5x the Fed's, losses could be much more meaningful.

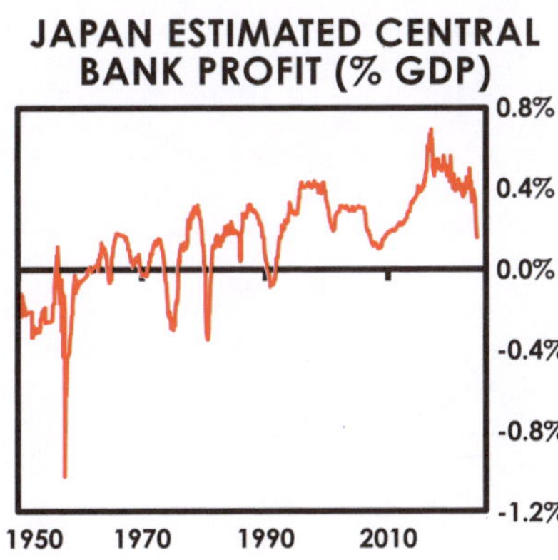

NOTE: MY FAILURE TO COVER A LOT

While it might seem like I covered a lot in this review of the period since 1945, what I left out was vastly greater than what I included. While I briefly looked at what happened in the United States, China, and Japan, I showed virtually nothing of what happened in the other developed powers (e.g., European powers) and Middle Eastern countries, and I barely mentioned most emerging countries, also known as the Global South (which includes many countries in Asia, Africa, Latin America, and Oceania). They all had and are having their Big Cycles. I am excited to say that with AI I am beginning to get my head around it all, and I have reason to believe that my digital self will evolve way beyond me to make sense of all these Big Cycles and communicate with you about them. (By the way, if you are interested in communicating with my digital self, you can receive updates on this AI initiative on my social media and by signing up at principles.com.)

Of the many countries I haven't been able to mention, it is worth taking a moment to look at rising countries with strong fundamentals (as reflected in my strength gauge that consists of 18 measures), like India, ASEAN countries (such as Singapore, Indonesia, and Vietnam), the UAE, and Saudi Arabia, which have benefited by being neutral vis-à-vis the power conflicts. A number of them are at take-off points in their developmental cycles because their people, governance systems, and capital markets are approaching being capable of competing in ways that they couldn't previously. Also, the conflicts between the United States and China are making the United States and China less desirable, which is driving capital, businesses, and talented individuals to these places. If you want to look at them more closely, I recommend that you look at my Country Power Index that summarizes the conditions and prospects of the top 24 countries. They are available for free at economicprinciples.org.

PART IV

LOOKING AHEAD

The first three parts of this book outlined the Big Debt Cycle based on my research of history and showed its mechanics in concepts, numbers, and historical examples. This final part, Part IV, applies the template to the present day, including my financial health and risk measures for central governments and central banks (Chapter 17) and my recommended solutions for the US given its current debt projections and pending problems (Chapter 18). Then, to conclude the book, I attempt to look into the future using my previously described template for how the machine works, taking into consideration the current and projected conditions of all the major forces that together make up the Overall Big Cycle. (Chapter 19).

CHAPTER 17

WHAT MY INDICATORS SHOW

In making my assessments of risks, I weigh a number of factors, many of which I have described and the most important of which are shown in the following table. The table shows these indicators across major countries as of my writing this in March 2025. Though they aren't all of my indicators and they are not enough to convey the whole picture, they paint a good enough picture. Think of this table as a dashboard that paints a rough, current picture of health in order to assess central government and central bank long-term debt risks. In addition to showing risks from existing and projected debt and debt service levels, it includes measures of whether a country has a reserve currency because being a reserve currency country—i.e., having one's currency widely accepted around the world as both a medium of exchange and a storehold of wealth—is a great risk mitigator, especially if the country is a good place to invest, as is currently the case for the US and its money and debt.

By looking at the indicators in the table, you can get a pretty good picture of what a country's debt risks are. You can see that the US has very large central government debts (which is a big risk) and low liquid savings/reserves (which means it has little protection from its debts), but its currency is the dominant world reserve currency (which is a great mitigator of the risk), which the US is undermining by a number of things it is doing (which I won't reiterate because it would be too much of a digression). From all this, you can see that its financial well-being hinges on maintaining its existing reserve currency status. You can also see that the Japanese central government has very large debts (which is a big risk) that are denominated in its currency (which mitigates the risk) and relatively large FX reserves (which reduces the risk). You can see that China has relatively big debts (which is risky), its debts are denominated in its own currency (which is risk-mitigating), it has relatively big reserves (which are risk-mitigating), it has a currency that is not widely accepted around the world as a storehold of wealth (so there isn't much support from that), and the attraction of and usage of its capital markets by foreign investors—while they were moderately large—are falling fast (which lessens the protection it would get from having more). You can also see that Singapore, Norway, and Saudi Arabia currently have good income statements and balance sheets that have much more in liquid assets than they have in debts, and you can get that sort of picture for the other countries shown.

ASSESSING CENTRAL GOVERNMENT AND CENTRAL BANK LONG-TERM DEBT RISKS: GOVERNMENT DEBT

	JPN	USA	BRZ	GBR	CAN	SAF	TUR	EUR	CHN	IND	MEX	KOR	AUS	SWE	CHE	NOR	RUS	SAR	SGP
Govt Assets vs Govt Debt (% Ctry GDP)	-183%	-96%	-70%	-87%	-45%	-59%	-22%	-76%	-63%	-40%	-27%	-15%	-21%	-22%	84%	383%	19%	94%	108%
Govt Debt (% Ctry GDP)	215%	99%	81%	92%	50%	73%	26%	85%	90%	56%	40%	49%	35%	32%	15%	14%	14%	26%	177%
Govt Debt 10Yr Fwd Projection (% Ctry GDP)	214%	122%	114%	101%	53%	79%	15%	87%	112%	67%	36%	40%	40%	26%	12%	0%	15%	47%	158%
o/w Held by Central Bank	92%	13%	21%	23%	9%	1%	0%	30%	1%	4%	0%	1%	11%	7%	0%	0%	-	0%	2%
o/w Held by Other Domestic Players	96%	57%	52%	45%	16%	51%	16%	41%	87%	48%	28%	38%	8%	18%	11%	6%	-	16%	-
o/w Held Abroad	27%	29%	8%	24%	25%	22%	9%	14%	2%	3%	12%	10%	15%	7%	3%	8%	-	11%	-
Significant Share in Hard Currency?	NO	NO	NO	NO	NO	YES	YES	NO	NO	NO	YES	NO	NO	NO	NO	NO	YES	YES	NO
Govt Interest (% Govt Revenue)	8%	22%	38%	8%	7%	18%	15%	8%	3%	42%	16%	5%	3%	2%	2%	0%	4%	-	-

Note that government debt is calculated for the central government only, except for China, where general government debt plus local government financing vehicles is used.

ASSESSING CENTRAL GOVERNMENT AND CENTRAL BANK LONG-TERM DEBT RISKS

		JPN	USA	BRZ	GBR	CAN	SAF	TUR	EUR	CHN	IND	MEX	KOR	AUS	SWE	CHE	NOR	RUS	SAR	SGP
LIQUID RESERVES	FX Reserves (% Ctry GDP)	32%	3%	11%	5%	5%	14%	4%	9%	20%	16%	13%	23%	4%	11%	99%	17%	33%	40%	84%
	Sovereign Wealth Assets (% Ctry GDP)	-	-	-	-	-	-	-	-	7%	-	-	11%	12%	-	-	380%	-	80%	201%
OTHER HEALTH MEASURES	Total Debt (% Ctry GDP)	486%	340%	181%	258%	377%	139%	167%	169%	289%	181%	130%	325%	219%	322%	300%	323%	233%	89%	353%
	Current Account 3Yr MA (% Ctry GDP)	4%	-4%	-2%	-2%	-1%	-1%	-6%	2%	2%	-2%	-1%	3%	-1%	6%	7%	21%	5%	5%	19%
RESERVE CURRENCY STATUS	World Trade (% of Trans in Ctry FX)	2.6%	52.6%	0.9%	9.2%	1.8%	0.4%	0.7%	15.4%	3.6%	0.4%	0.8%	0.9%	1.7%	0.6%	1.2%	0.5%	0.9%	0.5%	0.6%
	World Debt (% External Debt in Ctry FX)	1.5%	80.7%	0.2%	1.5%	1.3%	0.0%	0.2%	10.4%	1.0%	0.3%	0.2%	0.3%	0.7%	0.0%	0.4%	0.0%	0.0%	0.0%	0.0%
	World Equity (% of Global Market Cap)	4.7%	65.7%	0.4%	3.0%	2.6%	0.3%	0.1%	6.5%	5.9%	1.9%	0.2%	0.9%	1.5%	0.7%	1.9%	0.1%	0.1%	0.0%	0.3%
	World Central Bank Reserves (% in Ctry FX)	6.0%	57.0%	0.0%	5.0%	3.0%	0.0%	0.0%	20.0%	2.0%	0.0%	0.0%	0.0%	2.0%	0.0%	0.0%	0.0%	0.0%	0.0%	0.0%

The "Sovereign Wealth Assets" row includes only the top 20 sovereign wealth funds globally. The figures provided for sovereign wealth don't include liquid assets controlled or influenced by the government. For example, in Japan, in addition to the foreign exchange reserves held at the Ministry of Finance, there are assets held at the government's pension fund (GPIF) and the state-owned bank (Japan Post). Excluding them seems appropriate to me because if I included them, I would have to account for their liabilities—i.e., I would need to add pensions and quasi-government entities across countries (e.g., CPP, US federal employee retirement funds, etc.). For reference: if I were to count all of the foreign assets held by these entities, my measure of Japanese reserve firepower would go up significantly—a big increase but still well short of the government's 215% of GDP in debt.

I aggregate indicators into models designed to show the risks and rewards of things happening.

LONG-TERM AND SHORT-TERM INDICATORS OF THE RISKS FOR CENTRAL GOVERNMENTS AND CENTRAL BANKS

Using the above and other previously described indicators, I measure both long-term risks (which I view like measuring the long-term risks of having a heart attack) and short-term risks (like measuring the heart attack actually happening and its damage) for both central governments and central banks. While short-term risks are often due to long-term vulnerabilities becoming manifest in sudden problems (like a person at long-term risk of having a heart attack actually having a heart attack), this isn't always the case. For example, a pandemic (like COVID) could happen, or a war could break out, even if the underlying long-term vulnerabilities are low, which would lead to greater short-term risks that will show up in this risk gauge rising. **My measures of both the long-term and the short-term risks for the US are shown in the charts that follow. Please know that while these are good indicators, they, like most leading indicators of someone having a heart attack, are very imprecise for previously explained reasons.**

THE US CENTRAL GOVERNMENT'S DEBT RISKS

The next chart on the left shows my measure of the US government's long-term debt risks, and the one on the right shows my measure of the US government's short-term risks going back to 1900. **At this time, I judge the long-term risks of US government debt to be very high because the current and projected levels of US government debt and debt service, and sales of new debt and debt to**

be rolled over, are the highest ever and there are big debt rollover risks ahead. In fact, I judge the US government's debt situation to be nearing the point of no return. By that, I mean that the debt and debt service levels are nearing those that cannot be reduced without great losses to debt investors because at such levels a self-reinforcing debt "death spiral" occurs due to the need to borrow to service debt and due to interest rates rising because the risks of holding the debt/currency become apparent. At the same time, I judge the short-term risks to be low because inflation and growth are relatively moderate, credit spreads are low, real interest rates are high enough for lender-creditors without being too high for borrower-debtors, and the private sector's income statements and balance sheets are in relatively good shape—good enough to tax if that is needed to help the central government's finances. However, if the demand for new debt sales and debt rollovers falls off and/or there is the selling of debt assets, that would quickly raise the short-term risk gauge. By the way, this gauge can change very quickly—e.g., overnight.

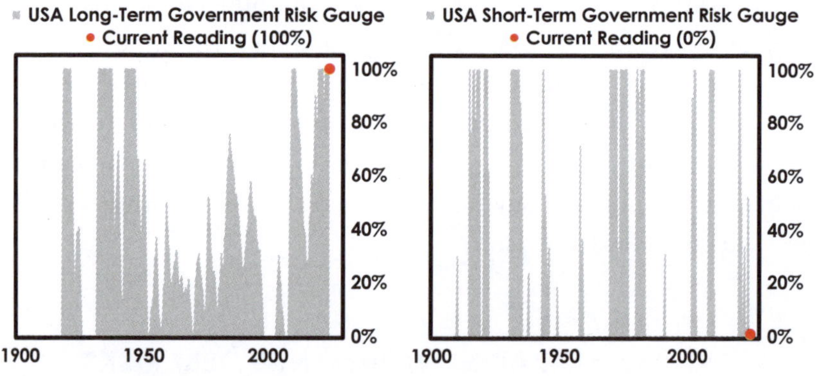

Next is a table showing some of the most important readings that feed into my long-term risk rating for the US central government. It's measured in Z-scores, or standard deviations above/below the mean. All you need to know is that above 2 is quite bad.

USA LONG-TERM RISK GAUGE CONSTRUCTION (UP = MORE VULNERABLE)

		Reading Today
Central Government Long-Term Risk	-	2.4z
Current Borrowing Need	-	2.4z
Current Borrowing Need (% Revenue)	39%	2.3z
Current Borrowing Need, If Roll Problems (% Revenue)	239%	2.5z
Projected Borrowing Need	-	2.8z
10Yr Forward Borrowing Need (% Revenue)	44%	2.8z
10Yr Forward Borrowing Need, If Roll Problems (% Revenue)	254%	2.9z
Share of Debt in Own Currency	100%	-2.0z

In short, it appears to me that there is a very high long-term risk of a US central government debt crisis of the sort I have been describing, but currently there is a very low imminent risk of that problem happening.

THE US CENTRAL BANK'S DEBT RISKS[51]

The following charts show my gauges of the long-term and the short-term risks of the Federal Reserve. While the long-term risk gauge is now higher than it has almost ever been because a) the

[51] This central bank risk gauge is based on timeless and universal principles developed from looking at many countries over long periods of time. It is based on:

1) How big the central bank's exposures are.
2) The size of the balance sheet and the vulnerability of its cash flows to interest rate changes, with consideration given to how profitable or unprofitable the central bank is today and how unprofitable it would be if interest rates changed adversely.
3) How strong the balance sheet is, e.g., how close the central bank is to running out of reserves (i.e., the number of months the central bank could sustain the current pace of reserve sales before running out).
4) The value of the debt/currency as a storehold of wealth. Based on logic and empirical evidence, countries' reserve currency statuses and track records of producing good outcomes make them more attractive to investors and therefore less risky.
5) The shares in this country/currency of world reserves, world trade, world capital flows, and world capital markets.

amounts of government debt held by the Fed are high, b) the losses taken by the Fed are the highest they have ever been, and c) the Fed has a poor net worth, these numbers are currently not large. So right now, the long-term risk is small but is in a place where it could accelerate very quickly. And, as of now, I measure the Fed's short-term risks to be relatively low because the US economy and markets are near their equilibrium levels. More specifically, while the reading is moderately bad relative to what it has been in the past, owing to a large balance sheet with few hard assets to back it up (with limited cash flow losses), it is not yet significant because the numbers remain very manageable and are nowhere near the levels that proved to be problematic for central banks in other countries in which the central bank problem became severe and led to a self-reinforcing downward spiral. Also, a) neither high and quickly rising inflation nor deflation and falling prices are a problem, b) the Fed is not actively monetizing debts but rather is slowly shrinking its debt holdings, and c) the Fed isn't encountering currency changes that are so large that they would affect inflation and growth enough to affect its monetary policy.

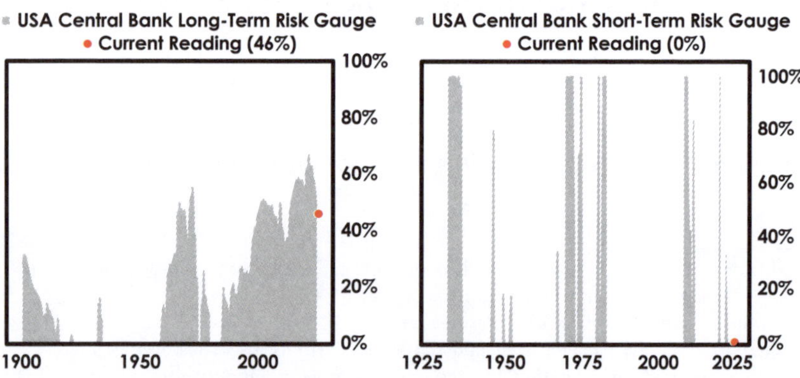

In fact, the US economy would at this moment in time appear to be in an excellent equilibrium level judging by its levels of growth, inflation, real interest rates, and central bank debt monetizations, which can create the mistaken impression that all is now good. But all is not good because there is the government debt supply-and-demand picture, which we've discussed, that is growing like a cancer, and the Fed's existing balance sheet has losses that would rise if interest rates rose, leading to its capital falling in a debt crisis. Besides increasing the financial risks, such a confluence of events would increase the risk to the Fed's independence because the Fed's actions would be put under greater political scrutiny, which, if confidence in the Fed's independence is undermined, would likely contribute to a negative reinforcing cycle because the confidence in the value of money being maintained would be undermined. At this time, we are a relatively long way from that. **The two things that we should expect not to happen but if we see them happen should be viewed as big red flags that are signaling that the real value of money and debt are at great risk are 1) another round of quantitative easing to increase liquidity and force real interest rates down and 2) the central government gaining control over the central bank.**

Next is a table showing some of the most important inputs to my long-term risk rating for the US central bank. You can see that the central bank's income statement looks not particularly bad, but the balance sheet looks about as vulnerable as it has ever been because of the large amount of money (74% of GDP) and the small amount of reserves (3% of GDP). The income statement doesn't look bad because, while the central bank is unprofitable, the magnitude is relatively small.

Also, as shown in the table, the United States has the world's dominant reserve currency, its capital markets are dominant, and the dollar has been a mediocre storehold of wealth. When I net these factors, I see the US as a good storehold of wealth, which reduces long-term risk.

Having said that, it should be noted that these supports can deteriorate very quickly as they did for prior world powers and their currencies. For a review of the declines of the British pound and the Dutch guilder before it, please reference my book *Principles for Dealing with the Changing World Order* at economicprinciples.org.

LONG-TERM RISK GAUGE CONSTRUCTION (UP = MORE VULNERABLE)

		Reading Today
Central Bank Long-Term Risk	-	**1.0z**
Central Bank Income Statement	-	**0.2z**
Current Central Bank Profitability (% GDP)	-0.2%	0.1z
Central Bank Profitability If Rates Rise (% GDP)	-0.4%	0.2z
Central Bank Balance Sheet	-	**1.0z**
Unbacked Money (% GDP)	71%	0.3z
Reserves/Money	-	1.5z
Months of Reserve Sales Before Running Out	-	0.0z
Currency Is Bad Storehold of Wealth Gauge	-	**-2.0z**
Reserve FX/Financial Center	-	**-3.3z**
Share of Reserves in Currency	57%	-1.9z
Financial Center Status (Z)	-	-2.7z
Safety and Stability for Investors	-	**-0.8z**
Institutional Quality	-	-1.2z
Rule of Law (Z)	-	-1.1z
Internal Conflict (Z)	-	0.3z
Macroeconomic Track Record	-	**-1.2z**
Volatility of Growth (Ann)	**2.2%**	**-0.8z**
Volatility of Inflation (Ann)	**1.4%**	**-2.1z**
Long-Term GDP Per Capita Growth	**1.5%**	**0.0z**
History of Losses for Savers	-	**1.1z**
Long-Term Real Cash Return (Ann)	**-1.4%**	**0.7z**
Long-Term Gold Return (Ann)	**9.8%**	**0.8z**

Please keep in mind that these indicators only reflect the debt/financial part of the picture and not the complete picture, and that the other big forces will have a great impact on this picture just as this picture will have a big impact on the other forces (i.e., domestic conflict, international conflict, acts of nature, and technology changes), so what we don't know is very large relative to what we do know.

CHAPTER 18

MY 3% 3-PART SOLUTION

This chapter is a quick and easy read for those who want to get the key points without spending too much time. It also provides thoughts and numbers that those who are analytical might want to spend some time pondering, so I recommend it for everyone.

I want to make this clear and easy to remember. If you keep in mind the number 3, that will help you remember that:

- **The budget deficit should be cut to 3% of GDP (from what it is currently projected to be by the CBO, about 6% of GDP), and**
- **These cuts can come from 3 sources (spending cuts, tax increases, and interest rate cuts, with interest rate cuts being the most impactful).**

If the president and those in Congress agree that they need to do that, and they agree on a bipartisan backstop approach to doing that (I will suggest an option), they will achieve the goal of greatly reducing the odds of the US government going broke.

That's it in a nutshell. I will now explain.

THE PICTURE AS I SEE IT

It appears to me that:

1. **Policy makers who are working on getting the debt issue under control (some have given up on the idea) are approaching the problem from the bottom up, by which I mean by working on which spending cuts and/or which tax increases are better than others, rather than working from the top down, by which I mean by looking at how much it will take in total to meet the goal, then looking at the three big levers that government policy makers can pull to reduce the deficit (i.e., spending cuts, tax increases, and interest rate reductions), and finally deciding which spending cuts, which tax increases, and which interest rate changes to make.**
2. **Policy makers are so tied up in arguing about the particulars in order to get exactly what they want that they have made the likelihood of a disastrous outcome—either not limiting the debt or having a bad government shutdown—much greater than the likelihood of an attainable good outcome.**

To tackle this problem, I believe that they should 1) work from the top down, by which I mean agree on the size of the cuts to the deficit and the size of the deficit as a percentage of GDP that need to be made to stabilize the debt and 2) agree on a fallback plan that achieves the necessary budget cuts that would automatically happen if they can't reach agreement on the particulars. This fallback plan could be something like equal percentage cuts to all spending that can be cut and equal percentage increases on all taxes that can be increased so that combined they will achieve the goal if they can't agree on anything else, so they will be assured of having a deal. Then, they can go on and try to create a plan that they can agree is better than that one. **I will now propose a fallback plan that policy makers should be able to agree on.**

WHAT MY 3% 3-PART SOLUTION LOOKS LIKE

The following chart shows the US debt level as a percentage of government revenue. The current debt trajectory is shown with the blue dashed line, and based on how I understand the mechanics to work and on indicators of what is most likely to happen, it appears to me that to prevent the central government from going broke, policy makers have to change the government debt level trajectory to the green dashed line. Changing that trajectory will require some cut in spending, and/or some increase in tax revenue, and/or some cut in the interest rate on the debt such that these three moves in total will add up to cutting the deficit down to 3% of GDP. Such a deficit cut would lead to the debt burden being about 17% lower in 10 years than it would be if the US were to continue on its currently projected path (which amounts to debts being $9 trillion lower in 10 years). In 20 years, my 3% 3-part solution would make government debt 31% lower, which is $26 trillion lower. **Doing that would greatly reduce the risks of the central government, those who are lending to it, and all those who would also be affected by a big debt issue from suffering a "heart attack."**

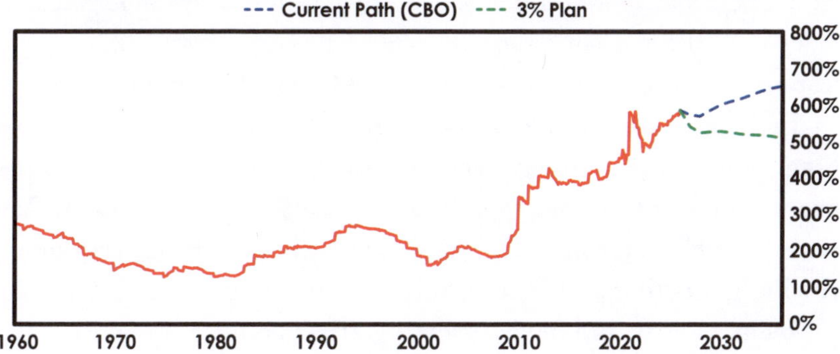

There are three main types of levers that can be pulled to control the deficit, and in Chapter 3 I showed tables that conveyed the effects of pulling them. To achieve the goal of stabilizing debt

relative to income, it would take about an 11% increase in taxes, about a 12% cut in spending, or about a 3% cut in interest rates, all else equal, if just one lever were used alone. Of course, any one of these numbers alone is way too large, so managing the adjustment will require a good combination of two or three of them.

Let's look more closely at those numbers, which are interesting because they show how much more powerful a change in interest rates would be than a change in taxation. For instance, interest rates falling by 1% is about four times more effective at reducing the debt-to-income ratio over the next 20 years than a 1% increase in tax revenue. **The numbers also show how much more powerful a change in taxation would be than a change in spending—a 1% increase in tax revenue is 1.2x more effective than a 1% reduction in spending** over the same 20-year time frame. But these estimates of the direct effects understate what the total effects are likely to be after accounting for the likely secondary effects. More specifically, a cut in interest rates is even more powerful than the estimate I gave you because, besides lowering government debt service payments, interest rate cuts would boost asset prices, which would raise capital gains tax receipts and be stimulative to the economy, and raise inflation, which would raise tax revenues. It's also worth noting that 1) the second-order effects of cutting spending would be negative for economic activity and thus negative for income taxes and 2) the second-order effects of raising taxes would also be negative because of the reduction in spending and economic growth.

In other words, there are two important takeaways. First, the biggest influence on the government's deficit is ironically not Congress, which determines spending and taxes—it is the Federal Reserve, which determines interest rates. Second, while trimming the budget deficit and cutting interest rates each reduces the debt problem, they would have offsetting effects on economic growth, inflation, and taxes. This means that if these actions are balanced well, the budget deficit can be reduced significantly without creating unacceptable effects on the economy.

Given that, if I were deciding for the president and/or Congress, I would want the Federal Reserve to lower the interest rate. I expect that the president and Congress will pressure the Fed to do that, but, of course, Congress and the president don't determine what the Fed does. **If I were on the Federal Reserve Board of Governors, I would be willing to work with the president and Congress to implement such a plan because a fiscal tightening** (which would have the first-order effects of reducing the deficit and being negative for economic growth and inflation) **in conjunction with a monetary easing** (which would also be deficit-reducing while being positive for economic growth and inflation) **looks like a great plan. It is obvious that a fiscal tightening with a monetary easing would be a good thing.** In fact, if Congress and the president enacted a significant deficit reduction, it would trigger a rally in bonds and a decline in interest rates that would help reduce the deficit. Some people worry about a cut in the fiscal deficit of that size being too negative on the economy, but that's not my worry because if the fiscal tightening were too negative on growth and inflation, it would trigger a monetary easing to rectify that. **So, what's the problem with cutting spending and raising taxes other than the political problem of anger from those who are getting less money from spending or who are paying more in taxes? I don't see it.**

A fiscal tightening with a monetary easing makes financial and economic sense because the biggest imbalance that now exists that should be rectified is between the central government's finances (it has dangerously too much debt and too much borrowing) and the private sector's finances (which are in relatively good shape, particularly in the booming areas of the market and the economy). This state of affairs came about because the Fed helped to fund the large budget deficits that allowed the big spending and the central government's debt problem to happen in the first place. So, the Fed cooperating to negate whatever pain that might come as a result of a large (3% of GDP) deficit cut would make sense, especially since the private sector has received lots of deficit-funded support, is now in pretty good shape, and could use some fiscal tightening, which the Fed could help manage with its monetary policy. It would bring private and public sector finances into better balance.

Who would suffer from the lower interest rate? While bond holders will get a lower real yield, they would benefit from interest rates falling because bond prices would go up, plus they would get a safer bond. The world would celebrate such an accomplishment, both because of the reduced US government debt risk and because it would demonstrate that the American political system can work well to solve at least this big problem. Also, other major markets like equities would benefit from those changes. So, just about everyone other than special interest groups should like the immediate effects of this plan.

Let's now play around with the numbers and these three levers to see what specific changes could get the 3% of GDP deficit goal achieved by making the adjustments come roughly equally from spending cuts, taxes, and interest rate cuts. That would take about a 4% cut in spending, a 4% increase in taxes, and a 1% cut in real interest rates. That way, policy makers would spread out where they get the 3% of GDP from so it's not too big for anyone, it's pretty politically agnostic, and the depressing fiscal effects would be offset by the stimulative monetary effects of the real interest rate cuts. That would be my solution to the problem with one possible modification: because those amounts of cuts in spending and increases in taxes would cause abrupt changes, I would phase these changes in over three years. As mentioned, I would try to make that a bipartisan fallback position to use if no other solution is reached because everyone would be relieved if policy makers could agree on an acceptable plan and negotiate the tweaks to it.

WHAT IF THE FED DOESN'T GO ALONG WITH THIS?

Of course, the Fed can't openly say that it will go along with this plan (though deals between the Fed keeping interest rates low while the government was cutting the deficit have been made in the past), so let's look at the possibility that Congress and the

president will have to make the changes come only from spending cuts and raising tax revenue by the same percentages. That percentage would be about 6% (i.e., cutting spending by 6% and raising taxes by 6%), which would also equal about a 3% of GDP deficit reduction. While those amounts of adjustments would be large by historical standards, I know that they can occur without problems if balanced well and I know that if they are too depressing to economic growth, the Fed will respond by lowering interest rates because that's what the central bank does when the economy and inflation are too depressed. **For these reasons, I know that if this 3% 3-part plan is followed it would be worlds better than if it is not followed.**

MY PROPOSED DEFICIT CUT COMPARED WITH PAST DEFICIT CUTS

While many will say that these changes are draconian, my study of past deficit cuts leads me to believe that they are very manageable if monetary policy is managed sensibly at the same time. Phasing in my plan and assuming the Fed will run monetary policy sensibly would lead to the adjustment looking something like what is shown in the blue dashed line, which is very close to the original 3% plan (green line).

USA CENTRAL GOVT DEBT LEVEL (% GOVT REVENUE)

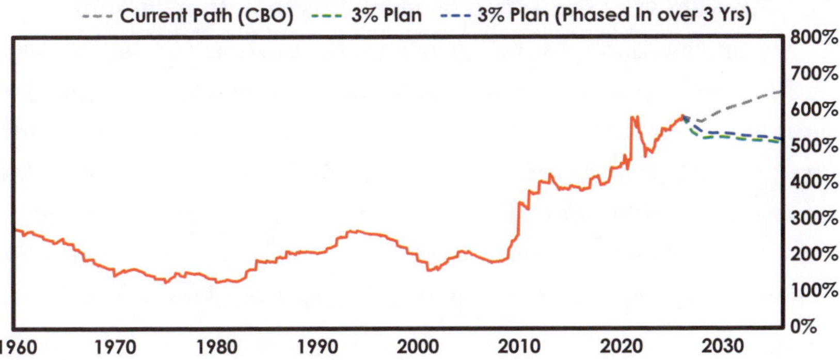

However, I need to point out a fly in the ointment. As mentioned, the numbers I showed are based on the bipartisan Congressional Budget Office's numbers. These numbers are based on the existing plan for the 2017 Trump tax cuts to roll off, so if they are extended as President Trump has promised to do, the deficit will be larger by an estimated 1.5% of GDP, so the deficit cut will have to be over 4% of GDP rather than about 3% to stabilize government debt-to-income.

While such a budget deficit cut is large, it's not very large by historical standards. The following table lists all major fiscal policy tightenings in all countries going back to 1960. It shows that big fiscal tightenings (3% of GDP or even much larger) went well if put into place when 1) growth was strong, 2) the monetary/currency policy was easy, and 3) debts were in currencies that the central bank could print. Notably, the fiscal tightening in these cases helped to lower bond yields, which reduced interest costs on the debt and encouraged private sector activity that raised taxes, and to the extent the fiscal tightening weakened the economy more than desired, it led to monetary easings that negated the fiscal tightening effects on the economy. **The most successful US case of cutting the budget deficit happened in the 1993-98 period, which took the deficit from 4% of GDP to a surplus of 1% of GDP (a 5% of GDP improvement) over those years, which would be like cutting the deficit by $1.5 trillion today. My plan would cut the deficit by much less than that amount.**

My timeless and universal principle about this is:

● ***When there are large government debts that are growing quickly so that large cuts to budget deficits are needed, the most important things to do are to 1) cut the deficit by enough to rectify the problem, 2) cut the deficit when economic conditions are good so the cuts are counter-cyclical, and 3) have monetary policy be stimulative enough to keep the economy strong in the face of such cuts.***

CASES WHERE SIGNIFICANT FISCAL ADJUSTMENTS WERE MADE

	Median (All Cases)	Median (Painless)	Median (Painful)
CASE DESCRIPTION			
Length	4	5	4
FISCAL OUTCOMES			
Chg in Primary Structural Deficit (% GDP)	5.7%	5.4%	6.3%
Share from Revenue Increases	59%	59%	54%
Share from Primary Spending Cuts	41%	41%	46%
MACROECONOMIC OUTCOMES (AVERAGE OVER ADJUSTMENT)			
Growth vs Potential	-0.3%	0.9%	-2.3%
UE Rate vs 10Yr Avg	1.0%	0.4%	2.6%
Slack	-1.1%	-0.5%	-1.7%
Inflation vs Target*	-0.2%	-0.5%	0.4%
Avg Bond Yield vs Starting Level	-0.6%	-1.2%	0.6%
DETERMINANTS OF ECONOMIC OUTCOMES			
Did Country Have Significant Hard Currency Debts?	10 of 40 Cases	0 of 21 Cases	10 of 19 Cases
Did Fiscal Changes Occur into Strong Domestic or Global Economy?	17 of 40 Cases	17 of 21 Cases	0 of 19 Cases
Did Fiscal Changes Coincide with or Produce Easier Financial Conditions?	25 of 40 Cases	17 of 21 Cases	8 of 19 Cases
Did Fiscal Changes Include or Coincide with Big Productivity Enhancing Reforms?	23 of 40 Cases	10 of 21 Cases	13 of 19 Cases

***Note for this and the following tables: before inflation targets were adopted, I use the trailing 10-year average inflation rate, bounded between 4.5% and 1.5%.**

CASES WHERE SIGNIFICANT FISCAL ADJUSTMENTS WERE MADE—PAINLESS CASES (1 OF 2)

CASE DESCRIPTION										
	BEL 82-87	ITA 90-97	SWE 93-00	DNK 83-86	IRE 87-89	NOR 93-97	CAN 94-97	GBR 94-00	NLD 96-00	AUS 86-88
Length	6	8	8	4	3	5	4	7	5	3
FISCAL OUTCOMES										
Chg in Prim Struct Dfct (% GDP)	10.6%	10.4%	10.2%	9.6%	7.9%	7.3%	7.2%	6.0%	5.8%	5.6%
Share from Revenue Increases	-	100%	100%	100%	0%	2%	21%	54%	6%	-
Share from Primary Spending Cuts	-	0%	0%	0%	100%	98%	79%	46%	94%	-
MACROECONOMIC OUTCOMES (AVERAGE OVER ADJUSTMENT)										
Growth vs Potential	-0.3%	-0.5%	1.1%	-	-	2.9%	0.9%	1.3%	1.8%	0.8%
UE Rate vs 10Yr Avg	0.8%	0.9%	3.6%	0.6%	2.6%	0.7%	0.1%	-1.5%	-1.2%	0.4%
Slack	-1.8%	-0.1%	-1.6%	-	-1.8%	-1.0%	-1.2%	0.0%	0.8%	0.8%
Inflation vs Target*	1.6%	0.2%	-0.2%	-	-1.4%	-2.5%	-0.2%	-1.1%	-0.4%	3.9%
Avg Bond Yield vs Starting Level	-3.4%	-2.7%	-2.7%	-6.6%	-3.2%	-2.2%	0.9%	0.6%	-0.7%	-2.1%
DETERMINANTS OF ECONOMIC OUTCOMES										
Did Country Have Significant Hard Currency Debts?	NO	NO	NO	NO	NO	NO	NO	NO	NO	NO
Did Fiscal Changes Occur into Strong Domestic or Global Economy?	NO	YES	YES	NO	NO	YES	YES	YES	YES	YES
Did Fiscal Changes Coincide with or Produce Easier Financial Conditions?	YES	YES	YES	YES	YES	YES	YES	YES	YES	YES
Did Fiscal Changes Include or Coincide w/Big Productivity Enhancing Reforms?	NO	YES	YES	NO	NO	NO	NO	YES	YES	YES

CASES WHERE SIGNIFICANT FISCAL ADJUSTMENTS WERE MADE—PAINLESS CASES (2 OF 2)

CASE DESCRIPTION											
	IND 03-07	JPN 79-85	USA 93-98	CAN 86-90	BEL 93-98	PHP 03-06	AUS 94-99	SWE 84-89	PLD 11-14	FRA 94-99	TLD 02-05
Length	5	7	6	5	6	4	6	6	4	6	4
FISCAL OUTCOMES											
Chg in Prim Struct Dfct (% GDP)	5.4%	5.3%	4.9%	4.8%	4.4%	4.2%	4.0%	4.0%	3.8%	3.8%	2.8%
Share from Revenue Increases	85%	79%	59%	44%	-	-	100%	60%	0%	29%	79%
Share from Primary Spending Cuts	15%	21%	41%	56%	-	-	0%	40%	100%	71%	21%
MACROECONOMIC OUTCOMES (AVERAGE OVER ADJUSTMENT)											
Growth vs Potential	2.0%	0.9%	1.2%	-0.1%	-0.1%	0.7%	1.2%	1.6%	0.0%	0.4%	2.1%
UE Rate vs 10Yr Avg	-	0.5%	-0.7%	-1.0%	0.9%	-	-0.4%	-0.6%	-1.7%	1.1%	-0.6%
Slack	-1.1%	-0.3%	-0.4%	2.1%	-1.2%	-0.5%	-0.3%	1.7%	-1.1%	-1.6%	0.4%
Inflation vs Target*	-0.6%	-1.0%	-1.2%	-0.3%	-1.4%	-0.2%	-0.2%	1.5%	-1.3%	-1.6%	-1.2%
Avg Bond Yield vs Starting Level	0.8%	1.8%	-0.5%	0.4%	-1.2%	-1.3%	0.8%	-0.4%	-1.4%	0.4%	-1.2%
DETERMINANTS OF ECONOMIC OUTCOMES											
Did Country Have Significant Hard Currency Debts?	NO	NO	NO	NO	NO	NO	NO	NO	NO	NO	NO
Did Fiscal Changes Occur into Strong Domestic or Global Economy?	YES	YES	YES	YES	NO	YES	YES	YES	YES	YES	YES
Did Fiscal Changes Coincide with or Produce Easier Financial Conditions?	YES	NO	YES	NO	YES	NO	NO	YES	YES	YES	YES
Did Fiscal Changes Include or Coincide w/Big Productivity Enhancing Reforms?	NO	YES	YES	NO	NO	NO	YES	NO	YES	NO	YES

CASES WHERE SIGNIFICANT FISCAL ADJUSTMENTS WERE MADE—PAINFUL CASES (1 OF 2)

CASE DESCRIPTION										
	GRC 10-14	IRE 11-14	GRC 90-94	ESP 10-14	HUN 07-09	PRT 11-14	PRT 81-84	NZL 87-94	DEU 96-99	ARG 24-24
Length	5	4	5	5	3	4	4	8	4	1
FISCAL OUTCOMES										
Chg in Prim Struct Dfct (% GDP)	16.6%	10.6%	10.0%	9.8%	9.0%	8.8%	8.6%	8.3%	6.9%	6.3%
Share from Revenue Increases	82%	4%	100%	14%	26%	68%	100%	100%	47%	0%
Share from Primary Spending Cuts	18%	96%	0%	86%	74%	32%	0%	0%	53%	100%
MACROECONOMIC OUTCOMES (AVERAGE OVER ADJUSTMENT)										
Growth vs Potential	-6.8%	0.9%	-1.2%	-2.9%	-5.2%	-2.8%	-2.4%	-0.9%	-0.7%	-
UE Rate vs 10Yr Avg	10.2%	5.3%	1.0%	9.4%	1.7%	4.7%	2.6%	2.6%	1.6%	-
Slack	-5.1%	-5.5%	0.0%	-4.1%	1.7%	-4.0%	-1.3%	-2.3%	-0.7%	-1.6%
Inflation vs Target*	-2.1%	-1.8%	11.6%	-1.2%	-0.7%	-0.7%	18.8%	2.3%	-1.5%	230.6%
Avg Bond Yield vs Starting Level	8.1%	-3.4%	-	0.6%	1.3%	1.1%	1.4%	-5.4%	-0.8%	-6.0%
DETERMINANTS OF ECONOMIC OUTCOMES										
Did Country Have Significant Hard Currency Debts?	YES	YES	NO	YES	YES	YES	NO	NO	NO	YES
Did Fiscal Changes Occur into Strong Domestic or Global Economy?	NO	NO	NO	NO	NO	NO	NO	NO	NO	NO
Did Fiscal Changes Coincide with or Produce Easier Financial Conditions?	NO	NO	NO	NO	NO	NO	NO	YES	YES	YES
Did Fiscal Changes Include or Coincide w/Big Productivity Enhancing Reforms?	YES	YES	NO	YES	NO	YES	NO	YES	YES	YES

CASES WHERE SIGNIFICANT FISCAL ADJUSTMENTS WERE MADE—PAINFUL CASES (2 OF 2)

CASE DESCRIPTION									
	ARG 01-04	ESP 92-97	HUN 12-12	HUN 96-96	DEU 92-94	NLD 81-83	TUR 00-01	ITA 11-12	MEX 15-17
Length	4	6	1	1	3	3	2	2	3
FISCAL OUTCOMES									
Chg in Prim Struct Dfct (% GDP)	6.1%	5.1%	4.2%	4.1%	3.4%	3.2%	3.1%	2.9%	2.5%
Share from Revenue Increases	88%	76%	61%	-	0%	39%	0%	100%	45%
Share from Primary Spending Cuts	12%	24%	39%	-	100%	61%	100%	0%	55%
MACROECONOMIC OUTCOMES (AVERAGE OVER ADJUSTMENT)									
Growth vs Potential	-2.8%	-0.7%	-3.3%	-2.2%	-1.9%	-2.4%	-10.3%	-1.8%	-0.7%
UE Rate vs 10Yr Avg	2.6%	1.4%	2.7%	-	0.7%	5.8%	2.4%	1.9%	-0.7%
Slack	-10.4%	-1.6%	-5.6%	-1.7%	0.6%	-3.4%	-5.8%	-0.1%	1.7%
Inflation vs Target*	5.5%	-0.1%	-1.6%	18.1%	1.8%	0.4%	47.9%	0.3%	0.4%
Avg Bond Yield vs Starting Level	37.9%	-1.5%	-2.1%	-	-1.0%	-0.2%	0.9%	0.6%	0.6%
DETERMINANTS OF ECONOMIC OUTCOMES									
Did Country Have Significant Hard Currency Debts?	YES	NO	YES	NO	NO	NO	YES	YES	NO
Did Fiscal Changes Occur into Strong Domestic or Global Economy?	NO	NO	NO	NO	NO	NO	NO	NO	NO
Did Fiscal Changes Coincide with or Produce Easier Financial Conditions?	NO	YES	YES	YES	YES	YES	NO	NO	NO
Did Fiscal Changes Include or Coincide w/Big Productivity Enhancing Reforms?	NO	YES	NO	YES	YES	YES	NO	YES	YES

MORE SPECIFICALLY, WHICH EXPENSES SHOULD BE CUT AND WHICH TAXES SHOULD BE RAISED?

While I am tempted to get into what I believe are the relative merits of the different specific types of spending cuts, tax increases, and interest rate cuts, I'm not going to do that because I don't think there is any reason that my preferences should matter.[52] It also would be too big of a digression and would lead to all sorts of arguing with all sorts of people who have different preferences. The problem of all sorts of people having all sorts of preferences that they will fight for and not being able to resolve their disagreements is to me the biggest problem that we face—i.e., as a country and a civilization—which is that there is so much arguing over the exact ways to prevent the disaster that it won't be prevented. That's why I am recommending the equal and proportionate cut in spending and increase in taxes as the fallback plan if no other plan can happen. Then, once that is in place, as has been proposed in the past, policy makers could authorize a bipartisan fiscal commission to examine the debt issue and propose specific alternatives that are preferable to the fallback plan. But frankly, I don't care exactly how congressional policy makers do it nearly as much as I care that they do it.

Nonetheless, let's look at the constraints that must be considered.

A selection of highly impactful potential spending cuts and tax increases and their impacts are shown in the following table. This list of items came primarily from the bipartisan Congressional Budget Office, which most policy makers refer to. **Looking at that list tells me that tweaking existing spending programs and taxes in moderate, tolerable ways could achieve the 3% of GDP deficit goal without unacceptable pain. This list also shows the revenue that**

[52] To say a little more, because my goal would be to raise broad-based productivity, I would a) make sure that spending cuts and tax changes do not hurt those who can least afford them and do not hurt high-productive functions like education, which are shown to be most effective in increasing broad-based productivity, and b) cut taxes and regulations in areas that would free up productive spending and improve efficiency where possible.

can be brought in by tariffs (which during many periods of history have been a greater source of government revenue than anything else). According to the CBO, 10% tariffs on all imports could bring in about 0.6% of GDP. Also, if Elon Musk's claim that he can cut the budget deficit by $2 trillion is half true (i.e., if DOGE can cut the budget deficit by $1 trillion), that would be 3% of GDP. There are several other radical changes and considerations on the table so I'm confident that one way or another policy makers can do it, and I like some of the aspirations as I'm all in favor of radically improving the efficiency of the government and the economy. **So, it's not hard for me to imagine how a pragmatic "grand bargain" between reasonable Republicans and Democrats could be reached. My only question is whether the people involved will operate together logically to do sensible things.**

Now is the time for policy makers to put up or shut up. To be clear, whatever form of grand bargain cuts the deficit to about 3% of GDP is good with me. **That leads me to conclude that if our representatives in Washington don't get a debt limit deal done, it will be because of their lack of reasonableness and their inability to compromise—not because a good and workable plan is beyond their reach. Because the failure to reach an agreement will produce a much bigger problem than reaching an agreement along the lines of my 3% solution, it seems to me that the electorate should hold their representatives in Congress accountable to get a debt limit deal done**.

In the following table are some of the choices and their effects on the budget deficit, which were put out for informational purposes mostly by the Congressional Budget Office. I am sharing them simply to convey a picture of the alternatives.

SAMPLE OF OPTIONS FOR REDUCING DEFICITS THROUGH SPENDING CUTS

"3% PLAN" TARGET REDUCTION IN SPENDING = ~1% OF GDP

	Savings over 10 Yrs	Est Annual Savings	Est Deficit Impact	Share of Target Cuts*
Cutting Government Benefits That Go to High Earners	$Bln	$Bln	% GDP	
Phase Out VA Disability Payments That Go to High Earners	384	38	0.10%	10%
Decrease Social Security for Higher-Income People (5yr Phase In)	197	20	0.05%	5%
Limiting Entitlements and Transfers				
Lower Implicit Subsidies for Medicare Advantage Plans	489	49	0.13%	13%
Overall Cap on Federal Spending for Medicaid (Adj for Inflation)	459	46	0.12%	12%
Eliminate Federal Farm Subsidies	311	31	0.08%	8%
Uniform Social Security Capped at 150% of Federal Poverty Level	283	28	0.08%	8%
Use Chained Inflation for Social Security and Mandatory Programs	278	28	0.07%	7%
Limit Transfers to States and Health Providers for Medicaid	241	24	0.06%	6%
Raise Full Retirement Age for Social Security from 67 to 70 (Phased)	95	9	0.03%	3%
Reduce Payments for Medical Education at Teaching Hospitals	94	9	0.03%	3%
Reducing Discretionary Spending				
Limit Military Personnel to ~1 Million People (<20% Reduction)	1,118	112	0.30%	30%
Rescind Inflation Reduction Act Climate and Energy Provisions	1,045	105	0.28%	28%
Limit Annual Non-Defense Spending Growth to 1.5%	592	59	0.16%	16%
Reduce Highway and Education Transfers to States by 33%	406	41	0.11%	11%
25% Reduction in Diplomatic Programs, Health and Military Aid	187	19	0.05%	5%
Total Potential Savings from Spending Cuts	6,179	618	1.67%	167%

"Share of Target Cuts" figures shown against a target of roughly 1% of GDP improvement in the deficit from each lever. Sources: CBO, Joint Committee on Taxation, Penn Wharton Budget Model

SAMPLE OF OPTIONS FOR REDUCING DEFICITS THROUGH TAX INCREASES
"3% PLAN" TARGET INCREASE IN SPENDING = ~1% OF GDP

	Savings over 10 Yrs	Est Annual Savings	Est Deficit Impact	Share of Target New Revenue*
Tax Increases Targeted at High Earners	**$Bln**	**$Bln**	**% GDP**	
Apply Social Security Taxes to Incomes over $250,000	1,427	143	0.38%	38%
2% Increase in Income Tax Rates for Four Highest Brackets	570	57	0.15%	15%
Impose Net Investment Income Taxes on Business Income	420	42	0.11%	11%
Lower Contribution Limits on IRAs and 401(k)s	187	19	0.05%	5%
Increase Medicare Part B Premiums for High-Income People	72	7	0.02%	2%
Remove Deductions and Tax Subsidies				
Cap Tax Benefits of Itemized Deductions to 4% of Income	736	74	0.20%	20%
Cap Ability to Pay Pre-Tax for Employer Health Insurance	521	52	0.14%	14%
Eliminate Mortgage Interest Deduction	349	35	0.09%	9%
Include Veterans' Disability Payments in Taxable Income	235	23	0.06%	6%
Remove Step-Up in Basis on Inherited Assets with Capital Gains	197	20	0.05%	5%
Remove Tax Credits for Post-Secondary Education	130	13	0.04%	4%
Other Increases in Taxes				
5% VAT Tax (ex-Necessities like Food and Healthcare)	2,180	218	0.59%	59%
Enact 10% Tariffs on All Imports to the US	2,100	210	0.57%	57%
Enact 60% Tariffs on All Chinese Imports	700	70	0.19%	19%
Tax on Greenhouse Gases ($25 Per Ton Emissions), ex-Gasoline	700	70	0.19%	19%
Remove Tax Exemptions on US Corporations' Foreign Income	340	34	0.09%	9%
Increase Tax on Financial Transactions from 0.002% to 0.01%	297	30	0.08%	8%
Require Half of Advertising Expenses to Be Amortized over 10 Yrs	177	18	0.05%	5%
Increase Corporate Income Taxes by 1%	136	14	0.04%	4%
Uniform Alcohol Tax of $0.25/oz of Pure Alcohol (Indexed)	102	10	0.03%	3%
Raise Taxes 2% on Long-Term Capital Gains/ Qualified Dividends	103	10	0.03%	3%
Total Potential Revenue from Tax Increases	**11,678**	**1,168**	**3.15%**	**315%**

"Share of Target Cuts" figures shown against a target of roughly 1% of GDP improvement in the deficit from each lever. Sources: CBO, Joint Committee on Taxation, Penn Wharton Budget Model

In considering which spending to cut, when one looks at the possibilities, one quickly notices that about 70% of the non-interest spending is considered "mandatory"—i.e., it is either contractually required or politically nearly impossible to cut. The breakdown is shown in the following chart.

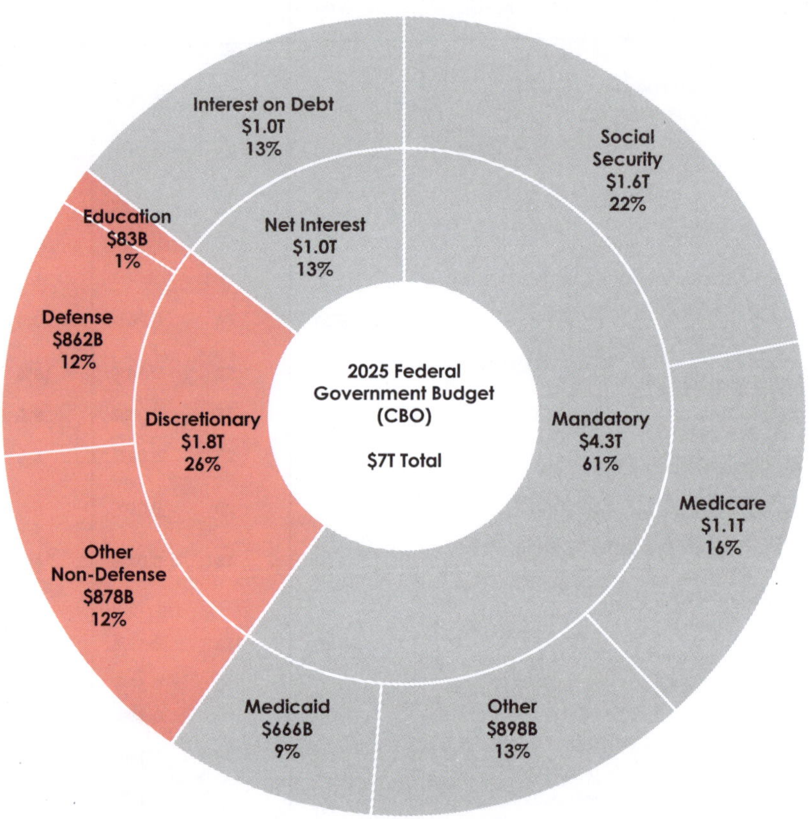

That said, in the "mandatory" spending part of the budget, there are a number of relatively modest changes that could have big impacts. For instance, two changes to Social Security (phasing in an increase to the retirement age from 67 to 70 and using a more realistic inflation measure to calculate the increase in benefits), which wouldn't affect virtually anyone immediately, would produce about a tenth of the required spending cuts.

The roughly 30% of spending that is "discretionary" that Congress has to reauthorize every year (which is shrinking fast as a share of spending because entitlement programs are growing) **includes defense spending (which is almost half of the discretionary budget), medical care for veterans, rental assistance for low-income households, funding for transportation, medical and scientific research, education transfers to states**, and hundreds of other functions of the government. Because a bill needs to be passed every year to authorize this spending, these are the easiest to cut (though they have not been cut). If you cut just from these "discretionary" items to achieve the goal of cutting spending by about 4%, that would require 15% cuts in these on average. I find the distinction between discretionary and non-discretionary spending to be a bit arbitrary because cuts can be made to both. **The important thing is getting to a reasonable mix that adds up to a deficit reduction of 3% of GDP to get the deficit down to 3% of GDP.**

DO IT NOW! DO IT COUNTER-CYCLICALLY!

To re-emphasize: When there are large government debts that are growing quickly so that large cuts to budget deficits are needed, the most important things to do are to 1) cut the deficit by enough to rectify the problem, 2) cut the deficit when economic conditions are good so the cuts are counter-cyclical, and 3) have monetary policy be stimulative enough to keep the economy strong.

Now is an exceptionally good time to implement a significant debt limit plan because:

- It is much better to reduce government deficits in good economic times than to wait for a debt crisis to happen in bad times.
- The US economy is near full employment, growth is moderately strong, inflation is a bit high, and the private sector's

income statements and balance sheets are in pretty good shape (mostly because the government took on the burden, though it should probably shift at least some of it back).
- If the plan is not implemented now, the debt problem will grow and be more difficult to deal with. That is especially true because the debt cycle is now at the stage in which more borrowing and more debt are needed to service existing debts, so they are increasing in a self-reinforcing and compounding way.

Implementing this plan now would be a confidence booster that would have all sorts of beneficial knock-on effects. **It's also worth noting that there are other, less commonly discussed ideas out there that could have a big impact on the debt picture. I'm in favor of marking the government's assets to market, creating a US government sovereign wealth fund, and exploring a US-backed stablecoin if these things can be done well. Imagine if the government's assets were managed economically—i.e., if they were valued, bought, sold, and/or developed economically rather than not even looked at economically, as is the case now—and imagine there was a well-funded, well-run sovereign wealth fund behind the government's financing and debt. That's an interesting subject for another time.**

In concluding this chapter, I want to reiterate that even with the best of budget plans, there are very big uncertainties that can throw them off. For example, we don't know if there will be wars that will cost more and worsen the budget deficits, or if there will be bigger-than-expected productivity gains from new technologies that will produce higher incomes and tax revenues that will reduce budget deficits. There are many such uncertainties that will undoubtedly disrupt these projections, so the ranges of possibilities around them are large. **To me, that suggests that US policy makers should be more, not less, conservative in dealing with the government's finances because the worst thing possible would be to have its finances in bad shape during difficult times.**

APPENDIX: LOOKING IN MORE DETAIL AT THE EFFECTS OF DIFFERENT SPENDING, TAX, AND INTEREST RATE CHANGES ON THE DEFICIT IN THE US

Achieving the goal of stabilizing government debts relative to government revenues is kind of like playing with a Rubik's Cube, in that changing one lever changes the impact of all the others. The following tables show how different combinations of government spending cuts, tax increases, and interest rate changes would lead to different outcomes for the government's debt-to-income ratio.

The first table shows the status quo—what the US government debt picture looks like in 20 years if there are no changes in revenue, spending, or real interest rates from those now projected by the Congressional Budget Office. In that baseline scenario, US government debt will reach over 130% of GDP in 20 years. However, it's important when doing these calculations to compare debt levels to tax revenue, not nominal GDP. GDP is often used by default, but that can be misleading because levels and changes in tax revenue can be very different from levels and changes in GDP. When dealing with government finances, what matters are the revenues and expenses of the government. Translating this projection into a share of government revenue, the US is projected to reach debt that is 7.2x government income, up from about 5.8x right now.

To give you a sense of how the different pieces interact, I also show in this table how this projection would change as the government changes its spending (x-axis, with spending declining as you move to the right) and/or revenues (y-axis, with taxes rising as you move down). **This shows how challenging it is to stabilize the debt if lower real rates are not part of the solution—it requires relatively large cuts in spending and increases in revenue.**

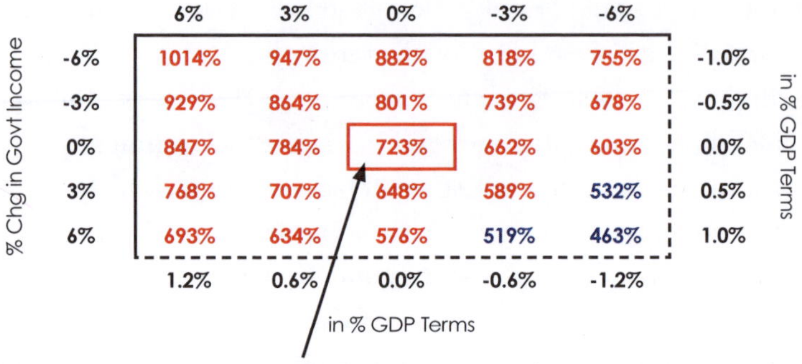

GOVT DEBT-TO-INCOME IN 20 YRS
ASSUMING CBO INTEREST RATES
CURRENT DEBT/INCOME = 583%
BASELINE PRIMARY DEFICIT = 12% OF INCOME (CBO)

% Change in Government Spending (columns); % Chg in Govt Income (rows)

% Chg in Govt Income	6%	3%	0%	-3%	-6%	in % GDP Terms
-6%	1014%	947%	882%	818%	755%	-1.0%
-3%	929%	864%	801%	739%	678%	-0.5%
0%	847%	784%	723%	662%	603%	0.0%
3%	768%	707%	648%	589%	532%	0.5%
6%	693%	634%	576%	519%	463%	1.0%
in % GDP Terms	1.2%	0.6%	0.0%	-0.6%	-1.2%	

In the following tables, I show the same sensitivity if real interest rates fell by 1% or 2% (i.e., if they end up roughly 1.5-2.5% below real growth rates). These grids help you see the impact of different policy mixes.

GOVT DEBT-TO-INCOME IN 20 YRS
IF REAL INTEREST RATES FALL 1%
CURRENT DEBT/INCOME = 583%
BASELINE PRIMARY DEFICIT = 12% OF INCOME (CBO)

% Change in Government Spending (columns); % Chg in Govt Income (rows)

% Chg in Govt Income	6%	3%	0%	-3%	-6%	in % GDP Terms
-6%	831%	773%	717%	661%	607%	-1.0%
-3%	782%	724%	668%	612%	558%	-0.5%
0%	732%	674%	618%	563%	508%	0.0%
3%	681%	624%	567%	512%	457%	0.5%
6%	629%	572%	515%	460%	405%	1.0%
in % GDP Terms	1.2%	0.6%	0.0%	-0.6%	-1.2%	

GOVT DEBT-TO-INCOME IN 20 YRS IF REAL INTEREST RATES FALL 2%
CURRENT DEBT/INCOME = 583%
BASELINE PRIMARY DEFICIT = 12% OF INCOME (CBO)

% Change in Government Spending (columns); % Chg in Govt Income (rows)

% Chg in Govt Income	6%	3%	0%	-3%	-6%	in % GDP Terms
-6%	725%	672%	620%	569%	519%	-1.0%
-3%	680%	627%	575%	524%	474%	-0.5%
0%	634%	581%	529%	478%	428%	0.0%
3%	587%	534%	482%	431%	381%	0.5%
6%	540%	487%	435%	384%	334%	1.0%
in % GDP Terms	1.2%	0.6%	0.0%	-0.6%	-1.2%	

Finally, I show how much of each lever you'd need to pull on its own. For instance, just cutting discretionary spending would require nearly 50% cuts to those programs, while just cutting interest rates on the government debt would require them to fall by around 3%. That's why I like my 3% 3-part solution—because it spreads the adjustments across the levers.

HOW THE US CAN STABILIZE DEBT-TO-INCOME IN THE NEXT 10 YEARS

Central Government Debt Today (% GDP)	**100%**
Central Government Debt Today (% Revenue)	**583%**
Proj Debt in 2035 (% GDP, CBO)	**118%**
Proj Debt in 2035 (% Revenue, CBO)	**648%**
Proj Nominal Growth Rate (CBO)	**3.9%**
Proj Real Growth	**1.9%**
Proj Inflation	**2.0%**
Proj Effective Nominal Interest Rates (CBO)	**3.5%**
Current Interest Rate (Avg 3M and 10Yr)	**4.5%**

If Lower Interest Rates Were the Only Lever. . .

Interest Rate Required to Stabilize Debt	**1.0%**
Change in Interest Rates vs Current Interest Rate	**-3.5%**
Change in Interest Rates vs CBO's Proj Avg Interest Rate	**-2.5%**

If Higher Inflation Were the Only Lever. . .

Required Inflation Rate to Stabilize Debt	**4.5%**
Change in Inflation Required (vs Current Proj Inflation)	**2.5%**

If Cutting Expenses Were the Only Lever. . .

% Spending Cut Required to Stabilize Debt	**12%**
% of Discretionary Spending	**47%**

If Raising Tax Revenue Were the Only Lever. . .

% Revenue Increase Required to Stabilize Debt	**11%**

CHAPTER 19

WHAT THE FUTURE LOOKS LIKE TO ME

In this chapter, I try to look into the future using my measures of where things now stand and my principles about how changes occur, which are based on what I think are the most important cause/effect relationships. I expect that you will find this chapter very controversial, very interesting, and very valuable.

***He who lives by the crystal ball is destined to eat ground glass* is an adage I learned early in my investment career. It has stuck with me ever since because it has repeatedly proven true. I know that whatever success I have had has been more due to my knowing how to deal with what I don't know than with anything I do know. So I will begin by explaining a bit about how I bet on the future.**

BETTING ON THE FUTURE

From very early on in my investment career, I based my decision-making approach on seeing the cause/effect relationships that drive what happens in markets and economies. I saw how the cause/

effect relationships that I identified interacted with everything to drive how all things happen as a sort of perpetual motion machine that drives developments over time. Seeing how this perpetual motion machine has driven everything that has happened led me to believe that everything (other than the quantum world) is predestined and that if we had a perfect model that took every cause/effect relationship into consideration, we could almost perfectly forecast the future. I believe that the only thing standing in the way of that perfect forecasting is our ability to understand and model all those cause/effect dynamics—and that we will get much closer to achieving this with AI.

Most people don't see things that way. They believe the future is unknowable and that destiny doesn't exist. I am confident that this view is by and large wrong now, and I believe that it will quickly become even more apparent that it is wrong to those who seek, obtain, and use the understandings that are increasingly available to us. In my own career, I found success by building AI expert decision-making systems to describe these cause/effect dynamics; in the future, the way that I—and I presume others—will model things will be through more advanced forms of AI such as generative AI and explainable AI.

To be clear, while having a perfect model that gives a nearly perfect picture of what the predestined future looks like would be great, I don't expect that my model will come close to that, so my goal is simply to have a crude, quickly evolving model that gives me a leg up relative to the competition and relative to the position I would be in if I didn't have the model. **I have found that this works well because, though forecasting exactly, or even nearly exactly, is now impossible because there are too many determinants that are themselves highly uncertain and together determine what happens, there are many things about the future—such as death, taxes, the life cycles of individuals, demographic shifts, the effects that people's DNA and environments have on them, and untold other cause/effect relationships—that are relatively knowable and good indicators of roughly what will happen. I especially look for big, unsustainable conditions and I position myself to bet that they won't be sustained.**

I play my betting/investing game by knowing as much as possible about the timeless and universal cause/effect relationships of these relatively knowable things, and I build this understanding into templates/models of how things are likely to unfold.

Because the causes come before their effects, if I know the cause/effect relationships better than my competitors, I can anticipate what will happen better than they can and, as a result, do very well in the investment game. I have found great value in building this approach into market-positioning systems that have been back-tested and can be used in an investment game plan that I execute. I constantly compare how conditions are evolving and how my bets are performing relative to my expectations. If the results are inconsistent with my expectations, I diagnose why and improve my decision-making systems. The computerized expert systems I use are designed to make decisions like I would, just better than I could because they can simultaneously and quickly process a lot more than my brain can.[53]

While I've done very well as a global macro investor betting on the future in this unique way, I am wrong a lot (at least one-third of the time relative to what the markets are expecting) and I am never exactly right. **Because I know that it takes only one really bad bet or a series of moderately bad bets to knock me out of the game, I am extremely risk-averse, so I have built great risk controls. I control risks through diversification of my good risky bets rather than by avoiding risky bets.** To me, the "Holy Grail of Investing" is to find and make 15 or more great uncorrelated bets.

I have followed this approach for about 35 of my 50-plus years as a professional investor. I am as hooked on playing this game as I have ever been, though now I want to pass along what I've learned rather than keep it to myself. It is of course up to others to decide whether what I'm sharing is of value, but I know that from my own experience

[53] I won't digress further into how I invest here, but if you're interested in learning more about my investment approach, I recommend that you take my Dalio Market Principles course, which you can find information on at principles.com.

it is. **I have made a lot of money betting on the cause/effect relationships I described earlier in this book—relationships between the short-term and long-term debt and political cycles, acts of nature, and humanity's inventiveness creating new technologies. These relationships are also logical and have appeared across thousands of years of history. I am sure that they are the biggest and most important forces, even though there are still a lot of key unknowns and uncertainties.**

Now that I have that explanation out of the way, I will tell you what I conjecture about the future. Please remember that I use my template to see things differently than most people and that I am especially drawn to situations that I assess to be more likely to happen than most people think. This means the outcomes I am anticipating are not reflected in the price, so they are good things to bet on. Also keep in mind that I am not fully sure of anything, except death and taxes.

LOOKING AHEAD USING MY TEMPLATE AND MY INDICATORS

You now know how I believe monetary orders, domestic political governance orders, and international orders evolve, break down, and transition driven by the five big forces I've outlined earlier and won't repeat here. I use my Big Cycle template and my indicators to show me where we are in these cycles and anticipate what will happen, and to make investments I convert this conceptual template into a much more specific analytical decision-making system. I will use these concepts to convey where I think things stand and what I expect.

I will start with my big-picture summary of how I see things as of my writing in March 2025:

1. **The US and the existing world order are about 80 years into, which is about 90-95% through, the Big Cycle that began in 1945. The Big Cycle is like the human life cycle**

in that it progresses through relatively knowable stages, and while knowing about this cycle won't tell you exactly what will happen, it will tell you a lot about what is likely to happen and roughly when. I broke this Big Cycle up into the six stages that I described in *Principles for Dealing with the Changing World Order* and touched on in this book. By my measures, the Big Cycle is in Stage 5, which is on the brink of great conflicts and seismic shifts.

2. **The US and other major economies are about five years into, which by my measures is about two-thirds through, the 13th short-term debt/economic cycle of the post-1945.** As explained, this short-term debt/economic cycle interacts with domestic political and international geopolitical cycles, acts of nature developments, and new inventions to drive the shorter-term cycle swings that typically take about six years, give or take about three years. While knowing about this short-term cycle won't tell you exactly what will happen and when, it will tell you a lot about what is likely to happen and roughly when.
3. **There are some big, unsustainable imbalances that make good bets because they likely won't be sustained—most importantly, it is a good bet that the amount of borrowing and buying and piling up of debt assets and liabilities being faster than income growth won't be sustained.**
4. **We are at the maximum point of not knowing what actions will be taken and what effects they will have because the new leadership in the US has only been in power for a few weeks and President Trump seems to be more inclined to do previously unimaginable things than any president in the last 80 years—and perhaps any president ever.**

By my measures, the current configuration of conditions is most analogous with those that existed in 1905-14 and 1933-38 and many prior times in many countries throughout history, which, as

just noted, is what I call Stage 5 of the Big Cycle. During Stage 5, countries are overindebted, inefficiently run, divided, and threatened by other countries, so there is a strong tendency for leaders with populist, nationalistic, protectionist, militaristic, and autocratic approaches to emerge.

By studying history, we can see that such challenging times have <u>always</u> led to much more autocratic governance because democracies become too divisive to be effective, and their leaders lose their abilities to compromise effectively. At these times, only power matters so those who get it and become the more autocratic leaders in positions of power tend to be more inclined to engage in conflict, not cooperation, with both their internal and their external opponents. **The new leaders <u>always</u> vow to fight to improve national strength and are more willing to engage in economic, geopolitical, and military conflicts, which bring them to the brink of major conflicts and big changes in the monetary order, the domestic political order, and the world geopolitical order.**

By my measures, this is where <u>all of the major powers</u> now are—i.e., they are overindebted, inefficiently run, and divided—and it is this configuration of conditions that is increasingly leading to the emergence of more nationalistic, protectionist, militaristic, and autocratic leaders and policies. These leaders, especially President Trump in the US, want to fight to improve national strength and are more willing to engage in economic, geopolitical, and military conflicts to win. Recent events are by and large following the classic Big Cycle template that I have laid out and that has brought the world to the brink of great conflicts and big changes. **To be clear, these changes don't have to be bad ones because what they will be like is still in the hands of those who control the levers of power.**

Let's now look a bit more closely at each of the five forces and what's happening with them, using as a guide some of the principles I shared earlier in this book. I will focus mostly on the United

States because it is the most important country by most measures and its changes will have the biggest effects on what will happen to the world, though the other G7 countries and China all are in similar positions and intertwined in this Big Cycle, and all countries will be affected by them, while also affecting what happens. It's also worth noting that, along with all of what you read from here, there is the demographic force to reckon with. This will lead to a lot of older people who won't be working and will be expensive to support (because of healthcare costs) at the same time that the workforce will be shrinking, so that only a small percentage of people will be truly productive.

1. The Debt/Money Force

Regarding where we are in the Big Debt Cycle, as shown earlier in this book, by my measures the US and most major countries (the other G7 countries and China) are overindebted, in the late stages of their Big Debt Cycles, and have to frequently rely on Monetary Policy 3 (i.e., big fiscal deficits that are funded by central banks buying the debt). As a result, if their long-term Big Debt Cycle issues are not controlled in some way, the probability of an unwanted major restructuring/monetization of debt assets and debt liabilities that are denominated in the major reserve currencies happening is very high—something like 65% over the next five years and something like 80% over the next 10 years. This is because the debt assets and debt liabilities are already very large, and they are projected to rise to significantly higher levels that will make it increasingly difficult to have interest rates high enough and money tight enough to satisfy the lender-creditors without having interest rates so high and money so tight that they will hurt the borrower-debtors. The following charts show the average total debt and debt service as a percent of GDP going back to 1900 across the G7 countries.

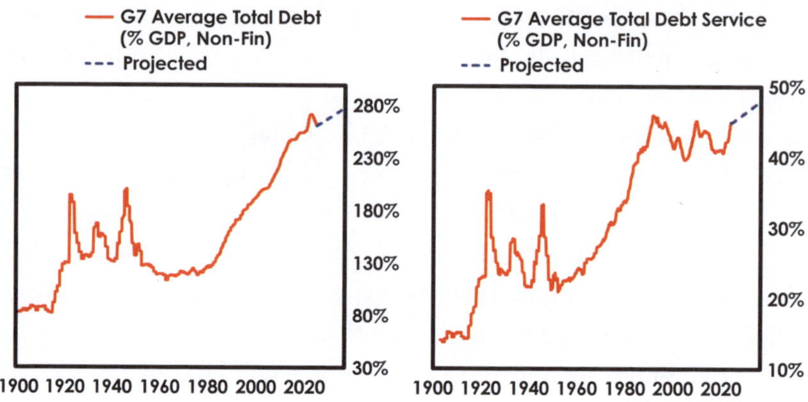

As described earlier, the next big red flag to watch out for that would signal that a debt crisis is about to happen is significant selling of government debt assets (e.g., bonds) by existing holders of them. This would come together with the issuing and sales of new government debt to create a huge supply relative to the demand, which would put central banks in the position of having to choose between letting nominal and real interest rates rise a lot or printing a lot of money and buying long-term government debt to keep these interest rates down, thus devaluing debt and money. **It seems to me that now is a good time to remember the following principle:**

- ***During times when there is too much debt relative to the quantity of money that is needed to service debts, the need to either increase the amount of money that exists and/or cut the amount of debt there is leads governments to break their promises and do some combination of a) raising the amount of money and credit, b) reducing the amount of debt (e.g., by restructuring it), and/or c) preventing the free-market ownership and movement of the hard money (e.g., gold). At such times, there is a run away from bad money to good money that the government wants to stop. This often leads to prohibiting good money from being freely held and freely moved.***

Clearly, it is in these countries' interests to not have such large debt burdens. As I have seen by studying history, when countries were in analogous positions, they reduced their debt burdens using

various, seemingly extreme ways that were then, and would be now, considered unimaginable. These extreme actions have included freezing debt payments, seizing assets of adversary nations, imposing confiscatory taxes and capital/foreign exchange controls, defaulting on debts/extending maturities, and changing the type of money in circulation (by de-linking it from a hard asset like gold or creating a new type of money).

I'm not saying it's certain that these things will happen, but I do want to point out that these kinds of radical changes were made by much more conventional leaders than Donald Trump, like Franklin D. Roosevelt and Richard Nixon. While at this time I consider most of these to be more unlikely possibilities than high probabilities, there is no doubt in my mind that, one way or another, leaders must manage the debt supply-and-demand issue well. It is important to be aware of the risks these extreme actions present and stay tuned as things change. In my opinion, my 3% 3-part solution in conjunction with a well-coordinated "beautiful deleveraging" in which the deflationary ways of deleveraging (e.g., fiscal tightening and debt restructuring) are balanced with the inflationary ways of deleveraging (e.g., the easing of monetary policy and debt monetization) would be best. **In any case, the days of borrowing much more than can be paid back to support excess consumption by unproductive people are coming to an end. Going forward, the primary goals will be to simultaneously increase productivity and diminish the burden of the debt (which will also diminish the value of the debt and money).**

As mentioned above, the US and most major countries are probably now about two-thirds into their short-term cycles. This puts them close to their equilibrium levels, judging by real and nominal economic growth and interest rates and inflation rates. The monetary tightening that began in March 2022 ended the last paradigm in which the US Fed and other G7 central banks gave away lots of money and credit for free. Starting in or around March 2022, the Fed and most other central banks shifted from a) monetary policies that were great for borrower-debtors and bad for lender-creditors and inflationary to b) monetary policies that were slightly tight (by my measures). As a result of this tightening and supply chain problems lessening, inflation rates declined to levels that are now modestly above their stated targets, which has led these central banks to gradually ease. Most countries are now in a new paradigm in which central banks are having a relatively neutral monetary policy with relatively moderate conditions, depending on the country (e.g., economic growth is stronger in the US, particularly in the tech sector, and weaker in other G7 countries), though the UK, France, and some developing countries like Brazil are encountering the sort of government debt supply-and-demand problems that I described earlier in this book. By and large, nominal and real interest rates now appear about right—i.e., high enough to be acceptable for lender-creditors without being so high that they are too problematic for borrower-debtors—judging by inflation and growth rates alone. But they are not high enough (by my measures) given the fiscal supply-and-demand dynamic explained in this book.

Additionally, this is all impacting different companies in different sectors very differently—in fact, more so than at any time I can remember—because of the disruptive changes that are underway. The main reason that debt service didn't rise to new highs while debts increased over the last few decades is that interest rates went down from 1980-81 until the recent rise. Since actual debt service payment changes lag interest rate changes (because interest rates on fixed-rate debt don't rise until the debts mature), we should expect debt service payments to continue to rise to catch up with current interest rates. Based on inflation and growth readings as of this writing in March 2025, a Fed easing is not appropriate now. That begs the question of how the Fed, which is essentially the central banker for the world, is going to run a monetary policy that works for most everyone. I think that is a virtually impossible job that will subject the Fed to much more criticism and interference. Given the circumstances and the history of what happens with central banks at such times, the independence of the central bank should not be taken for granted.

This most recent short-term debt cycle tightening was a bit different from other historical examples in two ways. First, because there was an engineered big shift in wealth to the private sector from the government sector (which is now carrying a lot of the debt and borrowing a lot to support the private sector), the private sector is currently in pretty good financial shape while the government sector is having financial problems, as previously described. In most developed economies, most importantly in the three major reserve currency economies—the US, the Eurozone, and Japan—the central governments have been and are still borrowing a lot to make distributions to households, and this is hurting these governments' finances and threatening them in the ways described throughout this study. Said differently, in recent years central government and central bank income statements and balance sheets deteriorated so that household and corporate income statements and balance sheets would improve. This has created a safer environment for the private sector because central governments and central banks don't have to worry about their debt problems as much, don't get squeezed for money as much, and don't have to worry about market losses as much.

The second thing that makes this short-term debt cycle less typical is that the picture of the private sector is one of abnormally large divergences between companies. The tightening that began in 2022 hurt some sectors much more severely than other sectors, and technological, political, and geopolitical changes created big divergences. More specifically, in the most recent short-term debt cycle tightening, the overlevered, cash-short, interest-rate-sensitive, and/or bubble companies and investors who invested in them were hurt while the cash-flush, interest-rate-insensitive, financially sound, and/or hot-tech-related companies and their investors did great. Also, even with the wealth transfer from the government sector to the private sector, wealth gaps have continued to increase, with the relatively uneducated bottom 60% of the population in bad shape while the top 1% (about 3 million people) who are amazingly well-educated and productive contributors to the boom areas are being tremendously rewarded in their jobs and in the investments that they own. This is most obviously exemplified in the large number of unicorn companies that are coming up with amazing new things that are enhancing productivity and producing billionaires (on paper) at a fast pace.

By my measures, there is a significant risk that both a debt squeeze and an economic downturn will simultaneously happen two or three years from now.

WHAT ABOUT THE MARKETS?

In looking at the markets, it is helpful to start with the following principle:

● ***There is always a current most popular meme that just about everyone believes. It is reflected in the price and is bound to be wrong in some way. These memes typically are due to a mix of extrapolating what happened before and emotional considerations. Also, most investors typically don't take into consideration market pricing. In other words, they tend to identify what has been a great investment (e.g., a strongly performing company) as great, and they don't pay enough attention to its pricing, even though its pricing (whether it is cheap or expensive) is the most important thing. At this time, it is typical for almost everyone to be looking to make money by buying assets that they believe will go up (rather betting on them going down), and they quite often use leverage.***

At the time of my writing this in early March 2025, the most popular meme is that we should be optimistic about the future because by and large things are now good, AI companies are great and will make things better, and the Trump administration will improve things because there are many inefficiencies and weaknesses that need to be fixed. He will fix them because he is taking a strong, practical, capitalist, and business-like approach and he is working with Elon Musk, who has an amazing track record of making brilliant inventions and world-changing products. To summarize the meme, the United States has demonstrated that it has "American exceptionalism."

I believe that this meme about American exceptionalism has

merit, but at the same time, by my measures, it is now more than reflected in the prices and there could be other big problems ahead. More specifically, I have no doubt that the US is exceptional in having a well-developed system. It is characterized by:

1. innovation,
2. well-developed capital markets that finance smart risk-taking in the pursuit of profits (which by and large naturally produce cost efficiencies and survival of the fittest), and
3. a well-developed legal system in which most people know the rules of the game and disagreements can be resolved without fighting to produce exceptional successes when measured against key performance indicators (KPIs) like total wealth and power.

At the same time, the system is producing great gaps in education levels, productivities, incomes, wealth, power, and opportunities that are extremely difficult to rectify and that threaten the long-term health of the country. **The big debt issue of there being too much debt relative to the demand for it will almost certainly lead to big fundamental changes in the monetary system, which will change what money is and how it works, which will happen either before the crisis in an attempt to prevent it or in response to the crisis. At a high level, while there are variations in how each of these debt crisis cases plays out, it almost always becomes relatively undesirable to hold the debt assets (e.g., bonds) compared with other storeholds of wealth that don't lose buying power when the value of money goes down.**

It's also worth noting that during Stage 5 of the Big Cycle, which we are now in, the domestic debt/economic situation is greatly affected by the domestic political and social order force, the international geopolitical force, acts of nature, and changes in technology. It is now the case that the internal political and external geopolitical conflicts that most countries are in are having bigger effects on countries' finances than at any time since the 1930s. For example, onshoring, friendshoring, and other forms of ensuring that critical supplies cannot be cut off by foreign enemies have become more important economic policy drivers than cost efficiency. This is happening for the first time since World War II; it is costly and typically leads to more indebtedness. Likewise, countries' finances are also having bigger effects on the internal political and external geopolitical conflicts than at any time since the end of the last Big Cycle.

As far as emerging countries are concerned, they break down into two types: those that are overcoming their obstacles and surging ahead economically and financially (e.g., India, Indonesia and most other ASEAN countries, and the Gulf Cooperation Council countries) and those that are falling further behind (e.g., poor and disorderly developing countries, especially those that have very little money and are adversely impacted by climate change). It is logical, and it appears to be the case, that the financially strong, orderly, and relatively geopolitically neutral countries that have the best people and the most rewarding systems are doing the best and will continue to do the best. That is because I still believe that ● ***globalization is an unstoppable force***. Despite the growing nationalism and the increased desire of many countries' leaders to protect and control, I am seeing vastly more globalized deal-making that brings together people of all nationalities who have money to brainstorm on how to do deals with each other than I did 10 years ago. The people and what they are doing are very multinational and becoming more so fast. This has been an unstoppable evolutionary trend that has existed throughout history and is accelerating.

2. The Domestic Order and Disorder Force

As for where we are in the short-term political cycle, **since Donald Trump and the Republican Party won the 2024 elections by a large enough margin to avoid disputes about who won, the US has had an orderly transfer of power. The principle that applies to such transitions is:**

● ***At the beginning of a new popularly chosen leader coming to power—e.g., in the first 100 days of a new presidency—there is a***

honeymoon period and great optimism. That is when dreams of great changes and great improvements exist and before realities and criticisms of how the new leader has shaped and handled them set in. As time passes, typically the big promises the leader made to get elected become difficult to deliver and bad things happen so disappointment sets in, critics and enemies become bolder, and support wanes. All this makes fighting to stay in power harder, which often leads to more extreme actions to make that happen.

After just a few weeks of the new administration, it should not be a controversial statement that Donald Trump wants to dictate policies rather than have a classic "let's work together across party lines" approach to governing. This confrontational approach is an extension of how great internal political conflict has become in recent decades. The following charts show two measures of how internal political conflicts in the US are among the most severe in history. The first one shows how conservative Republicans in the Senate and House and how liberal Democrats in the Senate and House have become relative to the past. Based on this measure, they have become more extreme, and their divergence has become larger than ever before. While I'm not sure that's exactly right, I think it's by and large right.

IDEOLOGICAL POSITIONS OF THE MAJOR PARTIES

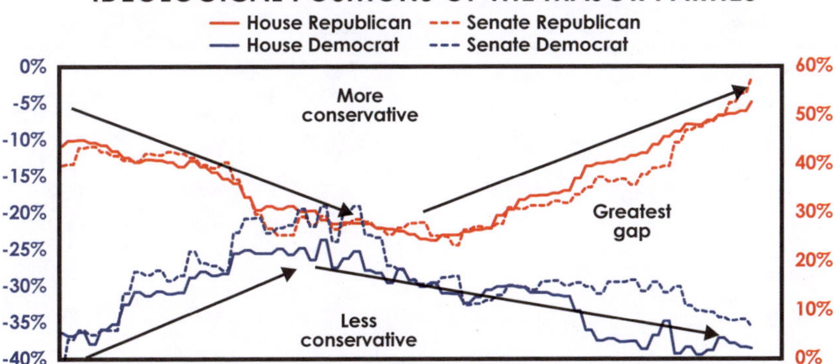

Also, votes along party lines for the average member of Congress are the highest ever. This continues to be reflected in the reduced willingness to cross party lines to compromise and reach agreements. In other words, the political splits in the country have become deep and intransigent.

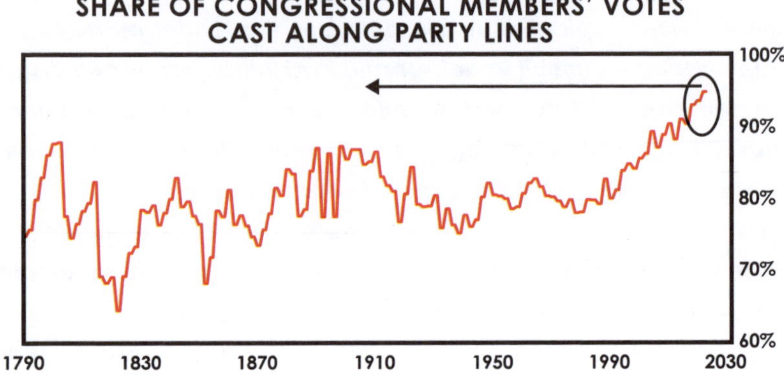

The fact that this is a global phenomenon and that it is happening in different degrees in different countries is captured in the next table, which shows an increasing majority of people surveyed in many countries saying that there are very strong or somewhat strong conflicts between people who support different political parties in their own country.

% WHO SAY THERE ARE VERY/SOMEWHAT STRONG CONFLICTS BETWEEN PEOPLE WHO SUPPORT DIFFERENT POLITICAL PARTIES IN THEIR OWN COUNTRY

	2022	2021	Diff
France	74%	65%	9%
Germany	68%	56%	12%
Spain	68%	58%	10%
Canada	66%	44%	22%
UK	65%	52%	13%
Netherlands	61%	38%	23%
Belgium	53%	46%	7%
Singapore	43%	33%	10%
Sweden	43%	35%	8%

The following chart shows the average global levels of political polarization since 1900.[54]

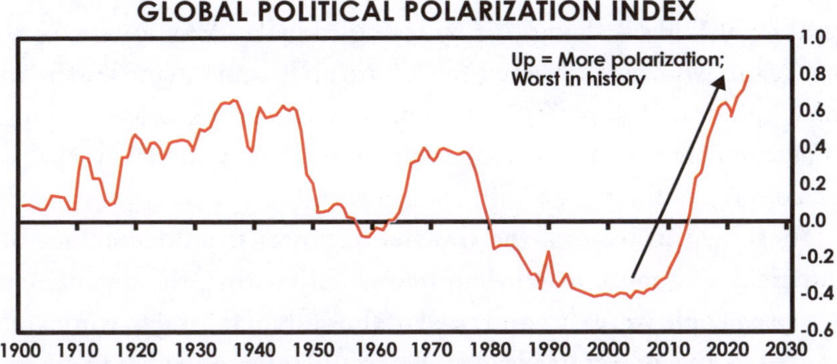

These are just a few measures of many that reflect high and rising internal conflict. It appears clear that, as the gaps in people's productivity, wealth, and values grow along with levels of dissatisfaction about how their democracies are working, it leads to more populist conflict and more policies that are like those in the 1905-14 and the 1933-38 periods. As I explained earlier, such times of conflict are often when transitions toward more autocratic forms of government happen.

- ***When democracies fail, autocracies come in.***

Within countries, intensifying populist conflicts between those of the hard right, those of the weak middle, and those of the hard left are now taking place, with big political shifts (mostly toward the hard right) and revolutionary changes resulting from them. In this environment in which those who are productive are rewarded and those who are unproductive suffer, the least productive and the poorest will suffer the most. **As history shows us, this situation typically has threatening consequences.**

- ***In times of disorder, financial, political, and military power matters more than laws, and authoritarianism works better than weak,***

[54] This was sourced from "Varieties of Democracy," a project run out of the University of Gothenburg in Sweden to create standardized global databases covering five indicators of governance and civil society.

disorganized collectivism. We are now seeing the dramatic part of the movie being played out by Donald Trump and his administration taking control of the US to try to reverse its decline to "make America great again." He is doing this by trying to make America competitive again, while at the same time we are also seeing many leaders in many countries, industries, and companies, and people broadly trying to outcompete the others. That competition is now so vicious that it includes the willingness to kill competitors.

As shown in history, the transfer of power from democracy to autocracy was more often than not orderly within the democracy because people were sick and tired of the system failing to work and wanted to give power to a leader who would take control of the mess and make it work well. Clearly this is now happening. But it has also always been the case that, after transfers of power, ● ***new leaders during periods of great conflict take steps to consolidate power—and more autocratic leaders do so more forcefully.*** Because the opposition remains threatening, it has to be dealt with so that its ability to threaten is reduced, which will likely be done by the leader and the party in power increasingly taking control of the law. We are now seeing this happen in the US through the president's use of executive orders. As always, we will see how far this will go when what the executive leader wants to do and what the other parts of the tripartite government want to do (i.e., the judiciary and Congress) come into conflict.

We should expect that there will be more fights—legal and otherwise—between factions and particularly between the president/executive branch and the other branches of government (especially the judicial branch) and between the federal, state, and local governments. These fights will make clear who really has the power. In a limits-of-power-testing battle between the power of the executive branch of government and the judicial branch of government, the judicial branch will lose because the executive branch has much more control over the powers of enforcement. In fact, the Department of Justice is part of the executive branch of government so is under presidential control. The powers of enforcement are the army and the National Guard and state and local police, with the president having control over the first two and the judicial branch having control over none. For these reasons, it was easy for Donald Trump to order dropping the case against New York City Mayor Eric Adams. **We should expect many more power struggles. I have little doubt that the president will win most of these.**

Different people have different views of whether this kind of leadership is a good thing or a bad thing. In Chapter 8, I described how the approaches of a strong CEO and those of a demagogue can be indistinguishable as both are people who take control and make radical changes with the goal of making radical improvements. That is certainly the case with Donald Trump. Is Donald Trump a demagogue? According to Plato, a demagogue is a political leader who gains power by appealing to people's emotions, fears, prejudices, and desires, often using manipulative rhetoric. Demagogues typically stir up populist sentiment and promise easy solutions to complex problems, often at the expense of truth or rational discourse. The question is what will the controls be and how far will Trump push things? Unlike for a CEO, there is no board for the US president. Are there effective regulators in place? If so, it is not clear to me who they are.

When I say that the policies President Trump is using to "make America great again" are remarkably like the policies that those of the hard-right countries in the 1930s used, that should not be controversial. It would be fair to argue that his attempts to maximize the power of the presidency by bypassing the other branches of government are analogous to the ways that Andrew Jackson (of the right) and Franklin D. Roosevelt (of the left) did, though he is even more aggressive than they were. We will see how far he will take it. In the typical historical case, ● ***in times of great conflict, aggressive leaders work to eliminate the opposition by threats and damaging action, by making changes in the law that give the leaders special powers, and by taking increased control over the media to produce pro-government propaganda. If conflicts with internal or external opponents become severe, laws and punishments targeting the opposition will be imposed.***

While the changes to government that President Trump is making are radical in terms of intended cost savings and must be done quickly to be successfully accomplished, there are negative consequences to these cuts because many people who will be hurt by them will fight back and valuable support systems will be weakened or eliminated. For example, my wife works to help the poorest students in the worst neighborhoods who suffer from inadequate nutrition and rely on school lunch programs that are being eliminated, which will have terrible second-order consequences. Second-order consequences like these should be taken into consideration when thinking about what the future will look like after the radical changes are made.

Remember that ● ***to be successful the system must produce adequate conditions for most people.*** **Will that happen? The challenge in the US is that there is and has been a deep and pervasive rot in our education, family, and social systems that has resulted in many children not being brought up to lead productive, civil, and healthy lives.** This is a multigenerational problem that is nearly impossible to fix, especially with fragmented leadership and inadequate resources directed to dealing with it. **Currently, only a small percentage of the population is highly productive and prosperous. More specifically, the top 1% of people (and increasingly machines) are making revolutionary changes. They, along with the next 9% who help them, together make up the top 10% and are doing great. The next 30% are doing so-so, and the bottom 60% are doing terribly—i.e., they are net costs rather than net contributors.** (On average, they have attained less than a sixth-grade reading level and get more in public assistance payments than they pay in taxes.) The Trump administration's policies are aimed at raising productivity by shifting more money, power, and freedom into the hands of those who are most productive. This will have second-order consequences that everyone, especially those in the Trump administration, should consider. It's not easy to manage and improve a country that has been mismanaged and in such a mess while also keeping people happy at a time when democracy is fracturing. **I recommend regularly checking on how those in the bottom 60% are doing and feeling.**

3. The International Order and Disorder Force

We are now seeing the international order changing in ways that are typical at this stage in the Big Cycle—i.e., there is a shift from a more cooperative, multilateral world order that pursues common interests (e.g., trade) to a classic great power conflict in which there is a more confrontational, unilateral world order that pursues self-interest through the bold use of financial, political, and military power. As described earlier, this is the part of a Big Cycle when there is a shift toward authoritarian, confrontational leadership. As is classic in Stage 5 and as we are seeing now, there is a type of world war going on that has turned more violent locally (e.g., Russia versus Ukraine, Israel versus Iran and its proxies) but has not yet turned violent between the leading global powers (the US and China).

At this stage, it is increasingly true that ● ***the strong prey on the weak.*** As a result, the weak empire should worry. Which is the weak empire? President Trump, Vladimir Putin, and everyone including the Europeans know that **Europe is weak and easy prey**, Russia will likely be an enemy of Europe, and Trump's "America First" policy will likely lead to it not defending Europe. Also, everyone knows that Trump is hard-right, so he is inclined to align the US with those who are hard-right and capable of fighting, and to use both carrots and sticks to make people and countries to do what he wants them to do. That is what is driving the reshaping of the new world order and the "allied powers" side led by the US. **It is also important to remember that at this stage in the Big Cycle** ● ***alliances often change fast as circumstances change quickly and winning is more important than loyalties.*** For example, Germany and Russia quickly switched from allies to enemies in World War II. **We should expect alliances to change fast and in previously unimaginable ways**—e.g., it would not surprise me if Trump's US and Putin's Russia align, with China becoming more isolated as there is no true love and fidelity between Russia and China. **Likewise, we might find Europe and China more**

aligned than Europe and the US. These sorts of previously unimaginable changes have often occurred at this stage in the Big Cycle. We will learn a lot shortly.

As far as the great power conflict between the US and China goes, it cannot be objectively disputed that the United States has been in relative decline and that the conflicts with China are increasing. This is clearly shown in the following charts. The one on the left shows my measure of the total powers (including my 21 measures of power) and the one on the right shows my gauge of the intensity of the US-China conflict. It shows the great power conflict and the Thucydides Trap dynamic in action.

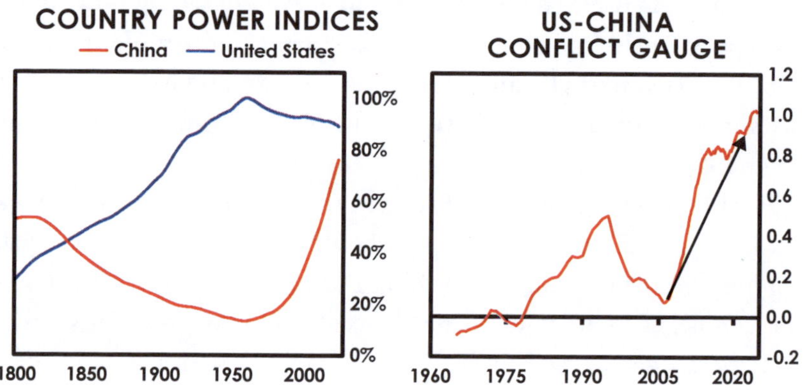

President Trump is seeking to reverse that relative decline at the same time as the US and China are clearly in a war that has not yet become a military war. It is not clear at this time (early March 2025) exactly what US-China relations—or, more broadly, international relations—will be like.

I don't expect a military war between the US and China in the foreseeable future because both sides know that it would lead to mutually assured destruction. I think the only thing that China would go to war over is a real threat to its sovereignty, which includes the Taiwan issue. Also, I don't think any American president would go to war unless there was an existential threat (like losing TSMC's chip production). At the same time, I could imagine that President Trump would be willing to negotiate Taiwan away under the right terms for the right, big price. Trump and Xi are strongmen running great powers and will have regular conversations to negotiate directly with each other. Both want to avoid a military war and existential threats to their countries while each would also love to eliminate the other as a threat.

The only way I can see either side winning a war is by secretly building a technology of overwhelming power that can be deployed without triggering an intolerable retaliation so that simply demonstrating it to the other side would lead to some form of capitulation. This has been done throughout history. This would be akin to the secretive development of the atomic bomb and the displaying of its power to the Japanese via the attacks on Hiroshima and Nagasaki. To be clear, I am not ruling out such a scenario because I am sure that both countries are working on the development of mind-blowingly powerful technologies that remain secret.

No one on either side believes that the US-China relationship will go back to what it was. Though neither side wants military war, the US and China are currently engaged in other types of war, including diplomatic, cyber, and trade wars in which they are severely threatening and hurting each other. It is not disputable that there is a deep-seated belief that the other side is an enemy and is doing very harmful things to the other. This is risky because the most important and threatening stuff is going on in secret, so it can't be controlled unless it is self-controlled, which, under the circumstances, neither side will do.

Still, my bet is that China will try to stay out of an overt fight for geopolitical dominance outside its region while a) acting to build great power that can be used to harm those who harm it and b) moving to achieve the unification of Taiwan with China, which is widely believed to be a goal that President Xi, who is now in his early 70s, would like to achieve in his lifetime. For those reasons, as mentioned above, if I were the Taiwanese, I would worry about my country being used as a negotiating chip for the US to offer to China in return for great concessions. Of course, such a deal would have to eliminate any semiconductor chip vulnerabilities for the US that would result in

China controlling Taiwan. I also expect China to continue to build important relationships in the Global South using both its economic and geopolitical power because that is a huge market for its very attractively priced manufactured goods and construction companies.

While governments are becoming more nationalistic and protectionist, the world, investors, and businesspeople have become more interdependent than at any time in history, and investment and business deal making are more international than ever before. For that reason, what is happening domestically affects what is happening internationally, and vice versa, more than ever before, and what is happening economically is affecting what is happening geopolitically, and vice versa, more than ever before. This is having policy, investment, and business implications. For example, the need to win the tech war is leading to top-down, government-directed domestic and international policies for chip production, data center investment and development, electricity production, embargoes on technologies, sanctions, CFIUS and reverse CFIUS tariffs, global talent acquisition, etc. **To me, the big questions are how practical the respective world leaders are, how they and their opponents will deal with each other, and how orderly and smartly things will be managed when times get tough. My take is that international investment and business deals will get easier and increase in number rather than get harder and fewer.**

Keep in mind that while that is what I think about the world's geopolitical order, I'm not sure of anything.

4. The Force of Nature (Droughts, Floods, and Pandemics)

We certainly cannot overlook the power and impacts of nature. As I described in Chapter 8, throughout history acts of nature have killed more people than wars and toppled more orders than all the other four forces combined. It is likely that in the years ahead, acts of nature will increase in frequency and be very costly. Given how heavily indebted and burdened with other demands the world's major nations now are, very little is going to proactively prevent and prepare for the high costs of a changing natural world. But the costs will be incurred regardless—either by paying to prevent the damages or paying to fix things after damages occur from intolerably hot weather, droughts, floods, rising sea levels, health problems, damage to the oceans that will change currents and sea life, species loss, and many other things likely to happen in the years ahead. This will require significant amounts of money being spent to adapt to these changes. For countries in the Global South that are experiencing big effects from climate change and don't have the resources to address them, this could lead to domestic conflict and emigration. Displaced people in turn will strain other countries, as we are already seeing with immigration in the US and Europe, making both domestic and international politics more unstable.

5. The Technology/Human Productivity Force

While the trends of the first four forces appear to be worsening, the technology force has never, in the whole history of humanity, been more powerful than it is now and will be over the next few years. It looks to me like we are now at the brink of a new era in which machine thinking will supplement or surpass human thinking in many ways, like how machine labor supplemented and surpassed human labor during the Industrial Revolutions. Just as we saw that doing math in our heads and remembering facts became much less important with the invention of computerized tools that do these things, and just as we have gone to Google (or its equivalents) to find information rather than gathering information in more traditional ways, we will soon be going to computers to get our instructions on what to do when we are in different situations because the computer will come up with better guidance more quickly than we can.

Over the next five years, we will see dramatic advancements in most areas. Creating the AI capabilities is just the beginning of the

AI applications. I know that in my area of investing where I and Bridgewater have been doing AI investing through expert systems for decades, the opportunities that are being developed are nearly unbelievable. The days of people making decisions in their own heads are ending. I and others at Bridgewater have experienced and capitalized on this (r)evolution via the computerization of investment decision making, so I'm excited by what will be happening.

Because these technologies will impact almost everything, there will be exceptionally big differences between the performance levels of countries, investors, and companies who use them well. Those who know how to use these tools effectively will be rewarded, and those who fail to do so will be penalized. It is worth noting, however, that from an investment perspective, it is not totally clear how much money will come in relative to the costs that will go out to invest in and create these new technologies.

The US and China are now the main competitors in designing these powerful new technologies, and how effective they are will have big impacts on their economic and military powers, though several countries are also developing and benefiting from these new technologies. While the US is ahead of China in developing the most advanced semiconductor chips and weak in its production of them, China is close behind in the development of advanced chips, ahead in producing less advanced chips much less expensively, and ahead in deploying AI. There will certainly be a lot of effort from both sides to gain an advantage over the other in this race, both by stealing/borrowing what the other side has and trying to defend one's own gains. I keep in the mind the principle that ● ***by and large, intellectual property protections don't work.*** While deep secrets that are protected with great effort (like the development of the atomic bomb) might be able to be kept hidden, anything that is openly used can almost instantly be replicated. Also, legal systems do a poor job of enforcing intellectual property protections. For these reasons, we should assume that most good ideas that are openly shown and are liked a lot will be replicated in about six months.

I should also make clear that AI isn't the only important technology shaping the relative power of nations. There are many technologies beyond chips and AI that the US and China are the main real competitors in, including quantum computing, gene editing and other biotech, robotics, space, etc. China, which is home to 20 of the 40 best computer science programs in the world,[55] is a formidable adversary to the US in the technology competition.

In conclusion, I am very excited and optimistic about the revolutionary improvements that are likely to take place as the result of inventive/practical people being put together with capital that gets them the resources that they need (perhaps most importantly, these new AI technologies) and operating in great environments that are conducive to advancement. Of course, new technologies are double-edged swords. For example, they have advanced how we can do each other harm as well as how we can do each other good. As shown in the following charts, there have been exponential improvements in real GDP and life expectancy. This is because of the accelerating, compounding rate of growth of knowledge, which should continue due to the way it is compounding via AI.

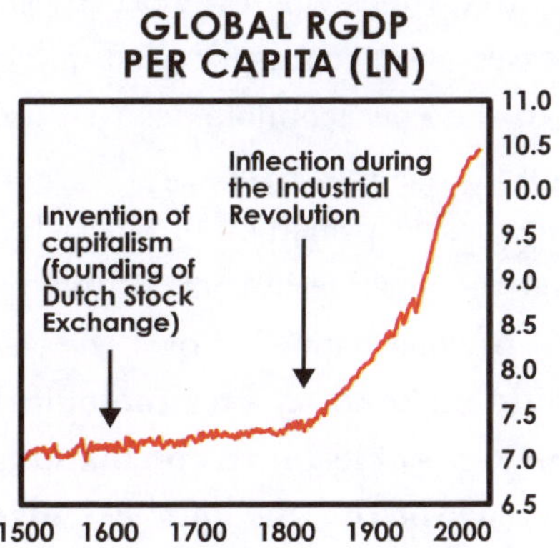

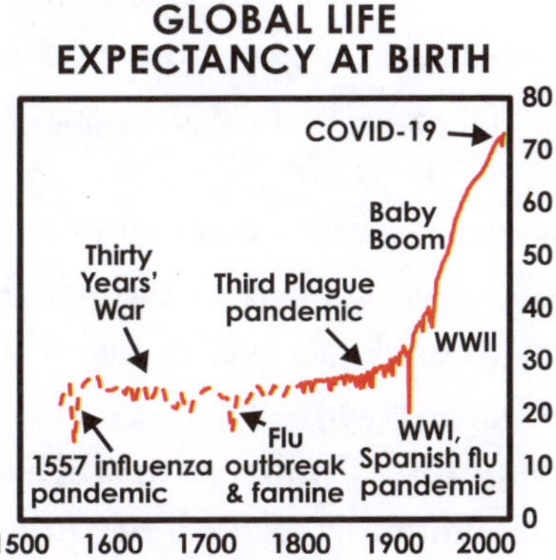

[55] Source: *US News & World Report* Best Global Universities for Computer Science rankings for 2024-25.

WHERE DOES THIS LEAVE US?

To conclude where I started, what I don't know is much greater than what I do know, and as I write this in early March 2025, I am at a maximum point of uncertainty. That's because the Trump administration took office just 40 days ago and its big moves to change the monetary, US political, and geopolitical world orders have just begun. At the same time, I also know that whatever changes we see happen will happen in similar ways for similar reasons to how they have happened many times before, though with contemporary twists. So, it appears to me that the changes in these orders will likely continue to track my template, which is based on the patterns of the past and the logical relationships between the five big forces.

Looking at where things are headed over the next few years, **I believe that very powerful technological advances will most likely not be enough to overpower the headwinds coming from the other forces**. I derived this view by looking at the amazing digital/computer/internet boom that we have experienced since 1985 and at the impacts of great discoveries and advances in technologies (e.g., railroads, steam engines, electricity, flight) at times when the other four forces turned negative. I used these cases as references for what might happen over the next 30 years due to the new technologies that are coming in AI, robotics, quantum computing, biotech, etc., and I asked myself what effect those prior technologies' leaps had on productivity.

More specifically, I estimated that the positive impacts of today's new technologies will be about 150% of what happened over the last 30 years. **By my measures, this would make today's technological revolution the most powerful ever in terms of its impact on markets and economic conditions. But my back-of-the-envelope calculations also show that this positive force will not be enough to negate the headwinds of debt, internal conflict, external conflict, climate change, and demographics.** Similarly and interestingly, when I looked at other periods of high inventiveness such as in the Industrial Revolutions and the 1920s, what I saw is that the productivity-improving powers of the great new technologies were normally squelched when the other forces of the Big Cycle turned negative. **So, it appears to me that the most important factor for the years ahead is that the other forces are managed well.**

I am confident that the next 5-10 years will be a period of enormous changes in all the major orders, and that going from now until then will feel like going through a time warp into a very different reality. Many countries, companies, and people who are now up will be down, and those who are down will be up. How we think and what we do will be very different, in ways that we can't possibly anticipate.

I also know that there are better and worse ways to play this set of circumstances, and the best way is to play the probabilities, diversify well, and stick with sound fundamentals. As far as the best places to be, I believe that they are the countries that get these fundamentals right—i.e., those that educate their people well so they are skilled and civil and have access to an environment of great opportunity for them to be productive, that earn more than they spend so they have strong national income statements and balance sheets, that have internal order rather than disorder, that have low risks of being in an international war, that have low risks of experiencing harmful acts of nature, and that benefit the most from changes in technology.[56] **Having great human capital will matter most.**

As I explained earlier, ● ***the biggest, most important force is how people deal with each other.* If people treat their problems and opportunities as being shared and they focus on getting the best outcomes for the whole without damaging each other, they will likely get the best possible results. For example, as described in the last chapter, it is now possible for government leaders to manage their countries' debts and monies well—e.g., for the US to cut its deficits down to 3% of GDP—which would greatly reduce the risks of**

[56] If you are interested in monitoring my KPIs of how countries are doing in these dimensions, you can find my updated Country Power Index at economicprinciples.org.

a government debt market/economic crisis. Similarly, domestic and world orders, acts of nature, and the managing of the amazing new technologies will have much better outcomes if those who have their hands on the levers of power work well together.

Unfortunately, I believe that an objective examination of how likely these things are to transpire would conclude that **the chances of cooperation for mutual benefit are not good. The reality is that the events that have brought the Big Cycle to where it is today have left strong beliefs within most factions that the people in the opposing factions are doing them harm—and that the time has come to fight and win at all costs. Those in the opposing factions also believe that they must fight to win at all costs. We know from history that extreme factionalism kills.**

Hopefully this picture makes people worry and motivates them to do what is still in their power to do to improve things, which brings me to a final principle: ● *If you're not worried, you need to worry—and if you're worried, you don't need to worry.* That's because worrying about the things that can go wrong will protect you, while not worrying about them will leave you exposed.

I hope you find good principles to prepare for the interesting times ahead.

Ray

ABOUT THE AUTHOR

Ray Dalio has been a global macro investor for more than 50 years. In 1975, he founded Bridgewater Associates from his two-bedroom apartment and built it over four decades into the largest and most successful hedge fund in the world and the fifth most important private company in the US, according to *Fortune* magazine.

Dalio grew up a very ordinary middle-class kid on Long Island and started investing when he was 12 years old. Over the course of his career, he has become a renowned author and speaker, an advisor to top policy makers, and one of the "100 Most Influential People in the World," according to *TIME*. *CIO* and *Wired* have called him "the Steve Jobs of investing" for his uniquely inventive and industry-changing way of thinking. He has also been named by *Forbes* as one of the 50 most generous philanthropists in the US.

In 2017, he decided to pass along the principles behind his success in a series of books and animated videos. His 2017 book *Principles: Life and Work* was a No. 1 New York Times Best Seller and the No. 1 Amazon business book of the year, has sold more than 5 million copies worldwide, and has been translated into over 30 languages. His 2021 book *Principles for Dealing with the Changing World Order* was also a New York Times Best Seller and has sold more than 1 million copies worldwide. Dalio has also created a series of 30-minute animated YouTube videos ("How the Economic Machine Works," "Principles for Success," and "Principles for Dealing with the Changing World Order"), which have together been watched more than 250 million times. His 2018 book *Principles for Navigating Big Debt Crises* was well-received by economists, policy makers, and investors.

In this latest book, *How Countries Go Broke: The Big Cycle*, Dalio is for the first time sharing his unique template for understanding the final stages of what he calls the "Big Debt Cycle" and showing how these stages help drive to the "Overall Big Cycle" that governs the kinds of radical monetary, political, and geopolitical changes we are seeing in the world today.